Ex Libris

American Furniture

AMERICAN FURNITURE 1994

Edited by Luke Beckerdite

Published by the CHIPSTONE FOUNDATION

Distributed by University Press of New England

Hanover and London

CHIPSTONE FOUNDATION BOARD OF DIRECTORS
Luke Beckerdite   *Executive Director*
Nancy Carpenter
Dudley Godfrey, Jr.
Charles Hummel
Brock Jobe
W. David Knox, II.   *President*
Jere D. McGaffey
Philip L. Stone
Mrs. Stanley Stone   *Chairman*
Allen M. Taylor   *Vice Chairman*

EDITOR
Luke Beckerdite

BOOK AND EXHIBITION REVIEW EDITOR
Gerald W. R. Ward

ASSOCIATE EDITOR
Catherine E. Hutchins

EDITORIAL ADVISORY BOARD
Luke Beckerdite, *Executive Director, The Chipstone Foundation*
John Bivins, Jr., *Conservator and Decorative Arts Consultant*
Edward S. Cooke, Jr., *Associate Professor, Department of the History of Art, Yale University*
Wallace Gusler, *Director of Conservation, Colonial Williamsburg Foundation*
Morrison H. Heckscher, *Curator of American Decorative Arts, Metropolitan Museum of Art*
Brock Jobe, *Deputy Director of Collections, H. F. du Pont Winterthur Museum*
Robert F. Trent, *Curator and in charge of furniture, H. F. du Pont Winterthur Museum*
Gerald W. R. Ward, *Associate Curator, American Decorative Arts & Sculpture, Museum of Fine Arts, Boston*
Gregory R. Weidman, *Curator, Maryland Historical Society*
Philip D. Zimmerman, *Museum and Decorative Arts Consultant*

Cover Illustration: Bust ornament of a desk-and-bookcase, Philadelphia, ca. 1765. (Collection of Mr. and Mrs. George M. Kaufman.)

Design: Wynne Patterson
Photography: Gavin Ashworth, New York, New York

Published by the Chipstone Foundation
Distributed by University Press of New England, Hanover, NH 03755
© 1994 by the Chipstone Foundation
All rights reserved
Printed in the United States of America   5 4 3 2 1
ISSN 1069-4188
ISBN 0-87451-681-1

Contents

Editorial Statement *Luke Beckerdite*	VII
Preface *Allen M. Taylor*	IX
Introduction *Luke Beckerdite*	XI
Identifying and Understanding Repairs and Structural Problems in Windsor Furniture *Nancy Goyne Evans*	3
Architect-Designed Furniture in Eighteenth-Century Virginia: The Work of William Buckland and William Bernard Sears *Luke Beckerdite*	29
Leon Marcotte: Cabinetmaker and Interior Decorator *Nina Gray*	49
John Cogswell and Boston Bombé Furniture: Thirty-Five Years of Revolution in Politics and Design *Robert Mussey and Anne Rogers Haley*	73
Flat Gates, Draw Bars, Twists, and Urns: New York's Distinctive, Early Baroque Oval Tables with Falling Leaves *Peter M. Kenny*	107
Jean Berger's Design Book: Huguenot Tradesmen and the Dissemination of French Baroque Style *Robert A. Leath*	137
A Masonic Master's Chair Revealed *Susan Buck*	163

English Furniture Pattern Books in Eighteenth-Century America   173
America
Morrison H. Heckscher

The Work of Clotworthy Stephenson, William Hodgson   207
and Henry Ingle in Richmond, Virginia, 1787–1806
Sumpter T. Priddy III and Martha C. Vick

Book Reviews   234

Portsmouth Furniture: Masterworks from the New Hampshire Seacoast, organized and edited by Brock Jobe; review by David L. Barquist

American Tables and Looking Glasses in the Mabel Brady Garvan and Other Collections at Yale University, David L. Barquist; review by John Hays

Clock Making in New England, 1725–1825: An Interpretation of the Old Sturbridge Village Collection, Philip Zea and Robert C. Cheney, edited by Caroline F. Sloat; review by Thomas S. Michie

New England Natives: A Celebration of People and Trees, Sheila Connor; review by Gerald W. R. Ward

Recent Writing on American Furniture: A Bibliography   247
Gerald W. R. Ward

Index   257

Editorial Statement

American Furniture is an interdisciplinary journal dedicated to advancing knowledge of furniture made or used in the Americas from the seventeenth century to the present. Authors are encouraged to submit articles on any aspect of furniture history, essays on conservation and historic technology, reproductions of transcripts of documents, such as account books and inventories, annotated photographs of new furniture discoveries, and book and exhibition reviews. References for compiling an annual bibliography also are welcome.

Manuscripts must be typed, double-spaced, illustrated with 8" × 10" black-and-white prints or transparencies, and prepared in accordance with the *Chicago Manual of Style*. Computer disk copy is requested but not required. The Chipstone Foundation will offer significant honoraria for manuscripts accepted for publication and reimburse authors for all photography approved in writing by the editor.

Luke Beckerdite

Preface

The Chipstone Foundation was organized in 1965 by Stanley Stone and Polly Mariner Stone of Fox Point, Wisconsin. Representing the culmination of their shared experiences in collecting American furniture, American historical prints, and early English pottery, the foundation was created with the dual purpose of preserving and interpreting their collection and stimulating research and education in the decorative arts.

The Stones began collecting American decorative arts in 1946, and by 1964 it became apparent to them that provisions should be made to deal with their collection. With the counsel of their friend Charles Montgomery, the Stones decided that their collection should be published and exhibited.

Following Stanley Stone's death in 1987, the foundation was activated by an initial endowment provided by Mrs. Stone. This generous donation allowed the foundation to institute its research and grant programs, begin work on three collection catalogues, and launch an important new journal, *American Furniture*.

Allen M. Taylor

Introduction

Luke Beckerdite

The articles in this volume of *American Furniture* span nearly three hundred years of furniture design, production, and use; nevertheless, they have many points in common. Robert Leath's article on Jean Berger's drawing book and Morrison Heckscher's comprehensive annotated catalogue of English design books in eighteenth-century America deal with the dissemination of furniture styles and ornamental details. Luke Beckerdite's article on architect-designed furniture in eighteenth-century Virginia, Sumpter Priddy and Martha Vick's study of Clotworthy Stephenson, Henry Ingle, and William Hodgson, and Nina Gray's profile of the life and work of Leon Marcotte explore the relationships between architecture and furniture design. Peter Kenny's article on New York baroque tables and Robert Mussey and Ann Haley's article on John Cogswell are rich contextual studies that show how European and English furniture forms were introduced into the colonies and modified to suit local tastes and craft traditions. Nancy Evans' article on Windsor seating furniture documents historical methods of repair, modification, and alteration, whereas Susan Buck's essay on the treatment of an important Ohio Masonic chair reveals how furniture conservation has benefited from recent scientific developments in the painting conservation field. The themes shared by these diverse articles underscore the importance of viewing American furniture as a continuum extending from historic antecedents in England and Europe to the present.

The 1995 volume will be a special issue on regional diversity and innovation in American furniture. With several multidisciplinary articles focusing on furniture, craft, and regional identity, this volume will include both object-oriented and context-oriented scholarship and show how material culture is often a direct manifestation of the social, economic, and cultural patterns of a given region. As with other issues of *American Furniture*, we hope this one will help forge a link between social history, American studies, and the decorative arts.

American Furniture

Figure 1 Detail of the rear face of the bow of a bow-back Windsor armchair, John Letchworth, Philadelphia, Pa., ca. 1787–1792. Yellow poplar (seat), maple, oak, hickory, and black walnut (arms and arm supports) (microanalysis). H. 37", W. (arms) 20 7/8", D. (seat) 17 3/4". (Courtesy, Winterthur Museum, acc. 57.99.2.)

Figure 2 Fan-back Windsor armchair, southeastern Pennsylvania, ca. 1764–1770. Yellow poplar (seat). H. 40 1/2", W. 26 1/2", D. 23 1/4". (Courtesy, Chester County Historical Society, West Chester, Pa.; photo, Winterthur Museum.)

Nancy Goyne Evans

Identifying and Understanding Repairs and Structural Problems in Windsor Furniture

▼ PROBLEMS IN Windsor furniture can be difficult to detect. Paint may conceal repairs, new parts, or old elements foreign to the original fabric of a piece of furniture. Collectors, dealers, curators, and furniture historians must be able to recognize and interpret irregularities in structure and design if they are to make wise purchase decisions and accurate object assessments. The detection of problems in Windsor furniture is, first and foremost, a matter of common sense and of training the eye and mind to recognize deviations from standard production. To analyze and understand puzzling features and to reach intelligent conclusions about the integrity of a piece of furniture, it is important for the collector or curator to allow sufficient time to make a thorough examination.

Like most utilitarian furniture, Windsor chairs have suffered from daily use and occasional abuse. Legs have been worn down through constant movement across floors or from exposure to dampness. Stretchers have been worn flat or broken from serving as footrests. Seats have split as a result of hard knocks or internal faults in the wood. Joints have broken under stress and strain. Bows, spindles, and delicate arm rails have cracked from being subjected to abnormal pressure as the wood dried and lost much of its elasticity.

Collectors and curators encounter multiple types and levels of repair and restoration. The most elementary condition is the honest repair, that is, one that retains all the original furniture parts and introduces little or no new material at the damage point. A restoration introduces new elements to replace those that have been broken, badly damaged, or lost, and such restoration work may be minor or major. An alteration involves the addition of a new feature to an existing form or the modification of one or more original element(s) to meet a specific need or condition. As a result, the function of the furniture may be changed slightly or even significantly. Reconstructions are usually a mix of old and new furniture parts to create forms that may be substantially changed in appearance, and sometimes in function, from the original objects. A reproduction is a close copy of a period object made for sale, usually at a popular price. A few reproductions have been created to deceive; others have been deliberately distressed at a later date for the same purpose. Enhanced objects are those made more desirable by the addition of decoration, an unusual feature, such as a headrest extension to a chair back, or documentation to a maker, frequently for fraudulent purposes.

Figure 3 Detail of the seat bottom of the chair illustrated in fig. 2. (Photo, Winterthur Museum.)

Repairs

Repair work has been part of Windsor chairmaking for more than two centuries. The versatile William Caulton, an upholsterer from London who settled in Williamsburg, Virginia, in 1745, readily announced his ability to make or mend Windsor chairs. Half a century later, specialists working in highly competitive markets attracted customers by promising "neat and durable" repairs executed in a "workmanlike manner" on "the shortest notice" for "reasonable" or "moderate" terms.[1]

A fragile part of a Windsor chair is the bow. Subjected to stress and resin loss during steaming and bending, weakened by holes drilled to socket the spindles, and made brittle as the wood dries out, bows frequently crack and break, especially at the points where holes have been bored and in the areas of greatest compression. Repairers have addressed the problem by various means: gluing, inserting an internal spline, replacing a section of bow with new wood, fastening a wooden or metal brace across the break.

Breaks in the bows of armchairs are particularly common adjacent to the rectangular mortises cut to socket the arms (fig. 1). The wood is thin at these points, and any unusual stress transferred through the arms can cause damage. The illustrated detail from a Philadelphia chair shows a vertical metal brace spanning a horizontal break to secure the joint and provide additional structural strength. The metal piece, which is held by screws, lies on the rear surface of the bow. Braces are often mounted in inconspicuous places and may be inset to conceal the repair.

Over the years, seat cracks and splits have been repaired in various ways, depending upon the severity of the damage. Minor cracks have at times been secured with small, flat pieces of wood called keys set into the surface of the seat crosswise to the break. The shrinkage indicates that a rectangular key inserted in the seat top of a 1790s fan-back side chair made by a Tracy family member in New London County, Connecticut, has been in place a long time. Like the seat, the key is made of chestnut, a wood highly favored in eastern Connecticut and Rhode Island for Windsor chair bottoms. The butterfly-shaped key on the seat bottom of a bow-back chair from the Boston shop of William Seaver and James Frost was part of the original construction, which suggests that a small but repairable crack developed during the shaping process. When the repair was completed, the partners placed their identifying brand on the seat bottom. By chance, part of the Frost surname extends across the butterfly.[2]

Handymen working during the last two centuries have often repaired split seats by simply gluing the break and screwing or nailing a board to the lower surface. Some repairers have chamfered the board edges to minimize the visual intrusion of the extra piece of wood. Another solution is the seat replacement, which requires considerably more skill since it necessitates disassembling the chair. The procedure appears to have been uncommon, although in 1836 partners Thomas J. Moyers and Fleming K. Rich of Wytheville, Virginia, were called upon twice by the same customer to place a new "plank in [the] bottom of [a] chair." The 25-cent charge for each repair represented about one quarter the cost of a new chair.[3]

An unusual, although not unique, seat repair made with iron clamps to a tall fan-back armchair of southeastern Pennsylvania origin, probably in the late nineteenth or early twentieth century, was perhaps executed in part by a metalsmith. One clamp is visible at the center top of the seat (fig. 2). The crack, which follows the wood grain, runs diagonally from side front to side back. The unusual orientation of the wood fibers is typical of a small group of Philadelphia-area Windsors constructed before the Revolutionary War that have rear seat extensions and bracing spindles in the English fashion. Two other clamps were affixed to the lower surface of the seat near the front and back to complete the repair (fig. 3). The right-angled tips of all the clamps penetrate the wood and are secured from the opposite surface by rivets and square iron washers. An embossed metal tag nailed over one of the clamps on the lower surface identifies the repairer (name obliterated) as a resident of Christiana, Pennsylvania, a small village on the border of Lancaster and Chester counties. The medial stretcher, which is not original, probably was replaced at the time the seat was repaired.

Another uncommon repair employing a metal clamp is one made to a child's low chair of western Connecticut origin (fig. 4). Probably as a result of hard use, the right back post was loosened at the seat joint, and the up-and-down motion of the loose standard substantially increased the size of the socket, making a normal repair difficult. The metal bar clamp that now secures the joint has a right-angled tip at the top, which passes through the post and is clinched over at the back. The threaded lower end extends through the basswood seat and is held fast by a square bolt and washer.

The crest piece may have been repaired at the same time as the post, since one of the nails holding it in place is also clinched over at the back. Screws were also added to provide further stability to the crest, which otherwise rested on rabbets cut into the post faces, a method borrowed from fancy chair construction. Originally, the top piece would have been held in place by screws inserted only from the back of the posts, countersunk and puttied over before painting. The decoupage decoration, a later addition, was a popular ornamental form from the late nineteenth century.

Figure 4 Child's square-back Windsor side chair, George Dewey, Litchfield, Conn., 1815–1824. Basswood (seat, microanalysis). H. 20 1/4", W. (crest) 12 3/4", D. (seat) 12 3/4". (Private collection; photo, Winterthur Museum.)

Restorations

A relatively common nineteenth- and twentieth-century restoration in Windsor furniture is the addition of a modeled or carved block of wood to the lower half of an eighteenth-century scrolled and knuckled handgrip (fig. 5). The unrestored arm terminals in figure 5 illustrate the original construction method: the flat surfaces of the grips and scroll blocks were glued together and the parts further secured with wooden pins or internal metal sprigs (headless brads).

A restoration encountered occasionally is the new lip affixed to the upper back edge of the crest in a nineteenth-century tablet-top chair. Seat rolls may be missing or replaced in other nineteenth-century chairs, since they were simply glued and nailed in place. As the glue dried out and the fasteners became loose, the small attachments fell off and were lost in the course of time.

Figure 5 Sack-back Windsor armchair, Rhode Island, 1780–1790. White pine (seat), maple, oak, and birch (microanalysis). H. 36 13/16", W. (arms) 25 1/4", D. (seat) 15". (Courtesy, Winterthur Museum, acc. 65.836.)

A common, and usually obvious, seat restoration is a patch to fill in a large, centered hole cut out of the plank in the nineteenth or early twentieth century to accommodate a commode pan. An early reference to this practice is in the Hartford, Connecticut, accounts of Philemon Robbins, who in 1834 undertook a customer's order for "making hole to large Chair." Often those who patched the chairs in later years did not contour the

Figure 6 Sack-back Windsor armchair, Connecticut-Rhode Island border region, 1790–1800. White pine (seat), maple, and oak (microanalysis). H. 41 3/4", W. (arms) 24 1/2", D. (seat) 16 1/2". (Courtesy, Winterthur Museum, acc. 65.3027.)

replacement disk to follow the original seat modeling, perhaps because a pillow or cushion would conceal the difference. An exception is the craftsman who carefully retrofitted a chair made by Thomas Cotton Hayward of Charlestown, Massachusetts, with a contoured patch. Except under a raking light, modern paint disguises the seat-top repair, although the restoration is plainly visible on the bottom surface.[4]

Replacement stretchers added to furniture in the nineteenth century or later are frequently close imitations or adaptations of the original braces. The modern examiner may find the evidence in disturbed joints or the chronology of paint layers. Other replacements may be more obvious and even use old parts, although making distinctions between the original fabric of a chair and later additions can still pose problems for the collector or curator. Figure 6 illustrates the restoration of two of the three stretchers in a chair, perhaps carried out before the mid-nineteenth century. The medial brace is stylistically different; indeed, the simulated bamboo turning is incompatible with the overall character of the other roundwork. Of the remaining two braces, logic suggests that the bulbous right one is original, since its profile relates more directly to the swelled elements in the legs. An examination of the layers of paint supports this hypothesis and suggests that the original painted surface was bright green over a grayish primer. The paint chronology also confirms that the right front leg, although smaller in diameter than the others, is original. The critical issue is not so much the diameter of the leg as it is the length of the individual elements and the character of the secondary turnings, including the leg tops and the heads of the two balusters.

Replacement stretchers are common because sitters often rested their feet on the chair rounds. Stretcher and chair round are terms used interchangeably in eighteenth- and nineteenth-century accounts. Samuel Douglas of Canton, Connecticut, replaced three rounds in two chairs when he repaired them in 1828. At Deerfield, New Hampshire, True Currier renewed four stretchers in a single chair in the 1830s. Householders frequently had their chairs repainted when repair work was carried out. Solomon Cole of Glastonbury, Connecticut, charged nine pence apiece to paint five chairs in 1799. The new stretcher put in one of them cost six pence.[5]

Pressure could cause legs to crack at the seat joints, and exposure to rough and damp surfaces could wear away the bottoms of legs as far up as the stretchers. When Abraham Low of Freehold, New Jersey, wrote in his accounts, "rep[aired] a winsor chaer with feet & a stritcher" in 1817, it is likely that he replaced the legs in their entirety since contemporary terminology equated *feet* with *legs*. Furthermore, it was simpler, less expensive, and more satisfactory to produce completely new turnings than to patch old ones. Preserving as much as possible of the original fabric of a chair was of little concern.[6]

Leg repairs made by late-nineteenth- and twentieth-century woodworkers are of several types. It is fairly easy to detect the open mortise-and-tenon joint, formed by uniting the original leg, which has been slotted at the bottom, and a new lower section cut with a rectangular tenon at the top (fig. 7a). If the repairer instead used a round-tenon joint (fig. 7b), the dowel-like tenon is completely concealed, but a faint circular line is frequently visible at the juncture of the two pieces of wood. A round-tenon joint executed at a natural crease between turned elements (fig. 7c) is often difficult to discern, and it may be stylistic evidence only that suggests a restoration. A leg from a chair of closely related design with similar round-

Figure 7a–7d Detail of Windsor chair legs. (Left to right) probably York Co., Pa. (*a*), and Rhode Island (*b–d*); 1800–1815, 1785–1790, 1790–1800 (*c–d*). Maple (legs, microanalysis). H. 38 7/8", 43 7/16", 37 1/2", 39 1/2"; W. (arms) 23 1/2", 24 13/16", 25 1/4", 23 3/16"; D. (seat) 18 3/4", 16", 15 5/8", 15 1/2". (Courtesy, Winterthur Museum, acc. 65.837; 59.1628; 69.230.)

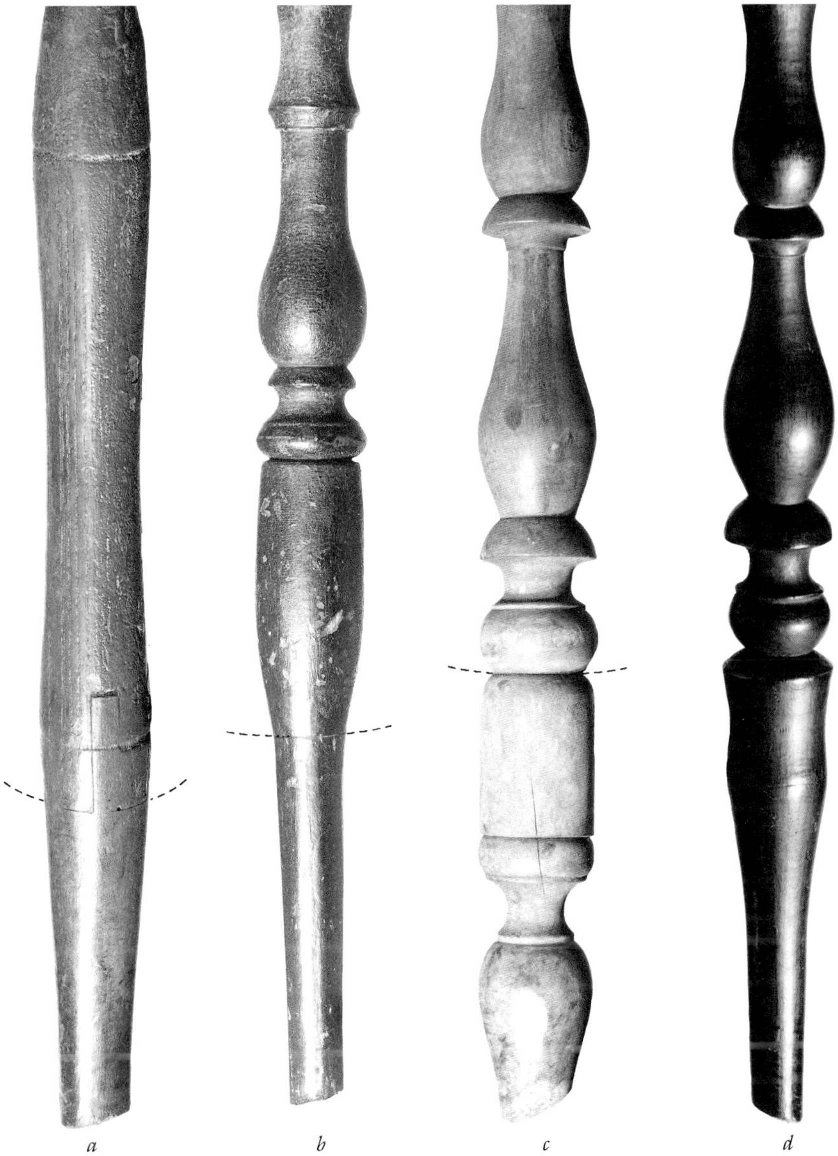

work above the cylinder (fig. 7*d*) shows that figure 7*c* has been restored. The lower legs in figure 7*c* were missing below the stretchers (which are original), and the restorer wrongly guessed that the chair originally had ball-type feet. The stylistic clue to the problem feet lay in the shortness of the cylinder. (Of further note, the wood grain differs slightly in the new and old work.) Had the legs been restored accurately, the new work might have gone undetected, especially if covered with one or more coats of paint. When a new joint is tight and the wood grain in the original leg and the restoration matches or is concealed by paint, X-ray analysis is often the only way to determine that the legs are pieced out.

Figure 8 illustrates a chair with legs replaced at an early date. All parts of the chair, with the exception of the legs but including the stretchers, were originally finished with a coat of bright, medium green paint over a gray primer. The second coat, which is the base coat on the legs, was a light, chalky blue green.

Figure 8 High-back Windsor armchair, Rhode Island, 1760–1770. Maple and ash (microanalysis). H. 42 1/16", W. (arms) 28", D. (seat) 16 1/8". (Courtesy, Winterthur Museum, acc. 65.3025.)

The question of originality arose because figure 8 is part of a group of unusual Rhode Island cross-stretcher chairs (fig. 9) produced before the revolution and the only one with a peg-like profile below the stretchers. Close comparison of the legs in figures 8 and 9 reveals a striking similarity as far down as the stretchers, suggesting that the repairer had that part of the old leg to copy. Below the stretchers, the turning profiles are completely different, which suggests the original feet had been completely destroyed. A likely

Figure 9 High-back Windsor armchair, Rhode Island, 1760–1770. Maple and hickory (microanalysis). H. 42 7/8", W. (arms) 26 5/8", D. (seat) 21 3/4". (Courtesy, Winterthur Museum, acc. 59.1667.)

explanation is that the feet had been exposed to dry rot, for even severe breakage would not have damaged all the feet beyond recognition nor allowed the stretchers to survive unscathed.

The leg repairs to the low stool with the sizable seat in figures 10 and 11 are unusual. Wallace Nutting, the early twentieth-century furniture connoisseur and author, illustrated the stool in at least three of his publications dating in the 1920s and twice identified the owner as George F. Ives, an early

Figure 10 Low Windsor stool, New England, 1850–1870. White pine (seat), maple, white pine, and birch (microanalysis). H. 13", W. (seat) 17 3/4", D. (seat) 11 3/8". (Courtesy, Winterthur Museum, acc. 59.1659.)

Figure 11 Underside of the stool illustrated in fig. 10. (Photo, Winterthur Museum.)

Figure 12 High-back Windsor armchair, Philadelphia, Pa., ca. 1754–1760. Yellow poplar (seat), maple, oak, and ash (microanalysis). H. 42", W. (arms) 28 3/4", D. (seat) 17 3/4". (Courtesy, Winterthur Museum, acc. 59.1572.)

collector from Danbury, Connecticut. The bulk of the Ives collection was housed in the Ives Tavern and Colonial Museum, an eighteenth-century inn originally in Brookfield, Connecticut, re-erected in nearby Danbury. In the "Illustrated Partial List of Items" at the Ives estate sale in 1924, the stool was pictured in the tavern kitchen and identified as item no. 668. The stool sold for forty-five dollars, but whether it entered the Henry Francis du Pont collection at Winterthur directly or at a later date is ambiguous, for it is not mentioned among the list of Ives estate purchases du Pont recorded.[7]

Only two of the stool legs are original. They, along with the seat, retain what is probably the original grain-painted surface in medium and dark brown over pinkish tan. The seat shows evidence of combing, or streaking; the maple legs are mottled and speckled like a pottery glaze.

The three replaced legs are most visible in figure 10. That at the extreme right front was hand whittled of pine, probably by a late-nineteenth-century owner, and is an amazingly good copy given the technique. The left and center front birch legs, possibly early-twentieth-century replacements, are close copies of the original supports in profile and in wear patterns but bear only a light, smeared coat of black paint on the wood. Whether the stool was originally a rare asymmetrical five-legged seat is unclear. Certainly, from the wear at the socket, a fifth leg would appear to have been in place from an early date.

Heavy restoration compromises the integrity of figure 12, a classic early Pennsylvania-type high-back chair long sought by connoisseurs as a cornerstone for their collections. Three features suggest a 1750s date: pronounced incline of the arm rail, attenuated arm posts, and baroque-style medial stretcher. Restoration work starts with the crest, which is a modern replacement colored with a red stain under the present dark varnish. The dimensions from top edge to bottom are greater than usual, the central hump is narrower and higher than common, and the base is almost an inch thick. The ridges of the spiral on the volute-carved ends show almost no wear or damage. Surface aging of the wood, common in old oak (fig. 13), is absent on this crest. Shrinkage, another typical condition that causes the wood of the crest to mold around the spindle tips in surface bulges that are visible or at least apparent to the touch on crest pieces of eighteenth-century chairs (fig. 14), is missing from figure 12.

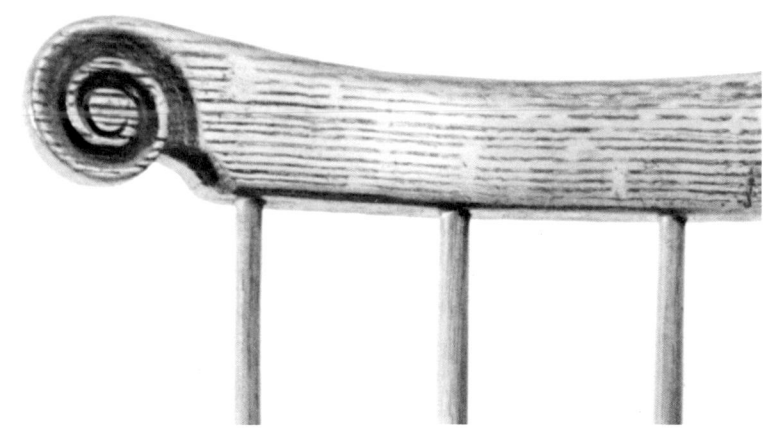

Figure 13 Detail of a crest scroll of a high-back Windsor armchair, Philadelphia, Pa., ca. 1765. Yellow poplar (seat), maple, oak, and hickory. H. 44 5/8", W. (arms) 25 5/8", D. (seat) 16". (Private collection; photo, Winterthur Museum.)

Figure 14 Detail of a crest end of a high-back Windsor armchair, Philadelphia, Pa., ca. 1768–1776. Yellow poplar (seat), maple, oak, and hickory (microanalysis). H. 40 11/16", W. (arms) 26 1/8", D. (seat) 14 3/8". (Courtesy, Winterthur Museum, acc. 59.1546.)

A diagonal break above the third short spindle at the right rear of the arm rail in figure 12 was repaired with nails, glue, and an outside patch. The rail was restored forward of this point. The first long back spindle adjacent to the repair was broken in two within the rail but not repaired. Both handgrips were restored (fig. 15). The rail ends were sawed off in rabbets (seen from the inside faces), leaving the short edges on the top surface only one-eighth inch forward of the holes drilled for the posts. The grips, each with a flaring side piece, are deeply carved with long grooves to produce knuckled scrolls that were completed by the attachment of separate carved blocks at the lower front edges. Nails hold the rabbets fast, and two large, round wooden pins visible on the inside and outside faces of the rail and handgrips further secure the joints.

In structure and design, the rail ends and handgrips are incorrect for the 1750s. The rail should continue forward on the inside edges to the ends of the grips, with the flaring joined pieces on the outer edges only. Moreover, the knuckled grip is rare in early high-back chairs with D-shape seats and bent arm rails. It was more common on 1760s high-back chairs of rounded-oblong seat and optional on the 1760s sack-back Windsor. As for the design of the handgrips in figure 15, the grooves are abnormally long and deep and positioned too closely together.

The finish on figure 12 suggests that most spindles, short and long, may be replacements, for only one short stick bears traces of the original green paint over a gray primer coat. There is also no evidence of original paint on the right post. That support was likely broken when the rail was cracked through at the rear corner. The new turning is almost an exact copy of the post at the left, an unusual circumstance since variations are generally noted between old and new work, especially in the interpretation of fine elements such as disks, spools, and collars. The feet, which are also restored, show the same attention to turned detail.

The seat plank provided other information about the structural history of the chair. A small, now-plugged hole indicates that the rail was once stabilized by a vertical iron rod between the first and second short spindles behind the right post. (There is no matching hole in the new right rail section.) The many small nail holes and nails on the chamfered edge beneath the sides and back of the seat and the single tacking line on the upper seat edge at the front indicate that the plank was once stuffed.

Each foot bears only a coat of dark varnish, although traces of the original green paint are on other elements of all four legs. The connections between the ring turnings above the feet and the leg cylinders are abrupt and somewhat sharply edged; the crevices lack the typical paint and varnish buildup common at these points. Furthermore, the left front foot is socketed slightly off-center, causing the ring turning to extend somewhat beyond the cylinder at the left side.

The extensive restoration of figure 12 was probably carried out in the early twentieth century. Other repair work was undertaken in 1965 before the true condition of the chair was recognized. A crack in the upper part of the left rear leg was stabilized, and the left front leg was patched in several places.

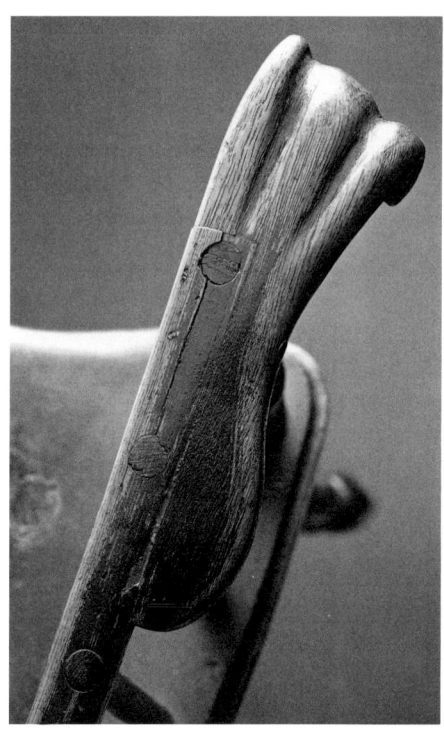

Figure 15 Detail of an arm terminal of the chair illustrated in fig. 12. (Photo, Winterthur Museum.)

Figure 16 Square-back Windsor side chair converted to rocker, Cornelius Timpson and John Vangelder, New York City, 1799–1801. Yellow poplar (seat), maple, and other woods. H. 29 ½", W. (rockers) 21 ⅛", D. (rockers) 21". (Courtesy, Winterthur Museum, acc. 81.41.)

Alterations

The most common alteration made to Windsors in the nineteenth and twentieth centuries was the addition of rockers. Account books from the late eighteenth century onward are filled with entries for such work, although they do not always distinguish between conversions and replacements of broken or worn rockers. On May 30, 1800, Silas Cheney put rockers on a chair for Tapping Reeve, founder of the Litchfield Law School in western Connecticut, and charged him 1s., or about 16½ cents. Elizur Barnes of Middletown on the Connecticut River charged a customer 75 cents in 1822 to convert a chair for rocking and included in the charge the cost of heightening the back, probably with a headrest, an alteration that suggests the chair was a Windsor. At Erie, Pennsylvania, a chair to be altered was in need of repair when taken to furniture maker George Landon in 1819 for "rockers and foot and stretchers."[8]

Surviving chairs that were converted into rockers are usually easy to identify. The chair in figure 16 is typical. The legs are cut off at an odd point (just below the simulated bamboo grooves), stretchers are almost at rocker level, and the attachment method is relatively crude. In the original construction of rockers, the legs are designed and turned to fit the shallower space between the seat and rockers, the stretchers are generally placed several inches above the rockers, and legs and rockers are united by one of three methods: round toes or rectangular tenons in the leg bottoms are socketed into the rockers; thick leg bottoms are slotted to receive slim rockers; or rabbeted leg bottoms are fitted with rockers on the outside or inside surfaces. Original rocker joints are secured by wooden pins, nails, or countersunk screws. Rocker conversion joints are usually rabbeted. In original rabbeted, and sometimes slotted, rocker construction, the long leg extensions adjoining the rockers are generally chamfered at the bottom, providing a neat finish and ensuring smooth rocking. Leg chamfers and rockers in chairs made originally for rocking have the same finish coats found on other parts of the chair, unless repairs or wear have compromised the surfaces.

In addition to the rocker conversion, the chair in figure 16 has undergone both a repair and a restoration. The right back post has been evened off near the bottom and reattached to the post extension that sockets into the seat. The left post has been replaced, and its smooth paint contrasts with the irregular finish on the rest of the chair. Unrestored damage remains at the post-and-crest joints.

A somewhat rare alteration involves converting a chair to a new function by adding a writing leaf to an armchair or even a side chair. Such leafs are generally smaller than customary to allow a user to slip into the confined seating space of the "new" piece of furniture. Sometimes the arm beneath the leaf has been modified to accommodate the writing board. An additional leaf support, usually a shaved stick or a metal brace, may be mounted at an acute angle between the bottom of the leaf and the spindle platform at the perimeter of the seat.

Nineteenth- and twentieth-century alterations carried out because of damage to a piece of furniture are relatively common. Chair backs are par-

Figure 17 Fan-back Windsor side chair, northeastern coastal Connecticut, 1790–1800. Basswood (seat), maple, and hickory (microanalysis). H. 30 3/8", W. (crest) 18 3/8", D. (seat) 15 7/8". (Courtesy, Winterthur Museum, acc. 59.2081.)

ticularly vulnerable to mishaps, because as the wood dries out, the back structure loses its elasticity and becomes brittle. Pressure exerted by a sitter or the accidental tipping over of a chair could and did result in cracked or broken posts, bows, and spindles, or damage to the entire top structure. Some owners chose to convert high-back armchairs with broken tops to low-back chairs simply by sawing off the spindles flush with the top of the arm rail. These low-back chairs with slim, steamed and bent arm rails are particularly easy to identify. Chairs made originally with low backs have

Figure 19 Detail of the front leg-seat joint of the chair illustrated in fig. 18. (Photo, Winterthur Museum.)

Figure 18 Bow-back Windsor side chair, Connecticut-Rhode Island border region, 1795–1805. Cottonwood (seat), maple, oak, and hickory (microanalysis). H. 34 9/16", W. (seat) 14 5/16", D. (seat) 16 1/2". (Courtesy, Winterthur Museum, acc. 64.1173.)

heavy, three-piece sawed rails to compensate for the pressure of the sitter's body in this confined area. Chairs with sawed off high backs are structurally unsound; the weight of the sitter is concentrated within the short back rather than being distributed over a taller form.

A side chair that sustained back damage was offered without caveat at auction as long ago as 1926 (fig. 17). A backward fall probably cracked or broke the spindles and posts near the crest. Rather than replace all the vertical parts, the repairer chose to modify the structure by whittling or shaving the upper part of all the elements to produce tips of the correct size for

Figure 20 Triple sack-back Windsor settee, eastern Connecticut or Rhode Island, 1790–1805. White pine (seat), maple, oak, and hickory (microanalysis). H. 40 1/2", W. (arms) 81 3/4", D. (seat) 23 5/8". (Courtesy, Winterthur Museum, acc. 59.151.)

reinsertion into the original crest. The crude tapering of the uprights, including the once-turned back posts forming the ends, is readily apparent. Fan-back side chairs with low backs are uncommon. When they were made, chairmakers fitted them with turned end posts modified in element length to fit the shorter space, much as they reduced the leg height in a rocking chair.[9]

An unusual alteration is pictured in figures 18 and 19. At some point, probably during the late nineteenth century, an owner lowered the height of the chair about one inch but did so with an unorthodox method. He had the rear legs cut off at the bottom and the front legs reworked at the top (fig. 19). The height adjustment of the legs necessitated shifting the side stretchers to minimize the front-to-back slope. Normally, stretchers are positioned an inch or more below the ring turnings in the legs, but the repositioning of the sockets in the back legs necessitated partially piercing the ring turnings. The original holes were plugged.

Even without the alteration, the turned work of figure 18 is out of the ordinary. Although the profiles of all four legs are similar, there is a pronounced difference in the diameter of the turnings of the front and back legs. The intent of the maker must have been to provide additional structural strength at the chair back, where the weight of the sitter concentrates. His concern with structural stress is further expressed in the prominent, ringlike collars at the leg tops (the front ones now removed) immediately

Figure 21 Detail of the right front seat corner and arm supports of the chair illustrated in fig. 20. (Photo, Winterthur Museum.)

adjacent to the seat bottom: rings prevented further penetration of the legs through the plank. The leg features, in combination with the thickly shaped seat and the aberrant character of the bow with its pendent "ears," identify the chair as the product of a rural craftsman.

Only four multiple-arch, sack-back Windsor settees made in the late eighteenth century are known (fig. 20). Other examples were reproduced in the 1930s by John M. Bair of Abbottstown, Pennsylvania, and Wallace Nutting, who described his as a "triple bow back ten legger." The chronology of paint layers in figure 20—an aged dark brown over green, both over green on a gray primer—indicates that the replaced parts include the bottoms of both handgrips and part of the undercarriage at the left end: the two rear legs, the two front-to-back stretchers, and the companion medial stretcher. The furniture researcher's greater challenge in this piece of furniture is understanding what has happened above the base.[10]

Beginning forward of the arm posts, both ends of the seat plank have a series of plugged holes (fig. 21). That both assemblies have the same paint coats as the rest of the settee ruled out restoration of the arms as an explanation and allowed two other questions. Did the chairmaker make a mistake in laying out the upper structure, or did the purchaser request an alteration while the work was in progress? The discovery that the seat is pieced at the front—a longitudinal seam passes through the post sockets and in front of the legs—and the discovery that the seat and the pieced front bear all the paint coats of the other original parts, led to the conclusion that someone decided to remove a piece of the plank, altering the settee some years after its manufacture. Spaced wooden pins, visible along the front edge of the seat, secure the two pieces of wood.

In its present state, the settee plank measures 23 5/8" from front to back, a reduction of about 2" from its original size as determined by the alteration made to the arms. A survey of six other long Windsor seats of late eighteenth-century date indicates that 19 1/4" to 21 1/2" is the usual depth of the settee form; this one is still 2 or more inches deeper than average. Further investigation shows that the arms were shortened at the rear corner joints and that, in the process, an entire spindle unit about 2" in length was removed at each end of the settee. The uprights beneath the arms were relocated in new holes, and the old sockets were plugged up. In its present dimension the seat is at maximum depth for comfortable seating. Two inches more must have made it uncomfortable to several generations of owners before one of them took action. A closely related settee with eight (rather than ten) legs still retains its full depth plank. It has ten short spindles beneath each arm instead of the nine in figure 20.[11]

Reconstructions

The Windsor illustrated in figure 22 is a reconstruction of a chair that began its life as a sack-back armchair, with a bow confining the tops of the long spindles inside an arc springing from the bent arm rail, in the manner of the chairs in figures 5 and 6. The principal evidence for this reconstruction is two plugged holes in the rail, one at each side between the first and second

Figure 22 Sack-back Windsor armchair, Connecticut-Rhode Island border region, 1790–1800. Maple, oak, and other woods; dimensions unknown. (Former collection of J. Stogdell Stokes; photo, Philadelphia Museum of Art.)

short spindles, where the bow ends were attached. The awkward proportions of the short, narrow back in relation to the breadth of the chair and the fragile, unfinished appearance of the top piece are neither structurally nor aesthetically compatible with the basic chair design. The full swelled short sticks and the slight inward sweep from bottom to top apparent in the end sticks suggest that the long end spindles once arced outward in decided bends within a bow. All parts except the top piece appear to be original to the chair. The long sticks look to be full height or close to full height. There is good compatibility of the turned work below and above the seat, espe-

Figure 23 High Windsor stool, eastern United States, probably New England, style of 1795–1810. Basswood (seat) and maple (microanalysis). H. 27 ½", Diam. (top) 14"–14 ¼". (Courtesy, Winterthur Museum, acc. 58.120.4.)

cially in the baluster heads and the profiles of the spools and rings. The large, rounded-oblong contoured seat with its thick, slightly canted sides, together with the turned work, suggest a Connecticut-Rhode Island origin.

Tall stools, because of their size and function, have been subject to considerable wear, stress, and strain. Over time seats have been marred, legs broken, and stretchers worn down. The seat and three of the stretchers in figure 23 are old parts, bearing evidence of several coats of paint under the present outer coat of green, which covers a dark brown finish. The worn state of the early paint coats, however, makes it ambiguous whether all the old parts are original to the same stool. One of the high stretchers and most, if not all, of the legs were considerably worn or broken, because all are new parts. The condition of the stool fits with an entry for a high stool that a Newark, New Jersey, firm took to local chairmaker David Alling in 1838: "To mending seat & putting new legs & rounds to one shop stool." The high stretcher at the right side in figure 23 exhibits deterioration from use comparable to that in the other three braces, but the wear is artificial: the top left surface is irregular, and the back edge is sharply angular and lacking the soft rounding that resulted from wear on the other braces. The legs are newly turned, and all bear signs of "distress" in the form of rounded nicks, large and small, gouged into the surface with a sharp cutting tool. Large nicks are plainly visible in the left front leg at the points of the bamboo grooves; small nicks fill the long space between the rings.[12]

Reproductions
Although several writing chairs of the pattern illustrated in figure 24 are known, the materials, profiles of the turnings, and the structure are completely unorthodox for the supposed late-eighteenth-century date of this chair. Except for the interior boards of the drawers, which are yellow pine, the chair is made of black walnut, a wood rarely used by American Windsor chairmakers. A small group of cross-stretcher Rhode Island Windsors made before the Revolutionary War was constructed almost entirely of maple (figs. 8, 9). Nathaniel Dominy V of East Hampton, Long Island, made a set of mahogany low-back Windsors in 1794 for a customer who supplied the material from his mahogany grove in Honduras. Walnut Windsors were sold at Philadelphia during the 1760s, but apparently few were made; only one cabriole-leg chair in the English style is known. The modestly curved, thick-bottomed balusters, especially those of the legs, have more the character of late-nineteenth-century than eighteenth-century work (compare them with those in figs. 2, 5–7, 12, 17–18, 20 and 22). The wood surface is rough, and there is no evidence of paint coats beneath the outer black varnish. The stretcher turnings are similar to eighteenth-century braces, however side stretchers with fancy ring turnings are uncommon features on eighteenth-century Windsors.[13]

The construction methods employed in this chair are peculiar by eighteenth-century standards. The arm-rail assembly consists of four units: the two arms, a center-back section that meets the arms at flat butt joints, and a center-back capping piece with short ogee tips. The four pieces of wood

Figure 24 Low-back Windsor writing-arm chair, eastern United States, probably Virginia, possibly nineteenth century in style of ca. 1768–1776. American black walnut and yellow pine (microanalysis). H. 30 1/16", W. (arms) 39 3/8", D. (seat) 18 3/8". (Courtesy, Winterthur Museum, acc. 59.1394.)

Figure 25 Detail of the seat bottom of the chair illustrated in fig. 24. (Photo, Winterthur Museum.)

are secured with screws from the bottom at the side back joints, a normal procedure in low-back construction, and with pins at the ends of the capping piece. Usually, eighteenth-century low-back rails consist of three pieces of wood only. In Rhode Island construction the arms meet at the center back in a butt joint and are capped by a shaped, ogee-ended top piece. The arms in Philadelphia chairs terminate at the back corners, and the center back section is one solid piece of wood cut with rabbets at the ends to form lap joints.

The seat is made of four boards rather than the usual single thick plank. Two boards form the top surface, and two the bottom, each set held together with two or three butterfly keys. These keys may be seen on the seat bottom (fig. 25) and near the back of the seat top in a line with the brass knob (not original) on the seat drawer. (Other butterfly keys secure the two pieces of the writing leaf on the bottom surface near the inside front edge.) The crosswise joints of the top and bottom seat boards do not coincide, although both are located toward the back of the chair. The two layers of wood are held together with screws, countersunk at spaced intervals around the bottom perimeter of the seat (fig. 25). Originally, the screw holes were covered over with a composition material, most of which has dried up and fallen out. The screws, which have flat tips and exhibit little taper in the shaft, have a tinned finish and date to the mid-nineteenth century or later. The horizontal seam marking the joint between the two board layers is visible across the seat front (fig. 24).

One researcher has suggested that the writing chair and two close mates were made originally for use in a courthouse during the late nineteenth century. The explanation is plausible. At least one chair has a Virginia background, having been recovered near Richmond in the early twentieth century. The walnut tree was common in Virginia, and by the late nineteenth century wide planks would have been difficult to secure and expensive to buy, which would explain why the chairmaker might purchase boards and piece up the seats. Yellow pine as a secondary wood supports a southern provenance.

Though the Virginia writing-arm chair appears to be a straightforward, late-nineteenth-century adaptation of a colonial American design that has

Figure 26 High-back Windsor armchair, Wallace Nutting, Framingham, Massachusetts, 1930s in style of 1780s. Pine (seat) and oak. H. 43 $^{15}/_{16}$", W. (arms) 26 $^{11}/_{16}$", D. (seat) 22 $^{1}/_{8}$". (Courtesy, Winterthur Museum, acc. 77.54.)

Figure 27 Continuous-bow Windsor highchair, Wallace Nutting, Framingham, Mass., 1930s in style of 1790s. White pine (seat), birch, and oak (microanalysis). H. 37", W. (arms) 15 1/8", D. (seat) 12 3/4". (Courtesy, Winterthur Museum, acc. 58.635.)

Figure 28 Detail of the leg and stretcher joint of the chair illustrated in fig. 27. (Photo, Winterthur Museum.)

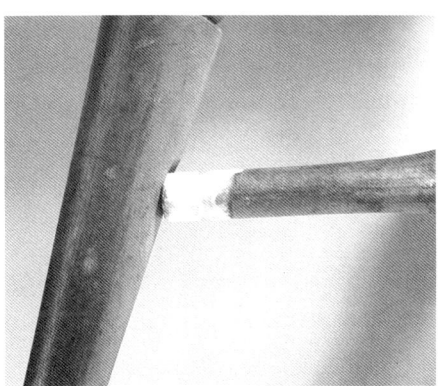

been misinterpreted in the twentieth century, there are many eighteenth-century-style reproductions made early in the twentieth century that are creating problems for the unwary. One of the prominent, early-twentieth-century producers of reproduction furniture was Wallace Nutting, who wrote several books on antiques and first issued a catalogue of his reproduction line in 1930. Some of Nutting's forty-four designs for Windsor furniture are obvious adaptations rather than true copies. Figure 26 is an adaptation that has bold, overstated features. Were this chair to be distressed and painted over many times, the single most revealing feature of its modern provenance would be the seat, which has an exaggerated inward ramp at either side front. Other telltale characteristics are the mechanically precise arms, the sizable crest piece, the exaggerated swells in the spindles, and the trademark turnings—full, oval-bodied roundwork, which represents the epitome of good design, that is present in about half of Nutting's Windsor production. When viewed, even from a distance, the chair is "too good to be true."[14]

One of Nutting's most successful, and most convincing, eighteenth-century-style Windsor designs is a child's highchair with a continuous bow (fig. 27). Indeed, this chair, which has been "aged," passed for many years as a period piece. In some places the light pea green paint is dry and irregular; in other places it is worn away, exposing the shiny patina of the bare wood. Some of the turnings show wear, notably the rings of the medial stretcher, although upon reflection it is obvious that no child's feet would have reached that far. The seat has several checks and many small nicks on the finished surfaces. The bottom has a lightly tooled appearance. The chance drying out of one of the stretcher-and-leg joints brought the truth to light. The partially exposed stretcher tip looked too white where the paint ended. Further investigation revealed that the end was mechanically formed rather than roughly shaped with a knife (fig. 28), and the flat-bottomed leg socket was hollowed out with a center bit rather than with a round-nosed spoon bit, the premier boring tool of the Windsor chairmaker until the mid-nineteenth century. Nutting's trademark turnings are present in the highchair, along with the exaggerated spindles. The design is illustrated in his catalogue as no. 210 and priced at forty-two dollars. Even as early as 1930, Nutting commented in general that some of his furniture was being passed off as antique: "A child's high chair made by me, and sold as new for nineteen dollars, was artificially aged and resold for a cool thousand. Nobody but the maker could have discovered the imposition."[15]

Moving from the honest reproduction to the "aged" replica and then to the out-and-out fake is only a few short steps. The early Pennsylvania-type Windsor illustrated in figure 29, which was probably made purely to deceive, has several obvious design and structural faults. Peaked-center crest pieces are uncommon in Windsor design. Wallace Nutting used peaked crests in at least four of his chairs, any one of which could have served as a general model for the independent entrepreneur who made this chair. This thick interpretation has a particularly sharp center point, roughly tooled top edges, and crudely carved volutes with irregular spirals and roughly chiseled hollows.

Figure 29 High-back Windsor armchair, eastern United States, probably Pennsylvania, twentieth century in style of ca. 1754–1760. Yellow poplar (seat), oak, hickory, and pear (microanalysis). H. 41 $^{11}/_{16}$", W. (arms) 25", D. (seat) 15 $^{13}/_{16}$". (Courtesy, Winterthur Museum, acc. 59.1609.)

The small round wooden pins securing the long end and center spindles of the peaked-crest chair are abnormally precise, and the spindles themselves are unusually slender at the tops. The sticks almost seem to be buckling under the weight of the crest (compare the spindles in figs. 12 and 29). The long outer spindles are socketed half an inch or more short of normal placement near the crest scrolls. Below the arm rail tapered spindles vary noticeably in thickness and are crudely shaped in ridges with a drawknife or comparable tool, as is visible under the right arm. The three-piece rail construction with diagonal lap joints at the back corners is correct for a Pennsylvania chair; however, the long ogee-shaped tongues extending onto the arms are not. The upper curves should be longer and more gradual, and the outer tips should be molded in shallow steps (see figs. 5 and 20).[16]

Problems with the turned work are less obvious to the untrained eye. The general plan is correct, but the profiles exhibit subtle variation from the norm (see fig. 12). The upper element in the arm posts is more baluster-like than budlike, and the bulging body of the long baluster is barrel shape rather than round or tear-drop shape, with somewhat angular transitions to the adjacent necks. The long swelling bodies in the leg balusters are more typical of work executed in the 1760s and later. Short, fully rounded swells typify the 1750s (see fig. 12). Saucer-like collars at the baluster tops are incorrect for any period of Pennsylvania work. The feet are simplistically interpreted (compare figs. 2 and 29) and the stretcher turnings are heavier than normal. Furthermore, the paint extends all the way to the bottom tips without any sign of wear.

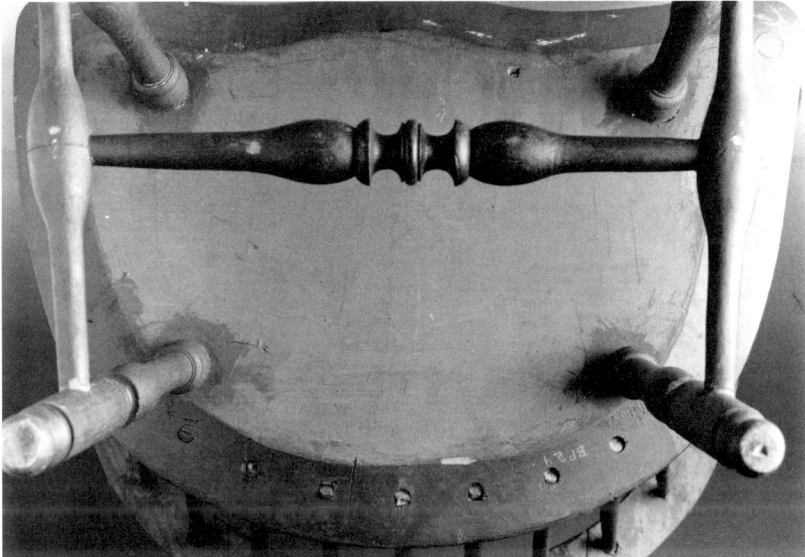

Figure 30   Detail of the seat bottom of the chair illustrated in fig. 29. (Photo, Winterthur Museum.)

The upper surface of the seat plank is reasonably well modeled, however the underside lacks any discernable plane marks running lengthwise with the grain of the wood (fig. 30). Planing was a common technique used by Windsor chairmakers to "dress," or smooth, the bottom of a seat plank. Instead, there are shallow gouge marks at right angles to the wood grain. The seat bottom, which is normally unpainted, has the same gray paint and varnish finish that is found on all the chair parts except the long spindles and the crest. The outer surfaces of the chair are further finished with brownish red paint and varnish.

Another peculiarity of the seat bottom is the presence of open spindle sockets around the back. Normally, the spindle tips are socketed within the plank. Since the short spindles beneath the arms are not exposed and the gray underpaint of the chair is absent from the long spindles and crest, it appears that the original back sticks were also concealed. Either the chair suffered damage to the back soon after being made in the early twentieth century, or the design was altered from low-back to high-back form to make it more salable. In either case, the repairer would have found it easiest to replace the back spindles by opening the sockets at the bottom and tapping out the stumps.

Figure 31 Detail of name brand on seat bottom of low-back Windsor armchair, Philadelphia, Pa., ca. 1760. H. 28 1/4", W. (seat) 24 13/16", D. (seat) 17 1/8". (Courtesy, Independence National Historical Park, Philadelphia; photo, Winterthur Museum.)

Enhancements

Windsors form the largest group of documented American furniture, yet the number of labeled, stenciled, signed, and branded objects is small. Brands are most numerous and usually identify original makers, although a few can be associated with original and subsequent owners. Some brands are modern additions made with period or new irons to enhance the value or appeal of an object. These marks have been placed on the furniture with intent to deceive.

Windsor brands are usually located on the plank bottom. All those on furniture dating before 1840, and most dating before 1850, bear names formed of letters with serifs (fig. 31). Letter height generally falls into the 3/8" to 5/8" range. The vast majority of craftsmen's brands includes an initial and a last name. Two-initial names are less common, and last names alone, except for partnerships, are unusual. Occasionally, given names are contracted, such as Ek. for Ezekiel or Ia. for James.

A brand that reads S.O.PAINE in upper-case, serif letters was probably made with a period iron, but its application on three (or more) period Windsor chairs is of twentieth-century date, probably before 1966 when one of the chairs was acquired for an institutional collection (fig. 31). The key to identifying the brand as a modern enhancement lies in the styles and regional characteristics of the chairs it marks. One is a fan-back side chair made in the Connecticut-Rhode Island border region; another is a Rhode Island sack-back armchair. Both date to the 1790s. The third chair is a Philadelphia low-back Windsor with ball-foot legs, made about 1760. All strikes of the brand are positioned near the center back of the seat bottom, where an impression could be made without the interference of legs and stretchers in the framed chair. The current desirability and enhanced value of documented antique furniture is a development of the early twentieth century, when researchers first began to link makers and products.

Problems in Windsor furniture run the gamut from the simple to the complex. Honing individual identification skills requires extensive examination and study of both authentic and compromised pieces of furniture to establish patterns of systematic investigation and to develop the thought processes essential to recognizing, understanding, and interpreting structural compromises in antique Windsors. The connoisseur's skills are further enhanced through knowledge of styles, construction methods, and regional characteristics. Like other investigative disciplines, the process is one of continued development and refinement.

1. Advertisements of Richard Caulton in *Virginia Gazette* (Williamsburg, Va.), November 28–December 5, 1745; Harmon Vosburgh and (?) Childs in *Hall's Wilmington Gazette* (Wilmington, N.C.), February 9, 1797; Reuben Sanborn in *Columbian Centinel* (Boston, Mass.), January 1, 1806; Gilbert Ackerman in *Albany Register* (Albany, N.Y.), August 31, 1798; Lemuel Adams in *Norfolk Herald* (Norfolk, Va.), July 11, 1801.

2. The Tracy family chair is in the Winterthur Museum, Winterthur, Del., acc. 59.1399. The Seaver and Frost chair is privately owned.

3. Thomas J. Moyers and Fleming K. Rich Account Book, 1834–1840, Joseph Downs Collection of Manuscripts and Printed Ephemera, Winterthur Museum Library, Winterthur, Del. (hereafter cited as DCM).

4. Philemon Robbins Account Book, 1833–1836, Connecticut Historical Society, Hartford, Conn. (hereafter cited as CHS). The Hayward chair is privately owned.

5. Samuel Douglas and Son and Waite Garret Account Book, 1810–1858, Connecticut State Library, Hartford, Conn.; True Currier Account Book, 1815–1838, DCM; Solomon Cole Account Book, 1794–1809, CHS.

6. Alexander Low Account Book, 1784–1826, Monmouth County Historical Association, Freehold, N.J.

7. Wallace Nutting, "The Windsor Chair," *Antiques* 1, no. 2 (February 1922): 74; Wallace Nutting, *A Windsor Handbook* (1917; 2d ed., Framingham and Boston: Old America Co., n.d.), p. 88a; Wallace Nutting, *Furniture Treasury* (1928; reprint ed., New York: MacMillan Co., 1966), fig. 2753; "The George F. Ives Collection of Antiques," *Antiques* 5, no. 5 (May 1924): 273–88.

8. Silas Cheney Ledger, 1799–1817, Litchfield Historical Society, Litchfield, Conn. (microfilm), DCM; Elizur Barnes Account Book, 1821–1825, Middlesex Historical Society, Middletown, Conn. (microfilm), DCM; George Landon Account Book, 1813–1832, DCM.

9. *The Early American Collection of Mr. and Mrs. G. G. Ernst*, January 20–23, 1926 (New York: American Art Galleries, 1926), lot 402.

10. John M. Bair, *Antiques of the Future* (Abbottstown, Pa.: John M. Bair, n.d.), p. 47; Wallace Nutting, *General Catalogue, Supreme Edition* (1930; reprint ed., Exton, Pa.: Schiffer, 1977), fig. 515, p. 93. Cornucopia, a late-twentieth-century furniture-making shop in Harvard, Mass., is also handcrafting Windsor settees of this pattern.

11. Nutting, *Furniture Treasury*, fig. 1636.

12. David Alling Account Book, 1836–1854, New Jersey Historical Society, Newark, N.J. (microfilm), DCM.

13. Charles F. Hummel, *With Hammer in Hand: The Dominy Craftsmen of East Hampton, New York* (Charlottesville, Va.: University Press of Virginia, 1968), fig. 185. Sheed and White advertisement in *South Carolina Gazette* (Charleston, S.C.), June 23, 1766, as quoted in Alfred Coxe Prime, comp., *The Arts and Crafts in Philadelphia, Maryland, and South Carolina, 1721–1785* (Philadelphia: Walpole Society, 1929), pp. 188–89; Milo M. Naeve, "An Aristocratic Windsor in Eighteenth-Century Philadelphia," *American Art Journal* 11, no. 3 (July 1979): 67–74.

14. Nutting, *General Catalogue*, fig. 415.

15. Nutting, *General Catalogue*, fig. 210, p. 4.

16. Nutting, *General Catalogue*, figs. 209, 309, 412, 440.

Figure 1 Charles Willson Peale, William Buckland, Annapolis, Maryland, 1787. Oil on canvas. 36 1/2" × 27". Peale completed this portrait thirteen years after Buckland's death. Buckland is depicted working on elevations and plans for the Mathias Hammond House. (Courtesy, Yale University Art Gallery; photo, Museum of Early Southern Decorative Arts.)

Luke Beckerdite

Architect-Designed Furniture in Eighteenth-Century Virginia: The Work of William Buckland and William Bernard Sears

▼ DURING THE eighteenth century, architects occupied a socioeconomic position higher than master builders, house joiners, and other artisans in the building trades. Many leading British architects, such as William Kent and Robert Adam, were tastemakers who designed landscapes, buildings, and a broad range of decorative arts for the nobility and wealthy merchant elite. Horace Walpole noted that Kent was "consulted not only for furniture . . . but for plate, for a barge, [and] for a cradle. . . . So impetuous was fashion that two great ladies prevailed on him to make designs for their birthday gowns. . . . One he dressed in a petticoat decorated with the columns of the five orders; the other like a bronze, in a copper colored satin with ornaments of gold."[1]

Colonial American records occasionally refer to builders as architects, but most of these individuals were tradesmen, entrepreneurs, or gentlemen esteemed for their technical expertise, ability to oversee a workforce, and basic knowledge of classical form and detail. Few were architects in the strict sense of the word, and fewer still ventured into other areas of design. Perhaps the most notable exception is William Buckland (1734–1774), a talented individual whose designs for public and private buildings and furniture in Virginia and Maryland justify his claim to the title architect (fig. 1). Because Buckland's career as a builder is adequately discussed in several books and articles, this article will focus on his furniture designs, on the artisans that executed them, and on the architectural context of the furniture.[2]

Buckland was born in the parish of St. Peter's-in-the-East, Oxford, England, in 1734 and trained as a joiner by his uncle, James Buckland of London. His apprenticeship, from April 5, 1748, to April 1755, coincided with one of the most dynamic periods of British furniture and architectural design. From 1720 to 1750, Palladian classicism dominated almost every aspect of design. To create harmonious decorative schemes, architects and cabinetmakers designed furniture and other decorative artifacts along architectural lines. A side table design by William Jones is representative, having a frieze with a scrolling fret and bead-and-reel and egg-and-dart moldings (fig. 2)—classical architectural details appropriate for the friezes of stair landings, door and window entablatures, and chimneypieces. The large pendant shell, florid leafage, masks, and heavy scrollwork represent a synthesis of the Palladian and baroque styles. Jones and many other designers of the time supplemented their ornamental repertoire with details derived from late-seventeenth- and early-eighteenth-century Netherlandish, German, and French designs.[3]

Figure 2 Design for a pier table illustrated on pl. 27 of William Jones's *The Gentleman or Builder's Companion* (1739). (Courtesy, Winterthur Library: Printed Books and Periodical Collection.)

Figure 3 Gunston Hall, Mason Neck (Fairfax County), Virginia, 1750–1760. (Photo, Gavin Ashworth.)

The baroque style largely was out of fashion when Buckland began his training, but the classical tradition and the concept of furniture as an extension of interior architecture remained in vogue. During the early 1740s, the naturalistic ornaments favored by the adherents of Andreas Pallado (1508–1580) evolved into the rocaille and cocaille forms, exaggerated scrollwork, and jagged leafage of the rococo style that was at the time termed "French" or "Modern." While an apprentice, Buckland saw the rococo style expand, encompassing Chinese and Gothic elements. Thomas Chippendale's *The Gentleman and Cabinet-Maker's Director* (1754), published in the final year of Buckland's apprenticeship, was the first British furniture design book to integrate successfully the seemingly disparate tastes of the rococo style.[4]

If Buckland's career is any indication of his training, he had a thorough knowledge of classical architecture and of the practical aspects of building prior to his arrival in the colonies. He also understood the nuances of French, Chinese, and Gothic tastes and their application to furniture and architectural design. All of this knowledge he applied in his first commission.

On August 4, 1755, approximately four months after his apprenticeship expired, Buckland signed an indenture with Thomson Mason of Fairfax County, Virginia, agreeing to serve Mason or "his Executors or Assigns in . . . Virginia" for four years "in the Employment of a Carpenter &. Joiner." In turn Buckland received free passage to the colonies, food, lodging, and an annual salary of £20 sterling. Thomson Mason acted as an agent for his older brother George, a prominent northern Virginia planter who had recently begun building a house later called Gunston Hall, "a substantial brick mansion, 40 by 70 feet," bounded by the Potomac River and Pohick Creek about ten miles south of Alexandria (fig. 3).[5]

Although the exterior walls of Gunston Hall probably were complete

Figure 4 Portico on the south front of Gunston Hall. (Photo, Gavin Ashworth.)

Figure 5 Central hall in Gunston Hall. (Photo, Gavin Ashworth.)

Figure 6 Detail of one of the appliqués on the arch spandrels in Gunston Hall. Yellow pine. (Photo, Gavin Ashworth.)

when Buckland arrived in November, it is likely that he designed the portico on the "south front" overlooking Mason's formal garden and the river (fig. 4). The portico closely resembles a garden temple in William Paine's *The Builder's Companion and Workman's General Assistant* (1758).[6] Both designs are based on a hexagon and have Doric friezes, broad engaged pilasters, and Gothic arches. Only in England and her colonies was the Gothic taste an important component of the rococo style.

The floor plan of Gunston Hall is similar to many other five-bay Virginia houses. On the first story there is a wide central hall that extends from front to back, accommodates the stair, and provides access to four rooms of approximately equal size (fig. 5). Both the hall and the southwest parlor are almost completely within the classical tradition. The hall has a Doric entab-

Figure 7 Carved stair bracket in Gunston Hall. Walnut. The scroll volute originally had an applied rosette. (Photo, Gavin Ashworth.)

Figure 8 Southwest parlor of Gunston Hall. The chimneypiece and carved elements painted white are restorations. (Photo, Gavin Ashworth.)

lature and fourteen engaged pilasters, two of which act as imposts for elliptical arches. Functioning as a support for the floor at the top of the stair, the arches have keystones with toed-back moldings, a large pendant drop, and carved spandrel appliqués (fig. 6). The tattered leaves of the appliqués are in the rococo style, but most of the surviving carving in Gunston Hall is relatively naturalistic and more akin to British work of the 1730–1740 period. This naturalistic style is most evident in the carving on the stair brackets and in the southwest parlor (figs. 7, 8).

The southwest parlor is the most ornate room. The windows, doors, and cupboards have Doric pilasters, entablatures, and pediments (cupboards and doors), and they are decorated with intricate frets, carved appliqués, and "leaf grass," egg-and-tongue, and rope moldings. Cupboards of this

Figure 9 Front and side views of the keystone over the arch of a cupboard in the southwest parlor of Gunston Hall. Yellow pine. (Photo, Gavin Ashworth.)

type probably derived from Roman acdicules, or sculpture niches, and like their ancient prototypes, the keystones on the Gunston Hall cupboards probably supported ceramic vases or busts (fig. 9).

Buckland's acute understanding of classical form and detail was the result of his training and his familiarity with published designs. His estate inventory included fifteen architectural design books, furniture design books, and builders' guides. He probably purchased most of the books before immigrating, but at least four were published after his arrival. Buckland frequently borrowed designs from these sources. The acanthus appliqués on the windows and doors in the southwest parlor, for example (fig. 8), are based on the crossette appliqués in plate 75 of Batty Langley's *The City and Country Builder's and Workman's Treasury of Designs* (1740), a book he owned.[7]

Buckland's treatment of the northwest room reflects the eighteenth-century fascination with the Orient (fig. 11). Passion for the Chinese taste was well established in English architecture before Buckland's move to Virginia, in part owing to publications such as William Halfpenny's *New Design's for Chinese Temples, Triumphal Arches, Garden Seats, Palings &c.* (1750) and George Edwards' and Matthew Darly's *A New Book of Chinese Designs* (1754). However, there is no design in these books that precisely matches Buckland's treatment of the windows and doors, which suggests that he was either working from memory or simply borrowing conventional "Chinese" details, such as scalloped cresting and imbricated consoles, from published sources. The only book in Buckland's library with similar details was Chippendale's *Director* (see fig. 16).[8]

For the execution of his designs, Buckland relied on local artisans, and a suit for back wages brought by journeyman joiner James Brent against Buckland provides information on the tradesmen in his crew. On July 6, 1763, Brent presented to the court a detailed list of his delinquent wages and expenses incurred on Buckland's behalf, including "37 1/2 days work at Colo. Masons" in 1761 and a "Pare Shoes to Bernard Sears" in 1759. Sears's son, Charles Lee Sears, reported that

> his fathers passage to Virginia was paid by George Mason, who claimed his services until the amount was claimed by labor. In his spare moments, he practiced wood carving. When the time of his service was about completed, Mr. Mason noticed some of the carved pieces of wood. . . . He employed [Sears] . . . to do the carved work in Gunston Hall.

Although it is doubtful that William Bernard Sears was a novice carver when Mason first employed him, other aspects of this oral tradition are confirmed by Sears's obituary, which stated that he was "a native of England" and that he "lived for a considerable time in the family of George Mason of Gunston."[9]

The designs of the carved moldings, appliqués, and other ornaments in Gunston Hall probably represent the collaborative efforts of Sears and Buckland. Buckland undoubtedly furnished Sears with working drawings and selected engravings from design books; however, Sears was entirely responsible for their interpretation in wood. His carving style is so distinc-

Figure 10 Detail of the casement molding for the door leading from the hall to the southwest parlor of Gunston Hall. (Courtesy, Museum of Early Southern Decorative Arts; photo, Luke Beckerdite.)

Figure 11 Northwest parlor of Gunston Hall. (Photo, Gavin Ashworth.)

tive and, in many respects, so unconventional that it is as identifiable as a signature. For example, the large husks (or bellflowers) on the spandrel appliqués and stair brackets have tiny, lancet-shaped "eyes" (folds between the individual lobes of the leaves) rather than the more typical U- or teardrop-shaped openings, unnecessarily complex edges, and deeply fluted and undercut lobes (see figs. 6 and 7). In many instances, the carving appears uncertain and labored-over rather than "workmanlike."

Buckland and Sears also worked together on a side chair, one of at least four made for Gunston Hall (fig. 12). Several details on the chair are related to a design for a Chinese chair in the first and second editions of the *Director* (see fig. 14). Although far from being identical, the relief-carved fret on the legs of the Gunston Hall chair and the pierced fret represented in the engraving have Gothic arches with tiny trefoils, pairs of confronting C scrolls, and lozenge-shaped strapwork. In addition, both chairs have brackets with opposing C scrolls. The scrolled ends of the brackets on Mason's chair are virtually identical to those on the stair brackets (see figs. 7 and 13). Sears shaded both with a very small U-shaped gouge, and he used the same tool to cut short paired flutes in the hollow of the large scrolls on the chair brackets. Similar paired flutes are on the tattered leaves of the spandrel appliqués and "leaf grass" moldings above the pendant and on the door casement at the entrance to the southwest parlor (figs. 6, 10, 13).[10]

A subsequent owner converted the side chair to an easy chair, and in all probability, the crest rail and splat of the side chair were already severely damaged or missing. The seat rails were planed to accommodate a board seat, but the adaptive use does not necessarily account for the heavy planing visible on the inner edges of the stiles. Repairs and alterations on eighteenth-century chairs often are the result of a sitter falling over backwards. Normally the splat breaks out of the crest rail and shoe, and the stile tenons break out of the crest rail. If Mason's chair had a splat that attached to the

Figure 12 Fragment of a side chair attributed to William Buckland and William Bernard Sears, Fairfax County, Virginia, 1756–1761. Walnut. The conversion to an easy chair occurred about 1850. (Courtesy, Museum of Early Southern Decorative Arts; photo, Wes Stewart.)

Figure 13 Detail of the front leg and bracket of the chair fragment illustrated in fig. 12. (Photo, Wes Stewart.)

inner edges of the stiles, the stiles may have been damaged enough to warrant planing. Chippendale illustrated several chairs with splats attached in this manner, most of which were "Gothic chairs" and "Chinese chairs" with fret backs (fig. 14).[11]

The structure of Mason's chair indicates that the joiners working under Buckland's direction were unfamiliar with the construction of seating forms. In fact, certain aspects of the construction resemble house joiner's work. The materials are unusually heavy—the leg stock is 2 1/8" × 1 3/4", and the rails are 1 1/4" thick—and the joints are marked with Roman numerals as on the framing members of eighteenth-century houses.[12]

Two other products of Buckland's shop are shown in an early photograph of the northwest room (fig. 15). Mounted on the west wall are remnants of two ornamental canopies, probably for the display of ceramics (see the reproduction canopies in fig. 11). Rabbets on the edges of the backboards suggest that they had small scrolled trusses like those flanking the door

35   ARCHITECT-DESIGNED FURNITURE

friezes below. The roof boards shown in the photograph appear to be original; however, they probably had nailed-on scalloped moldings that complemented the design of the doors. The ceramics rested on the protruding central section of each door head, so the entire ensemble functioned as an architectural version of the small cabinets capping several china cases in the *Director* (fig. 16).[13]

Most of the interior work in Gunston Hall was completed when Buckland's indenture expired in 1759. On November 8, 1759, Mason wrote the following recommendation on the back of Buckland's indenture:

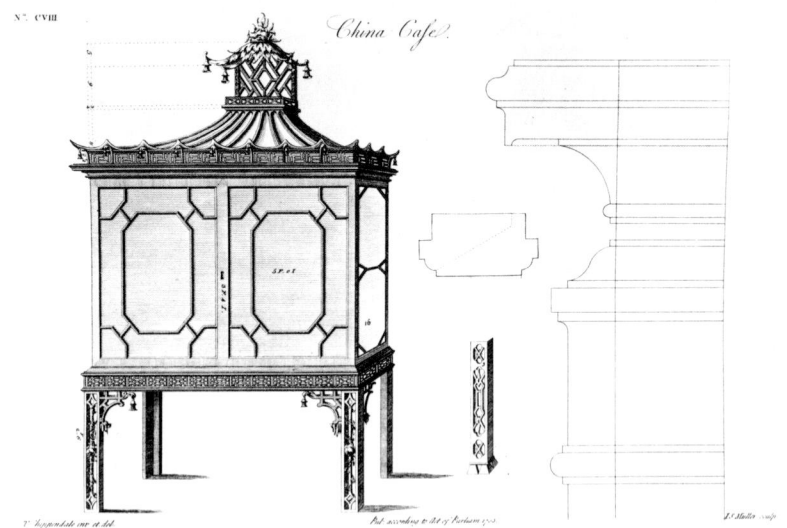

Figure 14 Design for a Chinese chair illustrated on pl. 25 in the first and second editions of Thomas Chippendale's *Gentleman and Cabinet-Maker's Director* (1754, 1755). (Courtesy, Museum of Early Southern Decorative Arts; photo, Wes Stewart.)

Figure 15 Detail of one of the canopies shown in an early photo of the northwest parlor of Gunston Hall. (Courtesy, Gunston Hall.)

Figure 16 Design for a china case illustrated on pl. 108 in the first and second editions of Chippendale's *Director*. (Courtesy, Museum of Early Southern Decorative Arts; photo, Wes Stewart.)

William Buckland came to Virginia with my Brother . . . who engaged him in London and had a very good Character of him there; during the time he lived with me he had the entire Direction of the Carpenters &. Joiners Work of a large House. . . . I can with great Justice recommend him to any Gentleman . . . & I think him a complete Master of the Carpenter's &. Joiners Business both in Theory &. Practice.

Mason's endorsement and social connections probably helped Buckland secure other commissions. One year later, Buckland received £93.2.0 from Truro Parish for unspecified work on the new glebe house, and in late 1760 or early 1761 the estate of John Ferguson paid him £0.15.0 for a coffin.[14]

Buckland moved to Richmond County, Virginia, in 1761 and settled near the town of Warsaw. On December 6, 1761, Buckland purchased large quantities of lamb, mutton, and beef from John Tayloe, II (1721–1779), a wealthy Richmond County planter who was in the process of either completing or remodeling his house, Mt. Airy, and who had hired Buckland to design and supervise the installation of the interior woodwork (fig. 17). As at Gunston Hall, the masonry work at Mt. Airy probably was already complete before Buckland's arrival. A fire in 1844 gutted the interior, but the surviving masonry supports and joists in the cellar suggest that the house

Figure 17 Mt. Airy, Richmond County, Virginia, 1750–1765. Reminiscent of pl. 58 in James Gibbs's *A Book of Architecture* (1728), Mt. Airy is made of reddish brown sandstone blocks with limestone trim. (Courtesy, Museum of Early Southern Decorative Arts; photo, Luke Beckerdite.)

Figure 18 Detail of a fragment of cornice molding from Mt. Airy. Yellow pine. (Courtesy, Museum of Early Southern Decorative Arts; photo, Luke Beckerdite.)

had symmetrically arranged rooms, a wide central hall, and possibly a marble floor. Entries in Tayloe's account book and lawsuits brought before the Richmond County Court suggest that Buckland worked for Tayloe for nearly three years from December 1761 to November 1764.[15]

A few fragments of carved cornice molding survived the 1844 fire (fig. 18). On these, the leaves on the ogee molding below the dentil course have undercut lobes and short parallel gouge cuts, as do those on the spandrel appliqués and door casement moldings that William Bernard Sears carved for Gunston Hall (see figs. 6 and 10). This similarity suggests that Sears joined Buckland's workforce at Mt. Airy, a conclusion supported by the

Figure 19 Pier table attributed to William Buckland and William Bernard Sears, Richmond County, Virginia, 1761–1771. Cherry with beech. H. 31 3/4", W. 45 3/8", D. 29 3/4". The marble top is approximately 1 1/4" thick. The two front foot blocks are early replacements. (Colonial Williamsburg Foundation, acc. 9364; photo, Gavin Ashworth.)

very rarity of carvers in eighteenth-century Virginia, particularly in areas like Richmond County where there were no large towns to support specialized tradesmen.

Among the many original furnishings that survived the 1844 fire are a pier table and a sideboard table attributed to Buckland and Sears (figs. 19, 25). The architectonic form of these tables and their carved details suggest that Buckland designed them to complement the interior woodwork in the house, much as he would have learned to do in England. Tables and large case pieces such as library bookcases were the furniture forms most often designed by eighteenth-century architects.[16]

The pier table is the more architectural of the two (fig. 19). It has massive scrolled legs that derive from large, early-eighteenth-century architectural trusses (also referred to as brackets and consoles), some of which have acanthus carving and deep, toed-back molding on the front face and strapwork and husk or acanthus carving on the sides. The central shell-and-acanthus ornament on the table is relatively underscale, but as with other Buckland designs it has precedents in British architectural and furniture design (compare figs. 2 and 19).

The materials and construction of the table suggest that it was built by Buckland's house joiners. The legs are made of mediocre stock 3 1/2" × 5"—dimensions suitable for rafters, purlins, minor floor joists, and studs—and

Figure 20 Detail of the construction of the pier table illustrated in fig. 19. (Photo, Gavin Ashworth.)

Figure 21 Detail of the construction of the pier table illustrated in fig. 19. (Photo, Gavin Ashworth.)

Figure 22 Detail of the shell-and-acanthus ornament on the front rail of the pier table illustrated in fig. 19. (Photo, Gavin Ashworth.)

have deep checks on the back edges, particularly where they are notched to help support the rails (fig. 20). The joiners used a saw with a relatively thick blade to cut the rail tenons and mortises for the three cross braces under the top. The shoulders of the tenons are cut at a 45-degree angle to abutt the angled faces of the notched leg stiles. The mortise-and-tenon joints are secured with glue and large wooden trunnels (pegs), some nearly 3/8" in diameter (fig. 21). (In conventional furniture joinery, mortise-and-tenon joints are either glued or glued and pinned with small trunnels.) Glue and large wrought finish nails attach the rail moldings and shell-and-acanthus appliqué (fig. 22). These nails would have been quite visible when the table was new. The rails and narrow boards with carved gadrooning form a shelf for strips of figured cherry that frame the marble top (fig. 21). Apparently the joiners miscalculated the dimensions of the marble, since they chopped out rabbets in the front and back rail *after* assembling the frame and chiseled rough bevels on the adjoining edges of the marble top. The joiners also made the table too low, an error that they corrected by adding 1½" blocks under the foot plinths (fig. 19). (The two original blocks on the rear legs are fastened with four large, rose-head nails that are set in counterbored holes.)

In designing the pier table, Buckland repeated several motifs that he used in Gunston Hall. The strapwork and husks on the sides of the legs (fig. 23) are enlarged versions of those on the keystones in the southwest parlor (fig. 9). On both there are stippled grounds, strapwork, floral volutes, and acanthus husks with stems that end abruptly rather than flow back into the volute. One can envision the table standing in a room where its ornamental details are repeated on the trusses and keystones of major architectural components (i.e., door and window entablatures, cupboards, and chimneypiece).

The carving on the pier table is more workmanlike than most of the carving in Gunston Hall. With conventional "eyes," subtle convex and concave surfaces, and delicate shading flutes, the acanthus leaves on the table legs are

Figure 23   Detail of the carving on the sides of the legs of the pier table illustrated in fig. 19. (Photo, Gavin Ashworth.)

Figure 24   Detail of the acanthus carving on the front legs of the table illustrated in fig. 19. (Photo, Gavin Ashworth.)

Figure 25 Sideboard table attributed to William Buckland and William Bernard Sears, Richmond County, Virginia, 1761–1771. Walnut. H. 33 1/2" (not incl. the 1 1/2" marble top), W. 42 1/2", D. 25 1/2". The fret, portions of the applied carving on the front rail, and several of the foot moldings are replaced (see fig. 31). (Courtesy, Museum of Early Southern Decorative Arts, acc. 3425; photo, Gavin Ashworth.)

more naturalistic in appearance than those on the stair brackets and keystones in Gunston Hall (compare figs. 9 and 24). Although the quality of Sears's work improved with time, he continued to use many unconventional techniques. He cut short paired flutes on the convex lobes of the shell and on the acanthus leaves, strapwork, and back edges of the legs of the pier table (see figs. 20, 22–24), on the brackets of Mason's side chair (fig. 13), and on certain architectural elements both in Mt. Airy and Gunston Hall (figs. 6, 10, 18). Sears seems to have been uncomfortable leaving any surface plain. On the table he used a single-point tool to stipple the ground on the sides of the legs and around the acanthus leaves on the front faces (figs. 23, 24), whereas, most of his contemporaries used gang-punches with four to eight points for stippling.

In contrast to the conservative Palladian style of the preceding example (fig. 19), Buckland based his design for the sideboard table on plate 38 in Chippendale's *Director* (figs. 25, 26). He also incorporated an intersecting circular fret and bold egg-and-tongue and rope moldings (figs. 25, 27), details used in the southwest parlor in Gunston Hall (fig. 8) and probably in the room in Mt. Airy where the table stood.[17]

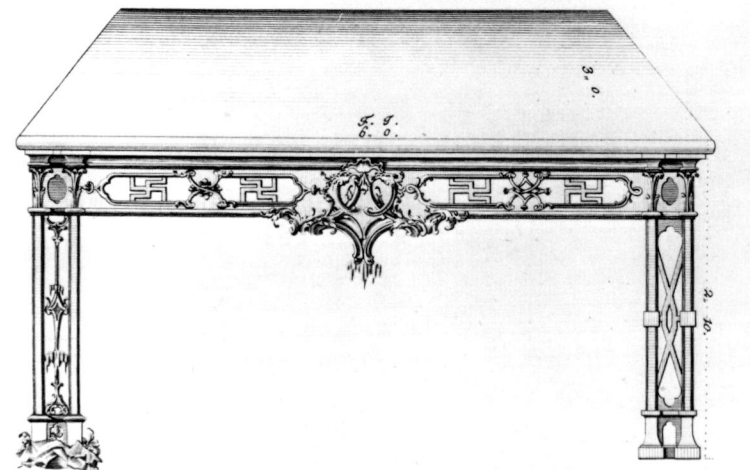

Figure 26   Design for a sideboard table illustrated on pl. 38 in the first and second editions of Chippendale's *Director*. (Courtesy, Museum of Early Southern Decorative Arts; photo, Wes Stewart.)

Figure 27   Infrared photograph of the side rail of the sideboard table illustrated in fig. 25. The fret on the side rails was identical to the fret on the front rail. (Courtesy, Colonial Williamsburg Foundation; photo, Hans Lorenz.)

Figure 29   Detail of the construction of the sideboard table illustrated in fig. 25. (Photo, Gavin Ashworth.)

Figure 28   Detail of the construction of the sideboard table illustrated in fig. 25. (Photo, Gavin Ashworth.)

In construction, the sideboard table is even more unusual than the pier table (figs. 28, 29). In addition to having the moldings and appliqués attached with large finish nails, the sideboard table has poorly cut haunched tenons and mortises that are completely open at the bottom. The tenons are glued and pinned with trunnels only slightly smaller than those on the pier table (fig. 27). Although Chippendale had little to say about the structure of his sideboard table in the 1754 and 1755 editions of the *Director*, in the 1762 edition he advised, "Feet and Rails . . . are cut through; which gives it an airy look; but will be too slight for Marble-Tops. Therefore the Tops will be better made of Wood." Tayloe evidently found this structural incompatibility to be the case. The triangular blocks nailed in the leg recesses and the L-shaped braces screwed to the stiles and rails probably postdate the table's construction by only a few years (fig. 29).[18]

Figure 30 Detail of the carving on the front rail of the sideboard table illustrated in fig. 25. (Photo, Gavin Ashworth.)

Figure 31 Pre-conservation detail of the carving on the front rail of the sideboard table illustrated in fig. 25. (Courtesy, Museum of Early Southern Decorative Arts; photo, Luke Beckerdite.)

The carving is unusually fussy for Sears, but it reveals a great deal about his methods (figs. 30, 31). The near absence of carving tool marks on the rails indicates that he glued the sawn appliqués to a board (probably with a paper interface) and carved them before attaching them to the table. With the exception of the moldings and flowers glued and nailed in the recesses at the top of each leg, all of the leg and foot carving is cut from the solid (fig. 32). Like the circular fret on the front rail, the carving on the table probably echoed architectural details in the room where it stood. The small husk just below the egg-and-tongue molding, for example, is very similar to the leaf carving on the cornice fragments in Mt. Airy (figs. 18, 30, 31).

Carving also links the sideboard table to a Gothic-style table that may have been among the original furnishings of Mt. Airy and that belonged to

a "Miss I. T., [of] Virginia" when it appeared in the "Riddles &. Replies" section of *Antiques* in March 1943 (fig. 33). Minute details of the carving are not discernable in that illustration, but the husks, scrolls, and acanthus leaves on the front rail are remarkably similar to those on the rail of the sideboard table (see figs. 30, 31, 33). Several of the scroll volutes have small leafy wings like those adjacent to the circular fret of figure 25.[19]

Buckland based his design for the Gothic table on elements for a French chair illustrated on plate 17 in the first and second editions of the *Director* (fig. 34).[20] Faint color shifts on the legs of the table suggest that it had

Figure 32 Detail of the leg of the sideboard table illustrated in fig. 25. (Photo, Gavin Ashworth.)

Figure 33 Sideboard table attributed to William Buckland and William Bernard Sears, Richmond County, Virginia, 1761–1771. (*Antiques* 43, no. 3 [March 1943]: 142; photo, Wes Stewart.)

Figure 34 Design for a French chair illustrated on pl. 17 in the first and second editions of Chippendale's *Director*. This engraving is not in the third edition (1762). (Courtesy, Museum of Early Southern Decorative Arts; photo, Wes Stewart.)

applied rosettes (on the circles between the piercings) where the *Director* engraving shows a small husk. Buckland's occasional reliance on the *Director* for furniture designs is logical, considering that he lacked formal training as a cabinetmaker.

The only other known piece of furniture with a possible connection to Buckland's shop is a fretwork sideboard table illustrated in Wallace Nutting's *Furniture Treasury* (fig. 35).[21] The legs appear to be constructed in a manner similar to those of figure 25 (see also fig. 32). To recess the frets, the joiner planed a wide groove in the face of each leg before sawing out the design. Most furniture frets are based on flowing or repetitious patterns, but those on the rails of figure 35 have a static quality reminiscent of eighteenth-century railing designs and a scale more suited to architecture than furniture.

Buckland and Sears probably parted company soon after completing their work at Mt. Airy. Between April 1765 and August 1768, Sears was in or near Loudoun County, Virginia. Buckland remained in Richmond County where his shop continued to produce furniture and architectural components. He described himself as a "Joiner & Cabinett Maker" when, on

Figure 35   Sideboard table possibly from the shop of William Buckland, Fairfax or Richmond County, 1755–1771. Materials and dimensions not recorded. (Wallace Nutting, *Furniture Treasury*, 2 vols. [Framingham, Ma.: Old America Co., 1928], 1: pl. 744; photo, Luke Beckerdite.)

April 2, 1765, he took John Randall of King George County, Virginia, as his apprentice. The following February Robert Wormley Carter wrote, "Buckland this day brought home my Bookcase cost £6.0.0 also put up my Chimneypiece of carved work, £2.10.6 . . . also a plan of a house £1.1.6 . . . this Plan he drew some time agoe." John Tayloe also may have referred to furniture from Buckland's shop when he informed Landon Carter that "8 chairs and 2 elbow ones . . . are in Buckland's hands to sell."

On March 25, 1771, Buckland wrote Robert Carter:

> I have long hopd for an opertunitie of being imployed (in the way of my Profesion) in some jobb under yr. Honr. . . . I have now some of the Best Workmen in Virginia among whom is a London Carver a masterly Hand. . . . Should yr. Fondness for Work of that kind and Drawings induce you to call in I shall ever Remember the Honr. done me.

The following November, Buckland, his London carver, and at least three other tradesmen from his Richmond County shop moved to Annapolis to complete the construction of a house that Edward Lloyd IV had recently purchased from Samuel Chase.[22]

In a November 7, 1772, letter of attorney to Benjamin Branham, Buckland described himself as an "Architect." This was the beginning of a new phase in Buckland's career, one in which he hoped to exercise fully his talents as a designer. Unfortunately Buckland died twenty-five months later, and the interior of the Chase-Lloyd house and the exterior of the Mathias Hammond house are the only documented work surviving from his Maryland period. As with the furniture and interior details he did with Sears, these important buildings show that Buckland was indeed one of colonial America's greatest *architects*.[23]

1. Peter Ward-Jackson, *English Furniture Designs of the Eighteenth Century* (London: Victoria & Albert Museum, 1958), p. 3.

2. For more on Buckland, see Rosamond Randall Beirne and John Henry Scarff, *William Buckland, 1734–1774: Architect of Virginia and Maryland* (Baltimore: Maryland Historical Society, 1958); William Voss Elder, III, "The Adams-Kilty House in Annapolis," *Maryland Historical Magazine* 60 (September 1965): 314–24; Elizabeth Brand Monroe, "William Buckland in the Northern Neck," M.A. thesis, University of Virginia, 1975; Barbara A. Brand, "The Work of William Buckland in Maryland, 1771–1774," M.A. thesis, George Washington University, 1978; and Luke Beckerdite, "William Buckland and William Bernard Sears: The Designer and the Carver," *Journal of Early Southern Decorative Arts* 8, no. 2 (November 1982): 6–41; "William Buckland Reconsidered: Architectural Carving in Chesapeake Maryland, 1771–1774," *Journal of Early Southern Decorative Arts* 8, no. 2 (November 1982): 42–88; and "William Buckland Reconsidered: Architectural Carving in Virginia and Maryland, 1755–1775," M.A. thesis, Wake Forest University, 1985. Beckerdite refutes several attributions made by other authors.

3. Beirne and Scarff, *William Buckland*, p. 1. Joiner's Company Register of Apprentice Bindings, 6:47v, Guildhall Library, London. For more on the Palladians and furniture design, see Michael I. Wilson, *William Kent, Architect, Designer, Painter, Gardner, 1685–1748* (London: Routledge & Kegan Paul, 1984); and Ward-Jackson, *English Furniture Designs*, pp. 7, 8.

4. For more on early rococo designs, see Ward-Jackson, *English Furniture Designs*, pp. 13, 14, 38–40; Morrison H. Heckscher, "Lock and Copland: A Catalogue of the Engraved Ornament," *Furniture History* 15 (1979): 1–23, and pls. 1–67B; and Elizabeth White, comp., *Pictorial History of British 18th Century Furniture Design: The Printed Sources* (Woodbridge, Suffolk: Antique Collector's Club, 1990), pp. 38, 39. For more on Chippendale, see Christopher Gilbert, *The Life and Work of Thomas Chippendale* (New York: MacMillian Co., 1979).

5. Indenture between William Buckland and Thomson Mason, August 4, 1755, George Mason Papers, Gunston Hall Plantation, Mason Neck, Virginia. *Alexandria Gazette and Daily Advertiser*, September 4, 1817. As quoted in Beirne and Scarff, *William Buckland*, pp. 25, 26.

6. Paine's "Plan, Elevation, &. Section of a Gothic Temple" is reproduced in White, *Pictorial History*, p. 136.

7. Frederick D. Nichols, "The Importance of William Buckland," *Buckland: Master Builder of the 18th Century* (Mason Neck, Va.: Regents of Gunston Hall, 1977), pp. 8–9. Batty Langley's *The City and Country Builder's and Workman's Treasury of Designs* (London, 1740), pl. 75. The author thanks John Bivins for the Langley references. Buckland's inventory listed "Gibbs Designs" (James Gibbs, *Book of Architecture* [1728]), "The London Art" (William Salmon, *Palladio Londonensis, or the London Art of Building* [1734, enlarged ed. 1738]), "Hopuss' Measurer" (Edward Hoppus, The Practical Measurer [1736]), Langley's "Gothic Architecture" and "Essay on ditto" (Batty Langley, *Gothic Architecture* [1747], and probably *The City and Country Builder's and Workman's Treasury of Designs* [1740]), Swan's "British Treasury," "Architect," and "Carpenter's Instruction" (Abraham Swan, *The British Architect; or The Builder's Treasury of Staircases* [1745], *A Collection of Designs in Architecture* [1745], and *Designs in Carpentry* [1759]), "Ware's Designs" (Isaac Ware, *A Complete Body of Architecture* [1756], "Chippendale's Designs" (Thomas Chippendale, *The Gentleman and Cabinet-Maker's Director* [1754, 1755]), "Johnsons Carver's Designs" (Thomas Johnson, *One Hundred & Fifty New Designs* [1761]), "Lightholder's Designs" (Thomas Lightoler, *The Gentleman & Farmers' Architect* [1764], or William Halfpenny, Thomas Lightoler, and Robert Morris, *The Modern Builder's Assistant* [1742]), and an unidentified volume by Robert Morris ("An Inventory of the Goods and Chattels of William Buckland, 1777," Anne Arundel County Inventories, 125:337).

8. William Halfpenny's *New Design's for Chinese Temple's, Triumphal Arches, Garden Seats, Palings &c.* (1750). "An Inventory of the Goods and Chattels of William Buckland."

9. The earliest description of Brent's account is in Berine and Scarff, *William Buckland*, p. 37. Beirne and Scarff's footnote for the suit ("Richmond County Order Book 15, July 1763–1764, f. 293") is an incorrect citation for the original order book entry of July 6, 1763 (Richmond County Court Order Book 15, pp. 143–44, Richmond County Court House, Warsaw, Virginia). Moreover, the authors' footnote is for a brief order book entry rather than for the detailed account that they describe in *William Buckland*. Accounts and other forms of evidence exhibited in court are separate from the order books and are stored unbound under the heading "court papers." I have been unable to locate the detailed account described in *William Buckland*, but a handwritten transcript is in the Beirne and Scarff personal notes (William

Buckland Manuscripts, Maryland Historical Society, Baltimore) and appears to have been traced from the original account. Brent's account of time against Buckland (£50.6.8½) and other enumerated expenses totaled £58.2.8½. The grand total after subtracting debits (£36.9.8) and adding interest (£1.4.5) was £15.17.5, which the Richmond County Court awarded him on March 5, 1765 (Richmond County Court Order Book 15, p. 387). Further indications of the accuracy of Beirne and Scarff's copy is a debit entry in Brent's account, "To Cash pd. Charles Hammond 59/6—£2.19.6" (Buckland Manuscripts). On October 3, 1763, James Hunter & Co. sued Buckland for £3.1.11 (Richmond County Court Order Book 15, p. 183). As evidence Hunter & Co. presented Charles Hammond's account, which had a June 10, 1762, entry, "To Cred. James Brent—£2.19.6 (Richmond County Court Papers, 1763). The quote regarding Sear's passage to Virginia is in Susan A. Plaskett, *Memories of a Plain Family, 1836–1936* (Washington: Franklin Press, 1936), p. 16. This oral history reportedly passed from Charles Lee Sears to Plaskett's mother. *Alexandria Herald*, May 4, 1818.

10. The chair is marked IV on the front seat rail and is probably from a set of six or more. Thomas Chippendale, *The Gentleman and Cabinet-Maker's Director* (1754; reprinted, London: J. Haberkorn, 1755), pl. 25. The first and second editions (1754, 1755) generally contain the same plates. The 1762 edition varies considerably.

11. Chippendale, *Director* (1755), pls. 21–25.

12. Although aspects of the joinery are crude (e.g., heavily undercut stretcher tenons), in many respects the chair is overbuilt. The seat rail tenons are unusually large, and they are secured with enormous pegs.

13. The author thanks John Bivins and Susan Bourchardt for information on the canopies. Mr. Bivins made copies of the now-missing canopies, substituting pagoda-shaped hoods for those shown in the photograph. For more on the display of ornamental ceramics, see Anna Somers Cocks, "The Nonfunctional Use of Ceramics in the English Country House During the Eighteenth Century," in Gervase Jackson-Stops, Gordon J. Schochet, Lena Cowen Orlin, and Elisabeth Blair MacDougall, eds., *The Fashioning and Functioning of the British Country House* (Washington: Distributed by the University Press of New England for the National Gallery of Art, 1989), pp. 105–215.

14. Buckland Indenture. Pohick Church, *Minutes of the Vestry: Truro Parish Virginia, 1732–1785* (Annandale, Va.: Baptie Studios, 1974), p. 82. Estate Papers of John Ferguson, Fairfax County Will Book B-1, 1752–1767, p. 357.

15. Accompanying Buckland were his wife, Mary Moore, and their daughter Mary. The date of their marriage is unknown, but their daughter was born on September 3, 1758 (Nichols, *Buckland: Master Builder,* p. 9). Buckland sporadically purchased provisions from Tayloe through August 23, 1768 (Account Book-Letterbook of Stephen Loyde [1708–1711], Account Book-Letterbook of John Tayloe [1687–1747], Account Book-Letterbook of John Tayloe [1721–1799, 1717–1778], Virginia Historical Society, Richmond). For more on Mt. Airy, see Thomas T. Waterman, *The Mansions of Virginia, 1706–1776* (Chapel Hill: University of North Carolina Press, 1945), pp. 253–61. The author thanks Marc Winger for information on the original interior plan of Mt. Airy. Only one entry for Buckland in Tayloe's account book dates after November 1764 (Account Book-Letterbooks of Lloyd, Tayloe, and Tayloe). John Tayloe provided security for Buckland in two lawsuits, one in 1763 (*John Tarpley* vs. *William Buckland*, July 6, 1763, Richmond County Court Order Book 15, p. 143) and another in 1764 (*Hugh Walker* vs. *William Buckland,* September 4, 1764, Richmond County Court Order Book 15, p. 312).

16. The author thanks Morrison Heckscher for calling the pier table to his attention.

17. The sideboard table is illustrated in all three editions of Chippendale's *Director*. Buckland also used an intersecting circular fret on the door entablatures in the "dining room" of the Chase-Lloyd house in Annapolis.

18. Thomas Chippendale, *The Gentleman and Cabinet-Maker's Director,* 3d ed. (1762; reprinted, New York: Dover, 1966), p. 8. Although the leg blocks are secured with eighteenth-century wrought finish nails, microscopy by Colonial Williamsburg furniture conservator Cary Howlett indicates that the blocks and table have slightly different finish histories. John Bivins conserved the sideboard table in 1983.

19. *Antiques* 43, no. 3 (March 1943): 142.

20. Chippendale, *Director* (1755), pl. 17.

21. Wallace Nutting, *Furniture Treasury,* 2 vols. (Framingham, Ma.: Old American Co., 1928), 1: pl. 774. The author thanks Charles Phillips for this reference.

22. *John Orr* vs. *William Bernard Sears,* April 8, 1765, Loudoun County Court Order Book

B, 1762–1765, p. 8. *William Beard* vs. *William Bernard Sears,* September 11, 1766, Loudoun County Court Order Book C, 1765–1767, p. 195. Summons for William Bernard Sears, Thomas Sorrell, and John Lewis, August 8, 1768, Loudoun County Court Order Book D, 1767–1770, p. 93. Randall Indenture, April 2, 1765, Richmond County Deed Book 12, p. 611. Richmond County indentures frequently were recorded in deed books and proven later in court. Randall's indenture was proven on May 6, 1765 (Richmond County Court Order Book 15, p. 404). Beirne and Scarff stated that Buckland took Randall as an apprentice in 1763 (Beirne and Scarff, *Buckland*, p. 44); however, I was unable to locate corroborating evidence. Memorandum Book of Robert Wormley Carter, February 6, 1766, folder 19, Carter Family Papers, Manuscript Department, Earl Gregg Swem Library, College of William and Mary, Williamsburg. John Tayloe to Landon Carter, January 3, 1768, folder 2, Carter Family Papers. William Buckland to Robert Carter, March 25, 1771, Carter Family Papers, Virginia Historical Society, Richmond. The earliest reference to Buckland working in Maryland is November 1771 ("Account between Edward Lloyd and James McCubbin," November 1771, William Cooke Papers, Maryland Historical Society). Edward Lloyd purchased Samuel Chase's unfinished house in July 1771 (James Bordley, Jr., "New Light on William Buckland," *Maryland Historical Magazine* 46 [June 1951]: 153–54). The tradesmen who accompanied Buckland to Annapolis were joiners John Ariss Callis, John Randall, and Samuel Bailey, and probably the carver Thomas Hall. Callis described himself as a resident of Annapolis in a letter of attorney to Richmond County lawyer, Benjamin Branham (John Ariss Callis to Benjamin Branham, recorded November 7, 1772, Richmond County Court Order Book 17, p. 527). Both Randall and Bailey are listed in Buckland's inventory (Anne Arundel County Inventories, 125:337). A carver named Thomas Hall ran away from Buckland in December 1773 (*Maryland Gazette*, December 16, 1773). Hall probably was the London carver mentioned in Buckland's letter to Robert Carter (William Buckland to Robert Carter, March 25, 1771).

23. William Buckland to Benjam Branham, recorded November 7, 1772, Richmond County Deed Book 13, pp. 457–59. *Maryland Gazette*, December 15, 1774. Several items listed in Buckland's estate inventory reveal that his Annapolis shop made furniture:

1 large white Picture frame	2.0.0
2 ditto blacked	1.0.0
5 Table frames @ 4/ Each	1.0.0
1 Small Picture frame part finished	0.3.0

Anne Arundel County Inventories, 125:337. No furniture from Buckland's Annapolis shop is known.

Nina Gray

Leon Marcotte: Cabinetmaker and Interior Decorator

▼ HERE, FOR *instance, is my house.... It is superbly furnished. Mrs. P. and I don't know much about such things. She was only stringent for buhl, and the latest Parisian models, so we delivered our house into the hands of certain eminent upholsterers to be furnished, as we send Frederic to the tailor's to be clothed. To be sure, I asked what proof we had that the upholsterer was possessed of taste. But Mrs. P. silenced me, by saying that it was his business to have taste, and that a man who sold furniture naturally knew what was handsome and proper for my house.... The furnishing was certainly performed with great splendor and expense.... They are there, because my house was large ... and because, as Mrs. P. says one must have buhl and* or molu, *and new forms of furniture, and do as well as one's neighbors, and show that one is rich.*[1]

In this passage of *The Potiphar Papers*, George William Curtis expressed the intense desire felt by many mid-nineteenth-century New Yorkers for the most stylish furniture and decoration. Curtis's characterization of the "eminent upholsterer" capable of supplying "the latest Parisian models" fits an interior decorator such as Leon Alexandre Marcotte, renowned in his own day as a decorator and cabinetmaker whose clientele included the affluent and sophisticated elite of New York. Marcotte was among the upper echelon of cabinetmakers that included Herter Brothers, Alexander Roux, and Pottier and Stymus.

In the middle of the nineteenth century, New York was full of promise economically and culturally. Wealthy New Yorkers were enthusiastic for the French styles and fashions that they encountered in their trips abroad. As New York flourished financially, the demand for French articles grew, reflecting the influence of imports, immigrant tradesmen, and French-trained architects and designers.[2]

Marcotte was in a fine position to succeed in New York because of his partnership with Auguste-Emile Ringuet-Leprince (heir to a dynasty of French ébénistes), his knowledge and training in French design, and his connections with Paris, assuring his clients of the very latest style. Although a contemporary cabinetmaker, Ernest Hagen, wrote that "Marcotte and Co. worked principally in the pure Louis XVI style and ... [did] the very best work," the firm was proficient in many of the successive revivalist styles that dominated the latter part of the nineteenth century.[3]

Leon Marcotte, born on May 15, 1824, in Valognes, Manche, France, attended the École des Beaux Arts and trained as an architect in the studio of the leading neoclassical, rationalist architect, Henri Labrouste.

While working for Labrouste, he probably met Danish-born architect Detlef Lienau. Lienau and Marcotte both came to New York in 1848, and several years later, they became business partners. Marcotte's architectural background and training were an important foundation for the part of his business that encompassed interior architectural work and decoration. His furniture designs also have an architectural quality marked by particularly fine proportions.[4]

Marcotte's involvement with the furniture making trades began by the time that his sister, Marie-Felicité, married Parisian ébéniste Auguste-Emile Ringuet-Leprince in 1835. Ringuet-Leprince's reputation was well established through his descent from a line of ébénistes dating back to the late eighteenth century and through the prestige he gained by winning a bronze medal for a buhl table, an armchair, a priedieu, and a side cabinet at the 1844 Universal Exposition in London. During the 1840s Ringuet-Leprince built up a strong client base and network of referrals from wealthy Americans who bought furniture and decorations from him in Paris. One of Ringuet-Leprince's earliest American clients was Mathew Morgan of New York, who in 1842 redecorated his parlor in the *Louis Quartorze* style and subsequently advised his friend James Colles that Ringuet was "a man of good taste in his line." Other wealthy New York clients during the 1840s included Mrs. Samuel Jaudon, a Mrs. Henderson, a Mr. Deacon, and Delancy Kane, all of whom moved in the same social circle. Colles was an especially valuable client since he referred his friends to the Parisian establishment and promised Ringuet-Leprince, "We shall cheerfully continue to commend you to our friends whenever an opportunity offers. We are pleased and satisfied with various articles you have furnished us: they are in excellent taste and we thank you for your care and attention." The issue of good taste was

Figure 1 Ringuet-Leprince, Marcotte and Co. shop, 343–347 Fourth Avenue, New York, 1854. The showroom was separate from the factory, which was located at 55 West 16th Street. (Courtesy, New-York Historical Society.)

an important one, as Mrs. Jaudon explained: "We on this side feel as if everything was so much hansomer, and better, and desirable that comes from Paris."[5]

Ringuet-Leprince's prosperity was based on the wide range of services he provided, including furniture, tapestries, curtains, ornamental architectural elements, carpets, bronzes, and chandeliers, as well as advice concerning the overall effect of a room. In short, he acted as a decorator, albeit long distance. The 1848 revolution adversely affected his local trade, so Ringuet-Leprince focused his attention on the more promising New York prospects. On March 30, 1848, he wrote Colles:

> My intention . . . is to go in the autumn with my brother in law who is an architect. . . . Our business would be first to give projects for townhouses or any construction whatever. Second to make the inside decorations in papier maché or paper or carved wood. Third to furnish them with any kind of furniture from my factory in Paris, Aubusson, Lyon etc., after choice of my designs, patterns, etc.

Ringuet-Leprince and his brother-in-law, Marcotte, arrived in New York sometime toward the end of 1848 and set up business on lower Broadway. Marcotte was put in charge of the New York branch, Ringuet-Leprince returned to France, and a third man traveled between the two to fill the orders.[6]

It is possible to reconstruct the business, known successively as Maison Ringuet-Leprince (1840–1849), Ringuet-Leprince & L. Marcotte (1849–1860), and L. Marcotte & Co. (1860–1918), through the Paris and New York city directories, the New York copartnership directories, the credit ledgers of R. G. Dun, the 1855 New York census, and various receipts and personal documents. During the 1850s, Ringuet-Leprince & L. Marcotte relocated several times both in Paris and New York (fig. 1). The variety of professional titles, services, and products listed in the directories is broad: architect, cabinetmaker, decorator, furniture dealer, rug dealer, supplier and maker of bronzes, exporter, commissioned merchant in deluxe furnishings as well as in papers (presumably wallpapers), silk, woolen and lace materials for curtains and chair coverings, gas fixtures, chandeliers, art furniture, looking glass plates, and tapestries. In New York, Marcotte was in partnership with Detlef Lienau from 1851 to 1854.[7] Lienau subsequently designed Marcotte's factory and store (fig. 2) and worked with him on the Lockwood Mathews mansion in Norwalk, Connecticut.

In 1852 (Étienne Simon Eugène) Roudillon was listed in the Paris city directory as the successor to the Maison Ringuet-Leprince; however, Ringuet-Leprince was listed at the same address until 1858. The double listings suggest that Ringuet-Leprince found his New York business more promising and relinquished his French trade to Roudillon, while maintaining the Paris shop and/or factory solely for export purposes. This interpretation is supported by post-1858 Paris directories that list Ringuet-Leprince as a commissioned merchant.[8]

Bill headings specify that the Paris business operated under the name Ringuet-Leprince and that the New York branch was Ringuet-Leprince and

Figure 2   L. Marcotte & Co. shop, 29 East 17th Street, New York, ca. 1865. The Marcotte shop was an elegant beaux arts building located on Union Square just off Fifth Avenue, a fashionable address for the period. (Courtesy, New-York Historical Society.)

Marcotte. The 1855 New York census valued the building at 347 Fourth Street at $17,000. Living with Marcotte were his younger brother Charles, who was also a cabinetmaker, his mother, and a French-trained cabinetmaker, Augustus Fredin. Fredin is listed as a partner with Marcotte and Ringuet-Leprince in the copartnership directories from 1853 to 1857. The R. G. Dun appraisals began in 1854, and approximately every six months a representative called on Marcotte to write an evaluation and commentary on the business. The first entry on Ringuet-Leprince and Marcotte reveals that they imported both plain and "rich" furniture, but that a majority of their work was "ornamenting houses." The report valued the business at $50,000, noted the firm's potential for expansion, and described Marcotte as smart and reliable with "much artistic taste" and business acumen. The following year Dun reported that Ringuet-Leprince and Marcotte employed 150 second-class hands. By 1858 Ringuet-Leprince and Marcotte reportedly made "first class work for the best and wealthiest clients, at their own prices," and showed a large profit.[9]

With business thriving, Marcotte turned his attention to personal matters. On May 23, 1859, he married Louise-Marie de Rudder, the daughter of a Parisian painter. Their marriage certificate stated that Marcotte was residing in Paris. He may have been there making arrangements to assume the added responsibility of Ringuet-Leprince's approaching retirement.[10]

In July 1860, Ringuet-Leprince retired and the firm name changed to L. Marcotte & Co., with Marcotte in charge. Throughout the 1860s, the firm reported excellent profits, had good customers, and maintained good standing in the business community. In 1866, the Mercantile Agency (a forerunner to Dun and Bradstreet) gave L. Marcotte & Co. a high credit rating and estimated the pecuniary strength of the firm to be $50,000/$100,000. By 1869, this figure rose to $100,000, reflecting the growth of the company and the addition of a new factory (built 1867–1868) at 158–164 West 32nd Street. Lienau designed the factory as well as the shop and showroom built two years later (see fig. 2).[11] As this was a time of great expansion, Marcotte and Ringuet-Leprince made Adrian Herzog a partner in 1868. Herzog remained with the company until his death in the early 1890s.

The firm continued to grow rapidly during the 1870s, and R. G. Dun frequently described L. Marcotte & Co. as an "old and well established house" or an "old rich house." In 1874 the firm did $200,000 worth of business, and in 1878 it had stock valued at $200,000 and outstanding invoices totaling $50,000. Ringuet-Leprince sold his interest the following year, and Marcotte decided to make Paris his permanent residence, although he spent equal time in New York.[12]

Back in France, Marcotte advertised the services of the Parisian branch in great detail and relocated the shop from Avenue de Villars 15 to the more fashionable Avenue de l'Opera 11. In 1882, the New York branch followed suit by moving to 298 Fifth Avenue at 31st Street. R. G. Dun estimated the strength of the business to be $200,000 to $250,000, despite "strong competition" from other leading decorating firms such as Herter Brothers and Pottier and Stymus. The high ratings continued throughout the 1880s.

Figure 3 Armchair attributed to Ringuet-Leprince & L. Marcotte, New York or Paris, ca. 1854. Fruitwood and ebonized walnut with beech. H. 38", W. 22¾". (Metropolitan Museum of Art, acc. 69.262.3.)

Leon Marcotte died on January 25, 1887, in Paris at the age of 62, but L. Marcotte & Co. continued under the direction of Adrian Herzog and his family in New York and Edmond Leprince Ringuet in Paris. The last listing for the firm in Paris is 1911. The New York branch moved to Long Island City in 1918 and went out of business by 1922.[13]

During the last half of the nineteenth century, Marcotte's firm kept pace with what was fashionable and in demand. Most of the styles were historic revivals, but they were interpreted in a very distinctive manner. Included were the Louis XIV, XV, and XVI styles, all based on eighteenth-century French models, and the Renaissance revival, an eclectic blend of Henri II, François I, and Louis XIII styles. The aesthetic style—another important artistic movement of the late nineteenth century—was considerably more diverse, incorporating elements of Far Eastern, Middle Eastern, and European design. While R. G. Dun's ledgers and the Mercantile Agency

Figure 4 Ballroom in Chateau-Sur-Mer, Newport, Rhode Island. (Courtesy, Preservation Society of Newport County.)

show that Marcotte's firm did a tremendous amount of business, only a small portion of this work is documented by bills of sale and correspondence or attributable through connoisseurship.

Marcotte and Ringuet-Leprince are best known for their interpretations of the Louis XV and Louis XVI styles in a broad range of forms, each of which was offered at a variety of levels to accommodate different tastes and budgets. An armchair from a suite of two sofas, two armchairs, four side chairs, a center table, and a firescreen made for John Taylor Johnston, the first president of the Metropolitan Museum of Art, is a fine example of the firm's Louis XV-style furniture (fig. 3). The style was the last phase of the rococo revival, and Ringuet-Leprince & L. Marcotte's interpretation was particularly refined. A distinctive feature of their furniture is the almost spherical shape of scroll feet. Possibly imported from France, the elegant chased mounts on the Johnston chair are exceptional even for the firm's finest work. Johnston's father-in-law, James Colles, may have recommended Marcotte and Ringuet-Leprince to the Johnstons when they began decorating their new home on Fifth Avenue and 8th Street. Johnston was an important client for Marcotte; he was a central figure in New York society, and his family was a continual source of patronage.

William Shepard Wetmore of Newport, Rhode Island, and Samuel Colt of Hartford, Connecticut, also purchased Louis XV-style furniture. Wetmore was a wealthy New York City banker and merchant who retired about 1850 and hired architect Seth Bradford to built his Newport mansion, "Chateau-Sur-Mer." He commissioned Marcotte to design a suite of ebonized Louis XV-style furniture—four sofas, four armchairs, and eight side chairs—for the ballroom (fig. 4).[14] The gold floral brocade upholstery complemented the gilt-bronze mounts on the furniture and the gilt highlights on the shaded grey walls. Although based on Louis XV furniture, Marcotte altered the proportions to suit the nineteenth-century taste for robust, florid forms and broke from eighteenth-century tradition by using ebonizing and ormolu mounts on seating furniture.

Marcotte's work for Samuel Colt's house, "Armsmear," included architectural elements, furniture, upholstery fabrics, draperies, carpets, chandeliers, and lamps for the drawing room, dining room, office, library, bedrooms, and a dressing room. The New York shop made the furniture and architectural components, and the Paris shop furnished many fabrics and lighting devices. After receiving a letter from Marcotte advising him to "call at our establishment where you will find my brother-in-law to your entire disposition," Colt traveled to Paris and ordered two carpets, five chandeliers, and two lamps from Ringuet-Leprince. On November 26, 1856, Marcotte advised, "The parlour set of furniture same as the dining room are very nearly finished. This last one however I cannot complete as you have decided upon different covering in Paris. . . . For the three bedrooms of the second story I am hurrying the work as fast as possible but I have only one set of mahogany furniture ready. If you would decide to have your bedroom furnished with rosewood I could send you a set at once." Colt chose the rosewood suite, about which Marcotte assured him, "We have calculated to have everything substantial and made in the best manner and not too elaborate." There is more ornamental carving on the rosewood parlor furniture than on the ebonized suites with gilt-bronze mounts, as if Marcotte compensated for the absence of applied, gilded ornament (fig. 5).[15]

Henry Marquand, another of Marcotte's socially prominent New York clients, was the second president of the Metropolitan Museum of Art and may have been introduced to Marcotte by John Taylor Johnston. Marcotte probably made the center table illustrated in figure 6 for Marquand's Madison Avenue mansion. The table has an exceptionally bold stretcher and sculptural mounts that envelop the scrolled legs.

Marcotte's business blossomed with the growing popularity of the Louis XVI style in the 1860s and 1870s. As late as 1878, Harriet Spofford wrote, "Louis Seize is again the favorite of that fashion. . . . It is as well suited to the frivolities of the life too frequently led nowadays by the extraordinarily wealthy as more stable and solid and dignified furniture could."[16] Several of Marcotte's old clients, including Johnston, ordered new suites of Louis XVI-style furniture. The side chair illustrated in figure 7 is from a large suite—two sofas, six side chairs, two lyre-back chairs, two armchairs, a firescreen, two single-door side cabinets, and a three-door side cabinet—made

Figure 5 Armchair by Ringuet-Leprince & L. Marcotte, New York, 1856–1857. Rosewood. H. 38 1/2", W. 24 1/2", D. 22 1/2". (Courtesy, Armsmear; photo, E. Irving Blomstram.)

for Johnston's music room about 1860. As the chair demonstrates, Marcotte's Louis XVI-style pieces are typically richer and bolder than their eighteenth-century counterparts, and they often have gilt-bronze beading emphasizing the silhouettes.

A number of Louis XVI suites by L. Marcotte & Co. have survived. Although there are differences in the mounts and carving, there is little variation in the proportions and dimensions of each furniture form. The chairs illustrated in figures 8 and 9, for example, are virtually identical in measurement to other Louis XVI-style chairs documented to L. Marcotte & Co., but they have several unique features. The crest rails have a single arch rather than the usual *Chapeau de Gendarme* shape (reverse curve),

Figure 6 Center table attributed to L. Marcotte & Co., New York, ca. 1865. Beech with hickory, aspen, white pine, and oak. H. 30 ½", W. 51 ½", D. 37 ½". (Brooklyn Museum, acc. 86.4.)

Figure 7 Side chair from a set of six attributed to L. Marcotte & Co., New York, ca. 1860. Maple with pine. H. 37 ¾", W. 20 ¾", D. 17 ½". The tufted silk upholstery, four fluted legs, and high-quality mounts all show that this was one of the fancier suites of Louis XVI furniture. (Metropolitan Museum of Art, acc. 68.69.6–11).

and the twisted column arm supports, carving, and gilt-bronze mounts are very distinctive.

Marcotte's establishment offered several lines of furniture. At the high end were custom-designed pieces, such as those commissioned by Colt, and in the middle range were items or suites of furniture that could be embellished with a variety of structural and decorative options: turned and fluted legs, carving, gilt-bronze mounts, and expensive upholstery fabrics and details (compare figs. 7 and 10). This sort of semi-custom work probably accounted for a substantial portion of his business.

A Louis XVI side chair made by Marcotte for Eliphalet Wood of Irvington, New York, has extraordinary covers that Wood purchased at *Aux Genre Gobelins* in Paris, while on a grand tour of Europe in 1869 (fig. 11). After deciding that a Marcotte suite purchased second hand through Sypher and Company of New York was not suitable for the upholstery, Wood ordered a new suite from Marcotte (fig. 12). Except for the absence of a gilt-bronze bow-knot in the center of the crest rail, the chairs from Wood's second suite are identical to those from two other suites by Marcotte—one in the Metropolitan Museum of Art and the other in the Lockwood Mathews Mansion Museum. Wood's open-back side chair is an extremely elegant form marked by the repetition of the *Chapeau de Gendarme* shape. Marcotte used the term "Light Chair[s]" to describe open-back examples of this general form.

Whereas Marcotte's Louis XVI seating furniture was unmistakably nineteenth century, his designs for case pieces were more faithful to eighteenth-century prototypes. The earliest Louis XVI-style casework documented to Ringuet-Leprince & L. Marcotte is a marble-top rosewood cabinet with gilt-bronze mounts made for the drawing room at Armsmear for which Colt paid Leprince and Marcotte $280 in March 1857. The cabinet is similar in form to one L. Marcotte & Co. made three years later for John Taylor Johnston as part of a suite of three cabinets, all of which closely resemble

Figure 8 Side chair attributed to L. Marcotte & Co., New York, ca. 1865. Beech. H. 36 1/2", W. 20 1/4", D. 16 1/2". (Private collection; photo, Gavin Ashworth.)

French neoclassical forms (fig. 13). These parallel the 1860 Marcotte and Ringuet-Leprince advertisement offering "rich suites of Black Wood and Gilt" and "Black and Gilt Carved Centre Tables with . . . elegant Cabinets to Match."[17]

A library table with a history of ownership by Johnston's daughter, Emily Johnston de Forest, represents a slightly more interpretive version of the French classical style (fig. 14). Marcotte used expensive amboyna veneers, stained hornbeam banding, ivory stringing, and small amboyna-veneered tablets to create repetitive geometric patterns that complement the linear shape of the stretchers and vertical orientation of the legs. The corners of the top also have inlaid ivory scrolls, leaves, and stringing that are reminiscent of marquetry on eighteenth-century French furniture.[18] Here, too, Marcotte offered basic forms that a buyer could upgrade by choosing different legs, exotic veneers, metal mounts, marquetry, and carving. A library table made for Mr. Eugene Ketcltas, who purchased "Lansmeer" in

Figure 9 Armchair attributed to L. Marcotte & Co., New York, ca. 1865. Beech. H. 38 1/4", W. 21", D. 19 3/4". (Private collection; photo, Gavin Ashworth.)

Figure 10 Side chair attributed to L. Marcotte & Co., New York, ca. 1860. Beech. H. 38", W. 21 3/4", D. 19". (Private collection; photo, Glenn Castellano.)

Newport in 1870, is very similar to de Forest's, but it is made of different materials (fig. 15). Keteltas's table is inlaid with exotic woods in geometric and floral patterns and, in place of the carved acanthus leaves and ionic capitals, has gilt-bronze mounts. Keteltas's daughter, Edith, had married William Shepherd Wetmore's son George in 1869, and the newlyweds were ordering furniture for Chateau-Sur-Mer from Marcotte at the same time.

At the lower end of Marcotte's business was stock furniture. A simple work table is one of several stock items that Ogden Codman, Sr., purchased for "The Grange," his house in Lincoln, Massachusetts (fig. 16). Marcotte also sold Codman mantles and a variety of wallpapers and fabrics.[19]

In the omnipresent Renaissance revival style, which manifested itself in a number of subcategories romantically evocative of great ages of the past, such as Henri II, François I, and Louis XIII, Marcotte could draw upon architectural details, including columns, pediments, caryatids, and classical decorative motifs. Marcotte's firm was a leader in the production of

Figure 11 Side chair by L. Marcotte & Co., New York, 1869. Cherry. H. 33 1/2", W. 18", D. 18". (Courtesy, Smithsonian Institution, Washington, D.C.; photo, Peter Hill.)

Figure 12 Bill of sale from L. Marcotte & Co. to Eliphalet Wood, New York, 1869. The bill head delineates the range of services offered by Marcotte, as well as the address of the Parisian branch. (Courtesy, Winterthur Library.)

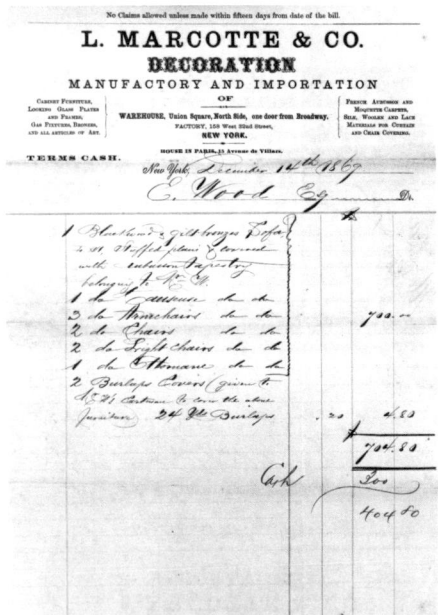

Figure 13 Cabinet attributed to L. Marcotte & Co., New York, ca. 1860. Fruitwood with oak and tulip poplar. H. 42 3/4", W. 72 3/16", D. 21 1/4". (Metropolitan Museum of Art, acc. 68.165.1a,b.)

Figure 14 Library table attributed to L. Marcotte & Co., New York, ca. 1872. Walnut, amboyna, and mahogany with pine. H. 30 3/4", W. 50", D. 29". (Metropolitan Museum of Art, gift of Mrs. Robert W. de Forest, acc. 34.140.1.)

Figure 15 Library table attributed to L. Marcotte & Co., New York, ca. 1870. Walnut, burl walnut veneer, and satinwood with oak and fruitwood. H. 30 7/8", W. 47", D. 27 1/8". (Private collection; photo, Glenn Castellano.)

Figure 16 Work table by L. Marcotte & Co., New York, 1869. Walnut and burl walnut veneer. H. 27", Diam. 18 1/2". This table is particularly "French" with delicately proportioned legs joined by a gracefully curved stretcher. (Courtesy, Society for the Preservation of New England Antiquities, acc. 1969.2126.)

Figure 17 Engraving of a sideboard made by Ringuet-Leprince & L. Marcotte for the Crystal Palace Exhibition, New York, 1853. (Silliman and Goodrich, *The World of Science, Art and Industry*, [New York, 1853], p. 47.)

Renaissance revival furniture in America. One of his earliest Renaissance revival pieces was a sideboard made for the Crystal Palace Exhibition in 1853 (fig. 17). Marcotte and Ringuet-Leprince were aware of the acclaim received by the sideboard that Alexandre Georges Fourdinois made for the London Crystal Palace Exhibition in 1851, and they chose to exhibit the same form to demonstrate that their work was equal to Fourdinois's.[20]

Samuel Colt ordered a large number of Renaissance revival pieces, including a side chair with scrolled arms and legs and arched ogee-shaped stretchers derived from Louis XIII designs and fringe and elaborate decorative nailing that were pure mid-nineteenth-century conventions (fig. 18). Likewise, Marcotte's desk for Armsmear is a rather loose interpretation of the *Bureau Mazarin*, a design distinguished by the number and shape of the legs and the H-stretcher (fig. 19). Marcotte's principal deviation from the historic model was the completely horizontal arrangement of the drawers.

A side chair from a dining-room suite in the Grange represents the other end of the financial spectrum in this line (fig. 20). On this stock item, the swan motif is derived from the early-nineteenth-century Empire vocabulary of Charles Percier and Pierre Fontaine, and the overall form of the chair and the incised decoration presage the Eastlake style (fig. 21).[21]

Marcotte's Renaissance revival designs occasionally resemble popular pieces derived from pattern books and periodicals of the day, with the major differences being the choice of woods and ornamental details. A suite of furniture Marcotte made for George and Edith Wetmore has a distinct American quality that contrasts with Marcotte's purer French designs (fig. 22). George's father, William Shepard Wetmore, had patronized

Figure 18 Chair by Ringuet-Leprince & L. Marcotte, New York, 1857. Oak. H. 44 1/2", W. 25 1/2", D. 25 1/4". (Courtesy, Armsmear; photo, E. Irving Blomstram.)

Figure 19 Desk by Ringuet-Leprince & L. Marcotte, New York, 1857. Walnut, oak, and mahogany with pine. H. 30", W. 60", D. 34". (Courtesy, Armsmear; photo, E. Irving Blomstram.)

Figure 20 Side chair by L. Marcotte & Co., New York, 1862. Butternut. H. 35 1/4", W. 18 3/4", D. 18 1/2". (Courtesy, Society for the Preservation of New England Antiquities, acc. 1969.767.1; photo, David Bohl.)

Figure 21 Detail of the side chair illustrated in fig. 20. (Photo, Nina Gray.)

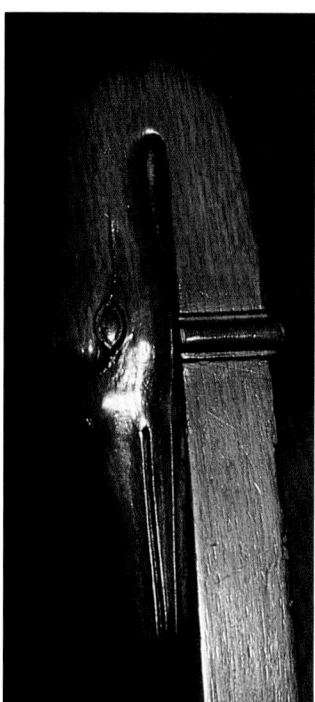

Figure 22 Suite of furniture by L. Marcotte & Co., New York, 1869. The suite is composed of a bedstead, armoire, dressing table, two night stands, a chaise longue, a commode, six side chairs, a linen press, and two wardrobe cabinets. (Courtesy, Preservation Society of Newport County.)

Figure 23 Library in the LeGrand Lockwood mansion, Norwalk, Connecticut, photograph ca. 1870. Financial and railroad entrepeneur, LeGrand Lockwood built the house in 1869. The divan and looking glass are on the left. (Courtesy, Lockwood Mathews Mansion.)

Marcotte and Ringuet-Leprince two decades earlier by purchasing a large Louis XV-style, ebonized suite for his ballroom.[22]

LeGrand Lockwood's mansion contains some of Marcotte's finest Renaissance revival work (figs. 23, 24). The original contents of the library included a throne-like black walnut and steel divan with a looking glass and a canopy.[23] Marcotte's furniture and interior decoration perfectly complemented the house design by his former partner, Lienau. The library has walnut woodwork and a parquetry floor—composed of five different species of wood—that repeated the star patterns of the door panels and the ceiling.

Marcotte's work of the 1870s brought him even more fame, and the exhibits at the Centennial Exposition at Philadelphia marked a high point in the firm's history. Marcotte displayed two interiors, an Henri II-style library and a Louis XIII-style dining room. The library had ebonized woodwork and furnishings, including a variety of seating forms upholstered in stamped leather and a large carved cabinet with enamel plaques and oxidized silver mounts. The dining room had walnut woodwork and a monumental, 9' cast-iron fireplace with carved *putti* and faience medallions. The exhibits were hailed as "a splendid illustration of the latest phases of decorative art, as employed by the French in the adornment of house interiors; . . . the best effort of its kind in the American Department," and Marcotte was praised for his "artistic design," "carving perfect in detail of execution and effect," and "beautiful proportions and excellent workmanship." An equal, if not greater, triumph was accorded Marcotte two years later at the Exposition Universelle in Paris where his ebonized cabinet won a gold medal (fig. 25). Critics judged the cabinet "a work of very great merit and beauty. . . . Although a production of the New World it competes with the very best work of the old. The American firm has assuredly shown that its home manufactures of the loftier order may in no way shrink from competition with the issues of the long established ébenistes of Paris."[24]

Marcotte's greatest known private commission—the 1877–1878 decoration of Cyrus Hall McCormick's house at 675 Rush Street in Chicago—occurred shortly after the Philadelphia exposition. Marcotte's bid of $60,597 for the furniture, decorations, and woodwork was higher than Herter Brothers' ($53,370) and Pottier and Stymus's ($53,742); yet, Marcotte received the contract.[25] The contract specified the materials to be used in each room, stated exactly what woodwork and trim Marcotte was responsible for providing, and noted where the building contractor's responsibilities ended and where Marcotte's began. These specifics proved advantageous to all parties since the McCormicks made several changes during the construction of their house.

The widely traveled McCormicks wanted their public rooms furnished in a variety of styles. The dining room had mahogany woodwork and a painted ceiling decorated with harvest scenes, an obvious reference to Cyrus McCormick's invention of the reaper (fig. 26). The sideboard that Marcotte provided for the dining room cost $800 and is a superb example of his best custom work. Designed in proportion with the room, the sideboard has

Figure 24 Detail of the library in the Lockwood mansion. The ceiling is particularly elegant and illusionistic in the manner in which the eight pointed stars surround the crosses. The blue and gold wallpaper is embossed like Moroccan leather. (Courtesy, Lockwood Mathews Mansion; photo, Gavin Ashworth.)

Figure 25   Engraving of a cabinet by L. Marcotte & Co., New York, 1878. (*Art Journal*, 1878.)

Figure 26   Dining room in the McCormick mansion, Chicago, 1880. The walls were covered with antique tapestry and the seating was upholstered with green stamped leather. (Courtesy, State Historical Society of Wisconsin.)

Figure 27   Drawing of a sideboard by Leon Marcotte, New York, 1877. Pencil on paper. (Courtesy, State Historical Society of Wisconsin.)

twisted Ionic columns, engaged pilasters, galleries, and arches that give it a strong architectural presence (fig. 27). The central panel of the lower section is carved with McCormick's initials.

Marcotte also decorated the hall in formal Renaissance revival style (fig. 28) and secured several of the decorations, including the hall lamp and the pair of Japanese vases on the mantel, from his Paris shop. The McCormicks visited Marcotte's establishment in Paris in 1879. Just prior to one of the McCormicks' trips abroad, Marcotte wrote,

> Your enquiring of the address of Mr. Herter's agent in Paris has made me think that you always contemplated to have the decorating and furnishing done by him. I have been told several times that Herter had some of the furniture already in hand. If such was the case I would be obliged to you to let me know of it as I would not like to interfere with Mr. Herter's plans and want to save my time about matters of no direct interest to me. I have done the part intrusted to me with my best ability and feel confident in having given to you capitol work. I would certainly like to complete the work but to do it with satisfaction I would like to know if you have entire confidence in my judgement.

Marcotte ultimately completed the furnishing of the McCormick mansion and Herter Brothers broke off their relationship with the McCormicks entirely in 1879.[26]

The following year, L. Marcotte & Co. provided furniture for rooms decorated by Herter Brothers in the Seventh Regiment Armory in New York City. The furniture was similar in formality to that in the hall of the McCormick mansion. Like the Lockwood Mathews mansion, the interiors of the Seventh Regiment Armory were contracted to a number of prominent decorators. L. Marcotte & Co. made furniture for the Board of Officers Room (fig. 29) and the Colonels Room. The presiding officer's chair (fig. 30) was the most elaborate piece of furniture made for the Board

Figure 28   Hall in the McCormick mansion, Chicago, 1880. (Courtesy, State Historical Society of Wisconsin.)

Figure 29   Board of Officers Room in the Seventh Regiment Armory, New York, 1880. (Woodcut from the *Decorator and Furnisher*, May 1885; photo, Gavin Ashworth.)

Figure 30   Presiding officer's chair by L. Marcotte & Co., New York, 1880. Mahogany. H. 64", W. 31", D. 29". (Courtesy, Seventh Regiment Fund, Inc.; photo, Gavin Ashworth.)

Room. Marcotte used Ionic pilasters for the back posts to complement the architecture of the room, and he incorporated a crest with ball finials and a shield carved with the number 7 to reflect the commission of the chair by the Armory.

Marcotte's aesthetic-style furniture encompassed all the exotic influences that came to bear on American interior design during the last quarter of the nineteenth century. "Mexican" is the term Marcotte used to describe an ebonized side chair that Ogden Codman ordered in 1869 (fig. 31). Possibly derived from the *chaise longue mexicane* illustrated in Victor Louis Quentin's *Le Magasin de Meubles*, the chair is a loose interpretation of that pat-

Figure 31 "Mexican" chair by L. Marcotte & Co., New York, 1869. Ebonized wood. H. 35 1/2", W. 20 1/2", D. 30". The plump scroll on the curve of the back is typical of Marcotte's work. (Courtesy, Society for the Preservation of New England Antiquities, acc. 1969. 2908.)

tern book's details.[27] Other stock pieces Codman purchased from Marcotte were a chair and firescreen in the Chinese style (fig. 32). Though their overall design clearly is Western, both pieces have "bamboo frets" and other Oriental details that kept Marcotte's designs in the vanguard of American work of the period. A self-conscious trendsetter, Marcotte was among the first to capitalize on the growing taste for Japanese, Far Eastern, Turkish, and Moroccan design in the 1870s and 1880s.

The aesthetic-style interiors, furniture, and decorations that Marcotte provided for the McCormick mansion were, by contrast to Codman's, extremely costly. Particularly intriguing are the library and music room, which would not be attributed to Marcotte were it not for the surviving contract, drawings, and bills that document his involvement (figs. 33, 34). The original plan for the library called for ebonized wood inlaid with tin, but the bookcases, mantle, door surrounds, cornice moldings, and other components installed by Marcotte were red-stained walnut. The shallow geometric carving on the bookcases and mantel is a superb American interpretation of Eastlake design. Each of the large armchairs upholstered in red silk with fancy trim and tassels cost $70, whereas the gilt side chairs with matching upholstery cost $60 (fig. 33). The library table, for which Marcotte charged $300, was the most expensive piece in the suite.[28]

Figure 32 "Chinese" side chair by L. Marcotte & Co., New York, 1869. Gilded wood. H. 28 ⅝", W. 20 ¼", D. 20 ⅞". (Courtesy, Society for the Preservation of New England Antiquities, acc. 1969.3528.)

Figure 33 Library in the McCormick mansion, Chicago, 1880. (Courtesy, State Historical Society of Wisconsin, photo ca. 1880.)

Figure 34 Music room in the McCormick mansion, 1880. (Courtesy, State Historical Society of Wisconsin, photo ca. 1880.)

Ebonized and inlaid with tin, the table provided a striking contrast with the walnut bookcases and other interior fittings. Marcotte's rich combination of materials and colors even extended to the wallpaper, which had a gold ground and blue tapestry designs.

The woodwork in the McCormicks' music room was maple, selectively decorated with exotic-wood marquetry with gilded incising (fig. 34). The delicate floral inlays complemented the marquetry of the ceiling and the shallow-carved capitals of the doorways and mantle. Marcotte's Paris factory made the over-stuffed chairs and sofa and upholstered them in plush fabric with Chinese-style motifs that harmonized with the exotic character of the room.[29]

The last interiors documented to Marcotte are those for the Vanderbilt family of New York. The Vanderbilts' sumptuous city residences and country houses were among the most ambitious domestic dwellings constructed during the late nineteenth century. William Henry Vanderbilt hired Marcotte to decorate the Fifth Avenue houses of his daughters Margaret Vanderbilt Shepherd and Emily Vanderbilt Sloane. In 1886, Marcotte wrote, "I feel very happy . . . that our plans have been accepted

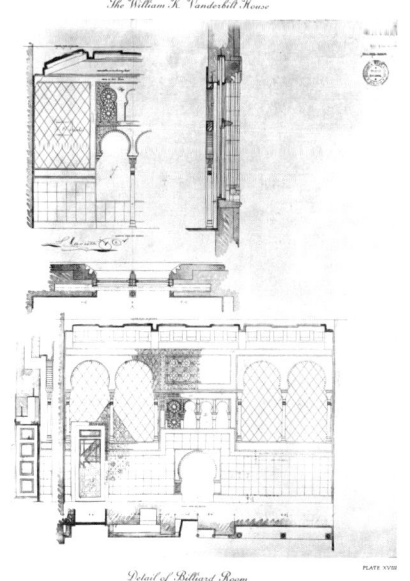

Figure 36 Billiard room in the William K. Vanderbilt house, New York, 1882–1883. (Illustration from John Vrenburgh Van Pelt, *A Monograph of the William K. Vanderbilt House* [New York: privately published, 1925], p. 58.)

Figure 35 Billiard room in the William K. Vanderbilt house, New York, 1882–1883. (Illustration from John Vrenburgh Van Pelt, *A Monograph of the William K. Vanderbilt House* [New York: privately published, 1925], pl. 18.)

and the contract signed a few days ago. This order is a very important one amounting to $120,000 for the woodwork only, and the decoration and furniture will certainly double that amount." Little is known about the furnishings of these two houses, but the interior of the Shepherd house was predominantly Renaissance revival, with heavily carved woodwork.[30]

Marcotte also worked for William K. and Alva Vanderbilt whose extraordinary French-style townhouse (designed by Richard Morris Hunt) was just up the street at 660 Fifth Avenue. The interiors of this house were among the most ambitious and sophisticated of the period. Mrs. Vanderbilt hired the most prominent decorators to furnish the rooms, including Herter Brothers and Jules Allard et Fils who created a Regence salon. The billiard room, decorated in the Moorish style, is the most exotic interior designed by Marcotte (figs. 35, 36). The room had a geometric frieze, recesses with Islamic-inspired serrated arches, walls covered with complex floral tiles and a geometric frieze, and a ceiling with three spiderweb blocks and a geometric border on either side.

Marcotte was actively involved with his firm until his death in 1887. L. Marcotte & Co. continued without change in title under the direction of Adrian Herzog and his family in New York and Edmund Leprince Ringuet in Paris before passing out of the family. The architectural firm McKim, Mead, & White hired L. Marcotte & Co. to provide architectural appointments for the library of the Robert W. Patterson house, built in Washington, D.C., between 1900 and 1903, and furnish a suite of white and gilt furniture for the Blue Room of the White House. Other than a few commissions recorded in the financial papers of architectural firms, little is known about the management and direction of L. Marcotte & Co. under Herzog and Ringuet. In general, the business seems to have lost strength after Marcotte's death, for the capital never exceeded $150,000 whereas previously it was closer to $250,000.[31]

Renowned for the quality and artistic integrity of his interiors, furniture, and decorations, his awards at international expositions, and his work for many of America's wealthiest and most socially prominent families, Leon Marcotte stood above many contemporaries in the decorating profession. The ever-opinionated Mark Twain summed up the esteem Marcotte aroused in a letter to the superintendent of construction of the Connecticut State Capitol:

> We have three rooms in our house which will prove to anybody that Marcotte knows his business. . . . [He] ought to have chance to bid. But thunder and blazes! These folks are bound to go to the wall before the gaudy rubbish of . . . nevermind. I won't mention names, though I could. New York is full of bastard furniture-constructors and decorators.[32]

1. George William Curtis, *The Potiphar Papers* (New York: G. P. Putnam, 1854), pp. 117–18.

2. For a contemporary comment on the "mania . . . for expensive French furniture," see Alexander J. Davis, *The Architecture of Country Houses* (New York: D. Appleton &. Co., 1850), p. 410. On the broader question of influence, see Kenneth Ames, "Designed in France, Notes on the Transmission of French Style to America," *Winterthur Portfolio* 12 (Charlottesville, Va.: University Press of Virginia, 1977), pp. 103–14; Peter Strickland, "Influence of the Second Empire on American Furniture," *Connoisseur* 119, no. 802 (December 1978): 256–63; and Marilynn Johnson et al., *19th Century America, Furniture and Other Decorative Arts* (New York: Metropolitan Museum of Art, 1970).

3. Elizabeth Ingerman, "Personal Experiences of an Old New York Cabinet-Maker," *Antiques* 84, no. 5 (November 1963): 580.

4. *Acte de Naissance*, M. le Maire, Valognes, Manche, France. César Daly, *Revue Generale de L'Architecture* 34 (1877): 60–61. American Institute of Architects, *Proceedings of the Annual Convention* (Philadelphia: AIA, 1870), p. 27. Marcotte is recorded as a lifetime member of the American Institute of Architects.

5. The Marcotte and Ringuet families may have been related prior to Leon and Marie-Felicitié's marriage, for Marcotte's mother's maiden name was Ringuet (*Acte de Naissance*). The author thanks Mme. Louis Leprince Ringuet for background information on Marcotte and Ringuet-Leprince. Further details are in the *Acte de Mariage*, Archives de Paris, kindly furnished by Mme. Denise Ledoux-Lebard. Auguste-Emile Ringuet-Leprince was the adopted stepson of the *tapissier* and *fabricant de meubles*, Julien-Daniel-René Ringuet (1777–1839). They were in business together from 1835 to 1839 (see Denise Ledoux-Lebard, *Les Ébénistes Parisiens du XIXe Siécle [1795–1889] Leurs Oeuvres et Leurs Marques* [Paris: Les Editions de L'Amateur, 1984], pp. 555–56). Emily Johnston Deforest, *James Colles, 1788–1883, Life and Letters* (New York: published privately, 1926), p. 130. Mathew Morgan to James Colles, March 30, 1848, James Colles Papers (hereafter JCP), New York Public Library. For more on Ringuet-Leprince's New York clients, see Mrs. Samuel Jaudon to Mrs. James Colles, July 14, 1844; Ringuet-Leprince to James Colles, January 30, 1845; James Colles to Ringuet-Leprince, April 23, 1845, James Colles to Ringuet-Leprince, November 29, 1845; Ringuet-Leprince to James Colles, December 31, 1845; James Colles to Ringuet-Leprince, November 29, 1845; Mrs. Samuel Jaudon to Mrs. James Colles, July 14, 1844; all in JCP.

6. R. G. Dun Ledgers, Baker Library, Harvard University. January 17, 1854, 191: 441. Auguste-Emile Ringuet-Leprince to James Colles, March 30, 1848, JCP.

7. In New York they were located at 477 Broadway from 1849–1854, 55 West 16th Street and 343–347 Fourth Street from 1854–1864 (Rodes New York City Business Directory; Trows New York City Directory; and Wilson's Business Directory of New York City). There are two documented projects by Lienau and Marcotte. The first is the Hart M. Shiff residence at 32 Fifth Avenue, New York, 1850–1852. Shiff was a French financier. The house was Second Empire in style, and Marcotte and Lienau were credited with some of the interior work. See Ellen Kramer, "The Domestic Architecture of Detlef Lienau, A Conservative Victorian," Ph.D. dissertation, Institute of Fine Arts, New York, 1957, p. 110. There is a drawing for a church on

Fifth Avenue, signed Lienau and Marcotte, in the Lienau Collection, Avery Library, Columbia University. The church was never built. Kramer believed that Marcotte came "to this country from France very highly recommended and with good contacts, so it is not unlikely that he may have been instrumental in getting Lienau some of his early commissions" (Kramer, "Domestic Architecture of Lienau," p. 85).

8. Ledoux-Lebard believes that Ringuet-Leprince sold his business to Étienne Simon Eugène Roudillon in 1853 (Ledoux-Lebard, *Les Ébénistes Parisiennes*, p. 563). In reference to the sale of Ringuet-Leprince's business to Roudillon, see Paris Almanach du Commerce 1853. There is no indication of a sale in the New York directories.

9. Numerous bills sent from New York and Paris during the 1850s are in the Samuel Colt Collection, State Historical Society of Connecticut. Dun Ledgers, January 17, 1854; September 15, 1855; April 5, 1858, 191: 441.

10. *Acte de Mariage*, Archives de Paris. An addenda to the marriage certificate in 1874 reported that Marcotte was living in New York with his mother, who was a *proprietaire* in the business.

11. *New York Tribune*, July 1, 1860. Dun Ledgers, July 1860; May 14, 1862; December 21, 1863; February 25, 1868; June 11, 1869, 194: 735. R. G. Dun and Company, *The Mercantile Agency Reference Book and Key, Containing the Ratings of the Merchants, Manufacturers and Traders Generally Throughout the United States* (New York: Dun, Barlow & Co., 1866). Department of Buildings, Boss Tweed Court House: New Building Docket #1067, 1867, filed 8/30, value $25,000, size: 95.6 × 40.4, height 51.61, no. of stories, 4, 5. Kramer, "Domestic Architecture of Lienau," p. 274. By 1878 the value of the company was $90,000 (Dun Ledgers, January 12, 1878, 194: 800).

12. Dun Ledgers, January 25, 1871; January 24, 1874 ; January 12, 1878; November 11, 1879, 194: 800.

13. Dun Ledgers, January 28, 1881; February 23, 1884, 194: A59. Marcotte obituary, *New York Daily Tribune*, January 26, 1887. It is not known why Edmond Leprince Ringuet reversed the order of his last name from Ringuet-Leprince.

14. For a profile of Chateau-Sur-Mer, see John Cherol, "Chateau-Sur-Mer in Newport, Rhode Island," *Antiques* 118, no. 6 (December 1980): 1220–25.

15. For a detailed account of the Armsmear commission, see Phillip Johnston, "Dialogues between Designer and Client, Furnishings Proposed by Leon Marcotte to Samuel Colt in the 1850s," *Winterthur Portfolio* 19, no. 4 (Winter 1984): 257–75. The letters, bills, correspondence, and drawings relating to this commission are in the Colt Collection, Connecticut Historical Society—Leon Marcotte to Samuel Colt, May 31, 1856; Bill from Ringuet-Leprince to Samuel Colt, Paris, November 7, 1856; Leon Marcotte to Samuel Colt, November 26, 1856; and Leon Marcotte to Samuel Colt, May 28, 1856. A drawing for this chair shows a cartouche-shaped back rather than the shield-back of the executed chair (Colt Collection). See also Johnston, "Dialogues," p. 270.

16. Harriet Spofford, *Art Decoration Applied to Furniture* (New York: Harper & Brothers, 1878), pp. 129–30.

17. For more on Colt's cabinet, see Johnston, "Dialogues," p. 268, fig. 16. Advertisement is as quoted in Marilynn Johnson, *19th Century America*, fig. 153.

18. Marilynn Johnson, *19th Century America*, fig. 155.

19. Richard Nylander, "Documenting the Interior of Codman House: The Last Two Generations," *Old Time New England* 71, no. 258 (1981): 84 ff.

20. On the Renaissance revival, see Kenneth Ames, "Renaissance Revival Furniture in America," Ph.D. dissertation, University of Pennsylvania, 1970; and Kenneth Ames, "The Battle of the Sideboards," *Winterthur Portfolio* 9 (Charlottesville, Va.: University Press of Virginia, 1974): 4, 8–27.

21. Marcotte's drawing for the chair is in the Colt Collection. The drawing is illustrated in Johnston, "Dialogues," p. 272, fig. 24. The chairs originally had springs and were covered in a figured enamel cloth. The bill from Marcotte is dated September 1863. The bills and correspondence relating to this commission are in the collection of the Society for the Preservation of New England Antiquities, Boston.

22. Other American cabinetmakers used the same design, which probably first appeared in a pattern book. Examples by Alexander Roux and George Henkels are in the Henry Shaw house in St. Louis and the Asa Packer mansion in the Borough of Tim Thorpe, Pennsylvania.

23. Other decorators involved in furnishing Lockwood's mansion were Herter Brothers and

George Platt. Leavitt Auctioneers sold the contents in New York (Leavitt Auctioneers, *Unique and Artistic Furniture from the House at Norwalk, Conn. of the Late Le Grand Lockwood*, October 30 and 31, 1873). The catalogue describes the furniture, but the present location of the pieces is not known.

24. *American Architect and Building News*, (December 1876): 413. Francis A. Walker, ed., *United States Centennial Commission International Exhibition, 1876, Reports and Awards, Group VI*, 5 vols. (Philadelphia: Lippincott, 1877), 5: 47. *Art Journal* (London: Virtue & Co. 1878), p. 144.

25. McCormick made copious notes comparing the estimates room by room, with columns for each firm and itemized entries for the architecture, frescoes, furniture, papers, lighting, and carpets (folder 2A, box 27, Cyrus Hall McCormick Papers, State Historical Society of Wisconsin, Madison). See also Pottier and Stymus estimates, July 2 and July 21, 1877; and Herter Brothers estimate, March 18 and May 25, 1877.

26. The hall furnishings are listed in bills from L. Marcotte & Co., Paris dated January 25, 1879, and February 4, 1879; Leon Marcotte to Cyrus Hall McCormick, September 26, 1878; and Cyrus McCormick, Peekskill Depot, to Mrs. C. H. McCormick, 5th Avenue Hotel, New York, June 23, 1879, all in the McCormick Papers.

27. Marcotte may have been inspired by a *chaise longue mexicane* illustrated in Victor Louis Quetin, *Le Magasin de Meubles*. The author found this illustration in a group of loose pages.

28. Invoice from L. Marcotte & Co. to Cyrus H. McCormick, October 19, 1877, McCormick Papers.

29. Letter from J. Rasch of L. Marcotte & Co. to Mrs. C. H. McCormick, January 7, 1880, McCormick Papers.

30. Leon Marcotte to Mrs. Cyrus Hall McCormick, June 25, 1880, McCormick Papers. Marcotte received $132,385.70 for the "hard woodwork" in the double house occupied by the Shepherds and Sloanes (John B. Snook Contract Book, p. 340, New-York Historical Society, New York). Their houses adjoined William Vanderbilt's residence at 640 Fifth Avenue. A late-nineteenth-century album in the New-York Historical Society documents the appearance of the public rooms of the Shepherd house. Nothing is known about the Sloan interiors.

31. *Trow's Copartnership and Corporation Directory for New York City*.

32. Mark Twain to General Franklin, Superintendent of Construction of the State Capitol of Connecticut, May 12, 1877, Mark Twain Memorial, Hartford, Conn.

Robert Mussey and Anne Rogers Haley

John Cogswell and Boston Bombé Furniture: Thirty-Five Years of Revolution in Politics and Design

▼ DURING the second half of the eighteenth century, bombé furniture was a signal expression of the prosperity and social status of many wealthy Bostonians. Cabinetmakers in other urban ports rarely incorporated the bombé shape in their work, but at midcentury Boston craftsmen embraced the new design and adapted it to suit local tastes and cabinetmaking practices. By 1775, a variety of bombé forms were available owing to competition between tradesmen and the search for more conspicuous totems of wealth by the merchant and professional classes.

Among the surviving bombé forms is an elaborate mahogany pulpit from Brattle Square Church (see figs. 3–5 later in this article) and four double-serpentine front bombé case pieces owned by merchant congregants. The pulpit, like other Boston bombé case pieces from the 1750–1775 period, has its swell placed low on the front and sides. Those forms from the 1775–1795 period evolved to combine less abrupt bottom-heavy shaping and double-serpentine facades.

The latter period encompasses the prime working years of John Cogswell (1738–1819), an Ipswich, Massachusetts, cabinetmaker who moved to nearby Boston about 1760. Cogswell's name has long been associated with Boston bombé furniture because of a magnificent chest-on-chest that bears his signature (see fig. 13 later in this article), but little has been written about his life and work. This article examines Cogswell's career and thirteen pieces of bombé furniture now attributed to his shop. The impact of the Revolution on Boston bombé design is explored, including the increasing French influence on the local culture and design aesthetic.[1]

Brattle Square Church and Bombé Design
The social, economic, and political forces that influenced bombé design at the beginning of Cogswell's career were manifest in the design and construction of Brattle Square Church and in the lives of many of its members. Four pieces attributed to Cogswell's shop were made for wealthy merchants who were members of that church: Thomas Amory, Joseph Barrell, Ebenezer Storer, and Gardiner Greene. Thomas Dawes (1731–1809), the designer and builder of the church, and at least three other congregants owned bombé furniture by other Boston cabinetmakers. In addition, the church had an imposing bombé pulpit, one of only three known to survive from the colonies. Prominently situated at the end of the central aisle, it was an emblem deliberately selected to reflect the elevated status of the members.[2]

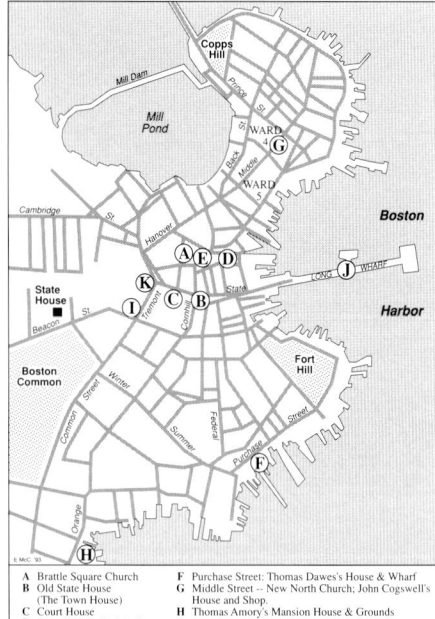

Figure 1 Sectional adaptation derived from *A New Plan of Boston From Actual Surveys By Osgood Carleton, With Corrections, Additions and Improvements*, Boston, 1800. (Adaptation, Eliza McClennen.)

Figure 2 Brattle Square Church, Boston, 1772–1773. Photograph by Josiah Johnson Hawes, Boston, 1859. Brattle Square Church was centrally located near the Town Market, Dock Square, Faneuil Hall, and the Province House. (Courtesy, Society for the Preservation of New England Antiquities.)

The first church in Brattle Square (1699) was known as the "Manifesto Church" for the congregation's inaugural proclamation of independence from religious dogma. By the middle of the eighteenth century, it was the leading social and philosophical forum for Boston's Congregationalist elite and, subsequently, a center of revolutionary resistance. Its congregation included merchants, politicians, lawyers, doctors, and many other wealthy and prominent Bostonians such as James Bowdoin, John Hancock, Samuel Adams, John Adams, Dr. Joseph Warren, William Cooper, Josiah Quincy, Samuel Otis, Joseph Barrell, Ebenezer Storer, Theodore Lyman, Thomas and Charles Bulfinch, John Erving, John and Jonathan Amory, John Fayerweather, Daniel Oliver, Thomas Boylston, and Peter Chardon.[3]

The church also functioned as a social center, and its architecture and furnishings reflected the wealth and taste of the congregation. A visiting Frenchman wrote, "the church is the great theater where they [American ladies] attend, to display their extravagance and finery. There they come dressed off in the finest silks, and overshadowed with a profusion of the most superb plumes. The hair . . . is raised . . . to an extravagant height, somewhat resembling the manner in which the French ladies wore their hair some years ago."[4]

By 1772, the old church building had become too small and dilapidated for the growing congregation. On February 6, 1772, John Hancock, seeking to curry the favor of the congregants, offered to contribute £1000 towards the erection of a new church provided that it was built on the site of the existing church. This location was central to the seats of government and the commercial districts (fig. 1). Construction of the new church (on the foundations of its predecessor) and the commission of its extravagant bombé pulpit occurred during the early 1770s, despite general economic and political turmoil. The church was the only major public building erected in Boston between 1765 and 1785.[5]

Painter John Singleton Copley (1738–1815) and mason/master builder Thomas Dawes both submitted designs for the church to the building committee. Copley's plan, although "admired for its elegance and grandeur," was rejected because of construction costs, and the contract for designing and building the church went to Thomas Dawes, a longtime friend and political crony of John Hancock. Dawes laid the cornerstone on June 23, 1772, and by July of the following year the church was completed (figs. 2, 3). The church commemorated Hancock's generosity by inscribing his name on an exterior quoin.[6]

Hancock's donation paid for the window glass, bell, pulpit, crimson silk damask pulpit furniture, deacon's seat, communion table, and seats for "the accommodation of poor widows and others belonging to the society, who are reputable persons and unable to furnish themselves with seats, &c." By personally selecting these lavish furnishings, Hancock focused attention on his largesse and raised his status in the church and society. Not coincidentally, Hancock's pew in the new church was adjacent to the pulpit at the head of the central aisle.[7]

The interior was "richly finished [in] the Corinthian order," and the

Figure 3 Interior of Brattle Square Church, photo 1866-1872. (Courtesy, Society for the Preservation of New England Antiquities.)

pulpit was "of mahogany, . . . the most elegantly finished work in town" (fig. 3). Although the soundboard does not survive, the pulpit is one of the most fully developed examples of late baroque Boston woodwork (figs. 4, 5). The overall design, based on a three-dimensional hexagon, is derived from Batty Langley's *City and Country Builder's and Workman's Treasury of Designs* (1740) (fig. 6). The rear of the pulpit from Brattle Square Church is open, and the facade has parallel returns on each side creating a reiterative bombé shape (fig. 7). The carving on the large ogee molding at the base of the pulpit is also derived from Langley's design, but the strapwork acanthus on the large torus molding is more reminiscent of late-seventeenth-century carving (fig. 5). Langley's *Treasury* was one of the design books advertised most frequently by Boston booksellers during the middle of the eighteenth century and was the primary source of designs for churches and church furniture. Dawes owned at least twelve architectural books including the *Treasury*, and his copy may have provided the inspiration for the pulpit.[8]

The raised panels of the pulpit initially appear to be joined in a conventional manner; however, the mahogany panels are carved from $4^{1}/_{2}$" to 5"-thick planks, and each is mitered at the corners and fastened with nails. Both the bevels and bordering quarter-round molding are cut from the solid. Only the central portion of the front panel is veneered (fig. 4).

According to one church pastor, "a temporary pine pulpit was first erected, that [the bombé pulpit] which was engaged by him [John Hancock] of Mr. Crafts not being finished when the house was occupied." Crafts also did approximately half of the overall carpentry work for the church. "Mr. Crafts" was probably William Crafts (1736–1800), a Boston house joiner who frequently worked with Thomas Dawes. Crafts held a series of minor town offices, serving at various times with Thomas Dawes and Joseph Barrell. Crafts built outbuildings for and made improvements

Figure 4 Pulpit attributed to William Crafts and William Burbeck, Boston, 1772–1773. Mahogany and mahogany veneer with white pine. H. 83⅝", W. 50⅛", D. 18¾". (Courtesy, Society for the Preservation of New England Antiquities, acc. 1975.195, and the Massachusetts Historical Society, acc. MHS 255 [base]; photo, David Bohl.)

Figure 5 Detail of the carving on the pulpit from Brattle Square Church. (Photo, David Bohl.)

to Hancock's houses on Beacon Hill and Queen Street over the period of a decade and made "3 elbow pieces, 1 Seat, 1 Shelf, 1 Draw, and 3 footstools" for Hancock's use at Brattle Square Church. Crafts's association with Dawes and Hancock underscores the importance of social and business connections for eighteenth-century artisans. Such relationships undoubtedly influenced Crafts's receiving the commission for the pulpit.[9]

Circumstantial evidence suggests that William Burbeck (Burbank) (1716–1785) may have carved the pulpit (figs. 4, 5). Burbeck was working in Boston by 1735, and during his career he collaborated on various projects with Dawes, Crafts, and Hancock. He also held minor town offices and belonged to some of the same influential organizations as these men, including the Ancient and Honorable Artillery Company, the Lodge of St. Andrew, the Massachusetts Charitable Society, and the Sons of Liberty.

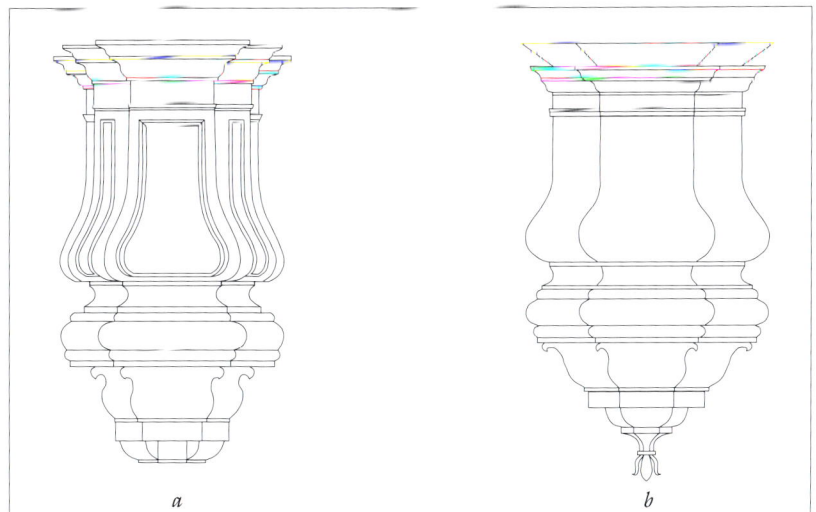

Figure 6   Design for a pulpit illustrated on pl. 112 in Batty Langley's *The City and Country Builder's and Workman's Treasury of Designs* (1740; reprint, London, 1756). (Courtesy, Society for the Preservation of New England Antiquities.)

Figure 7   Comparison of the pulpit from (a) Brattle Square Church and (b) pl. 112 in Langley's *Treasury*. (Drawing, Eliza McClennen.)

Like Dawes, Burbeck owned several English architectural design books including William Halfpenny's *Useful Architecture* (1752), William Salmon's *London Art of Building* (1734), James Gibbs's *A Book of Architecture* (1728), and three separate publications by Batty Langley, one of them probably the *Treasury*.[10]

The relationships between Burbeck, Crafts, Dawes, and Hancock went beyond those of artisan and patron, for they collaborated on several important public projects. For Burbeck, Crafts, and Dawes, such projects represented steady pay and an opportunity to interact with potential patrons. Furthermore, public service meant increased social standing and power in the community. Although these alliances clearly benefited the participants financially, the collaboration also resulted in several exceptional works of architecture.

As the most conspicuous and costly fixture in Brattle Square Church, the pulpit undoubtedly reflected the taste of the building committee and other influential congregants. The baroque curves and bold molding profiles of the pulpit certainly were comparable to those in the most fashionable Boston bombé furniture; yet, the reliance on thirty-year-old English Palladian designs expressed the fundamental conservatism of Boston's pre-Revolutionary craftsmen and merchants.

John Cogswell

John Cogswell was one of the few outsiders to break into Boston's relatively closed artisan community. During the early 1750s, he probably trained with a member of the Gooding family, a sixth-generation artisan family centered principally around Charlestown but with members also living in Boston and Cambridge. Cogswell married Abigail Gooding in 1762. The association with the Goodings probably gave Cogswell entrance into Boston's artisan community. Other social contacts may have been provided by Cogswell's father, Francis. A graduate of Harvard College and a moderately successful merchant, Francis had extensive business contacts in Nova Scotia, Quebec, Boston, and other New England seaports. He also represented Ipswich at the General Court of the Massachusetts Provincial Legislature in Boston from 1751 to 1754.[11]

Cogswell's early career coincided with the severe economic depression that followed the Seven Years' War. Higher taxes, rising inflation, and new duties and regulations caused a dramatic rise in the number of artisans on relief. These problems worsened during the Revolutionary War. Cogswell and allied tradesmen, such as Dawes and Crafts, subsisted by taking advantage of social, religious, fraternal, and political connections and by working within the caucus system. Burbeck relied on military pay.[12]

The caucus system emerged during the 1730s as a response to worsening economic conditions in Boston, but by midcentury it had become a powerful political machine and a means of soliciting patronage. John Adams described it in 1763:

> Caucas Clubb meets . . . in the Garrett of Tom Daw[e]s, the Adjutant of the Boston Regiment [Ancient and Honorable Artillery Company]. . . . There they smoke tobacco till you cannot see from one End of the Garrett to the other, . . . drink Phlip, . . . and . . . choose a Moderator, who puts Questions to the Vote regularly, and select Men, Assessors, Collectors, Wardens, Fire Wards, and Representatives are Regularly chosen before they are chosen in the Town. . . . They send Committees to wait on the Merchants Club and propose, and join, in the Choice of Men and Measures. Captn. Cunningham says they have often solicited him to go to these Caucas, they have assured him Benefit in his Business &c.[13]

Wealthy aristocrats held the most coveted town positions—as selectmen—but artisans and their political allies controlled many minor appointive offices. The most influential members of the Caucus Club functioned as ward bosses who secured votes during elections and helped "staff" town committees responsible for allocating funds with the "right tradesmen." Through churches, fire and militia companies, social clubs, mercantile organizations, and a variety of town offices, the Caucus Club influenced almost every group of voters in town. Moreover, it gave artisans the chance to interact with selectmen and other potential patrons.[14]

As leader of the Caucus Club, Dawes made certain that public funds went to trusted associates. By serving on town committees, such as the one appointed to consider his own "Scheem . . . for . . . preventing Chimneys taking fire," Dawes secured commissions for himself (the town hired him to implement the committee's recommendations) and other artisans in his circle.[15] Throughout his career, the small group of tradesmen he regularly worked with included Crafts, Burbeck, and Cogswell.

Although Boston-born tradesmen dominated the Caucus Club, Cogswell became involved shortly after his marriage. In 1763, the town appointed him constable, and the following year he participated in the annual "General Walk or Visitation of the Town" along with Dawes and merchants Ebenezer Storer, Edmund Quincy, and Timothy Newell. Cogswell's service to the town was not continuous, but he held several important positions. In 1779, for example, the town instructed him, Dawes, and painter/joiner Thomas Crafts (William Crafts's brother) "to procure Subscriptions to fortify the harbor." Intermittently, from 1770 to 1818,

Cogswell served as Scavenger (serving at various periods with carver John Welch and merchants Jonathan Amory and Joseph Barrell), Surveyor of Boards, Surveyor of Shingles (along with William Crafts), and Surveyor of Mahogany.[16]

On April 24, 1767, he purchased a house and shop at 49 Middle Street (now Hanover), in the center of the North End (fig. 1). This area encompassed Ward 4, where Cogswell held town offices and where Thomas Dawes was caucus leader. Many inhabitants of the North and South End were artisans, particularly shipbuilders and related tradesmen. In 1773, Cogswell's younger brother William, a minor merchant, married Thomas Dawes's sister, further cementing John's relationship with Dawes.[17]

Like many tradesmen, Cogswell fared poorly during the Revolution. In the 1771 Boston tax list, he is recorded as a cabinetmaker living with one other voting age adult, probably a journeyman. His real estate assessment was £16 and the value of his "Stock in Trade" was £60, an average figure for successful cabinetmakers in that year. In 1780, he is listed as a "Trader," having one "rateable poll [himself]" and £50 annual rent from his "Back House." With his trade disrupted, Cogswell had to find an additional source of income. On July 24, 1782, he petitioned the Suffolk County Inferior Court:

> That his business of a Cabinetmaker having almost failed, and the great loss he has met with by the depreciation of the Ennemey and the wanton depredations of the Ennemey when the Town was shut up, together with great sickness in his Family he has found himself under the necessity of opening a Shop for the Sale of West India Grocery Goods in order to support himself and his Family. . . . He shall experience but little profit unless he can obtain a License to retail Spirits . . . for his said Shop situated in Middle Street [see fig. 1].

The selectmen granted him an "Innholder & Retailer" license on August 28, 1782. The tax assessment for 1782 listed him as "Huxter," probably referring to his retail grocery trade.[18] For most Boston artisans, financial recovery depended on the renewed trade of their primary clientele—established merchants and new entrepreneurs such as Joseph Barrell and Elias Hasket Derby of Salem. Despite Cogswell's financial hardships, he secured at least one substantial commission shortly after the war: the costly chest-on-chest made for Derby in 1782 (see fig. 13).

Soon after his first wife's death early in 1782, Cogswell married Abiel (Abiall) Page, daughter of shipwright Edward Page, and continued forging commercial alliances with mariners. In 1785, his oldest daughter, Sarah, married Abiel's brother, Capt. Thomas Page, and Cogswell sold land on Bennett Street to Capt. John Skimmer. Cogswell may have used such connections to maintain a steady supply of groceries and other retail goods and to dabble in the venture cargo trade.[19]

In 1787, Cogswell was not listed as a cabinetmaker on the tax rolls, suggesting that the recovery of his trade was slow, but in 1788 he was. His assets grew during the 1790s; however, his tax valuations were less than those of cabinetmakers George Bright, Thomas Sherburne, and Gibbs Atkins. To supplement his income, Cogswell worked part-time as "surveyor of boards and shingles" from 1788 to 1818 and as "surveyor of mahogany" from 1799 to 1818. He died with an estate valued at $4,218.65, a figure indicative of moderate success.[20]

By the early 1780s, Cogswell had worked in Boston for more than twenty years. He, and at least one other unidentified cabinetmaker, updated traditional bombé forms by reducing the convex swell of the sides and fronts and by adding double-serpentine shaping to the facade. They adopted double-serpentine shaping about 1780, approximately the same time that Salem cabinetmakers began making case furniture with single-serpentine fronts. Imported English and French furniture with "commode" fronts and London design books, such as Thomas Chippendale's *Gentleman and Cabinet-Maker's Director* (1754) and Ince and Mayhew's *Universal System of Household Furniture* (ca. 1762), probably inspired the serpentine shaping.[21]

No French furniture of commode form has been documented in Boston before the 1790s; however, interaction between Boston and French armed forces, economies, cultures, and political systems increased significantly during and after the war. Although John Hancock, Reverend Samuel Cooper of the Brattle Square Church, and John Adams had been avowed enemies of France, each played a key role in recasting the erstwhile "demons" as saviors and as valuable political and economic allies after 1776. Hancock was a commander of the unsuccessful French-American assault on British forces in Newport and frequently entertained French naval officers and seamen at his mansion. Cooper became best friends with General Lafayette, and Adams spent 1778 to 1780 in France.[22]

From 1777 through 1784, a squadron of the French navy was quartered in Boston harbor. The navy was one of the few sources of specie in a town cut off from access to British currency and credit. Enterprising young men, such as Joseph Barrell, made fortunes privateering and provisioning the French, much as Thomas Hancock, John Erving, and Charles Apthorp had built fortunes in the 1750s and 1760s by provisioning British forces in the series of wars with the French. Marquis de Chastellux, a wartime visitor to Boston, noted in his diary, "[On the Hercule] was a young man of eighteen, of the name of Barrel, who had been two months on board, that by living continually with the French, he might accustom himself to speak their language, which cannot fail of being one day useful to him." William Burbeck, with his diverse skills, became the lead American fortifications engineer for Boston harbor, working throughout the war in close cooperation with French counterparts. His probate inventory taken in 1785 includes a French dictionary and several other French titles.[23]

The experience of merchant brothers John and Jonathan Amory was typical. Cut off by the war from their normal supplies of English credit and goods, they began trading with France and Belgium. John spent much of the war in Nantes, France, purchasing French fabrics and general merchandise that Jonathan resold in Boston. Returning home after the hostilities, John continued to import French dry goods for his customers and French furniture for himself. Evidence of growing affection for French goods is Ebenezer Storer's order of November 12, 1779, to "Mr. Jonathan Williams,

Merchant in Nantes," for a variety of yard goods suitable for upholstering a coach, a "neat gold watch made by . . . Gregson, Watchmaker at Paris," a French grammar book, a French dictionary, and other volumes. Years later, the Marquis de Chastellux recalled, "It is inconceivable how the stay of the [French] squadron has contributed to conciliate the two nations and to strengthen the connections which unite them. . . . The officers of our navy were every where received, not only as allies, but as brothers, . . . and they were admitted by the ladies of Boston to the greatest familiarity."[24]

The customary excesses of wartime life and the sudden exposure to French values had a profound influence on traditional Boston society. As early as 1778, General Warren observed that "all manner of extravagance prevails here in dress, furniture, equipage and living," and in 1779 Samuel Adams decried "that inundation of levity, vanity, luxury, dissipation." Both men saw a single cause: the French presence.[25]

A whole new set of customs, affectations, and social clubs sprang up to amuse the nouveau riche. Perez and Sarah Morton and others founded the "Sans Souci Club," modeling it on French manners, dancing, and entertainment. The club and the values it celebrated stood in sharp contrast to the simplicity and republican virtues to which Boston's traditional leaders clung. The dialectic of this clash was to dominate Boston life, politics, and taste for the next twenty years.[26]

The rise of a new cosmopolitan merchant elite and Bostonians' newfound taste for French art, literature, and culture created a fertile environment for artisans to develop and experiment with new forms and styles. Although the city's elite continued to embrace the bombé form in the decade following the Revolution, the stage was set for cabinetmakers to refine their designs and construction methods and depart from the heavier bombé forms of the pre-Revolutionary period.

Figure 8 John Singleton Copley, *Thomas Amory II*, Boston, ca. 1772. H. 49 3/4", W. 39 1/2". (Courtesy, Corcoran Gallery of Art, Museum purchase, funds provided by William Wilson Corcoran, acc. 1989.22.)

John Cogswell's Bombé Furniture

Sometime between 1780 and 1784, Cogswell made a serpentine bombé desk for Boston merchant Thomas Amory, Jr. (1722–1784) (figs. 8, 9). The desk features an innovative commode front and has the faint initials "JC" written in chalk on the left fallboard support. Although relatively difficult to execute, the double-serpentine shaping of the broken-stripe figured drawer fronts created a dramatic sense of movement. In addition, the drawer fronts are accentuated by the engraved chinoiserie brasses and the escutcheon plates. Birmingham trade catalogs of the 1770s illustrate several similar patterns (see fig. 12), but in the colonies this pattern is found only on Boston furniture.[27]

The desk has an unusual amphitheater interior with a central prospect door and serpentine- and concave-blocked drawers (fig. 10). The outer drawers slope back gently, and their shaping becomes flatter toward the top. This distinctive design occurs on only three other known Boston desk-and-bookcases, two of which are attributed to Cogswell's shop.[28]

The construction of the Amory case and its large drawers is somewhat less substantial than that of bombé pieces from the 1750–1775 period. During the

Figure 9 Desk attributed to John Cogswell, Boston, 1780–1784. Mahogany with white pine. H. 42 3/4", W. 37 3/8", D. 19 5/8". Only two serpentine front bombé desks are known. (Private collection; photo, David Bohl.)

Figure 10 Detail of the interior of the desk illustrated in fig. 9. The distinctive amphitheater design occurs on only three other desks, all of bombé form. (Photo, David Bohl.)

1750s and 1760s, Boston's cabinetmakers followed the English practice of cutting the sides from very thick planks so that the outer surface could be curved and the inner surface and drawer sides left vertical.[29] In contrast, Cogswell (or a tradesman in his shop) used chisels, large gouges, and a

Figure 11 Detail of the case construction of the desk illustrated in fig. 9. (Photo, David Bohl.)

Figure 12 Brass backplate and handle no. 1149 illustrated on pl. 55 in an anonymous brass founder's catalogue, England, n.d., ca. 1770–1780. Amory sold hardware and probably owned catalogues from English manufacturers who offered this pattern or a similar one. (Courtesy, Winterthur Library: Printed Book and Periodical Collection.)

"round" plane to cut two large hollows on the inner surface of the sides, leaving the flat, unplaned surfaces at the top and bottom of each hollow to function as drawer guides (fig. 11). This procedure reduced the weight of the case, allowed for larger drawers, and helped prevent warping. Another distinctive construction detail is the giant, square dovetail attaching the front base molding to the baseboard. Eighteenth-century Boston case pieces often have giant dovetails, but the dovetails typically have angled sides.

The drawer fronts have curved ends that project beyond the drawer sides and fit into a curved rabbet cut into the front edges of the case sides (fig. 11). This feature makes the sides of the Amory desk appear much thinner than they are. The drawer sides are vertical rather than being angled or curved to conform to the shape of the case. Like many Boston case pieces, the runners are nailed to the sides at the back of the case and attached to the drawer blades with a tongue-and-groove joint.

Amory may have used the desk in the counting room of his waterfront shop, since Boston merchants often sought to impress their clients and encourage orders by displaying imposing furniture in their places of business. Amory's desk also may have called attention to his firm's extensive inventory of brass hardware. No location was specified, however, for the "Mahogany Desk" valued at £9 in his 1784 probate inventory. The 1813 probate inventory of his son, Thomas Coffin Amory (1767–1812), included "1 Desk" and "1 Writing Desk," valued at $6 and $5, respectively. The desk presumably descended to his son, William Amory (1804–1888), whose brand "W. A." is on the right fallboard support of the desk and who instructed that his family portraits "be kept together as heirlooms in the possession of one person and in Boston or its vicinity." The desk is not listed in William's inventory, but it and the portraits descended to his eldest grandson, William Amory Gardner (1863–1930), whose brand "W. A. G." is on a backboard of the desk. The piece is listed in Gardner's inventory, and it descended from him to the present owner.[30]

An imposing chest-on-chest that reportedly belonged to Elias Hasket Derby (fig. 13) shares numerous construction details with the Amory desk, including the distinctive scooping out of the interior case sides. As the only piece of furniture with Cogswell's full signature, it represents a benchmark for identifying other examples of his work (fig. 14).[31]

The chest-on-chest separates into three sections: a lower case with four drawers, an upper case with five drawers, and a pediment. The pediment fits into a rabbet formed by the astragal molding directly below the upper fret band. It is decorated with an elaborate scrollboard appliqué, carved urn-and-flame finials, and floral garlands (of which only fragments survive) that descended from the rosettes (fig. 15).[32]

Part of the ornament may be from the shop of Boston carvers John and Simeon Skillin (Skillings). The bows, leaves, and flowers on the finial urns (fig. 16) are very similar to those on the chamfered corners of another chest-on-chest that originally belonged to Derby. The latter chest is attributed to Dorchester cabinetmaker Stephen Badlam and the Skillins based on work-

Figure 13 Chest-on-chest signed John Cogswell with carving attributed to the Skillin shop, Boston, 1782. Mahogany with white pine. H. 97", W. 44¼", D. 23½". (Courtesy, William Francis Warden Fund, Museum of Fine Arts, Boston, acc. 1973.289.)

Figure 14 Inscription on the top board of the lower case of the chest-on-chest illustrated in fig. 13. (Photo, Museum of Fine Arts, Boston.)

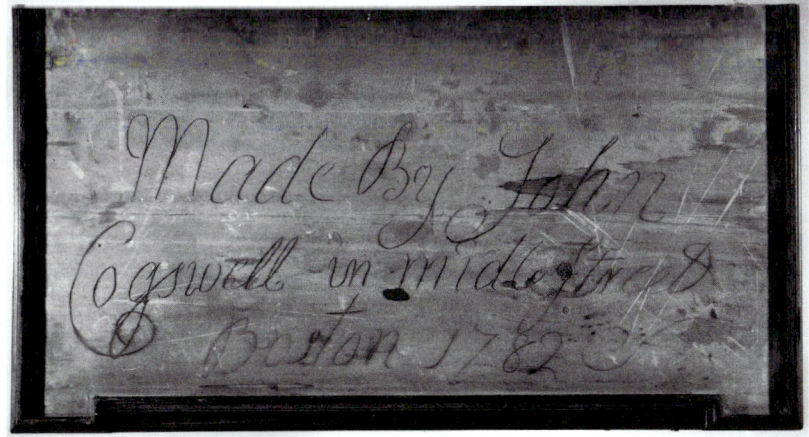

Figure 15 Detail of the pediment of the chest-on-chest illustrated in fig. 13. (Photo, Museum of Fine Arts, Boston.)

Figure 16 Detail of the finial, fret, and scrollboard carving on the chest-on-chest illustrated in fig. 13. (Photo, Museum of Fine Arts, Boston.)

manship and on their respective bills to Derby for £19, "exclusive of the carving," and £6.15.0 for "Carv'd work done for a chest of draws pr. bill given in."[33] The leaves, rosettes, and scrollboard appliqué on Cogswell's chest-on-chest are less competently carved than the finials (figs. 15, 16); however, such variations are common in the products of large shops that had journeymen and apprentices.

Elias Hasket Derby made a fortune through wartime privateering and the provisioning of French and American forces. He epitomized the new elite who prudish republicans like Abigail Adams described as an "aristocracy of money." Near the end of the Revolution, this new "aristocracy" represented one of the few sources of patronage for struggling artisans like Cogswell.[34]

Cogswell's reemerging shop probably made the bombé desk-and-bookcase illustrated in figure 20 in 1786. The cornice molding, scrollboard shape, Ionic pilasters, plinth and waist frets, and bombé sides are similar to those

Figure 17 Desk attributed to John Cogswell, Boston, 1770–1780. Mahogany with white pine. H. 42 1/2", W. 40 1/8", D. 20 3/4". (Private collection; photo, Will Brown.)

Figure 18 Detail of the chalk initials "JC" on the top board of the lower case of the desk illustrated in fig. 17. (Photo, Joseph Godla.)

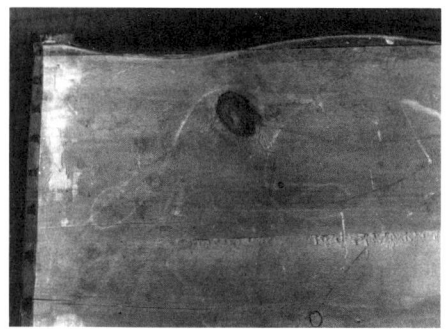

of the 1782 Derby chest-on-chest (fig. 13). The scrollboard carving on both pieces is by the same hand, suggesting that Cogswell maintained a business relationship with the Skillins. The carved rosettes originally had garland drops, and the base molding had a scrolled carved pendant that probably resembled the one on the Derby chest-on-chest.[35] The owner, however, opted for a traditional swelled front for the desk section rather than a serpentine bombé facade.

The construction of the desk section with straight interior sides is unusual for Cogswell's shop, occurring on only one other example (fig. 25). Over a twenty-year period, his shop developed four different treatments for the interior surfaces of bombé sides: to leave them vertical (see figs. 20, 25); to hollow (figs. 9, 13); to cut angled facets approximately parallel to the outer curve (figs. 33, 36); and to saw them parallel to the outer curve (figs. 17, 24, 40, 41, 43). Although these variations could represent the different work habits of journeymen, the later pieces attributed to Cogswell typically have faceted or parallel-sawn inner surfaces, suggesting that these techniques evolved from the more labor-intensive hollowing method.

An unusual two-part desk inscribed "JC" probably is the earliest case piece with parallel-sawn sides attributed to Cogswell (figs. 17, 18). Only two Boston two-part desks are known; however, the form was popular in England during the late-seventeenth and early-eighteenth centuries, and an imported example may have inspired Cogswell's design.[36] The case separates above the drawer blade between the second and third exterior drawers, making the desk portion easily transportable by the lifting handles. The mating ends of the case sides connect with angled joints that positively locate the two halves. Wear patterns on the adjacent surfaces of the two sections indicate frequent use.

The patron evidently wanted a writing compartment that was more functional than decorative, for the interior drawers are much plainer than was common for Boston desks of this period (fig. 17). The writing slide that doubles as a support for the fallboard is an extremely unusual feature for this type of desk.

Although the joinery is cruder than that typically associated with Cogswell, the basic structure of the desk is similar to the preceding examples. An important point of comparison in bombé furniture is the curve of the case sides. Cogswell used a template to inscribe or trace the bombé curve on the side boards, then he sawed, planed, and scraped the surfaces to their final shape. Because templates often differed significantly from one cabinetmaker to another, side shape can serve as a "signature" for a particular shop. The side shape of the two-part desk is almost identical to that of the Amory desk and very similar to that of the 1782 Derby chest-on-chest, but it is distinctly different from those made by other Boston cabinetmakers in the 1750–1780 period (fig. 19). The outward curve begins higher on the sides, thus minimizing the bottom-heavy appearance.

Cogswell's shop was probably also responsible for eight other pieces of serpentine bombé furniture. All share construction details with the preceding pieces, but the cases are generally lighter and the workmanship is more refined. As Boston's economy recovered, demands for opulent furniture increased, offering Cogswell an opportunity to continue perfecting the bombé form.

On seven of these examples, Cogswell cut the inner surfaces of the case sides parallel to the outer surfaces (see fig. 21), thus reducing the weight of the case and creating a larger space for the drawers. To accommodate this new structure, his shop developed three different methods for constructing case drawers. One piece has vertical drawer sides, two have angled drawer sides and projecting drawer fronts that fit into rabbets in the front edge of the case sides, and five have curved drawer sides. Despite these variations, all drawers have saw kerfs extending slightly beyond the end of each dovetail shoulder, suggesting one man's work (see fig. 22).

One desk-and-bookcase (fig. 24) and all the chests have drawer blades with identically angled dovetails that penetrate to within $1/8$" of the outer edge of the case side (see fig. 21) and cove-and-ovolo base moldings that were cut with the same (or very similar) planes and scratch cutters. Most of these pieces have similar base blocking, including large triangular glue blocks at the corners, and bear chalk inscriptions on the underside of the bottom boards: a chevron witness mark "^" or "X" across the glue joints and the word "Bottom" (see fig. 23).

The desks-and-bookcases in this group (figs. 24, 25) were made for Boston merchants Joseph Barrell (1739–1804) and Edward Brinley (1730–1809). The Barrell example has been substantially repaired and altered (fig. 24):

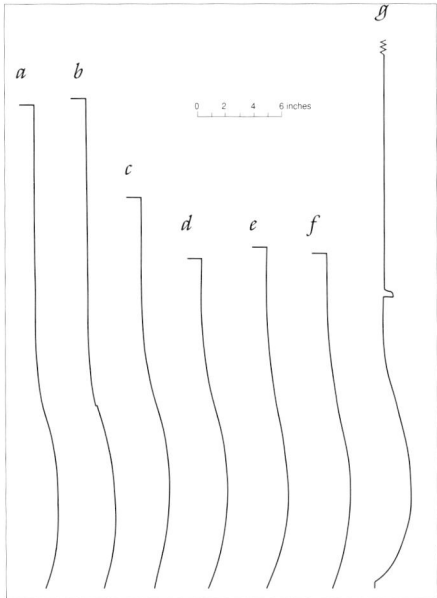

Figure 19 Comparative profiles of the sides of (a) Amory desk, fig. 9; (b) two-part desk, fig. 17; (c) chest-on-chest signed "John Cogswell," fig. 13; (d) Storer chest of drawers, fig. 33; (e) chest of drawers, fig. 43; (f) chest of drawers, fig. 40; (g) desk-and-bookcase signed "Benj. Frothingham" and "BF 1753" (Diplomatic Reception Rooms, U.S. Department of State, not illustrated). (Drawing, Eliza McClennen.)

Figure 20 Desk-and-bookcase attributed to John Cogswell, Boston, 1786. Mahogany with white pine. H. 99 1/4", W. 45 1/8", D. 22 7/8". This desk-and-bookcase has two inscriptions, "1786 AD" and "Jackson [?]." (Courtesy, Winterthur Museum, acc. 59.3414.)

Figure 21 Detail of the case construction of the chest of drawers illustrated in fig. 41. (Photo, Art Institute of Chicago.)

Figure 22 Detail of the drawer construction of the chest of drawers illustrated in fig. 41. (Photo, Art Institute of Chicago.)

Figure 23 Detail of the base construction and inscriptions on the desk-and-bookcase illustrated in fig. 24. (Photo, Winterthur Museum.)

the bookcase unit is a colonial revival replacement, possibly modeled on the original; the lower case was disassembled, and the sides were slightly reshaped.[37] The writing compartments of the Barrell and Brinley desks have serpentine- and concave-blocked drawers and receding cove moldings that are closely related to those of the Amory desk (compare figs. 10 and 26). This interior plan is very unusual for Boston desks, and its presence on the Barrell and Brinley examples strongly suggests that all of the pieces in the latter group are products of Cogswell's shop.

The carved figures on the Barrell desk-and-bookcase (fig. 24) probably represent Justice, Commerce, and Agriculture—subjects also depicted on Barrell's engraved bookplate. The figures are attributed to the Skillin's shop,

Figure 24 Desk-and-bookcase attributed to John Cogswell with figures attributed to the Skillin shop, Boston, 1780–1785. Mahogany with white pine. H. 95 1/2", W. 37 5/16", D. 20". (Courtesy, Winterthur Museum, acc. 56.23.)

Figure 25 Desk-and-bookcase attributed to John Cogswell with carving possibly by William Burbeck, Boston, 1780–1785. Mahogany with white pine. H. 82 1/16", W. 37 1/4", D. 20 9/16". (Courtesy, Winterthur Museum, acc. 57.1396.)

Figure 26 Detail of the writing compartment of the desk-and-bookcase illustrated in fig. 25. (Photo, Winterthur Museum.)

one of the few Boston carving shops capable of producing sculptural ornaments. Assuming that they are original to the desk-and-bookcase, these figures provide additional evidence that Cogswell contracted carving work from specialists.[38]

Barrell probably ordered the desk-and-bookcase for his Charlestown mansion, Pleasant Hill. Designed by architect Charles Bulfinch and completed in 1794, Pleasant Hill was modeled on "The Bagatelle," an oval-on-axis house just outside Paris. Bulfinch also purchased French books and furnishings for the house, making it one of the first Boston residences to integrate French furnishings and architectural detail. Like many post-Revolutionary Boston merchants, Barrell made the "grand tour" of France and lionized French culture as the supreme expression of ancient and modern ideals. As his desk-and-bookcase suggests, Barrell also had a fondness for sculpture. The grounds at Pleasant Hill featured a pond with "four ships at anchor & a marble figure in the center," and his estate inventory listed a "Lion &. Lioness . . . 6 Wood Figures . . . 4 Wooden Horses . . . 1 Stone Horse . . . 1 Image-Cupid . . . 2 Images-Gardner &. Wife," and two sculptures of Venus.[39]

A brass plaque attached to the inside of the bookcase section gives the line of descent: "Joseph Barrell/Hannah Barrell Joy [wife of Benjamin Joy]/ John Benjamin Joy/ Charles Henry Joy/Benjamin Joy." What may be the original purchase price, "37 11116 £64," is penciled in script on the bottom board. Although Barrell's 1805 probate inventory does not list household furnishings, legal action against his executor and son-in-law, Benjamin Joy, brought by Barrell's sons does. They accused Joy of absconding with assets, including money and a desk-and-bookcase. The court valued the desk-and-bookcase at $80, a phenomenal figure for a single piece of furniture.[40]

Although the Barrell and Brinley desks-and-bookcases are very similar in design, their construction varies. The major differences are that the Brinley example has fallboard supports, concealed drawer blade dovetails, straight

Figure 27 Detail of the upper case of the desk-and-bookcase illustrated in fig. 25. (Photo, Winterthur Museum.)

Figure 28 Detail of the carving at the top of the door and on the ogee head of the desk-and-bookcase illustrated in fig. 25. (Photo, Winterthur Museum.)

Figure 29 Detail of the carving on the lower rail of the door of the desk-and-bookcase illustrated in fig. 25. (Photo, Winterthur Museum.)

inner case sides, and vertical drawer sides (fig. 25). It also has spectacular rococo carving unlike that on any other piece of American furniture (figs. 27–29). Although scholars have cited the carving as evidence of French influence in Boston, the object's ogee head, its central acanthus ornament, and the thin rococo "columns" of the bookcase door are derived from a London design book (figs. 30–32).[41]

The carving is closely related to that on the pulpit in Brattle Square Church and may represent the work of William Burbeck. The acanthus leaves on the bookcase door have fully veined surfaces and edge profiles (from similar outlining cuts) like those on the large ogee molding and pulvinated frieze of the pulpit (figs. 4, 5, 27–29). Burbeck's involvement with the desk-and-bookcase is plausible considering his association with Cogswell in the caucus system, various fraternal organizations, and New North Church.

The composite pilasters flanking the bookcase door disguise narrow hinged doors that give access to shell-carved drawers and document compartments (fig. 27). These pilasters also may have served as visual "pedestals" for carved figures like those on the Barrell desk-and-bookcase. Details of this classical order are extraordinarily rare on colonial American furniture.

Figure 30   Design for a "Writing Table & Bookcase" illustrated on pl. 44 in the Society of Upholsterer's *Houshold Furniture in Genteel Taste, for the Year 1763* (London, 1763). (Courtesy, Cary Collection, Redwood Library and Athenaeum, Newport, Rhode Island.)

Figure 31   Detail of a design for a "Chimney Glass" illustrated on pl. 54 in the Society of Upholsterer's *Houshold Furniture in Genteel Taste, for the Year 1763* (London, 1763). (Courtesy, Cary Collection, Redwood Library and Athenaeum, Newport, Rhode Island.)

Figure 32   Designs for "Shelves for Books &c" illustrated on pl. 67 in the Society of Upholsterer's *Houshold Furniture in Genteel Taste, for the Year 1763* (London, 1763). (Courtesy, Cary Collection, Redwood Library and Athenaeum, Newport, Rhode Island.)

Figure 33 Chest of drawers attributed to the shop of John Cogswell, Boston, 1780–1795. Mahogany with white pine. H. 30 7/16", W. 35 7/8", D. 20". (Courtesy, Diplomatic Reception Rooms, U.S. Department of State, acc. 69.103; photo, Will Brown.)

Figure 34 Detail of the hardware on the chest illustrated in fig. 33. The brasses were regilded in 1989. (Photo, Will Brown.)

Equally distinctive are the carved ball-and-claw feet (fig. 25). (These were once cut off at the ankles but were retained and reattached during an early restoration.) The feet are singular in design and execution, with very square ankles and poorly developed toes and claws. Scaled-down versions of these feet are on three of the six related serpentine bombé chests (compare figs. 25, 38, 39, 41, 42), and identical ones are on a 1785 Boston desk-and-bookcase with a bust of Milton carved by the Skillins (Beverly Historical Society).

The left fallboard support of the Brinley desk-and-bookcase is inscribed in ink, "Bought this Desk Oct 15th 1828/ of my Father/ Total/ Edward Brinley." The prevalence of the name, Edward Brinley, and the wide dispersal of the Loyalist Brinley family during and after the war makes identification of the original owner very difficult. Edward Brinley (1730–1809), the third son of Col. Francis Brinley of Roxbury and a member of a family of merchants and distillers, and his son Edward II (1765–1823) died before the inscription date. Another Edward Brinley (1757–1852) was born in Newport, Rhode Island, and died in Perth Amboy, New Jersey (no desk-and-bookcase is listed in his inventory).[42]

Closely related to the desks-and-bookcases are six serpentine bombé chests of drawers, five of which are illustrated here (figs. 33, 36, 40, 41, 43). Cogswell may have referred to this form in 1769 when he invoiced Boston merchant Caleb Davis for a "mehogany Bewro."[43] Two of the chests have elaborate rococo hardware (figs. 33, 36), one set being identical to that on the Amory desk (compare figs. 9, 12, 37). Minor stylistic and structural vari-

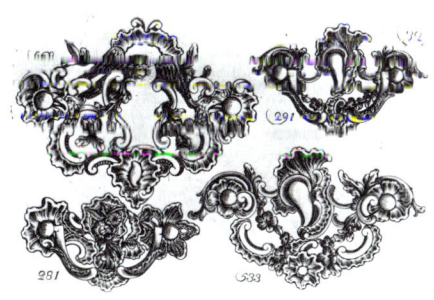

Figure 35 Brass patterns illustrated on pl. 32 of *Brass Founders Catalog of Accessories for Cabinetmakers and Upholsterers*, England, 1770s. For the brass of fig. 33, the backplate is derived from no. 568 and the handle from no. 533. (Courtesy, Winterthur Library: Printed Book and Periodical Collection.)

Figure 36 Chest of drawers attributed to the shop of John Cogswell, Boston, 1780–1795. Mahogany with white pine. H. 31 1/2", W. 35 3/4", D. 20 1/4". (Dietrich American Foundation on loan to the Metropolitan Museum of Art, acc. L.1980.29; photo, Metropolitan Museum of Art.)

Figure 37 Detail of a brass on the chest illustrated in fig. 36. (Courtesy, Dietrich American Foundation; photo, Will Brown.)

ations are present within the group of chests, but overall they are remarkably similar (see fig. 19 and appendix).

One chest belonged to Ebenezer Storer II (1729/30–1807) (fig. 33). Storer was in the dry goods business and had complex connections to both the merchant and artisan communities. During the early 1770s, he and John Hancock raised funds and oversaw the construction of Brattle Square Church. In 1780, Storer and John Adams were representatives to the Massachusetts Constitutional Convention, and, the same year, they joined with Thomas Dawes in founding the American Academy of Arts and Sciences. From 1752 until his death, Storer held several town offices including selectman. Widely recognized for his financial skills, he served as treasurer of Harvard University and kept the institution solvent during and immediately after the Revolutionary War.[44]

Storer was a radical Whig, and the British evidently offered a reward for his capture for he fled Boston in 1775 and looters raided his property at Sudbury and Portland streets. The preamble of his will states that his fortunes were diminished due to his dedication "in the late glorious revolution," however, Storer remained a wealthy man. His chest was probably among his most expensive furnishings and may be the "bureau" or the "case of drawers" listed in his probate inventory.[45]

Gardiner Greene (1753–1832), also a member of Brattle Square Church and an immensely rich merchant, owned another Cogswell chest (fig. 36). After working for many years as a merchant in Demerara, British Guiana, Greene returned to Boston, invested in real estate, and became the first president of the Boston branch of The United States Bank. At the time of his

Figure 38 Detail of the case and left front foot of the chest illustrated in fig. 36. (Courtesy, Dietrich American Foundation; photo, Will Brown.)

Figure 39 Detail of the side of the chest illustrated in fig. 36. (Courtesy, Israel Sack, Inc., N.Y.C.)

death in 1832, Greene's estate was worth $1,086,008.71. The appraisers valued his "Mansion House Estate" and other real estate at $186,900 and his "Personal Estate" (not itemized) at $899,108.71. Although Greene's house was destroyed in 1835, Martha Babcock (Greene) Amory's recollection of the interior provides some architectural context for Gardner's furniture:

> [In the dining room] . . . the carver had . . . fashioned in the panels on each side of the bow [window] elaborate designs of grapes, vines and leaves. . . . Arched recesses on each side of the chimney conveniently accommodated the generous beaufets. . . . The drawing-room, 35 or 40 ft in length by 25 in width, with two windows on the front looking down Court St. and a deep bold bow, with three more . . . and adorned with a finely carved wooden chimney-piece of delicate work whose subject . . . as I recall the rash charioteer and fiery steeds . . . must have represented Phoebus, with the horses of the Sun! Family pictures by Copley of stately dames and gentlemen in full powdered wigs hung upon the walls and glowed in the bright light.[46]

Inscribed "Green" (on the interior of the case), Gardner's chest reportedly descended through the family of his third wife, Elizabeth Copley Clarke. The gilt chinoiserie hardware, which is identical to that on Thomas Amory's desk, was among the most expensive available at the time (figs. 9, 37).[47] Except for having angled drawer sides, Greene's chest is virtually identical to the other five chests in the group (see the appendix on pages 104 and 105). Such minor structural differences may represent evolving shop practices, cost-cutting efforts, or the habits of different workmen in the same shop.

The chest illustrated in figure 40 is the only serpentine bombé piece said to have a Salem, Massachusetts, history. Oral tradition maintains that the chest originally belonged to Richard Sprague Stearns (1803–1840), the youngest son of Salem apothecary Dr. William Stearns (1754–1819); however, it is possible that he may have inherited the chest from his father or father-in-law Col. Joseph Sprague, a Salem distiller and merchant who had extensive family and business connections in Boston and Charlestown.[48]

Cogswell made the drawer fronts and case sides from large mahogany planks with relatively straight grain; however, the deep symmetrical shaping cuts across the grain revealing vibrant swirls, stripes, and ovals. For the top he selected dense, broken-stripe mahogany boards similar to those he chose for the sides of Gardiner Greene's chest (fig. 39).

The remaining chests have remarkably similar case dimensions and construction (figs. 41, 43). One has ball-and-claw feet carved by the same hand as those on the Greene and Sprague-Stearns chests and the Brinley desk-and-bookcase (figs. 25, 38, 40), and the other has simple ogee bracket feet with conventional Boston shaping like those of the Storer chest (figs. 33, 43).[49]

The production of the bombé furniture examined in this article occurred during and after the most tumultuous period of Boston's history. The Revolutionary War devastated the city's economy and created hardships at every level of society. It also provided opportunities for a few enterprising individuals, such as Elias Hasket Derby. Tradesmen, however, suffered

Figure 40 Chest of drawers attributed to the shop of John Cogswell, Boston, 1780–1795. Mahogany with white pine. H. 31 1/4", W. 36 1/8", D. 20 1/4". The chinoiserie hardware is replaced based on scars left from the originals. (Private collection; photo, Richard Cheek.)

Figure 41 Chest of drawers attributed to the shop of John Cogswell, Boston, 1780–1795. Mahogany with white pine. H. 31 3/8", W. 36 1/8", D. 20". This chest is the only one of the group that survives with remnants of the original finish. (Courtesy, Art Institute of Chicago, Helen Bowen Blair Fund, acc. 1979.499, photo copyright 1992. All rights reserved.)

Figure 42 Detail of the foot of the chest illustrated in fig. 41. (Photo, Art Institute of Chicago.)

Figure 43 Chest of drawers attributed to the shop of John Cogswell, Boston, 1785–1795. Mahogany with white pine. H. 30 1/4", W. 35 3/4", D. 21". (Private collection; photo, David Bohl.)

almost universally. Like many of his contemporaries, John Cogswell had to supplement his income by renting property and working in other occupations.

Postwar Boston was, in some respects, a different city. Although conservative citizens, such as Abigail Adams, opposed the growing cultural and economic ties with France and resented the wealth and status of the new merchant elite, society as a whole became more cosmopolitan and more receptive to new ideas and stylistic influences. This change in attitudes created a climate in which cabinetmakers, like Cogswell, could refine old furniture forms and techniques and develop new ones. His serpentine bombé designs are a direct manifestation of this environment, regardless of whether they reflect immediate or indirect French influences.

By taking advantage of alliances created through his marriages, educational and church affiliations, and the benefits afforded members of the Caucus Club, Cogswell was able to flourish in a trade traditionally dominated by long-established artisan families. His success attests to his ability to satisfy the demands of conservative patrons, who preferred traditional bombé furniture based on late baroque English examples, and those of more progressive clients who wanted commode facades, sculptural ornaments, and rococo carving derived from English design books. The fashion for bombé furniture began to wane about 1790 as Bostonians gradually embraced the neoclassical style. Cogswell adapted to this new style as well and continued to work in Boston for at least another decade.[50]

ACKNOWLEDGMENTS   The authors thank Mr. and Mrs. E. G. Nicholson for funding the initial research for this study and Brock Jobe for sharing his research on Boston cabinetmakers. Others who assisted are Luke Beckerdite, Ron Bourgeault, Douglas Brown, Michael Brown, Clement Conger, Edward S. Cooke, Jr., Wendy A. Cooper, Stephen Davis, Frederick Detwiller, Dietrich American Foundation, John M. Driggers, Julian Wood Glass, Joseph Godla, Ward Gregg, Morrison H. Heckscher, Ronald Hurst, Mary Itsell, Leigh Keno, Eulalie Langford, Bernard and S. Dean Levy, Martha McNamara, Tillie Massen, Thomas Michie, David Mitchell, Milo Naeve, Clark Pearce, Michael Podmaniczky, Deborah Rebuck, Nancy Richards, Harold Sack, Gail Serfaty, Diane Langford Swiger, Lee Taylor, Joe Twichell, Charles Venable, Gerald W. R. Ward, William Young, Philip Zimmerman, and the owners of the furniture. The support and patience of our spouses, Carol Stocker and Jack Haley, is especially appreciated.

1. Articles written about Cogswell include: Joseph Downs, "John Cogswell, Cabinetmaker," *Antiques* 61, no. 4 (April 1952): 322–24; and M. Ada Young, "Five Secretaries and the Cogswells," *Antiques* 88, no. 5 (October 1965): 478–85.

2. Samuel Dexter, William Greenleaf, and Josiah Quincy, Sr., owned bombé furniture by other cabinetmakers. Joiner Abraham Knowlton made a bombé pulpit for the First Church in Ipswich, Massachusetts, in 1749, and cabinetmaker John Folwell made one for Christ Church, Philadelphia, in 1769. For an illustration and description of the First Church pulpit, see Peter Benes and Philip Zimmerman, *New England Meeting House and Church: 1630–1850* (Boston: Boston University and the Currier Gallery of Art for the Dublin Center for New England Folklife, 1979), pp. 39–45. For an eighteenth-century engraving showing the Christ Church pulpit with its original soundboard and dove ornament, see Julia B. Leisenring and Patricia A. S. Forbes, *A Guide to Christ Church in Philadelphia* (Philadelphia: Pearl Pressman, Liberty Printers, 1990), pp. 4, 5.

3. Samuel K. Lothrop, *A History of the Church in Brattle Street, Boston* (Boston: Wm. Crosby and P. H. Nichols, 1851). Brattle Square Church Society Records, 1755–1805, "Votes and Proceedings of the Church and Congregation . . . Meeting in Brattle Street BOSTON," p. 41, Boston Public Library, Rare Books and Manuscript Department (hereinafter BPL, RBMD).

4. Abbé Robin, quoted in Nathaniel B. Shurtleff, *A Topographical and Historical Description of Boston* (3d ed., Boston: Rockwell & Churchill, 1890), p. 71.

5. Lothrop, *History of the Church*, p. 95.

6. Frederick C. Detwiller, "Thomas Dawes's Church in Brattle Square," *Old Time New England* 59, nos. 3–4 (January–June 1979): 3. Dawes was the third generation of a relatively prosperous family of Boston tradesmen. His educational background is unknown, but early records list his occupation as "mason" and "bricklayer." His public commissions include Harvard Hall, Faneuil Hall, the Province Hospital at Rainsford Island, the Town House (Old State House), Castle William, and the Light House. For more on Dawes and his public works, see Frederick C. Detwiller, "Thomas Dawes: Boston's Patriot Architect," *Old-Time New England* 68, nos. 1–2 (Summer–Fall 1977): 1–18.

7. Lothrop, *History of the Church*, p. 101. John Hancock Letter Book, Hancock Collection (hereinafter HC), Baker Library, Harvard Business School (hereinafter BL, HBS). Martha McNamara, "John Hancock's Gifts to the Brattle Square Church," unpublished paper, American Studies, Boston University, 1987, p. 10.

8. Folwell's pulpit for Christ Church is closer to Langley's design than the Brattle Square example (Leisenring and Forbes, *Guide to Christ Church*, p. 5). Detwiller, "Dawes's Church," p. 7; Helen Park, "A List of Architectural Books Available in America Before the Revolution," *Journal of the Society of Architectural Historians* 20, no. 3 (October 1961): 121; and George Francis Dow, *The Arts and Crafts in New England, 1704–1775* (Topsfield, Mass.: Wayside Press, 1927), pp. 221–23. Conversation with John Harris, April 27, 1993. Boston Athenaeum, Catalogue of Donations, January 7, 1809, p. 15. Most of Dawes's library survives in the Boston Athenaeum. The authors thank Frederick Detwiller for sharing his files on Dawes and notes on Dawes's library compiled by Abbott L. Cummings.

9. Lothrop, *History of the Church*, p. 101. James M. and William F. Crafts, *The Crafts Family, A Genealogical and Biographical History of the Descendants of Griffin and Alice Crafts of Roxbury, Massachusetts, 1630–1890* (Northampton, Mass.: Gazette Printing Co., 1893), p. 113. For more on Crafts's activities, see *A Report of the Record Commissioners of the City of Boston, Containing*

the Selectmen's Minutes from 1764 Through 1768 (Boston: Rockwell & Churchill, 1889), p. 219; *A Report of the Record Commissioners of the City of Boston, Containing the Boston Town Records, 1758 to 1769* (Boston: Rockwell & Churchill, 1886), pp. 108–9; Thwing Index, Massachusetts Historical Society (hereinafter MHS); *A Report of the Record Commissioners of the City of Boston, Containing the Selectmen's Minutes from 1776 through 1786* (Boston: Rockwell & Churchill, 1894), pp. 278–79. Crafts's account with John Hancock, settled October 13, 1783, HC.

10. William Burbeck was born on July 22, 1716, to Edward and Martha Burbeck of Boston (*A Report of the Record Commissioners of the City of Boston, Containing Births from A. D. 1700 to A. D. 1800* [Boston: Rockwell & Churchill, 1894], p. 111). He married twice, to Abigail Tuttle on September 3, 1737, and to Jershua Glover on October 7, 1749 (*A Report of the Record Commissioners of the City of Boston, Containing the Boston Marriages from 1700 to 1751* [Boston: Municipal Printing Office, 1898], pp. 227, 292, 337). Burbeck's earliest known commission was "a lion 7 foot and a half long" and "25 foot of freeze work" for the vessel *Industry* (William Burbeck to Captain Atkins, May 8, 1735, C. E. French Estate, MHS). Burbeck, Crafts, and Dawes played important roles in rebuilding Harvard Hall after it burned in 1764, and Hancock contributed money for the purchase of new books (John Hancock to Thomas Longman, October 28, 1765, HC). For more on Burbeck and his collaboration with Hancock, Dawes, and Crafts, see Herbert S. Allan, *John Hancock, Patriot in Purple* (New York: MacMillian Company, 1948), p. 92; Publications of the Colonial Society of Massachusetts, *Transactions, 1911–1913* (Boston: by the Society, 1913), vol. 16, p. 17; *A Report of the Record Commissioners of the City of Boston, Containing the Selectmen's Minutes from 1764 Through 1768* (Boston: Rockwell & Churchill, 1889), p. 281; *A Report of the Record Commissioners of the City of Boston, Containing the Selectmen's Minutes from 1776–1786* (Boston: Rockwell & Churchill, 1894), pp. 278–79; *A Report of the Record Commissioners of the City of Boston, Containing the Boston Town Records, 1770–1777* (Boston: Rockwell & Churchill, 1893), pp. 77–79; *Massachusetts Soldiers and Sailors of the Revolutionary War*, 17 vols. (Boston: Wright & Potter, 1896) 2:818; and Madelon Burbeck Baltzer, ed., *The Burbeck Genealogy* (Pembroke, Mass.: privately printed, 1959), pp. 1, 2, 8. Other publications have incorrectly attributed Burbeck's work at Harvard Hall, King's Chapel, and Faneuil Hall to his brother, Edward. William Burbeck Inventory, August 23, 1785, Suffolk County Registry of Probate (hereinafter SCRP), no. 18485, Massachusetts State Archives (hereinafter MSA), Boston. Although full titles for the Langley books are not given, they probably were the *Treasury* (London, 1740), *The Builder's Chest Book* (London, 1727), and *Gothic Architecture* (London, 1742). Dawes and Burbeck are the only Boston artisans known to have architectural design books listed in their inventories. Further information regarding Burbeck's work and library will be included in a forthcoming article by the authors.

11. E. O. Jameson, *The Cogswells in America, 1635–1884* (Boston: Alfred Mudge and Sons, 1884), pp. 24–39. Cogswell may have trained with Timothy Gooding, Jr., a Boston-area cabinetmaker (Brock Jobe and Myrna Kaye, *New England Furniture: The Colonial Era* [Boston: Houghton Mifflin, 1984], p. 15). *A Volume of Records Pertaining to the Early History of Boston, Containing Boston Marriages from 1752 to 1809* (Boston: Municipal Printing Office, 1903), p. 46. John and Abigail had two sons, but both died in infancy. Both were named Samuel Gooding Cogswell, after Abigail's father. For more on members of the Gooding (Goodwin, Godwin) family, see Thomas Bellows Wyman, *The Genealogies and Estates of Charlestown in the County of Middlesex and Commonwealth of Massachusetts, 1629–1818*, 2 vols. (Boston: David Clapp and Son, 1879), 1:414–22. For Francis Cogswell, see Clifford K. Shipton and John L. Sibley, *Sibley's Harvard Graduates, Biographical Sketches of Those Who Attended Harvard College*, 17 vols. (Boston: Massachusetts Historical Society, 1942), 6:235; Peter Faneuil to Francis Cogswell, June 13, 1737, HC; Francis Cogswell to Jacob Wendell, July 30, 1740, Suffolk County Registry of Deeds (hereinafter SCRD), book 59, p. 152.

12. The New North Church was an integral part of Cogswell's life. At least three of his four wives were members (Cogswell married Abigail Gooding on December 2, 1762; Abiel Page on March 19, 1782; Mary Caznau [Cazneau] on May 24, 1804; and Sarah Tuckerman in 1811), and his three surviving daughters married tradesmen in the congregation. Furniture making tradesmen belonging to the church included cabinetmakers James McMillian, Nathaniel Holmes, Thomas Dillaway, James Freeland, Abraham Hayward, Thomas Foot, and William Alexander; four members of the Ridgeway chairmaking family; upholsterers Samuel and Moses Grant; and carvers John Welch, Benjamin Luckis, John Skillin, William Burbeck, and Thomas Burbeck (*Records of the New-North Church in North-street, Boston, Gathered Oct[ober] 20th, 1714*, BPL, RBMD; *International Genealogical Index* [Salt Lake City, Utah: Church of

Jesus Christ of Latter Day Saints, 1982], microfiche M-0213). Francis S. Drake, *Life and Correspondence of Henry Knox* (Boston: Samuel G. Drake, 1873), pp. 26–27.

13. L. H. Butterfield, ed., *Diary and Autobiography of John Adams*, 4 vols. (Cambridge, Mass.: Belknap Press, 1961), 1:238.

14. For more on the Caucus Club, town offices, and tradesmen in Revolutionary era Boston, see Gary B. Nash, *The Urban Crucible: Social Change, Political Consciousness, and the Origins of the American Revolution* (Cambridge, Mass.: Harvard University Press, 1979).

15. *Boston Town Records*, 1758–1769, p. 97.

16. *Boston Town Records*, 1758–1769, p. 80. *Selectman's Minutes*, 1764–1768, p. 33. *Boston Town Records*, 1778–1783, p. 75. *Boston Town Records*, 1770–1777, p. 11, and passim.

17. Young, "Five Secretaries and the Cogswells," pp. 478–85; the authors were unable to document Cogswell's purchase of property on Middle Street. Jameson, *Cogswells in America*, pp. 24–29.

18. "A List of the Polls and of the Estates, Real and Personal of the several Proprietors and Inhabitants of the Town of Boston," 1771, MSA. *Assessors' Taking Books of the Town of Boston, 1780, for Ward 4*, BPL, RBMD. License of John Cogswell in Boston, July 24, 1782, Suffolk County Inferior Court Records, vol. 533, no. 93885. *Selectmen's Minutes, 1776–1782*, pp. 1090–91. *Assessors' Taking Books of the Town of Boston, 1782, for Ward 4*, BPL, RBMD.

19. Thwing Index, MHS. *The Records of the New-North Church In North-Street, Boston*, p. 27. John Cogswell to Capt. John Skimmer, January 10, 1785, SCRD, book 147, p. 2. The following year Cogswell purchased a shop and land near Middle Street (Benjamin Rumley to John Cogswell, March 22, 1786, SCRD, book 156, p. 35).

20. *Assessors' Taking Books of the Town of Boston, 1788, 1791–1799*, BPL, RBMD. *Boston Directory* (Boston: John Norman, 1789), *Boston Directory* (Boston: Manning and Loring for John West, 1796), *Boston Directory* (Boston: Rhoades and Laughton for John West, 1798), *Boston Directory* (Boston: John Russell for John West, 1800), *Boston Directory* (Boston: John West, 1803), *Boston Directory* (Boston: Edward Cotton, 1805–1807, 1809–1810, 1813, 1816, 1818). John Cogswell, Administrative Account, May 31, 1819, SCRP, no. 25458.

21. Serpentine bombé furniture by other Boston makers includes: a chest of drawers and desk-and-bookcase in the Rhode Island School of Design (Christopher P. Monkhouse and Thomas S. Michie, *American Furniture in Pendleton House* [Providence, R.I.: Rhode Island School of Design, 1986], pp. 63–65, 100, 101); a chest of drawers in the Museum of Fine Arts, Boston (Gilbert T. Vincent, "The Bombé Furniture of Boston," in Walter Muir Whitehill, Brock Jobe, and Jonathan Fairbanks, eds., *Boston Furniture of the Eighteenth Century* [Boston: The Colonial Society of Massachusetts, 1974], p. 182, pl. 128); a chest of drawers in the Winterthur Museum (Downs, *American Furniture*, pl. 165); a chest of drawers now in a private collection (Northeast Auctions, *The Collection of John Howland Ricketson III*, May 29, 1993, pl. 95); a desk and bookcase (owned originally by Thomas Dawes) in the Bayou Bend Collection (Harold Sack, "The Bombé Furniture of Boston and Salem, Massachusetts," *Antiques* 135, no. 5 [May 1989]:1080). For a detailed discussion of the evolution of the bombé form, see Vincent, "Bombé Furniture," pp. 137–96. For French style commodes in British design books, see Thomas Chippendale, *The Gentleman and Cabinet-Maker's Director* (London, 1754), pls. 37, 38; and Ince and Mayhew, *The Universal System of Houshold Furniture* (London, ca. 1762), pl. 41.

22. Allan, *Patriot in Purple*, pp. 357–63. Shipton, *Sibley's Harvard Graduates*, 11: 207–9.

23. Marquis de Chastellux, *Travels in North America, in the Years 1780–81–82* (New York: White, Gallaher, & White, 1827), p. 324. William Burbeck Inventory.

24. John Amory to Capt. William Dawes, September 23, 1779, Amory Collection, BL, HBS. On June 15, 1785, John Amory ordered "a very elegant French piano forte with French stand, leather cover, desk, complete set of strings, tuning hammer and fork" for £49 from Gilbert and Lewis DeBlois, Amory Collection (hereinafter AC), BL, HBS. John Amory to John Dowling, July 2, 1786, AC. Marquis de Chastellux, *Travels*, p. 336.

25. Charles Warren, "Samuel Adams and the Sans Souci Club in 1785" (Boston: Massachusetts Historical Society Proceedings, 1927), vol. 60, p. 319.

26. Warren, "Samuel Adams and the San Souci Club," p. 322.

27. Thomas, John, and Jonathan Amory were the sons of Thomas Amory, Sr. (1682–1728), one of Boston's most successful merchants and distillers. After inheriting a distillery, a mercantile business, and sizable fortunes, the brothers began to expand their business via a network of trade contacts in the West Indies, Holland, Belgium, France, the Azores and Nova

Scotia—Thomas, singly, and John and Jonathan as "J. & J. Amory." Their businesses included banking, mortgage lending, insurance, shipping, and manufacturing. Distilling remained a foundation of their wealth for three generations. For more on the Amorys, see Gertrude E. Meredith, *The Descendants of Hugh Amory, 1605–1805* (London: Chiswick Press, 1901). The Amory desk is one of the earliest Boston case pieces with chinoiserie hardware. For a 1770–1775 block front chest-on-chest made for Ebenezer Storer with virtually identical hardware, see Jonathan L. Fairbanks et. al, *Collecting American Decorative Arts and Sculpture, 1971–1991* (Boston: Museum of Fine Arts, 1991), p. 34.

28. These include the desk-and-bookcases illustrated in figs. 24 and 25 and another in the Maryland Historical Society (Gregory R. Weidman, *Furniture in Maryland, 1740–1940* [Baltimore: Maryland Historical Society, 1984], pp. 62–63, pl. 24).

29. See Vincent, "Bombé Furniture," pp. 150–51; and Sack, "Bombé Furniture of Boston and Salem," p. 1080.

30. Amory placed extensive orders for hardware from Sheffield and Birmingham, England, in 1781 (Jonathan Amory to Joseph Antt & Son, February 19, 1781; Jonathan Amory to Samuel Rogers, April 13, 1781, AC, BL, HBS). Thomas Amory Inventory, February 10, 1785, SCRP, no. 18252. Thomas Coffin Amory Inventory, October 21, 1816, SCRP, no. 24068. William Amory Will, 1888, SCRP, no. 81338. Correspondence between the authors and the current owner.

31. Fairbanks, *Collecting American Decorative Arts*, p. 36, n. 2. The authors were unable to substantiate any published account of Derby's ownership of the chest-on-chest. The piece also has three additional Cogswell signatures on the interior surfaces of lower backboards.

32. The design sources for the fret patterns are unknown. Thomas Dawes used a similar fret on three buildings: soffit of the portico of the Hurd house (Charlestown); entrance portico of the Mount Griddell house (Charlestown); soffit of the east entry to the balcony of the Old State House in Boston (the authors thank Frederic Detwiller for this information).

33. Gerald W. R. Ward, *American Case Furniture in the Mabel Brady Garvan and Other Collections at Yale University* (New Haven: Yale University Art Gallery, 1988), pp. 171–77.

34. Page Smith, *John Adams* (New York: Doubleday, 1962), pp. 527, 531. For additional biographical information on Derby, see Richard McKey, Jr., "Elias Hasket Derby, Merchant of Salem, Massachusetts, 1739–1799," Ph.D. dissertation, Clark University, 1961; and Sotheby's, *Important American Furniture, Folk Art and Folk Paintings*, October 25, 1992, sale no. 6350, lot 322.

35. For an early photograph of the desk-and-bookcase with incorrect finials, a Philadelphia-style ornament, and a replaced fallboard, see Wallace Nutting, *Furniture Treasury*, 2 vols. (Framingham, Mass.: Old America Company, 1928), 1: pl. 717. The desk-and-bookcase has long been considered a product of Cogswell's shop (see Joseph Downs, *American Furniture, Queen Anne and Chippendale Periods* [New York: MacMillan Company, 1952], p. 228; and Vincent, "Bombé Furniture," pp. 180–81).

36. The other two-part example is a desk-and-bookcase in a private collection, but it was not examined by the authors (the authors thank Alan Miller for this information).

37. Winterthur Museum object files for acc. 56.23 (Barrell) and 57.1396 (Brinley). The alterations are discussed in Michael S. Podmaniczky and Philip D. Zimmerman, "Two Massachusetts Bombé Desk-and-Bookcases," *Antiques* 145, No. 5 (May 1994): 724–31.

38. For more on the desk-and-bookcase, see Charles F. Montgomery, *American Furniture, The Federal Period* (New York: Bonanza Books, 1978), pp. 220–21. Winterthur Library: Printed Book and Periodical Collection. Dean Fales identified the figures as Hope, Industry, and Indolence (Dean Fales, "Joseph Barrell's Pleasant Hill," *Publications of the Colonial Society of Massachusetts* [Boston: by the Society, 1966], vol. 43, pp. 384–85). For an excellent study of the Skillins, see Sylvia L. Lahvis, "The Skillin Workshop and the Emblematic Image in Federal Boston," Ph.D. dissertation, University of Delaware, 1990. For an early example of desire for sculpture to adorn furniture, see Thomas Hancock to "J.T.," August 31, 1749, Hancock Family Papers, American Antiquarian Society, Worcester, Massachusetts.

39. Charles Arthur Hammond, "Where the Arts and the Virtues Unite: Country Life Near Boston, 1637–1864," Ph. D. dissertation, Boston University, 1982, pp. 85, 103–9.

40. Joseph Barrell Will, 1805, Middlesex County Registry of Probate, no. 1142. Henry F. Charles, George Barrell, and Samuel B. Barrell, *Statement of Facts Relative to the Conduct of Mr. Benj. Joy, Executor of the Last Will and Testament of Joseph Barrell* (Boston, 1816); and Benjamin Joy, *A True Statement of Facts in Reply to a Pamphlet lately published by C., H. F., G.,*

and S. B. Barrell (Boston, 1816). Joy stated that Pleasant Hill had cost $48,000, and that Barrell was indebted to him for $62,000 resulting from Barrell's investment in a failed Georgia land speculation. Barrell vs. Joy, August 18, 1818, Middlesex County Registry of Probate, no. 1142.

41. Aaron Mark Stein, "French Influences in American Furniture," *Antiquarian* 17, no. 3 (October 1931): 15, 18. Society of Upholsterer's, *Houshold Furniture in Genteel Taste, for the Year 1763* (London: printed for Robert Sayer, 1763). The authors thank Nancy Richards for the information on this design source.

42. Thomas Bridgman, *Memorials of the Dead in Boston; Containing Exact Transcripts of Inscriptions of the Sepulchral Monuments in the King's Chapel Burial Ground, in the City of Boston* (Boston: Benjamin B. Mussey & Co., 1853), p. 226. The Brinley family's Roxbury mansion, "Dachet House," was one of the grandest Boston-area residences: "All the paneling and woodwork consisted of elaborate carving done abroad. . . . Two cherubs carved in wood extended their wings . . ." (Charles Martyn, *The Life of Artemas Ward* [New York: Artemas Ward, 1921], pp. 167–68). State of New Jersey, Middlesex County Probate, no. 13093.

43. John Cogswell to Caleb Davis, November 4, 1769, Caleb Davis Papers, MHS. For an illustration of the receipt, see Young, "Five Secretaries," p. 484. This is the only known receipt for furniture signed by Cogswell. For a discussion of the term "bureau," see Robert F. Trent, "Matching Inventory Terms and Period Furnishings," in *Early American Probate Inventories* (Boston: Boston University for the Dublin Center for New England Folklife, 1989), pp. 20–21.

44. Documents pertaining to Storer's business are in the Ebenezer Storer & Son Papers, BL, HBS. Brattle Square Church Society Records, pp. 35–42. Shipton, *Sibley's Harvard Graduates*, 12:209–13.

45. Malcolm Storer, *Annals of the Storer Family, Together With Notes on the Ayrault Family* (Boston, 1927), p. 49. Storer was a supporter of the Non-Importation Agreement (Ebenezer Storer Papers, March 15, 1768, MHS). Ebenezer Storer Will, 1807, SCRP, no. 22829. Mary Storer, Administrative Account, February 10, 1775, SCRP, no. 15409.

46. Louise Brownell Clarke, *The Greenes of Rhode Island With Historical Records of English Ancestry, 1534–1902*, 2 vols. (New York: Knickerbocker Press, 1903), 1:150, 258–59. Gardiner Greene Inventory, February 18, 1833, SCRP, no. 30090. Probate records of Greene's descendants were not researched. Gardiner Greene married Elizabeth Clarke Copley (1770–1866), daughter of John Singleton Copley, in London in 1800. Martha Babcock (Greene) Amory to Charles Amory [no month/day] 1869, Library of the Boston Athaeneum.

47. The authors thank Deborah Rebuck of the Dietrich American Foundation for information from their files. This hardware is on a blockfront chest-on-chest originally owned by Ebenezer Storer in the Museum of Fine Arts, Boston, (acc. 1984.520), and the desk-and-bookcase illustrated in fig. 24 is in the Winterthur Museum (acc. 56.23). The hardware on the chest in fig. 40 is replaced. The form of its original brasses is unknown.

48. Tradition maintains that the chest originally belonged to Richard Sprague Stearns (1803–1840), but his birthdate makes that impossible. A bombé desk-and-bookcase attributed to Boston cabinetmaker Henry Rust descended to Richard and his wife, Theresa St. Agnau, from Richard's father or his father-in-law, Col. Joseph Sprague (1739–1808) (Charles Venable, *American Furniture in the Bybee Collection* [Austin, Texas: University of Texas Press in association with the Dallas Museum of Art, 1989], pp. 58–63). The bombé chest (fig. 40) supposedly descended in the same line and bears a crudely scratched "HR 1774" on a base glue block (clearly a modern addition), but the chest cannot be identified in any of the sources cited by Venable. The current owner purchased the chest at auction (Sotheby's, *Important American Furniture, Folk Art, Folk Paintings, and Chinese Export Porcelain*, October 24, 1991, sale no. 5500, lot 208).

49. Sack, "Bombé Furniture," p. 1079, pl. 2. The other chest is privately owned and has not been previously published.

50. A pair of square-back neoclassical side chairs and a spider leg table made by John Cogswell for his daughter are owned by a direct descendant.

Summary of Characteristics

Figure no.	Form	Current owner	Original owner	Date
9	Desk	Private collection	Thomas Amory, Boston	Before 1784
13	Chest-on-chest	Museum of Fine Arts, Boston	Family of Elias Hasket Derby, Salem	1782
17	Two-part desk	Private collection	—	—
20	Desk-and-bookcase	Winterthur Museum	—— Jackson ?	1786
24	Desk-and-bookcase	Winterthur Museum	Joseph Barrell, Boston and Charlestown	—
25	Desk-and-bookcase	Winterthur Museum	Edward Brinley, Boston/Roxbury	—
33	Chest of drawers	US Department of State	Ebenezer Storer I or II, Boston	—
36	Chest of drawers	Dietrich American Foundation	Gardiner Greene, Boston	—
40	Chest of drawers	Private collection	Poss. Joseph Sprague or Wm. Stearns, Salem	—
41	Chest of drawers	Art Institute of Chicago	—	—
43	Chest of drawers	Private collection	—	—
—	Chest of drawers	Private collection	—	—

Inscriptions	Profile of inner surface of case sides	Drawer-side profiles	Ends of drawer fronts	Triangular base brackets	Top-edge profile of drawer sides
"JC"; "WA"; "WAG"	Two large areas scooped out	Straight vertical	Project beyond drawer sides	No	Single bead
"John Cogswell In midle Street, Boston 1782"; "John Cogswell" 4 times on inner surface of backboards	Two large areas scooped out	Straight vertical	Project beyond drawer sides	No	Double bead
"JC"; cartoon of daisy	Curved	Curved to conform to case sides	Only one of four projects beyond drawer sides	No	Single bead
"1786 AD Jackson[?]"	Straight vertical	Straight vertical	Project beyond drawer sides	No	Single bead
"Bottom" in chalk on bottom board	Curved	Curved to conform to case sides	Flush with drawer sides	Yes	Double bead
"Bottom" in chalk on bottom board	Straight vertical	Straight vertical	Project beyond drawer sides	Yes	Double bead
"Bottom" in chalk on case bottom board	Angled facets	Angled	Project beyond drawer sides	Yes	Double bead
—	Angled facets	Angled	Project beyond drawer sides	Yes	Double bead
"Bottom" in chalk on bottom board	Curved	Curved to conform to case sides	Flush with drawer sides	Yes	Double bead
"Bottom" in chalk on bottom board	Curved	Curved to conform to case sides	Project beyond drawer sides	Yes	Double bead
None	Curved	Curved to conform to case sides	Flush with drawer sides	Yes	Double bead
"Bottom" in chalk on bottom board	Curved	Curved to conform to case sides	Flush with drawer sides	No	Double bead

Figure 1 Draw table, Dutch, 1660–1680. Oak and ebony. H. 32 5/8"; top: 36" x 59 3/4" (closed). (Courtesy, Old Dutch Church, North Tarrytown, New York; photo, Gavin Ashworth.)

Peter M. Kenny

Flat Gates, Draw Bars, Twists, and Urns: New York's Distinctive, Early Baroque Oval Tables with Falling Leaves

▼ THE SUBSTANTIAL body of surviving oval tables with falling leaves made in New York City and in the rural towns of the Hudson River Valley, Long Island, and central and northeastern New Jersey from the late-seventeenth through the mid-eighteenth century comprise a remarkable group that is structurally and ornamentally unconventional—in comparison to their New England counterparts—and redolent of a bold baroque design ethos. These tables present a brief but fascinating chapter in American furniture history and a peculiar interpretive challenge as by-products of Anglo-Dutch cultural fermentation in late-seventeenth-century New York.

In medieval times dining tables were the largest and most cumbersome pieces of furniture next to beds. They could be built-in or, as was sometimes the case with trestle tables, taken apart and either stored away or moved to another location. By the 1500s, however, societal changes began rendering these behemoths obsolete. Large, transient medieval households with mostly portable possessions gave way to smaller households occupying year-round dwellings. In the interest of conserving space in these furniture-filled interiors, joiners found ways of reducing the size of dining tables without sacrificing too much surface area.[1]

In England, two types of dining tables with relatively compact bases and tops that could be expanded or reduced in size emerged by about 1550. Furniture historian Victor Chinnery suggests that the earlier of the two designs consisted of a heavy, open-frame base and a fixed rectangular top with hinged, floor-length leaves attached to the ends. When raised, the leaves were supported by heavy lopers or draw bars pulled out from inside the frame. This rather awkward design apparently never came into wide use, but hinged or falling leaves, as they were known in the period, presaged subsequent advances in variable-top dining table design. A slightly later development was the considerably more elegant draw table, or "drawing" table as the form was referred to in sixteenth-century inventories. This design featured an open-frame base and a large rectangular top that rested loosely on a fixed transverse center board and had leaves inserted at either end. When drawn out from under the top, the leaves cantilevered off the frame on tapered rails that ran in tracks inside the aprons and were held in compression, at full extension, by the fixed transverse board. Draw tables were extremely popular in England and northern Europe during the late Renaissance and continued in production and use well into the baroque period.[2]

Tables with oval-shaped tops and falling leaves are most closely associated with the reigns of Charles II and James II, and, as furniture historian David Barquist suggests, they may be a purely English innovation. The genesis of the form may lie in the trend toward more relaxed, informal dining in late-seventeenth-century England. The oval shape tended to sublimate issues of precedence in seating.[3] Lighter and more portable than their earlier, variable-top counterparts, these tables could be set up in the center of the room for meals and stored with the leaves down against the wall after use. The leaf supports were no longer heavy lopers but stylishly turned auxiliary leg supports consisting of two uprights linked by parallel rails. The inner upright pivoted between the bottom edge of the side apron and the upper face of the side stretcher, giving the whole assembly the look of a swinging gate, hence the modern term—gate-leg table. Seventeenth-century appraisers generally described these tables by size, primary wood, or the shape or kinetic action of their tops.

Rectangular dining tables of traditional late medieval and Renaissance form, including draw tables, were made and used in New England from the 1630s onward, whereas oval tables with falling leaves first came on the scene there in the 1660s. One of the earliest references is the "Ovall Table" and set of twelve "Turkey worke chayres" in the 1669 estate inventory of Antipas Boyse of Boston.[4] From their inception, these tables were meant to harmonize with the sets of turkeywork, cane, and leather chairs sold by Boston merchants. Consequently, Antipas Boyse's oval table with falling leaves probably had the repetitive spherical turnings of the stylish, low-back "Cromwellian" chairs of the 1660s and 1670s, whereas examples from the 1680–1730 period had baroque twist, baluster, vase, and urn-shaped turnings resembling those of imported and domestic high-back cane and leather chairs.

A similar pattern of development seems to hold true for New Netherland and early colonial New York, although dining tables of the early rectangular form are exceedingly rare. Oval tables with falling leaves survive in considerable number, but the paucity of inventories dating before 1680 makes it difficult to determine if the form was in use in New York City as early as in Boston. It seems unlikely that it was, given that this apparently was a purely English furniture form and, as historian Michael Kammen has pointed out, Anglicization did not occur in New York on a large or permanent scale until nearly a generation after the English conquest of 1664.[5]

The 1686 estate inventory of Cornelis Steenwyck, one of the wealthiest residents of New Amsterdam and twice mayor, lists an "ovall table" as well as a dozen Russia leather and rush-seated chairs in the "kitchen chamber," a sort of common family living room. In the "great chamber" or best room, however, a "square table" valued at £10 is listed, along with a dozen "Rush leather Chyres" and two "Velvet Chyres with fine silver lace." The high value assigned to this table and the presence of fourteen chairs suggests that it was an especially fine example, possibly having an expandable top; an imported Dutch baroque draw table of rich rosewood and ebony immediately comes to mind. Physical and documentary evidence proves that draw tables were imported and used in New York Dutch homes long after the English conquest; the physical proof is witnessed in an oak and ebony example with a solid Phillipse family history (fig. 1), and the written record includes the "square table that pulls out" that was listed in the 1711 estate inventory of Margareta Schuyler of Albany.[6] Although draw tables and references to them are rare, it seems likely that they provided some competition early on for oval tables with falling leaves among this segment of the population, especially if the latter form was perceived as English.

Only a handful of late-seventeenth-century inventories list oval tables with falling leaves, and few references from any period specify their use. Englishwoman Charlotte Lenox's account of a sumptuous tea in the home of one New York Dutch family in the late 1730s or early 1740s describes how such tables were set up in a room and laid out with food and napery from the earliest period of their use:

> Immediately after the tea equipage was removed, a large table was brought out, and covered with a damask cloth, exquisitely white and fine; upon this table were placed several sorts of cakes, and teabread, with pots of the most delicate butter, plates of hungbeef and ham, shaved extremely fine, wet and dry sweetmeats, every kind of fruit in season, pistacchio and other nuts, all ready cracked. . . . The liquors were cyder, mead and Madeira wine. All these things were served in the finest china and glass.[7]

Figure 2 Oval table with falling leaves, New York City, 1700–1730. Mahogany with maple and yellow poplar. H. 30 1/8"; top: 58" × 72 1/4" (open). The table may originally have belonged to Philip Van Cortlandt (1683–1748) and his wife Catherine De Peyster (1688–1766?) who were married in 1710. (Courtesy, Historic Hudson Valley, Tarrytown, New York; photo, Gavin Ashworth.)

Tables with Draw-Bar Supports

The approximately sixty surviving early baroque oval tables with falling leaves can be divided into two broad categories based on their method of leaf support: those with pivot-leg supports (figs. 2, 3), and those with draw bars or lopers (fig. 4). The majority are of the former type. Although distinctive in their own right, New York tables with pivot legs follow a common English design formula adopted throughout the colonies in the late seventeenth and early eighteenth centuries. However, tables with draw-bar supports are unique to New York, and the seventeen surviving examples represent about 30 percent of the total.

Figure 3 Oval table with falling leaves, New York, 1720–1750. Red gum with yellow poplar. H. 28 1/2"; top: 35 1/2" × 45 1/2" (open). Branded twice on the underside of the stretcher are the initials ATB (conjoined), which may stand for Abraham Ten Broeck of Albany (1734–1810), an owner, not a maker. (Collection of Peter Eliot; photo, Gavin Ashworth.)

Figure 4 Oval table with falling leaves attributed to the Elting-Beekman shops, Kingston, New York, 1700–1730. Red gum and maple with pine and oak. H. 28 1/2"; top: 48 1/2" × 58" (open). The table was purchased by its current owner out of an old Hurley, New York, home. It retains its original top, although its far leaf is off and not included in this photo. The exaggerated shape on the edge of the thick top is characteristic of this shop tradition. (Private collection; photo, Gavin Ashworth.)

Draw bars or lopers are rudimentary support mechanisms. They appear on a few sixteenth- and seventeenth-century English dining tables with variable tops and on a few other early English table forms, but not on any English or Dutch tables directly analogous to the New York examples. The way the support system works is simple and obviously related to the mechanisms of the earliest draw tables and variable top tables with falling leaves.[8] Two wooden bars, rectangular in section, run in a slotted board (or track) mounted transversely inside the table frame (fig. 5). Square- or round-section pegs tenoned into the bottom of the bars engage the slots and serve as stops when the bars are drawn out from inside the frame through the openings in the side aprons (fig. 6). The draw bars are usually made of heavy stock, but a few are similar in scale and section to the lopers on early baroque, slant-lid desks (see figs. 7, 8). Draw bars may be partially responsible for the broad proportions of the tables on which they are used, since

Figure 5 Detail of the draw-bar track on the table illustrated in fig. 10. Pegs that are rectangular in section and inserted in the draw bar at an angle slightly less than 90 degrees are typical of tables attributed to the Elting-Beekman shops. (Photo, Gavin Ashworth.)

Figure 6 Detail of the draw bar on the table illustrated in fig. 4. A prominent feature of the draw bars on tables by the Elting-Beekman shops are cut fingerholds. (Photo, Gavin Ashworth.)

Figure 7 Oval table with falling leaves, New York or New Jersey, 1735–1760. Red gum and cherry. H. 26"; top: 38⁷⁄₈" × 43¹⁄₂" (open). (Courtesy, Art Institute of Chicago, gift of the Antiquarian Society through the Mr. and Mrs. William Y. Hutchinson Fund, acc. 1985.241.)

Figure 8 Detail of the draw bar and boxlike draw-bar guide inside the frame of the table illustrated in fig. 7. (Photo, Art Institute of Chicago.)

the frames had to be wide to accommodate draw bars of sufficient length to support the leaves. The wide, sturdy stance of the tables (figs. 9, 10) is complemented by proportionately stout legs, which consistently measure at least 2¹⁄₂" in diameter or larger, a stock size that allowed the turner to work deeply into the wood for dramatic effects.

Five of the tables with draw-bar leaf supports have bold, twisted legs and dramatic X- or double-ended Y-shaped stretchers (figs. 11, 12). The walnut example illustrated in figure 12 is probably the earliest of the draw-bar

Figure 9 Oval table with falling leaves, New York, 1700–1720. Cherry with maple. H. 27 1/2"; top: 44 1/2" × 47" (open). The smallish top, which is original, was affixed originally by long iron rivets that passed all the way through the aprons and were covered by face-grain plugs in the top. The drawer pulls have their original, late Jacobean-style cast backplates. (Collection of Peter Eliot; photo, Gavin Ashworth.)

Figure 10 Oval table with falling leaves, attributed to the Elting-Beekman shops, Kingston, New York, 1740–1770. Red gum with pine and oak. H. 28 1/8"; top: 50" × 60 3/8" (open). This is the only table with end drawers attributed to the Elting-Beekman shops. The draw-bar track inside the frame usually discouraged this feature. (Courtesy, Huguenot Historical Society, New Paltz, New York; photo, Gavin Ashworth).

tables. Its stretcher design parallels that of the 1660–1680 Dutch-made draw table owned by the Phillipse family (fig. 1), and the ovolo-and-bead rail molding matches that on the door frames of the four earliest surviving American *kasten*. That this distinctive molding has only been found on sev-

Figure 11 Oval table with falling leaves, New York City, 1690–1730. Red gum with yellow poplar and pine. H. 29 3/8" (minus top); frame 20 3/8" × 35 7/8". The top and finial on the crossed stretchers are modern replacements. The graining on the aprons and lower leg blocks probably dates to the early- to mid-nineteenth century. (Private collection; photo, Gavin Ashworth.)

Figure 12 Oval table with falling leaves, New York City, 1680–1710. Walnut with pine. H. 28 1/2"; top: 42 3/4" × 19" (center section only). The leaves, finial, and possibly the feet are modern replacements. (Courtesy, Winterthur Museum, acc. 59.5.)

Figure 13 Detail of the single-twist leg on the table shown in fig. 11. The leg tapers from a diameter of 2 5/8" at the ring on top of the bottom block to 2 1/8" at the top ring. The upper reel on the leg is skillfully diminished in proportion to the taper. (Photo, Gavin Ashworth.)

enteenth-century, Dutch-influenced furniture strongly suggests that the maker was of Netherlandish rather than English descent. If so, this table is a late-seventeenth-century Dutch New York joiner's adaptation of a new and unfamiliar English table form. To accommodate the Dutch-derived stretcher system, he had to utilize that most rudimentary of support mechanisms, the draw bar or loper, and in so doing created a new and distinctive Anglo-Dutch table form, one that today serves as a sensitive indicator of cultural blending in early colonial New York.[9]

The four other twisted-leg tables have a slightly different aspect due to

Figure 14 Oval table with falling leaves, attributed to the Elting-Beekman shops, Kingston, New York, 1770–1800. Red gum with yellow poplar and pine. H. 28 1/2"; top: 48 1/2" × 58" (open). This table has a history of ownership in the Vanderlyn family of Kingston and is in a remarkable state of preservation, retaining nearly the full original height of its feet. (Courtesy, Senate House State Historic Site, Kingston, New York; photo, Gavin Ashworth.)

their boxlike, dovetailed frames and separate legs pinned up into the corners (fig. 11). Although this construction initially appears rickety, it allows for a firm connection between the legs and the X-shaped stretchers. (Pinned legs can be rotated so that their bottom blocks face each other at opposite corners.) The difference between the boxlike frames with pinned legs and the mortise-and-tenon frame and leg construction is reminiscent of a change that occurred over time in American *kasten* design. Around 1700, boxlike, dovetailed base units with ball-turned feet pinned up into the front corners began to replace the heavy post-and-rail facade construction of seventeenth-century examples.[10]

Figure 15 Oval table with falling leaves, New York City, 1749–1763. Mahogany with red gum and yellow poplar. H. 29 1/2"; top: 71" × 78 1/2" (open). (Courtesy, Albany Institute of History and Art; photo, Gavin Ashworth.)

The twelve other tables with draw-bar supports all have box stretchers aligned with the frame and legs with a variety of early baroque turnings, including vases, rings, balusters, and urns (see figs. 4, 7, 9, 10, 14). Pivoting gate-leg supports could have been used on these examples, but for at least two reasons were not: the draw-bar system saved the expense of turning and

Figure 16 Oval table with falling leaves, New York, 1690–1730. (Wallace Nutting, *Furniture Treasury* [Framingham, Mass. 1928], 1: no. 943; current location unknown.)

Figure 17 Oval table with falling leaves, New York, 1690–1730. Cherry with yellow poplar. H. 27 1/2"; top: 47 1/2" × 36 1/8" (open). This table and the one in fig. 9 have lambs' tongues carved on the corners of their leg blocks. The reserve area on the face of the leg blocks are in the shape of baroque ogee arches as a result of this decorative carving. The moldings run on the flat gates are similar in scale and profile to the applied single-arched moldings on early high chests and other case furniture. (Courtesy, Wadsworth Atheneum, gift of J. Pierpont Morgan, acc. 1926.492.)

Figure 18 Oval table with falling leaves, New York City, 1690–1720. Mahogany with maple, yellow poplar, and oak. H. 28 7/8"; top: 40 3/4" × 44 1/2" (open). (Courtesy, Museum of the City of New York, gift of the Reynal family; photo, Gavin Ashworth.)

Figure 19 Oval table with falling leaves, New York City, 1700–1740. Mahogany with yellow poplar and oak. H. 28 3/8". Except for the use of turned versus plain stretchers, this table is nearly identical to the example illustrated in fig. 18 and is probably by the same hand. The top appears to be a modern replacement. (Courtesy, Colonial Williamsburg Foundation.)

framing the gate legs and avoided the annoyance of sitters occasionally having to straddle a pivot leg. Plain molded stretchers appear on all but one table (fig. 9), and they strike a slightly discordant note in the overall design when compared to the elaborate turnings. However, the stretchers and the broad overall proportions of the tables (figs. 4, 10) provide a visible link to earlier heavy, stretcher-base tables with stationary tops, such as the square table, a rare form now thought only to have been made in New England.[11]

Tables with Gate-Leg Supports

Gate-leg tables are of two types, classic examples with turned uprights and stretchers in the gates, and simpler ones with gates made from molded boards. Most prominent among the former type are the Sir William Johnson table (fig. 15) and the Van Cortlandt family table (fig. 2). The reputations of these two tables were established in the early years of this century when Esther Singleton and Luke Vincent Lockwood published them in their pioneering books on American furniture. Since then these tables have come to be considered the beau ideals of New York early baroque table design. (Wallace Nutting reproduced the Sir William Johnson table in the 1920s and went so far as to call it the "Supreme Gate Leg" in the catalogue of his reproductions.) Based on their massive scale and the quality of their design and workmanship, the reputations of these two tables are well deserved. What further distinguishes them as high-end luxury items is their primary wood, mahogany. Singleton considered the Van Cortlandt table an especially early example of the use of mahogany in the colonies, an observation that was astute and remarkably prescient; several New York tables made of mahogany with turned pivot-leg supports have since come to light (figs. 18, 19, 20, and another in the collection of the Monmouth County Historical Association in Freehold, New Jersey). Half a dozen examples of native cherry (fig. 21), walnut, and maple round out the classic gate legs, bringing the total up to twelve. Although it is fruitless to try to equate survival rates of specific types with their popularity, it is instructive to compare the iconic "William and Mary" gate leg with the other surviving New York oval tables with falling leaves to show that this design was only one of the options available to New Yorkers in the late seventeenth and early eighteenth centuries.[12]

Tables with gates made of flat boards account for the greatest number of New York oval tables with falling leaves. Of the approximately thirty examples known, only six have four legs and box stretchers (fig. 16); the balance have trestle bases with two uprights connected by flat low stretchers (fig. 17). These tables caught the eye of Lockwood and Nutting, both of whom illustrated examples in their books on American furniture. Nutting commented that tables of this design had recovery histories in Maine, New Hampshire, and Massachussetts; however, his failure to mention New York has clouded regional attributions ever since. Of all the known examples, only one (fig. 3) can be linked to a likely eighteenth-century Albany owner through a brand on the underside of its stretcher. Yet there are overwhelming reasons to attribute these tables to New York rather than to New

Figure 20 Oval table with falling leaves, New York City, 1740–1760. Mahogany. H. 28 1/2"; top: 53" × 67" (open). This is a considerably smaller version of the Sir William Johnson table (fig. 17). (Private collection; photo, Christie's).

England: most have been found and offered for sale by dealers in the Hudson River Valley; many are made of red gum, a wood used as a cheap substitute for mahogany in New York, but not in New England; and their turnings and leg-stock dimensions are clearly related to those of documented New York examples with draw bars and gate legs, but they bear little relation to those of New England tables.[13]

The tables with flat gates and trestle bases have tops that measure, on average, about ten inches less in overall length and width than the tops on their four-legged counterparts with draw-bar and gate-leg supports. (The Johnson and Van Cortlandt tables are excluded from this calculation because they are abnormally large.) Tops range in size from 36 1/8" × 47 1/2" (fig. 17) to 30" × 34 3/4" (fig. 22). The smaller tables may have been used for tea or light meals, or as service stations alongside grander, oval-topped dining tables; the larger ones could comfortably seat four and may have served as the principal dining table in some households.

The beauty of these tables is in their compactness and the ease with which they can be moved and stored. With the leaves down they are seldom over a foot wide (fig. 23). The 1724 room-by-room inventory of Gertruy Van Cortlandt's home in New York City suggests that she lived in a tall, two-storey, Dutch-style townhouse and used one of the smaller trestle-base tables there. On the first floor were an entry, front and back parlors, a closet, and a kitchen dependency. Listed "in the closet," not necessarily a closet as

Figure 21 Oval table with falling leaves, possibly Flushing, New York, 1690–1730. Cherry with pine. H. 27 3/8"; top: 45" × 61" (open). This table and three carved-top Boston leather chairs (one of which is illustrated here) were given to Washington's Headquarters by the Verplanck family between 1858 and 1872. A dressing table discovered in Flushing, Long Island, with closely related turnings, possibly by the same shop or school of makers, is illustrated in Jonathan L. Fairbanks and Elizabeth Bidwell Bates, *American Furniture 1620 to the Present* (New York, 1981), p. 65. (Courtesy, New York State Office of Parks, Recreation and Historic Preservation, Washington's Headquarters State Historic Site, Newburgh, New York; photo, Gavin Ashworth.)

Figure 22 Oval table with falling leaves, New York, 1690–1730. Red gum with yellow poplar. H. 26 1/4"; top: 30" × 34 3/4" (open). (Courtesy, Metropolitan Museum of Art, gift of Mrs. Eleanor G. Sargent, 1980.)

we think of one today but a small room adjacent to or between the parlors, were a total of nine pieces of earthenware, a stone jug, a whitewood chest, a candlebox, and "1 ovall table."[14]

Major structural variations indicate that these tables represent the work

Figure 23 End view of the table in fig. 3 showing the typical heavy dovetail joinery at the top of the upright where it connects to the thick board that supports the top. (Photo, Gavin Ashworth.)

Figure 24 Oval table with falling leaves, New York, 1720–1750. Red gum. H. 28 1/4"; top: 33" × 39 1/2" (open). This trestle-base table with flat gates differs from the two other illustrated examples in that its turned uprights are tenoned up into a cross piece at the top rather than dovetailed to a thick board. The severe warp in the top is typical of flat-sawn red gum, a notoriously unstable wood. (Colonial Williamsburg Foundation.)

of several shops. (Paired versus single board stretchers [figs. 17, 24] and mortise-and-tenon versus dovetail joints where the uprights meet the support structure of the top.) The consistent use of mortise-and-tenon and dovetail joints (fig. 23), suggest that most were made by joiners rather than turners. The tables are workmanlike and sturdy. The quality of their design and construction is superior to most New England shoe-foot, trestle-base tables with falling leaves, which typically have a turned stretcher joined higher up on the posts and vertically oriented rails supporting the tops (as opposed to the flat rails on the New York ones). Today, many of the New England examples are rickety and unstable, a condition as much attributable to their original design and construction as to their antiquity.

New York four-legged tables with flat gates (fig. 16) are a curious blend of the classic design with trestle-base examples. The end rails are like those on most four-legged tables, but the side ones are unusual in being turned flat side down and lapped into the tops of the legs so that they are nearly invisible and provide extra room for knees. Unlike all but one other New York falling-leaf table with plain box stretchers (fig. 7), the stretchers on these tables are oriented so that their broadest surfaces are in a vertical plane. This orientation relates well visually to the framing members of the flat gates.

Though the tables with draw-bar supports evidently are a hybrid Anglo-Dutch design, trestle-base tables with flat gates appear to be purely English in derivation. (Chinnery illustrates several closely related examples from England that he dates from the mid- to late-seventeenth century, but nothing similar is known in Dutch furniture.)[15] This indicates that unadulterated

Figure 25   Cane armchair, England, 1685–1688. Walnut. (Courtesy, Metropolitan Museum of Art, John Stewart Kennedy Fund, 1918.)

English joiners' designs were also popular among New Yorkers and makes the total lack of trestle-base tables with flat gates and New England histories of ownership that much harder to explain.

The Ornamental Elements of New York Tables with Falling Leaves
The turnings on oval tables with falling leaves were meant to harmonize with the sets of cane and leather chairs used with them and with other late seventeenth- and early-eighteenth-century furniture forms. During this period joiners and turners in America shared an Anglo-Dutch vocabulary of turned ornament that consisted of compressed or elegantly drawn ogee balusters, flat-topped urns, straight-sided tapered columns, smooth spheres and ellipsoids, rings, reels, and twists. All of these profiles except for the last are evident in an English cane armchair bearing the royal cypher of James II (1685–1688) and his consort Mary Beatrice in its crest (fig. 25). Less elaborately carved but similar high-back chairs were imported by North American colonists, and their turnings served as design sources for local joiners and turners who could copy certain passages verbatim or pick and choose among the various profiles to come up with inventive combinations that satisfied their creative impulses and suited the tastes of their clientele.

In New York, that taste seems to have run toward complexity and exuberance. Furniture historian Benno Forman pointed this out in his study of New York leather chairs. He cited a group of indigenous plain-top, high-back examples that are "rather stiff in their stance" but with "wonderfully elaborate turnings" as proof that, despite the heavy importation of Boston leather chairs, many New Yorkers preferred local variants. On the issue of the relative Dutchness or Englishness of these New York chairs, he was rightfully wary and noted a persistent problem with singling out design

Figure 26 Detail of a leg from the Van Cortlandt family table (fig. 2). (Photo, Gavin Ashworth.)

Figure 27 Detail of a leg from the table illustrated in fig. 9. The ball-shaped foot is a modern replacement as are most of the lamb's tongue carvings on the lower corners of the bottom leg block. (Photo, Gavin Ashworth.)

influences on early New York furniture. He specifically warned that such influences "could come directly from Holland, or France, or from England which had been influenced by Holland, or from Boston which had been influenced by England, which had been influenced by Holland."[16] The same problem exists for New York oval tables with falling leaves, although it is possible to identify a precise design source for the turnings on one subgroup of tables with draw-bar supports and possibly for the twisted leg as executed in New York.

Wallace Nutting unknowingly described one distinctive attribute of early baroque turnings in the caption he wrote for #943 in his *Furniture Treasury* (see fig. 16): "This rare turning or something different from the conventional is usually found with the trestle gate or the flat gate." By "different from the conventional" Nutting meant different from the bilaterally symmetrical ogee balusters found on many New England tables. New Yorkers showed a more adventurous spirit in the selection and arrangement of the elements used on table legs, opting for variety and visual complexity over symmetry. This quality is manifest in seven patterns of turned legs on the tables illustrated in this article: (1) twist (fig. 13); (2) stacked ogee balusters

Figure 28 Composite detail of legs from tables attributed to the Elting-Beekman shops at Kingston; left (fig. 4), center (fig. 10), right (fig. 14). (Photo, Gavin Ashworth.)

(figs. 26, 27); (3) large ogee baluster surmounted by a smaller, double-ended, compressed one with a short tapered column above (fig. 28a–c); (4) short urn with a large ogee baluster above (fig. 29a–c); (5) double-ended compressed ogee baluster surmounted by a large, single-ended one (fig. 22); (6) opposed end-to-end ogee balusters (figs. 7, 17); and (7) single elongated baluster (fig. 24).[17]

Certain consistencies among the patterns help to delineate a distinctive New York early baroque turning style. Several tables have flattened ball-shape feet, a well-defined reel on top of the lower leg blocks, and fat, full rings. Also distinctive is a double-ended compressed baluster—sometimes used above a large ogee baluster and sometimes below—that looks a little like an unfinished ball turning. The heavy leg stock and the visual complexity and dynamism of baroque design work hand in glove; the turner can exploit his reductive decorative techniques to the fullest and still maintain axial mass and strength in the legs.[18]

Twisted legs (fig. 13) are a rare feature in American furniture, found on only twenty surviving pieces: five Cromwellian-style leather chairs from Boston and one from Philadelphia or New York; two low-back chairs with

Figure 29 Composite detail of urn-and-baluster turned legs; left (fig. 18), center (fig. 21), right (fig 15). (Photo, Gavin Ashworth.)

board seats and twisted back spindles from Philadelphia; two oval tables with falling leaves, one possibly from New England and one from the South; and nine pieces of New York furniture, including the five tables with draw-bar supports (figs. 11, 12), three high chests, and one dressing table. Legs of this type are frequently said to be twist turned, but this description is something of a misnomer since it incorrectly implies that the twist is imparted in the turning process. The ball-shaped foot, rings and reels, and the essential cylinder are all turned, but the twist is formed with rasps and gouges while the leg blank is at rest in the lathe. There it can be rotated by hand as the artisan works his way around, guided by spiraling layout marks. Bringing a twisted leg to finished smoothness was painstaking work that obviously meant a higher sales price. All the New York examples are single twist, and all the New England, Pennsylvania, and southern examples are double. Benno Forman and Dutch scholar Jan Veenendaal both state that the single twist is more continental European than English; Forman calls the design French, and Veenendaal says that it is Dutch. Either way, it should not be surprising that the single twist only shows up in New York where French Huguenots, French-speaking Walloons, and Netherlandish

Figure 30 Carved top leather armchair, Boston, Massachusetts, 1695–1710. Maple and red oak. H. 53 1/4". (Courtesy, Winterthur Museum, acc. 58.553.)

furniture craftsmen and their customers formed a large segment of the population in the late-seventeenth and early-eighteenth centuries.[19]

Stacked ogee balusters (fig. 26) are found only on furniture from New York and the South Carolina low country, two areas with sizable populations of French Huguenots. The stacked balusters appear most frequently on trestle-base tables with flat gates (fig. 3) but are rare on those with turned gate legs and tables with draw-bar supports.[20] In all but one instance (fig. 9), the lower baluster in this stacked arrangement is shorter than the upper one, a disposition that contrasts with modern perception that smaller things should be stacked on larger ones but that is in perfect keeping with the tenets of baroque design where the emphasis was on dramatic tension and movement. With this seventeenth-century design principle in mind it is easier to understand a composition in which the lower baluster is consciously made squatter with a shorter neck to give it the appearance of being forced into compression by the pendulous baluster above.

A single baluster surmounted by a compressed double-ended baluster (fig. 28) appears on a group of tables with draw-bar supports made at Kingston in Ulster County (figs. 4, 10, 14). The apparent source for this design was the turned-arm supports on carved-top Boston leather armchairs like the one shown in figure 30 or in New York City versions of the same.[21] It is easy to imagine the genesis of this design occurring when, around 1700, a Kingston-area joiner was commissioned to make an oval table with falling leaves for use with a fine new set of Boston or New York City carved-top leather chairs recently acquired by a local householder. The turning, when expanded to table leg size, takes on an abstract quality visible especially in the center leg in figure 28, where each turned element looks as if it could be snatched from the stacked column of shapes by a deft hand.

Of the four remaining turning patterns, the one most frequently associated with New York—thanks almost exclusively to the renown of the Sir William Johnson table—is the urn and baluster (fig. 29). This pattern is directly traceable to seventeenth-century English oak and walnut oval tables with falling leaves, and it appears as part of the series of turnings on the stiles of the English cane chair shown in figure 25. In American oval tables with falling leaves, it is found in less than robust form on two related mid-eighteenth-century examples from Maine and on a total of five from New York (figs. 15, 18–21).[22] Three distinct variations of the urn and baluster are shown in figure 29. The most notable difference among the three is the lack of the well-defined reel on top of the lower block on the leg of the Sir William Johnson table (fig. 29, far right), a prominent feature of the other two legs. This deletion may indicate a drift away from the design tradition that spawned it. Otherwise, the turnings on the Johnson table are beautifully executed, something that should be expected from a first-rate New York City shop executing a major commission.

The fifth turning pattern—a large ogee baluster over a compressed double-ended one—is represented by the trestle-base table with flat gates illustrated in figure 22. The pattern also occurs on two other tables of the same form and on two walnut tables with box stretchers and turned gate legs probably made in New York City, but it is not found on any of the tables with draw-bar supports. The turning is not exclusive to New York and is found both in surviving architectural woodwork and freestanding furniture from southeastern Massachusetts. An inverted version of this pattern occurs on a curly maple table from Hempstead, Long Island, that has compressed double-ended balusters over the large ogee balusters with the reel that normally sits on top of the lower leg block nestled between them.[23]

Opposed ogee balusters on New York tables—turning pattern number six—have little except their general disposition in common with the rhythmic, bilaterally symmetrical turnings of New England oval tables with falling leaves. Only five New York examples with this leg turning are known, two of which (figs. 7, 17) have multiple fat rings at the top and bottom of the legs but otherwise appear to be unrelated. A trestle-base table at Winterthur (acc. 58.527), one of the few New York examples with turned gate legs, and another closely related table illustrated in Lockwood's *Colonial Furniture in America* both have short, fullsome ogee balusters with heavy filleted rings between them. The turnings on figure 17 are similarly configured but have much blunter looking rings that are generally similar to the turned arm supports on a great, plain-top, New York leather armchair at the Museum of Fine Arts, Boston, which Benno Forman believed to be the most thoroughly Dutch of all surviving New York leather chairs.[24]

The seventh and final turning pattern, a simple elongated baluster, is perhaps the least interesting visually (fig. 24). It appears on eight tables, including seven with flat gates, two with turned gates, and one with draw-bar leaf supports. Full-bottomed and drawn out to a columnar form above, the turnings on the table in figure 24 lack the well-defined lower reel, an omission that suggests that it is a fairly late example.[25]

Dating and Attributions to Makers and Locale
Not a single table discussed in this article can be assigned a precise date, place of manufacture, or maker based on signatures, inscriptions, or other documentary evidence. Traditionally, the method used for dating anonymous or poorly documented early baroque oval tables with falling leaves has been by the type of table-leaf joint employed—the tongue-and-groove joint thought to be the earlier form, and the rule joint believed to be the later one. This method was combined with that intangible quality so many collectors, dealers, and students of early furniture use in formulating their final subjective judgments on such matters—aspect. A measure of validity is brought to this dating process if additional "toe holds" are present, such as histories of ownership in a single family or other datable design features. A few New York tables offer such documentation, making dating slightly less subjective at least in a few instances.

One example of this dating method comes from the Johnson table (fig. 15), which has rule joints with short, half-round sections of wood glued at the table ends under the quarter-round section of the joints. This sophisticated conceit, the source of which was probably English, occurs only in New York in American work and appears with greatest frequency on late baroque (fig. 31) and rococo tables with falling leaves and cabriole legs. Another feature relating the Johnson table to late baroque and rococo case furniture made in New York is its drawer construction. (It is difficult to perceive the end drawers in the table's current condition because the original bail handle drawer pulls, which may have been similar in appearance to the type on the table in figure 31, have been removed and the post holes filled.) The secondary wood in the drawers is yellow poplar; the drawer bottoms are chamfered on all four edges and set into grooves; the top edges of the drawer sides and backs are softly rounded; and there are neat miter joints at the top back corners that echo the fine finish of the rule joints. The sophisticated rule joint and aspects of the drawer construction push the date of manufacture for the Johnson table toward 1750, and the circumstances of

Figure 31 Oval table with falling leaves, New York City, 1735–1765. Mahogany. H. 28"; top: 61" × 65 1/4" (open). Representing a later phase of the baroque style in New York City tables, this example is approximately contemporary with Sir William Johnson's table (fig. 15) and shares its use of mahogany and barrel-like rule joints. The cyma curves cut into the ends of the rail appear to be segments of the sweeping, cyma and half-round cutout shapes on the Johnson table drawer fronts. (Courtesy, Bernard & S. Dean Levy Inc., N.Y.C.; photo, Helga Studio.)

Johnson's life tend to confirm this date as well. Johnson was born in Ireland in 1715 and came to New York in 1738 at the age of twenty-three. Between 1749 and 1763, he built three houses along the Mohawk River, each increasingly grand to suit his growing prominence as an entrepreneur, politician, and royal government official in charge of Indian affairs on New York's western frontier.[26]

Although the rule joint can be used to shade the Sir William Johnson table toward midcentury, the exact date that this joint was introduced in the colonies is unknown. One of the earliest references to the joint is in the account book of Newbury, Massachussetts, joiner Joseph Brown, Jr., who charged £3 for a "table rule joynted" in 1741. Thirteen years later the joint is mentioned in the day book of New York City joiner Joshua Delaplaine, who charged John Devine £1 for a "bilsted [red gum] Rule Joynt table 3 fot bed [frame]." Rule joints were listed as an option in a 1757 Providence, Rhode Island, table of prices for joiners' work, which lists: "Maple rule Joynt tables @ £6 Pr foot; old fashen Joynts @ £5.10."[27] The "old fashen Joynts" probably were tongue-and-groove, and their listing as a less expensive option in 1757 cautions against dating tables by their leaf joints alone.

A second table rich in family tradition is illustrated in figure 18. Inset in the top is a brass plaque that delineates the table's descent from Catherine Bedloe (bapt. May 22, 1664) of New York City. Bedloe, the daughter of a Dutch merchant, married (n.d.) English merchant Thomas Howarding sometime before 1693, when their daughter Margaret was baptized. She married her second husband, wealthy Dutch New York surgeon Dr. Samuel

Staats, in 1707, and the table reportedly descended to her daughter Margaret, perhaps as part of her dowry, when she married Robert Livingston, Jr., in 1717. From Margaret Livingston the table descended through several generations to General Louis Fitzgerald, who inherited it in 1886 and probably was the person responsible for chronicling the history and affixing the plaque. Family histories are notoriously unreliable for dating furniture, but in this instance the survival of an original 1690–1720 backplate for a pendant drop and the tongue-and-groove leaf joints indicate that the table belongs to the generations of Catherine Bedloe or her daughter Margaret Howarding. Also, although it is possible that this style of drawer pull could have been used in the 1730s or 1740s, it is unlikely given the wealth and status of its original owners, who would have wanted hardware as up-to-date as possible.[28]

Figure 32 Detail of a wrought iron dovetail hinge on the table illustrated in fig. 18. (Photo, Gavin Ashworth.)

The original wrought iron hinges (fig. 32) are of a type termed "butterfly" hinge today, but in shop jargon of the period may simply have been called "dovetail."[29] On several New York tables, the dovetail hinges are fastened by a combination of rosehead nails and a single rivet peened over on both ends. The rosehead nails are short and do not pierce the face of the table top; the rivet also passes only partially through, its countersunk head camouflaged by a face-grain plug (fig. 33). The source of this riveted hinge detail is unknown, but it appears with great regularity on New York tables with pivot legs and draw bars.

A table from the Verplanck family is another example with tongue-and-groove leaf joints that can be dated to the first quarter of the eighteenth century. It and three carved-top Boston leather chairs (fig. 21) were donated to Washington's Headquarters between 1858 and 1872. In the 1882 *Catalogue of Manuscripts and Relics in Washington's Head-Quarters,* they were described as being "the altar furniture of the Reformed Dutch Church at Fishkill, brought from Holland by the Verplanck family in 1682." Although the Verplancks probably provided the church furniture, the overall design and secondary woods of these pieces indicate that they were made in New York rather than in Holland. Moreover, they are stylistically related and probably were made within a very short time of one another. If so, they are a rare survival, graphically demonstrating the decorative harmony between the turnings on tables and chairs alluded to earlier.[30]

Figure 33 Detail of the face-grain plugs that cover the countersunk rivet heads on the top of the table illustrated in fig. 10. (Photo, Gavin Ashworth.)

Attributions to makers and locale are similarly handicapped by the lack of documented examples. Logic dictates that some of these tables came from New York City shops, particularly those made of mahogany and black walnut, woods that had to be imported from the South. The tables made of these expensive woods appear to be the work of several different shops. Those illustrated in figures 15 and 20 and those in 18 and 19 represent the work of two different New York City shops because of their closely related turnings and because of the sophisticated rule joints on the former pair and the original use of oak pegs for the mortise-and-tenon joints on the latter pair. It is also conceivable that the Van Cortlandt family table (fig. 2) represents an earlier generation of the shop tradition that spawned the Johnson table (fig. 15).

New York City furniture tradesmen in the late-seventeenth and early eighteenth centuries had northern European and English names. Joiners (the tradesmen responsible for these tables) who were active between 1695 and 1727 included John Le Chevalier, Edward Hunt, Robert and Peter White, Edward Burling, Joshua Delaplaine, James and Daniel Gautier, John Kinder, Joseph Kingston, Thomas Grigg, Andrew Brested, Thomas and Jonathan Gleaves, Joseph Diviat, John Sibley, and Richard Berry. The account books of Joshua Delaplaine reveal that he made tables throughout his career (fl. 1718–ca. 1771). In a series of six separate transactions between 1721 and 1727, Delaplaine made tables ranging in value from 15s. to £1.11.0 in exchange for tools, hardware, fabrics, and other sundries that he acquired from Edward Burling, a Quaker joiner who became a freeman in 1683 and probably worked until his death in 1753. Burling undoubtedly resold the tables, all of which were probably made in the early baroque style. In 1753 Delaplaine made "a mahogany Dining table 5 foot 3 In. bed, 8 legs, 2 draws" for Elias Desbrosses and charged him £8.10.0. This table, on the other hand, could have resembled the relatively late Johnson table (fig. 15) or the eight-legged table shown in figure 31, or it could even have had modish new cabriole legs with ball-and-claw feet. Like Burling, Delaplaine was a Quaker. He took at least one Quaker apprentice (his first), Francis Warne. His business relationships with Friends extended well beyond New York, for he entered into a sales arrangement for two desks and a tea table with Newport cabinetmaker Christopher Townsend in 1745. Little attention has been given to the Quaker strain in New York furniture, but there is something about the precision and obsessive attention to detail in features like the barrel-shaped rule joint and the mitred top back corners of the drawers in the Johnson table and other eighteenth-century New York City case furniture that, though having no direct relationship to the furniture of Newport Quakers, is reminiscent of the quality and level of refinement apparent in John Townsend's labeled work. Burling, Delaplaine, and the many apprentices they trained could have been responsible for high-quality New York City furniture of this sort, and they were tradesmen worthy of greater scrutiny than that applied in this study.[31]

If the Johnson table possibly represents an Anglo-Quaker strain, the tables with draw-bar leaf supports, especially the walnut and red gum examples illustrated in figures 11 and 12, are more indicative of a northern European tradition. The walnut table is almost certainly city made, and the other table, although made of red gum, probably qualifies for the same distinction. The Delaplaine account books show that "bilsted" or red gum was a common commodity in New York City. What really sets the red gum table apart as the mature product of a talented urban craftsman are its well planned and excellently proportioned legs, which taper slightly in thickness from the bottom to the top (fig. 13).

Beginning around 1700, the draw-bar version of the early baroque oval table with falling leaves found expression in the Kingston area (Ulster County) of the Hudson River Valley—the only locale that has yielded enough related tables with histories to allow the identification of a distinct

Figure 34 Detail of the drawer from the table illustrated in fig. 10. (Photo, Gavin Ashworth.)

school outside of New York City. Of the eight tables attributed to this area, six have turnings derived from the arm supports of Boston and New York City carved-top leather chairs of the late 1690s and early 1700s (figs. 4, 10, 14) and the other two have cone-like, stubby columns at the top—details characteristic of the Ulster County school. One of the tables with twisted legs and a tradition of ownership in the Elmendorf family of Hurley (just outside of Kingston) could also be locally made given its history and the presence of these same short, tapered columns at the top of its rather horsey-looking, single-twist legs.[32]

The dominant shop tradition for the Ulster County region centered at Kingston and was presided over for generations by the Beekman and Elting families, beginning with Jan Elting (1632–1729) in 1672 and continuing into the nineteenth century with Thomas Beekman (1761–1814). The Elting-Beekman joiners made *kasten* of a consistent design for their principally Dutch and Huguenot customers from at least 1700 until after the Revolution, and evidence suggests they produced early baroque oval tables with falling leaves as well. The ogee moldings on the rails and stretchers of the tables match those used in the central sections of the massive *kast* cornices, and on the draw-bar table illustrated in figure 10, the end drawers are constructed (except for the lack of channeled sides) like those in the *kasten* (fig. 34).[33]

The working dates of the Elting-Beekman shop (fl. ca. 1672–1814) and the persistence of early baroque designs in Ulster County suggest that some of these eight tables may be earlier than others. Of the three tables included in this article (figs. 4, 10, 14), only the one illustrated in figure 14 has rule joints, and it appears to be the latest. This table also differs from the other two in having rails and stretchers with edge beading similar to the quirk and bead moldings found on late-eighteenth-century interior woodwork rather than ogee moldings. Its large baluster turnings are slightly drawn out at the neck and look a little flacid in comparison to those on the other two tables (figs. 4, 10). Aspect alone suggests that the table shown in figure 4 is the earliest. The legs are stouter (measuring 2 3/4" square), the baluster is full and strongly compressed, and the reel element is slightly taller than on either of the other Ulster County tables. In the end, however, it probably matters little which table predates the other. What these tables gloriously represent is a taste for bold, early baroque design, nurtured by a conservative, non-Anglo society throughout a century when many other New Yorkers successively embraced the late baroque, rococo, and early neoclassical styles. The table illustrated in figure 10 probably dates to the mid 1700s and is a wonderfully appealing object expressive of the culture that produced it. This object can stand on its own aesthetic merits regardless of the date it was made.

New York early baroque furniture has its admirers, many of whom believe that it is bolder in outline and more vigorous and diverse in its turned ornament than contemporary New England work. The early baroque New York oval tables with falling leaves examined here will strengthen this conviction for some and might even win a few converts.

More importantly, however, they provide, in the absence of written documents, the only record of the form's development in New York. Tables of purely English design with turned and flat gates reveal that some New Yorkers looked to England and Boston for the latest furniture forms and fashions. These New Yorkers would at first have been primarily of English extraction, or were non-Anglos who stood to gain from outward displays of allegiance to their new rulers. Conversely, the tables with draw bars suggest that there was a significant segment of New York society intrigued by English fashion but still reluctant to abandon completely their traditional European furniture forms and design aesthetic. The draw-bar table probably fell out of favor in New York City by 1740 as English culture became dominant, but it remained popular among the conservative, non-Anglo population of Ulster County, where it fell comfortably into the rhythm of rural life until the time of the Revolution. This is what places the form squarely in the canon of objects described as New York Dutch material culture. Included in this canon is the *kast*, which, it can be argued, is quintessentially Dutch. The draw-bar table, on the other hand, is not. Instead it is a wonderful hybrid that physically manifests Anglo-Dutch cultural blending in early colonial New York.

ACKNOWLEDGMENTS I would like to thank the following individuals for their kind assistance in the preparation of this article: Gavin Ashworth, Luke Beckerdite, Frank Cowan, Constance and Dudley Godfrey, Roger Gonzalez, Rich Goring, Tammis Groft, John Hays, Bill Hosley, Tom Hughes, Kate Johnson, Mel Johnson, Leslie Stratton-Le Fevre, Bill Lohrman, Johanna McBrien, Alan Miller, Bill Orser, Jonathan Prown, Frances Safford, Bob Slater, Robert Trent, Anne and Fred Vogel, Deborah Waters, Jack and Mary Ellen Whistance, and Martin Wunsch.

1. David L. Barquist, *American Tables and Looking Glasses in the Mabel Brady Garvan and Other Collections at Yale University* (New Haven, Conn.: Yale University Art Gallery, 1992), p. 118.

2. Victor Chinnery, *Oak Furniture: The British Tradition* (Suffolk, Eng.: Antique Collectors' Club, 1979), pp. 301–3.

3. Barquist, *American Tables and Looking Glasses*, p. 118. Gerald W. R. Ward, "The Intersections of Life, Tables and Their Social Role," in Barquist, *American Tables and Looking Glasses,* pp. 21–24. For the importance of the oval shape in baroque architecture and decoration, see Phillip M. Johnston, "The William and Mary Style in America," in Reinier Baarsen et al., *Courts and Colonies, The William and Mary Style in Holland, England, and America* (New York: Cooper-Hewitt Museum, 1988), pp. 72–74.

4. Barquist, *American Tables and Looking Glasses*, p. 118, states that oval tables with falling leaves "can usually be distinguished from smaller tables with stationary oval tops by their value and the presence of large sets of chairs used with them."

5. Two heavy rectangular tables, one with a trestle base and the other with a stretcher base, both possibly from New York, are illustrated in Dean F. Failey, *Long Island is My Nation, the Decorative Arts and Craftsmen, 1640–1830* (Setauket, N.Y.: Society for the Preservation of Long Island Antiquities, 1976), p. 27. The Dutch draw table in figure 1 and a second one illustrated in "In the Museums," *Antiques* 71, no. 1 (January 1957): 68, are the only two known examples of this form believed to have been made or used in New York. Michael Kammen, *Colonial New York* (Millwood, N.Y.: KTO Press, 1978), pp. 73–74, 91. Kammen cites population figures as follows: in 1665, 1,470 persons (of 254 listed for taxation, only 16 had English surnames); by 1676, the city had grown to more than 2,200 persons (of 302 taxables, 115 seem to have been English).

6. Cornelis Steenwyck Inventory, July 29, 1686, New York State Court of Appeals, New York State Archives, Cultural Education Center, Albany. This collection has been microfilmed

and is abstracted in Kenneth Scott and James A. Owre, *Genealogical Data from Inventories of New York Estates 1666–1825* (New York: New York Genealogical and Biographical Society, 1970). The Phillipse family table is at the Old Dutch Church, North Tarrytown, New York, where it is still in use by the congregation. The January 7, 1730, will of Catherine Phillipse (1652–1730) of New York City reads: "I give and bequeath to my Son in Law Adolph Phillipse Esq. & to his heirs for Ever . . . a Long table In Trust to and for the Congregation of the Dutch Church Erected at Phillipseburgh by my late Husband Frederick Phillipse decd" (typescript copy, files of the Old Dutch Church). For the Schuyler inventory, see Ruth Piwonka, "New York Colonial Inventories: Dutch Interiors as a Measure of Cultural Change," in Roderic H. Blackburn and Nancy A. Kelly, eds., *New World Dutch Studies: Dutch Arts and Culture in Colonial America 1609–1776* (Albany, N.Y.: Albany Institute of History and Art, 1987), p. 73. Piwonka gives the best and most succinct summary of the problems and opportunities presented by seventeenth- and eighteenth-century New York estate inventories, as well as a sampling of the few room-by-room ones available.

7. Cited in Roderic H. Blackburn and Ruth Piwonka, *Remembrance of Patria: Dutch Arts and Culture in Colonial America, 1609–1776* (Albany, N.Y.: Albany Institute of History and Art, 1988), p. 186.

8. Chinnery, *Oak Furniture: The British Tradition*, p. 301, figs. 3: 202, 3: 211, 3: 213. The supporting rails on draw tables also run in tracks but differ from lopers in that they are fixed to the undersides of the leaves and taper in length (the thinnest part of the taper toward the ends of the table, the thickest toward the center). This taper causes the leaves to rise to the height of the fixed center section of the top as they are drawn out from under it.

9. Something analogous to this occurs in late-seventeenth- and early-eighteenth-century New York tankards, which are an English form but have cut-card banding and meander ornaments that are more typically Dutch grafted onto them. For a discussion of the New York tankard as an Anglo-Dutch hybrid, see Gerald W. R. Ward, "The Dutch and English Traditions in American Silver," in Francis J. Puig and Michael Conforti, eds., *The American Craftsman and the European Tradition, 1620–1820* (Hanover, N.H.: Minneapolis Institute of Arts, 1989), p. 139. The ovolo-and-bead molding and the *kasten* on which it is found are illustrated and discussed in Peter M. Kenny, Frances Gruber Safford, and Gilbert T. Vincent, *American Kasten: The Dutch-Style Cupboards of New York and New Jersey, 1650–1800* (New York: Metropolitan Museum of Art, 1991), pp. 12, 36–43.

10. A table with apron construction similar to the example shown in figure 11, but that appears to be the work of a different shop, is illustrated in Blackburn and Piwonka, *Remembrance of Patria*, p. 174. The remaining two tables with twisted legs, one with a history of ownership in the Elmendorf family of Hurley in Ulster County, New York, and the other originally owned in the Van Bergen, Bronck, or Houghtaling families of Greene County, New York, have half-inch-thick rectangular plaques nailed on the corners that obscure the apron joints. These appear to be an original treatment, perhaps intended to give the tables a stronger, more joinerly appearance. The Elmendorf table is illustrated in *Antiques* 83, no. 6 (August 1963): 165, where the applied corner plaque is barely visible behind one of the table leaves. This table is still in the possession of descendants of its original owner, as is the one with the Greene County history that has never been illustrated. These two tables probably come from the same shop.

11. Robert Trent suggests that broad central frames on oval tables with falling leaves may be an early feature that points to the genesis of the form when leaves were attached to massive rectangular tables of traditional style. For Trent's comments, see *American Furniture with Related Decorative Arts, 1630–1830: The Milwaukee Art Museum and The Layton Art Collection* (New York: Hudson Hills Press, 1991), pp. 83–84. A square table with plain stretchers is also illustrated in the Milwaukee catalogue on p. 41. (Several others survive, including examples in the Nutting collection at the Wadsworth Atheneum, the Metropolitan Museum of Art, and the Historical Society of Old Newbury, Newburyport, Massachusetts.) In the Milwaukee catalogue, Trent argues that the Milwaukee and the Metropolitan Museum square tables, both being made of maple, may date as late as 1710. The possibility has yet to be considered that any of these could have been made in New York.

12. The Van Cortlandt family table and the Sir William Johnson table are illustrated and discussed in Esther Singleton, *The Furniture of Our Forefathers* (New York: Doubleday, Page and Company, 1900), pp. 256–60. The Johnson table is also in Luke Vincent Lockwood, *Colonial Furniture in America*, 2 vols. (2d ed., New York: Charles Scribner's Sons, 1921), 2:174–75. Wallace Nutting, *Wallace Nutting General Catalog, Supreme Edition* (1930; reprint, Exton, Pa.:

Schiffer Limited, 1977) p. 104. The table at the Monmouth County Historical Association, an exceptionally small example, is illustrated in *Antiques* 118, no. 1 (January 1980): 180.

13. Lockwood, *Colonial Furniture in America*, 2:179–80, Wallace Nutting, *Furniture Treasury* (Framingham, Mass.: Old America Company, 1928), nos. 942, 943. For additional illustrations of tables with flat gates, see Norman E. Rice, *New York Furniture Before 1840* (Albany, N.Y.: Albany Institute of History and Art, 1962), p. 17; Robert Bishop, *American Furniture 1620–1720* (Dearborn, Mich.: Edison Institute, 1975), p. 10; Charles T. Lyle and Philip D. Zimmerman, "Furniture of the Monmouth County Historical Association," *Antiques* 118, no. 1 (January 1980): 186; Charles T. Lyle, "Buildings of the Monmouth County Historical Association," *Antiques* 118, no. 1 (January 1980): 184 (the four-legged table with flat gates shown here is now in a private collection); and Failey, *Long Island is My Nation*, p. 28. A few trestle-base tables with turned gate legs and low flat stretchers are known. One that was owned by Miss C. M. Travers of New York is illustrated in Lockwood, *Colonial Furniture in America*, 2:179. Another closely related example attributed to New York is at Winterthur (acc. 58.527). A "flat gate" with a trestle base said to have descended in some Norwalk, Connecticut, families was sold at Sotheby's, *Fine American Furniture, Folk Art, Folk Paintings and Silver*, June 26, 1986, sale no. 5473, lot 112.

14. Piwonka, "New York Colonial Inventories," pp. 74–76. Like Cornelis Steenwyck, Van Cortlandt appears to have preferred not to use an oval table with falling leaves in her front parlor or best room. The large oak table in this room may have been a considerably older one with an expandable draw top since there were eighteen "chairs" and one "elbo cain chair" in the room. The inventory is salted with references to "old" objects, the most interesting one being the "old Holland case" in the chamber over the back parlor. Apparently, Gertruy Van Cortlandt maintained a "Dutch" household to the very end. For an informative analysis and reconstruction of Dutch townhouses in The Netherlands and colonial New York based on period documents, see Henk J. Zantkuyl, "The Netherlands Town House: How and Why It Works," in Blackburn and Kelly, eds., *New World Dutch Studies*, pp. 143–60.

15. Chinnery, *Oak Furniture: The British Tradition*, pp. 306–7.

16. Benno M. Forman, *American Seating Furniture 1630–1730* (New York: W. W. Norton & Company, 1988), p. 292.

17. A few New York oval tables with falling leaves exist with unique turnings, and more undoubtedly will surface in the future. The purpose of organizing the turning patterns into visually cohesive groups is to aid the reader in making comparisons and in discerning a distinct early baroque New York turning style.

18. Forman, *American Seating Furniture*, p. 290. Forman was the first to identify fat, full rings as a characteristic of New York early baroque turning on high-back leather chairs. The extra turned foot under the inner pivot leg of the auxiliary leg support, a typical New England feature, is seldom used.

19. Robert F. Trent, "17th-Century Upholstery in Massachussetts," in Edward S. Cooke, Jr., ed., *Upholstery in America & Europe from the Seventeenth Century to World War I* (New York: W.W. Norton & Company, 1987), p. 44, fig. 22. The Philadelphia board-seated chairs and the Philadelphia or New York leather chair are illustrated in Forman, *American Seating Furniture*, pp. 220–23. The two tables of possible New England origin are illustrated in Singleton, *The Furniture of Our Forefathers*, 1:200; and in Frances Clary Morse, *Furniture of the Olden Time* (New York: MacMillan Company, 1902), p. 220. The southern table is illustrated in *Antiques* 61, no. 1 (January 1952): 59. For the New York high chests, see Philip M. Johnston, "The William and Mary Style in America," in *Courts and Colonies*, p. 64; John T. Kirk, *American Furniture and the British Tradition* (New York: Alfred A. Knopf, 1982), p. 190; and Joseph Downs and Ruth Ralston, *A Loan Exhibition of New York State Furniture* (New York: Metropolitan Museum of Art, 1934), no. 34. The dressing table is in a private collection. The entire process from layout to finishing for both single- and double-twisted legs is clearly explained in "Twist Turning, Traditional Method Combines Lathe and Carving," *Fine Woodworking* 33 (March/April 1982): 92–95. For the continental European background of the single twist, see Forman, *American Seating Furniture*, p. 220; and Jan Veenendaal, *Furniture from Indonesia, Sri Lanka and India During the Dutch Period*, trans. by R. Robson-McKillop (Delft: Volkenkundig Museum Nusantara, ca. 1985), p. 31.

20. For coastal South Carolina furniture with stacked baluster turnings, see E. Milby Burton, *Charleston Furniture, 1700–1825* (Charleston: Charleston Museum, 1955), fig. 76 (a 1710–1720 stretcher table from Limrick plantation); and MESDA research file S-1273 (a 1710–1725 couch). The author thanks Luke Beckerdite for these references. The only

table with turned gate legs that has stacked balusters is the Van Cortlandt family table (fig. 2). Two draw-bar tables with this turning are known: figure 9 and a table (private collection) once owned by the Knickerbacker family (phone conversation with Roderick Blackburn, January 1992).

21. For an armchair attributed to New York with the same turning under the arm, see Forman, *American Seating Furniture*, p. 288.

22. The Maine tables are illustrated and discussed in Brock Jobe and Myrna Kaye, *New England Furniture: The Colonial Era* (Boston: Houghton Mifflin Company, 1984), pp. 270–71.

23. The trestle-base tables with this leg turning include one that descended in the Butler and Chichester families of Norwalk, Connecticut (Sotheby's *Fine American Furniture, Folk Art, Folk Paintings and Silver*, sale no. 5473, lot 112) and another advertised by Fred J. Johnston in *Maine Antiques Digest*, August 1990. One of the walnut tables with turned gate legs was sold at Sotheby's *American Heritage Auction of Americana*, January 30, 1982, sale no. 4785Y, lot no. 783 and subsequently offered for sale by John Walton, Inc., in *Maine Antiques Digest*, May 1983. The other is at the Van Cortlandt Mansion in Van Cortlandt Park, New York. Details of turned staircase balusters and a table leg from South Scituate and Marshfield, Massachusetts, are illustrated in Robert Blair St. George, *The Wrought Covenant* (Brockton, Mass.: Brockton Art Center/Fuller Memorial, 1979), pp. 41–42. For the Hempstead, Long Island, table, see Failey, *Long Island is My Nation*, p. 30.

24. The leather armchair is illustrated in Forman, *American Seating Furniture*, p. 290. For the trestle-base table related to the Winterthur example, see Lockwood, *Colonial Furniture in America*, 2:179. For the Museum of Fine Arts, Boston, armchair and a discussion of opposed ogee baluster arm supports in New York leather chairs, see Forman, *American Seating Furniture*, pp. 289–90. The fourth New York trestle-base table with opposed baluster turnings is in the collection of the Monmouth County Historical Association in Freehold, New Jersey, and on display at Marlpit Hall in Middletown. This table also has a full fat ring as a linking device between the balusters.

25. In addition to the trestle-base table with the elongated balusters illustrated here (fig. 24), other examples are illustrated in Lyle and Zimmerman, "Furniture of the Monmouth County Historical Association," p. 186; and in a Joseph Sprain advertisement in *Antiques* 106, no. 2 (August 1974): 161. The two classic "gate-legs" are illustrated in Thomas Smith Hopkins and Walter Scott Cox, *Colonial Furniture of West New Jersey* (Haddonfield, N.J.: Historical Society of Haddonfield, 1936), pp. 32–33 (it's possible that it is a Philadelphia table), and in Christie's *Important American Furniture, Silver and Decorative Arts,* June 2, 1983, sale no. 5370, lot 366. A fifth "flat gate" with four legs and low plain board stretchers is illustrated in situ in the Allen house, Shrewsbury, New Jersey, in Lyle, "Buildings of the Monmouth County Historical Society," p. 184. The table with draw-bar supports was owned by Roger Gonzalez and Frank Cowan in 1994 as were two additional flat-gate tables with stretchers and elongated-baluster legs.

26. An English pad-foot dining table with falling leaves and additional half-rounds glued beneath the rule joints is shown in John T. Kirk, *American Furniture and the British Tradition to 1830*, p. 324. The drawer's softly rounded top edges and mitered back corner joints are details that also appear on a New York City mahogany chest of drawers in the rococo style at the Brooklyn Museum (acc. 55.225) and on a fine New York City mahogany desk-and-bookcase in the same style at Winterthur, illustrated in Joseph Downs, *American Furniture, Queen Anne and Chippendale Periods* (New York: MacMillan Company, 1952), p. 224. I am grateful to Wade Lawrence for information on the Brooklyn Museum and Winterthur case furniture. For information on Sir William Johnson and his homes, see Kammen, *Colonial New York*, pp. 308–15, and Dumas Malone, ed., *Dictionary of American Biography*, 11 vols. (New York: Charles Scribner's Sons, 1961), 5:124–28.

27. Susan Mackiewicz, "Woodworking Traditions in Newbury Massachussetts, 1635–1745," M.A. thesis, University of Delaware, 1981. J. Stewart Johnson, "New York Cabinetmaking Prior to the Revolution," M.A. thesis, University of Delaware, 1964, p. 87. The full table of prices is given in Irving W. Lyon, *The Colonial Furniture of New England* (Boston and New York: Houghton Mifflin Co., 1891), pp. 265–66.

28. Museum of the City of New York, file for acc. 78.106.

29. The accounts between Joshua Delaplaine and Edward Burling list the purchase of numerous tools and hardware, including entries in 1730 and 1738 for dozens of "dovetails." For the Delaplaine and Burling accounts, see Johnson, "New York Cabinetmaking Prior to the Revolution," appendix F.

30. E. M. Ruttenber, *Catalogue of Manuscripts and Relics in Washington's Head-Quarters, New Burgh, N.Y., With Historical Sketch* (Newburgh, N.Y.: E. M. Ruttenber & Son, 1882), no. 616. The 1882 catalogue was based on an 1872 inventory of the contents of the house. A catalogue dated 1858, in the archives of Washington's Headquarters, lists the chairs but not the table. The author thanks Tom Hughes and Mel Johnson of Washington's Headquarters for these references. Forman, *American Seating Furniture*, p. 311. Forman dates Boston carved-top leather chairs no later than 1723 based on the account books and letters of Boston upholsterer Thomas Fitch. The gift of the Dutch draw table (fig. 1) to the Dutch Reformed Church after it was used for a couple of generations by the Phillipse family is a pattern that may also hold true for the Verplanck table and chairs.

31. The names of these joiners are taken from *The Burghers of New Amsterdam and the Freemen of New York 1675–1866*, in *Collections of the New-York Historical Society for the Year 1885* (New York: New-York Historical Society, 1886); and *Indentures of Apprentices 1718–1727*, in *Collections of the New-York Historical Society for the Year 1909* (New York: New-York Historical Society, 1910). Johnson, "New York Cabinetmaking Prior to the Revolution," appendices E–L and pp. 17–19.

32. In addition to the three Ulster County tables illustrated here, there are also examples with the same turning at the Chipstone Foundation in Milwaukee, Winterthur Museum (acc. 58.1028), and Senate House State Historic Site in Kingston, New York (acc. SH 1975.321). The Winterthur table reportedly descended in the Depuy-Schoonmaker family of Stone Ridge, Ulster County (phone conversation with Bob Slater of Fred J. Johnston Antiques [the firm that sold the table to H. F. du Pont], May 1989). The turnings on the sixth table (private collection, Kingston, N.Y.) feature well-defined reels surmounted by elongated balusters with short tapered columns above. This table was once the property of artist and designer Ivar Evers of New Paltz, and, like the table shown in figure 10, its short tapered columns are slightly convex, a reference to classically correct entasis. The seventh table has turnings comprised of a series of three compressed balusters surmounted by straight-sided, short tapered columns. This table, which was sold at the Copake Country Auction in 1986 (*Antiques and the Arts Weekly*, August 15, 1986), does not have a local Ulster County history, but its turnings are nearly identical to those on a desk-on-frame from the Kingston area illustrated in Blackburn and Piwonka, *Remembrance of Patria,* p. 178. The Elmendorf family table with twisted legs is illustrated in *Antiques* 83, no. 6 (August 1963): 165.

33. For more on the Elting-Beekman group of makers, see Kenny, Safford, and Vincent, *American Kasten*, pp. 23–26, 54–59.

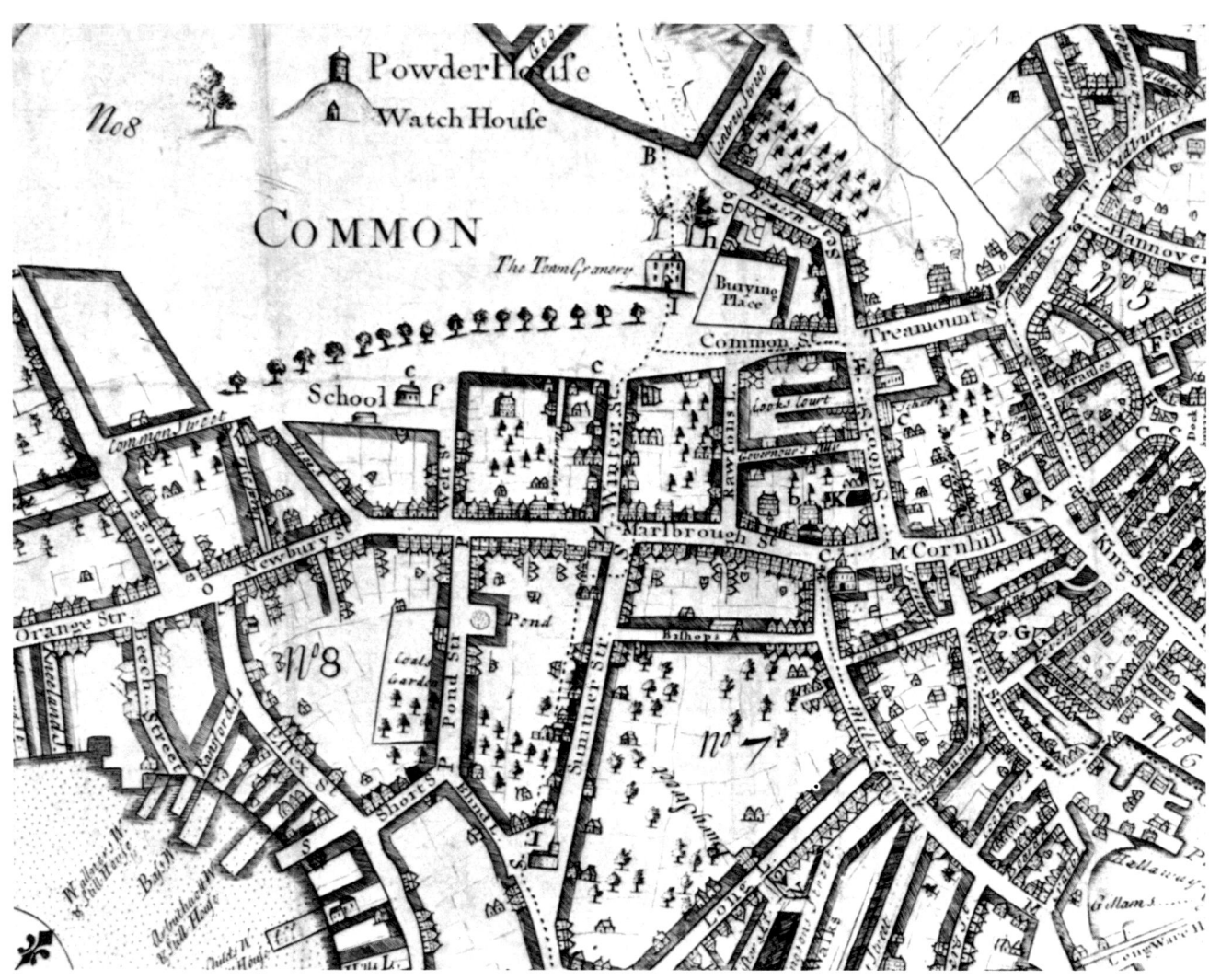

Figure 1 Detail of *A New Plan of ye Great Town of BOSTON in New England in AMERICA With the many Additional Buildings &. New Streets to the Year 1733*. Etching and engraving. 16 13/16" × 23". Originally drawn by John Bonner and engraved by Francis Deming, this map was revised by William Price and Thomas Johnston in 1733. Berger's residence was beneath Coal's Garden on the northwest corner of Pond and Short streets and the Huguenot Church (marked K) on School Street. (Courtesy, John Carter Brown Library, Brown University.)

Robert A. Leath

Jean Berger's Design Book: Huguenot Tradesmen and the Dissemination of French Baroque Style

▼ ART AND furniture historians traditionally have focused on the role of Huguenot-born court artisans, such as Daniel Marot (1663–1752), as the primary disseminators of French baroque style. But nearly a quarter million Protestants fled France after Louis XIV's revocation of the Edict of Nantes in 1685, and many of these refugees also were highly skilled tradesmen familiar with the court style that emanated from Versailles during Louis XIV's reign. Highly conversant in the baroque decorative vocabulary, such men were, because of their relocation, collectively more responsible than court artisans for the diffusion of French baroque style. The recently discovered design book of Jean Berger (fl. ca. 1718–1732), a Boston Huguenot painter-stainer, presents new evidence for the influence of Huguenot tradesmen among the middle classes in both Europe and colonial America.[1]

The painter-stainers of Berger's time were versatile artisans whose skills included ornamental painting, graining, marbleizing, gilding, japanning, and varnishing. The full extent of Berger's work may never be determined, but presumably he decorated buildings, ships, carriages, furniture, and a broad range of household objects.

Jean Berger probably was a member of the Berger (Bergier, Barger, Bargier) family that settled in Boston about 1685. The progenitor of this family, known only as "M. le Sr. Berger," was a merchant from La Rochelle who enjoyed the patronage of Jean Baptiste Colbert (1619–1683), France's minister of finance prior to the edict's revocation. Appointed as the king's lieutenant for the French colony of Acadia (now Nova Scotia) in 1684, Berger earned the ire of Quebec's Catholic hierarchy, who opposed placing "a most obstinate Huguenot" so close to the Protestant English colonies. In 1685, a group of Huguenots who arrived in Boston from La Rochelle via Casco, Maine, included one Philip Barger. Barger was subsequently a mariner and part owner of the brigantine, *Neptune*, which engaged in Boston's Carribean trade. At his death in 1703, Philip was survived by his widow Margaret and three children: Elizabeth (b. 1686), John (1688–1708), and Philip (1690–1721).[2] Owing to the scarcity of records for Boston Huguenots, the precise relationship between the Philip Barger family and Jean Berger remains unclear.

The design book and a few court cases involving Berger represent virtually everything known about his life and work. Written in both English and French, a sketchy family register at the back of the book records the birth of Berger's wife, Rachel, on October 16, 1686, and the death of his father-in-law on June 29, 1730. It also reveals that Berger had at least four children and was a member of Boston's sizable Huguenot community.[3] His approximate working dates can be extrapolated from the date 1718 on the frontis of the book, Berger's last known court appearance in 1732, and Rachel's appearance in court as a widow in 1736. Court records also indicate that Berger rented a house on the northwest corner of Pond and Short streets from Mary White, and that he leased a portion of the house to bookbinder Joseph Wheeler (fig. 1).

Ironically, the most important information regarding Jean Berger's career comes from the circumstances surrounding a personal tragedy. On December 17, 1719, a Frenchman named John Harristy attacked Berger along the docks of Boston harbor. Berger subsequently sued, charging Harristy "with force & Arms an Assault did make & him did beat, wound, & evilly intreat so that of his life it was dispaired." The court convicted Harristy and ordered him to pay damages totaling £19.3 plus Berger's court costs. The defendant then appealed his conviction.[4]

The evidence presented in Harristy's appeal provides a picture of the tradesmen among whom Berger lived and worked. Witnesses summoned to testify included physician Laurence Delhonde, merchant Temple Nelson, pewterer Thomas Smith (1678–1742), and "Felix Powell, who lives with Cooper the Painter." Powell's deposition described the assault:

> Felix Powell, Aged about 21 years upon his Oath being Sworne declares that Last Thursday Evening being ordered by his Master John Cooper painter to attend John Bergie, a French Painter about a peice of Painting work on board a Vessell at the Dock, but going on board met the said Bergie come from said Vessell with his Box of Paint and Brushes and he told me he would not work any Longer that night, at which time John Harristy a French man being the Same Person now present as a Defendant came up with him the said Bergie and Spoke to Each other in French, which the Deponant did not understand, and immediately the said Harristy fell upon the said Berger and struck him Severell Blows with a Stick he then had in his hand, and then in English threatened him that he would be up with him. The Plaintiff, after the Defendant had struck him, bid me take notice how he had abused him and so they parted.[5]

Delhonde stated that he had treated Berger's head wounds twice daily for over a month, using "Lotens, Imbrocations, fomentations, Ointments & Plaisters," and presented a list of medical expenses totaling £5.16.6. The court upheld Harristy's conviction, fined him an additional 20s. for the government, and released him on recognizance for good behavior for a period of one year. Rigger John Jarrard and chairmaker Samuel Mattocks, Jr., (b. 1678) provided sureties for Harristy in the amount of £25 each during the probationary period.[6]

Powell's master probably was New England artist J. Cooper, whom art historians have speculated was English-born artist John Cooper (ca. 1695–1754), son of London art dealer and print publisher Edward Cooper (ca. 1660–1725). Many of his paintings are signed "J. Cooper" or initialed and dated between 1714 and 1718 (fig. 2). Assuming these two painters are the same man, Berger's suit provides the first documentary evidence of John Cooper's presence in the colonies from 1718 to 1721.[7]

As a French-speaking artisan in a primarily English-speaking community,

Figure 2 *Lady with Jewels*, inscribed "J. Cooper 1714," possibly Boston. Oil on canvas. 14" × 12". (Courtesy, Peabody Essex Museum.)

Berger possibly had difficulty securing private patronage. Powell's deposition and suits involving Berger, Cooper, and other Boston tradesmen suggest that he frequently worked as a subcontractor. In 1721, Berger sued Cooper and his partner, apothecary Thomas Creese, Jr., for failing to honor a £5 note. The court ruled against Cooper and Creese and ordered them to pay the balance due on the note, plus Berger's legal expenses. Berger initiated another suit against Cooper later that year, but the artist failed to appear before the court. This court record is the last reference to Cooper in Boston, and it coincides with the career of the English-born artist who assumed his father's print-selling business in London around 1725.[8]

Creese's brother-in-law was William Price (d. 1771), a prominent Boston cabinetmaker, art dealer, and print publisher. Price advertised that he sold a variety of London-made prints and maps, oil paintings in carved and gilt frames, varnish, and "Jappan Work, viz. Chest of Drawers, Corner Cupboards, Large & Small Tea Tables, &c. done after the best manner by one late from London." Price in turn maintained a close business relationship with Thomas Johnston (1707–1767), who, in 1732, had trade cards advertising "Japaning, Gilding, Painting, Varnishing" at his shop on Ann Street.[9]

The chinoiserie drawings in Berger's design book identify him as one of Boston's earliest japanners, along with Nehemiah Partridge (d. ca. 1726) and Joshua Roberts (d. 1719). Furniture historians have identified two distinct schools of early Boston japanning. One includes tradesman Robert Davis (d. 1739) and his son-in-law, William Randle. Their work consists of large and loosely arranged chinoiserie motifs painted against a black ground with little attention to their relationship in any greater design. The other school centers around Thomas Johnston, Thomas Johnston, Jr. (1731–ca. 1776), and Daniel Rea (active 1767–1800), who had a "more integrated and ornate style." Their work typically features elaborately drawn chinoiserie scenes on both black and tortoiseshell backgrounds and baroque elements, such as winged cherubs' heads, fluted columns, and floral designs. Stylistically, Berger's drawings are closer to the japanning attributed to Johnston and the tradesmen in his sphere.[10]

At first glance, the drawings in Berger's book appear to be generally similar to those in John Stalker and George Parker's *Treatise of Japanning and Varnishing* (1688) (figs. 3 and 4) and Johan Nieuhof's *Atlas Chinensis* (1665), two standard pattern books for late-seventeenth- and eighteenth-century chinoiserie designs. But not one image is a direct copy from either work. Berger's designs are either original or borrowed from an unknown source, and they attest to the role of Huguenot artisans as transmitters of the fashion for chinoiserie. Marot used chinoiserie designs for porcelain rooms with lacquer paneling in two of his earliest commissions as a refugee—Binnenhof, The Hague (1685), and the castle at Honselaarsdijk (1686)—and later at Hampton Court and Kensington Palace (fig. 5).[11]

The watercolors and sketches on Berger's first six pages are reminiscent of those by French artists, Jean Cotelle (1607–1676), Jean Le Pautre (1617–1682), Paul Androuet Ducerceau (ca. 1630–1713), and Jean Berain

Figure 3 Designs for birds and insects illustrated on pl. 11 of John Stalker and George Parker's, *A Treatise of Japanning and Varnishing* (Oxford, 1688). (Courtesy, Winterthur Library: Printed Books and Periodical Collection.)

Figure 4 Designs "For Drawers for Cabbinets to be Placed according to yor. fancy" illustrated on pl. 18 of John Stalker and George Parker's, *A Treatise of Japanning and Varnishing* (Oxford, 1688). (Courtesy, Winterthur Library.)

(1639–1711), whose designs for ornament were published in the late seventeenth century (fig. 6). Based on mythology and ancient Roman wall paintings, their work defined the taste for baroque decoration "*a l'antique*" and greatly influenced Marot and other Huguenot emigrés.[12] Berger's first three drawings depict satyrs and nymphs in the French "*arabesque*" style, with Bacchic lions, cupids, and eagles amidst scrolling acanthus. Two of the drawings have cartouches with fleur-de-lis; one is supported by a heavily molded plinth dated 1718, and the other is surmounted by a shield with military trophies. Two intermediate pages present decorative borders with scrolling acanthus and lambrequin strapwork.

Painted decoration on buildings, ships, and furniture produced in early Boston was probably far more prevalent than the surviving evidence suggests. Until its destruction around 1833, the Clark-Frankland house (ca. 1715) had an ornate scheme:

> The flutings and capitals of the pilasters, the dentils of the cornice, the vault and shelves of the buffet, were all heavily guilded.... The peculiar decoration consisted of a series of raised panels filling these compartments, reaching from the surbase to the frieze, eleven in all, each embellished with a romantic landscape painted in oil colors, the four panels opposite the windows being further enriched by the emblazoned escutcheons of the Clarks, the Saltonstalls, and other allied families. Beneath the surbase, the panels, as also those of the door, were covered with arabesques. The twelfth painting was a view of the house upon a horizontal panel over the mantel, and beneath this panel, inscribed in an oval, was the monogram of the builder, W. C. At the base of the gilded and fluted vault of the buffet was a painted dove.

Although only two landscape panels survive from the Clark Frankland house, the interior of the Vernon house (ca. 1708) in Newport, Rhode Island, has several surviving japanned panels depicting Oriental figures and exotic birds and beasts.[13]

Finally, a closer look at the design book speaks directly about the life and work of Jean Berger. The two fluted columns and triangular pediment on the frontis frame the words "*Ses Jean Berger Qui A Fait Ses Ouvrage Dece Livrect A Baston Ce* MDCCXVIII" ("It is Jean Berger who has done this work in this book in Boston 1718"). The iconography provides immediate clues. Atop the pediment are two figures that define his work as an ornamental painter in early America, a male holding the anchor of commerce and a female looking into the mirror of beauty. The English motto "*Dieu est mon Droy*" on a tapestry at the base of the columns proclaims Berger's loyalty to his new sovereign, while the flaming heart pierced by two arrows between his initials in the center of the pediment serves as a reminder of Huguenot religious persecution.

Figure 5 Design for a chimney wall with lacquered panels and porcelain in Daniel Marot's, *Nouvelle chemenées faittes en plusieurs en droits de la Hollande et autres provinces,* Netherlands, ca. 1700. Etching and engraving. Like many of his contemporaries, Marot combined Oriental motifs with European baroque designs. (Courtesy, Cooper-Hewitt Museum, acc. 1988-4-48.)

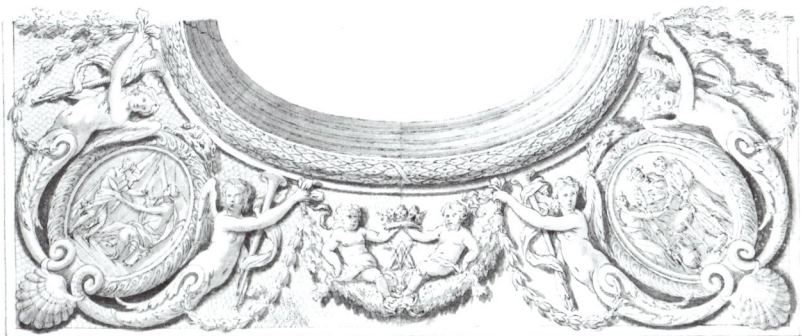

Figure 6 Ceiling design illustrated in Jean Cotelle's *Livres des Ornemens pour Plafonds* (Paris, ca. 1640). (Courtesy, Ashmolean Museum.)

Like Berger, thousands of Huguenot tradesmen fanned out across Europe and America seeking their religious freedom. In their wake, they spread knowledge of French taste and culture, greatly influencing their newfound communities. Jean Berger's design book survives as a remarkable testament to the work of these largely forgotten and unknown craftsmen. But several important questions remain unanswered. Where was Berger born, and when did he die? Where was he trained? What design sources did he use? Who were the other artisans with whom he worked, and how did he impact them? Does any of Jean Berger's work survive? The design book is presented here in its entirety for those interested in pursuing these questions.

153 JEAN BERGER'S DESIGN BOOK

ma fame est née a noële
Le bien heweex jour
Le 16 autobvre 1686

Mon bau pevre trovy est mort
de la picotte le 29 Juin 1730

David Dickson Married To
Mrs Margret Dickson
Sept the 21st 1786

David Dickson Married To
Mrs Margret D—

Mon Jany est venu au monde a baston le 16 septenbre 1722 a 4 heure du matin et a ette batiste par mr mersieu le 23 7bre 1722 Jayette parin madame Dupe marine dieu le benisse eternellem

Et est mor le 16 de may 1730 — 7 an 9 m.

Ma mariee est venu au monde Le 9° Juin 1725 a 10 heure du soir et a ette batiste le 13 madame mary jorin mareune Mr. franſoy max parin

Ma bette est venu au monde le Judy le 11 Janvier 1727 et a ette batise par le Reverant totoeur Cotelar en ma meson le 22 Janvier 1727 que dieu la benisse

Mariee est venu au monde le Lundy 19° may 1729 a menuit et a ette batise le 27 mardy de la grant cote, mr a border parin et la fame m° et la fame du tonneur

David Dickson Married Sept yr 21 1736

My Son David Borne Thursday June
The 16: 1737 and Baptized Sept 7th 1737
Mr Price Minister Capt pooler Chalie
and Mr Pohilip Jones Thuirites Mr Enos

Joseph Born ye 28 Day Augst
Babtizd 20th may 1741
Suertys Chr: Lughy Mr Eastick
Juler wth Wf Marthew Suith

Jos: By in June 1742

Frances Born 24 June at Six in morning 1743

Father of Margaret Berger b. 1686 Berger m. 1718

Frances' mother was Father Jean & Margaret Berger. Father David Dickson

this book from Cousin Kitty to me. Sara Julie Dehon wife of General Frederic Vaughan Abbot, Engineer Corps U.S.A.

Dehon is french & pronounced de Hon

1911 —

This book came to me, among Cousin Matilda & "Kitty" Parkers belongings in Cambridge Mass". where they lived (& died) in their Parents home Mr & Mrs Theodore Dehon Parker.

Frances Dickson, see opposite page, born 24. June at 3 in the morning 1743. she married the "French Immigrant Theodore Dehon in Boston 1759 — died Nov' 1804. Their son (8th child) became 2nd Bishop - Episcopal - of South Carolina Theodore II. D.D. L.L.D.

ACKNOWLEDGMENTS The author thanks Luke Beckerdite, Thomas Savage, and Robert Trent for helping prepare this manuscript and Rick Rhodes for his excellent photography of Jean Berger's design book. I am especially grateful to Anne Rogers Haley whose research greatly illuminated Berger's career.

1. For more on Marot and Huguenot court artisans, see Museum of London, *The Quiet Conquest: The Huguenots 1685–1985* (London: by the museum, 1985); and Reinier Baarsen, Gervase Jackson-Stops, Phillip M. Johnston, and Elaine Evans Dee, *Courts and Colonies; The William and Mary style in Holland, England and America* (Seattle: University of Washington Press for the Cooper-Hewitt Museum and Carnegie Museum of Art, 1988). Thomas Savage and I discovered the design book while researching a group of objects associated with Charleston merchant Nathaniel Russell (1738–1820). The book descended for eight generations in the family of Russell's son-in-law, Bishop Theodore Dehon (1776–1817). Berger was Dehon's great grandfather. The book and other Dehon family artifacts are on loan to Nathaniel Russell House, Historic Charleston Foundation.

2. For more on the Berger family, see Charles W. Baird, *History of the Huguenot Emigration to America*, 2 vols. (Baltimore: Regional Publishing, 1966), 1:143–45 2:210. Massachusetts State Archives, Boston, Commercial Series 1685–1714, vol. 7, pp. 79, 104–5. *A Report of the Record Commissioners Containing Boston Births, Baptisms, Marriages, and Deaths, 1630–1699* (Boston: Rockwell and Churchill City Printers, 1883), pp. 167, 178, 189.

3. Many of the names mentioned in this section are easily identifiable as members of Boston's Huguenot community. "*Mr. mersiee*," who baptized Berger's first child, almost certainly is the Reverend Andrew Le Mercier (d. 1764), rector of Boston's Huguenot church from 1715 until 1748. "*Madame dupe*," named as the child's godmother, probably is the wife of Jean Dupuis, or Dupee (d. 1734), an elder of the French church. "*Mr. fransoy masc*" probably refers to a member of the Mascarene family (Baird, *Huguenot Emigration*, 2:233, 239–45, 250–51). Berger's daughter Margaret married David Dickson on September 31, 1736, and the couple had three children: Frances, David, and Joseph. In 1759, Frances Dickson (1743–1804) married Huguenot perukemaker Theodore Dehon (d. 1796) (Christopher E. Gadsden, *An Essay on the Life of the Right Reverend Theodore Dehon, D.D.* [Charleston, S. C., 1833], pp. 41–44). Elizabeth Given vs. Rachel Berger, August 5, 1732, Suffolk County Supreme Judicial Court (hereinafter SCSJC), Index to Suffolk Files, 1629–1795, no. 32696, Massachusetts State Archives, Boston. Rachel Berger, March 26, 1736, SCSJC, no. 166715. Mary White vs. Jean Berger, November 24, 1726, SCSJC, no. 18926. Jean Berger vs. Joseph Wheeler, January 24, 1728, SCSJC, no. Z1296.

4. Jean Berger vs. John Harristy, undated, Suffolk County Court of Common Pleas (hereinafter SCCCP), Records Book, 1715–1721, p. 11, Massachusetts State Archives, Boston.

5. The witnesses are listed in Jean Berger vs. John Harristy, January 7, 1719/20, SCSJC, no. 163519. Powell's deposition is in Jean Berger vs. John Harristy, undated, SCSJC, no. 26989.

6. Jean Berger vs. John Harristy, March 15, 1720, SCSJC, no. 14839. Jean Berger vs. John Harristy, January 5, 1719/20, SCSJC, no. 13803.

7. Examples of J. Cooper's work are at the Yale University Art Gallery, the Winterthur Museum, the Peabody Essex Museum, the New York Historical Society, the Connecticut Historical Society, and the Wadsworth Athenaeum. For more on Cooper, see George C. Groce, "Who Was J(ohn?) Cooper (b. ca. 1695 – living 1754)," *The Art Quarterly* 18, no. 1 (Spring 1955): 73–82; James Thomas Flexner, *First Flowers of Our Wilderness* (New York: Dover, 1947), pp. 45–46; and Waldron Phoenix Belknap, *American Colonial Painting* (Cambridge, Mass.: Harvard University Press, 1959), pp. 223–25, 319–20.

8. Jean Berger vs. John Cooper and Thomas Creese, Jr., undated, SCCCP, p. 13. Jean Berger vs. John Cooper and Thomas Creese, Jr., March 3 and 7, 1721, SCSJC, no. 15234. John Cooper vs. Jean Berger, September 15, 1721, SCCCP, p. 110. Groce, "Who Was Cooper," pp. 78, 79. Painter Samuel Haley (fl. 1716–1724) sued Berger on September 19, 1722 (SCCCP, p. 422).

9. Sinclair Hitchings, "The Musical Pursuits of William Price and Thomas Johnston," in *Music in Colonial Massachusetts, 1630–1820* (Boston: Colonial Society of Massachusetts, 1985), pp. 84–87, 107. *Boston Gazette*, August 14–21, 1721; May 14–21, 1722; August 27–September 3, 1722; April 4–11, 1726. Sinclair Hitchings, "Thomas Johnston," in *Boston Prints and Printmakers* (Boston: Colonial Society of Massachusetts, 1973), pp. 87, 102, 107. Although there is no documentary evidence conclusively linking Berger with Price and Johnston, his involvement with Cooper and Creese suggests that Berger was part of an interactive circle of painters, japanners,

engravers, print sellers and art dealers associated with early Boston. For example, a portrait of Cooper's father, London art dealer Edward Cooper, was engraved by Peter Pelham (ca. 1697–1751), the mezzotint artist who emigrated to Boston in 1727 (Groce, "Who Was Cooper," p. 78).

10. For more on Boston japanning, see Sinclair Hitchings, "Boston's Colonial Japanners: The Documentary Record", and Dean A. Fales, Jr., "Boston Japanned Furniture," in Walter Muir Whitehill, Brock Jobe, and Jonathan Fairbanks, eds., *Boston Furniture of the Eighteenth Century* (Boston: Colonial Society of Massachusetts, 1974), pp. 49–75. The two early schools of japanning are discussed in Elizabeth Rhodes and Brock Jobe, "Recent Discoveries in Boston Japanned Furniture," *Antiques* 105, no. 5 (May 1974): 1082–91; and Morrison H. Heckscher, Frances Grubber Stafford, and Peter Lawrence Fodera, "Boston Japanned Furniture in the Metropolitan Museum of Art," *Antiques* 129, no. 5 (May 1986): 1046–61.

11. For more on Nieuhoff, see Leslie B. Grigsby, "Johan Nieuhoff's Embassy,"*Antiques* 143, no. 1 (January 1993): 136–43. Baarsen, Jackson-Stops, Johnston, and Dee, *Courts and Colonies*, pp. 15–18, 200–229.

12. Baarsen, Jackson-Stops, Johnston, and Dee, *Courts and Colonies*, pp. 62, 80–85, 95.

13. Baarsen, Jackson-Stops, Johnston, and Dee, *Courts and Colonies,* pp. 62, 175. As quoted in Abbot Lowell Cummings, "Decorative Painting and House Painting in Massachusetts Bay, 1630–1725," in Ian M. G. Quimby, ed., *American Painting to 1776: A Reappraisal*, (Charlottesville, Va.: University Press of Virginia, 1973), pp. 107–8. The surviving panels from the Clark-Frankland house are in the collection of the Society for the Preservation of New England Antiquities, Boston. For more on the Vernon house, see Allen Freeman, "Model of Restraint: Conservationists of Newport's Eighteenth-Century Vernon House," *Historic Preservation* 45, no. 1 (January/February 1993): 26–32.

Figure 1 John Luker, Masonic Master's chair, pillars, and candle stands, Vinton County, Ohio, 1870. (Courtesy, Museum of Our National Heritage; photo, David Bohl.)

Susan Buck

A Masonic Master's Chair Revealed

▼ O F A L L the conservation fields, furniture conservation has benefited the most from the alternative cleaning systems and ultraviolet light cross-section analysis first developed for the treatment of easel paintings.[1] This technology enables us to determine the original appearance of furniture, to interpret more accurately the intentions of the tradesman and patron, and to develop appropriate conservation treatments.

In the fall of 1991, the Society for the Preservation of New England Antiquities Conservation Center began treatment of an unusual suite of Masonic furniture owned by the Museum of Our National Heritage in Lexington, Massachusetts. The suite consists of a very large armchair, two tall pillars, and two candle stands (fig. 1). The armchair bears the signature "Manufact'd by John Luker" painted in gold-colored metallic powders on the front face of the medial stretcher and the name "Houston," also in gold, painted on the left leg. Luker evidently made and decorated the chair for J. H. M. Houston who served as Worshipful Master of Swan Lodge No. 358 in Swan, Vinton County, Ohio, from 1867 to 1873 (fig. 2).[2]

Although awkwardly constructed, with a combination of pegged mortise-and-tenon and dowel joints, the overall structure of the chair in 1991 was sound (fig. 3). As the Master's chair, it had served an important symbolic function, but it also had suffered from regular use and eventual abuse. In addition to considerable paint loss, there were major repairs to the G on the crest; and cracks in the legs, arm-seat joints, and seat were all filled with a brittle white substance. Holes on the underside of each foot indicated that the chair was fitted with casters at some point.

Upon initial examination, the background color of the chair appeared to be black, and the edges of virtually all the structural elements had red pinstripes that were somewhat obscured and irregular. The large G above the crest rail was highlighted with a pebbly blue paint, and the Masonic square and compasses were a mottled dark greenish brown (fig. 4). Although many motifs were illegible, a wide variety of painted Masonic symbols were visible on the splat, legs, stiles, and crest rail. However, these too were quite dark because of dirt and degraded varnish.

Paint loss, darkening, and irregularity on unprotected areas, such as the backs of the stiles and splat and the tops of the globes, indicated that the chair was exposed to excessive light, heat, and moisture.[3] The celestial and terrestrial globe finials and the tops of the arms and seat were especially worn and weathered. In addition, the base of the splat, the front of the splat shoe, and the legs had thick accumulations of an opaque, waxy material, and

Figure 2 Swan Lodge No. 358, Vinton County, Ohio. This photo probably was taken during the mid-1960s. (Courtesy, Museum of Our National Heritage.)

Figure 3 Pretreatment view of the Masonic Master's chair illustrated in fig. 1. (Photo, Susan Buck.)

Figure 4 Pretreatment detail of the G, compass, and square of the Masonic Master's chair illustrated in fig. 1. The surface of the square and dividers was corroded, and the G was encrusted with grime. (Photo, Susan Buck.)

the feet, arms, and stiles had unidentifiable brittle white accretions. Overall the surface of the chair was very uneven and unsightly. The confusing, unstable painted surfaces required careful analysis to characterize the paint and metallic powder layers and to identify the accumulated obscuring materials before experimenting with solvents or water-based cleaning systems.

I removed eighteen samples (100 to 300 microns in size) from painted and metallic powder design areas with a "harpoon," a sharp scalpel originally designed for eye surgery. By taking the samples from the edges of cracks and areas of loss, I avoided intruding into intact painted surfaces. I encased the samples in small half-inch cubes of polyester resin, cured them for twenty-four hours, ground and polished each at right angles to expose the cross-sections, and analyzed them with a fluorescence microscope at 125×, 250×, and 500× magnifications. A fiber-optic light source allowed me to compare the appearance of the various layers in visible light and in ultraviolet light. In visible light, shellac, plant resin varnishes, and glaze layers are very difficult to distinguish—they all look uniformly translucent brown or tan. In ultraviolet light they fluoresce (or glow) in characteristic ways: shellac fluoresces bright orange; plant resin varnishes (such as copal, mastic, dammar, and sandarac) fluoresce bright white; and plant resin-bound glaze layers appear brilliantly colored depending on the pigments contained in the glaze. In contrast, modern synthetic varnishes tend not to fluoresce and will often appear as very dull blue or lavender layers. To determine the organic materials in each layer I applied a series of fluorescent biological stains that help to identify oils, carbohydrates (starches, sugars, and gums), and proteins (hide glues, egg, or casein) in the binding mediums.[4]

The cross-sections revealed that the background color on the chair was not black but an intense blue glaze consisting of blue pigment particles suspended in a plant resin binder. That glaze had been applied on top of a white priming layer, although in several samples there was an intermediary gray paint layer that may have been an underdrawing. The cross-sections from the G had three layers on top of the blue glaze: a thick layer of silver-colored metallic powder, a layer of large glass-like blue particles, and another layer of blue glaze (figs. 5, 6). This combination originally produced a bright, highly reflective surface. The pinstripes were composed of intense red pigment particles in a plant resin binder (figs. 7, 8), the same medium used to suspend the silver- and gold-colored metallic powders of the Masonic designs. The outer finish surface was an irregular layer of degraded plant resin varnish, above which lay thick accumulations of wax and oily grime.

Application of the biological stains revealed the presence of oil in the binding mediums of all layers and the absence of proteins or carbohydrates. The similar composition of the binding mediums—all having oil-bound plant resin components—severely limited the treatment options for the chair. To remove the degraded varnish layer (to reveal the more intact surfaces below) I had to design a cleaning system that would solubilize *only* the outer plant resin varnish layer. Alternatively, I could achieve a more legible, aesthetically pleasing surface by saving the remnants of the early varnish coating and removing only the grime and wax layers.

Before proceeding with cleaning I also needed to identify the pigments and metallic powders. I began by scraping particles from protected areas of red pinstripes and blue glazes and from the pebbly surface of the G. Polarized light microscopy (PLM) techniques, microchemical testing pro-

Figure 5 Cross-section of the G of the Masonic Master's chair photographed in visible light at 125×: (1) white preparatory layer; (2) blue glaze layer; (3) thick pewter powder layer; (4) large smalt particle. (Photo, Susan Buck.)

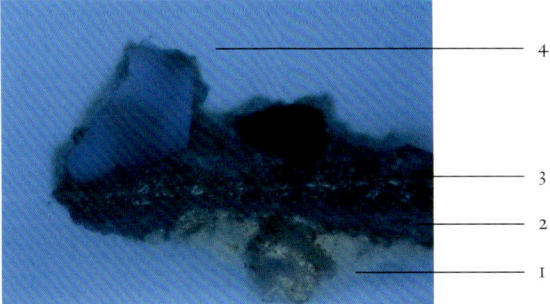

Figure 6 Cross-section of the G of the Masonic Master's chair photographed in ultraviolet light at 125×: (1) white preparatory layer; (2) blue glaze layer; (3) thick pewter powder layer; (4) large smalt particle. The fluorescence indicates that the blue glaze and metallic powders have a plant resin binding medium. (Photo, Susan Buck).

Figure 7   Cross-section of a red stripe on the Masonic Master's chair photographed in visible light at 500×. (Photo, Susan Buck.)

Figure 8   Cross-section of a red stripe on the Masonic Master's chair photographed in ultraviolet light at 500×. The fluorescence indicates that the preparatory layer, blue glaze, and red stripe have a plant resin binding medium and that there is an early plant resin varnish coating on the red stripe. (Photo, Susan Buck.)

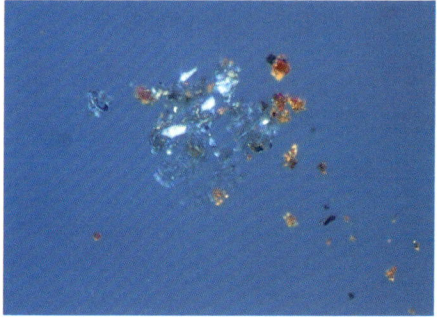

Figure 9   Red lead pigment particles with characteristic bright birefringence and isotropic Prussian blue particles photographed with transmitted light under crossed polars at 500×. (Photo, Susan Buck.)

cedures, and comparisons to known pigment samples revealed that the blue glaze pigment was Prussian blue, a high tint strength transparent colorant first synthesized in 1704 (fig. 9). It remains relatively stable when exposed to light and air, but if combined in oil and/or resin it appears greenish over time, and if exposed to alkalis it turns brown. When newly applied, the blue glaze was a deep, glossy, rich blue color; 120 years later it was a green-black. The chunky blue particles above the metallic powder layer of the G were smalt, coarse ground glass colored with cobalt. Smalt, a very stable pigment, is generally not affected by light, heat, or acids. The red pinstripe sample contained red lead and vermilion. Red lead, an ancient pigment noted for its brilliance and hiding power, is unstable and darkens when exposed to strong light and high humidity. Vermilion, also an ancient pigment that is intensely red with good hiding power, darkens when exposed to sunlight, especially if used in tempera or watercolor mediums. The combination of these pigments produced a brilliant red-orange color (see fig. 9).[5]

The components of the different metallic powder layers required identification by other analytical methods. A scanning electron microscope (SEM) revealed that the gold-colored powder was composed of brass (80 percent copper, 20 percent zinc). Unlike gold leaf or gold powder, brass powder corrodes and darkens if not protected by a varnish layer. The silver-colored powder was tin with a smaller proportion of lead and trace amounts of zinc—the traditional composition of pewter. Although pure tin powders are quite stable and not prone to tarnishing (unlike silver leaf and powder), the lead and zinc components guaranteed that this "pewter powder" corroded and darkened significantly. SEM analysis also confirmed earlier identifications of Prussian blue, red lead, and vermilion and determined that the primer contained white lead, zinc white, and calcite. The combination of white pigments created a very opaque, bright white ground coating. Application of intense blue glaze over this bright white ground would have created an effect of depth and translucency.[6]

The results of the analysis indicated that this chair would never reveal its true character unless the degraded varnish layer, thick accumulations of wax, and deposits of grime were removed, yet the cross-section samples and materials analysis indicated that cleaning these accumulations from the painted and metallic powder surfaces would be problematic (fig. 10). Polar and aromatic solvents (such as ethanol, benzyl alcohol, acetone, and xylene) would indiscriminately dissolve the varnish coating and underlying glaze layers, and any surfactant cleaning system in water (to remove the thick grime layer) would encourage further corrosion if the cleaner came in contact with the metallic powders.

The only solvent that appeared not to solubilize any of the glaze or powder layers was Stoddard Solvent, essentially a refined version of mineral spirits. Stoddard Solvent, however, left a white haze, suggesting that a substantial amount of wax remained on the surface and possibly in the paint and glaze layers below. Extensive tests produced only one cleaning system that was a moderately effective grime remover—saliva.[7]

After removing the wax with cotton swabs and Stoddard Solvent, I

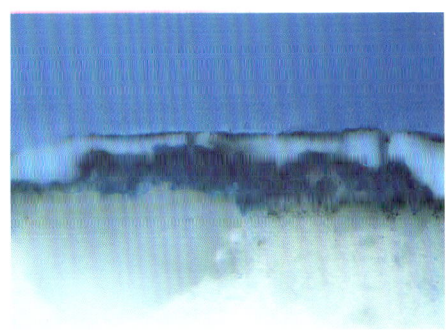

Figure 10 Cross-section of a protected surface under the seat of the Masonic Master's chair photographed in ultraviolet light at 500×. A thick layer of cracked, weathered plant resin varnish is visible above the blue glaze layer. (Photo, Susan Buck.)

Figure 11 Post-treatment view of the Masonic Master's chair. The painted surfaces under the seat are closest to the original colors. (Photo, David Bohl.)

mixed a trial batch of artificial saliva to simulate the viscosity and cleaning effectiveness of actual saliva. To speed the cleaning I raised the pH slightly with dilute sodium hydroxide and, to reduce the possibility of further metallic powder corrosion (because saliva contains water), added a water-soluble corrosion inhibitor to the solution.[8] The result was a controllable, effective cleaning solution to remove the grime layer on all the different design areas.

This procedure left intact the areas of remaining original plant resin varnish and, where the chair had not suffered abrasion or water damage (such as the lower portion of the splat and the sides of the legs), a smooth, somewhat glossy surface was recovered. Fortunately, I was able to save the early varnish layer where it still survived and reveal a pleasing, intensely colored surface. But the only area that remained comparatively intact and provides some sense of the brilliance of the original palette is the side of the right leg where the wide overhang of the seat protected the paints and glazes from exposure to sun, rain, and abrasion (fig. 11).

Using dental tools, I removed the small white accretions stuck to the legs and stiles of the chair, and I used a soft brush to gently push away the loose dirt and dust trapped around the large smalt particles; this surface was too fragile for any further cleaning. A spraycoat of a synthetic matte varnish that is reversible, protective, and appropriate in appearance proved to be the final step.[9]

Before cleaning, many of the painted and metallic powder symbols on the chair were partially or almost completely obscured. For Masons, these images represent the physical world, and they play an important role in conveying the practices and teachings of the Craft. It proved to be particularly significant that the chair was blue rather than black: "The color blue has always been associated with what is deemed beneficial: chastity, fidelity, immortality and prudence. The blue canopy of heaven is the covering of the Universal Lodge of Freemasonry." Some Masonic lodges are referred to as "Blue Lodges," and in many lodges the ceiling in the central room is painted blue, sometimes with lights or stars to simulate a night sky. Red also

Figure 12 Post-treatment detail of the splat and crest rail of the Masonic Master's chair. (Photo, David Bohl.)

had significance for Masons. It is the color of the Royal Arch symbol and denotes a fervor for knowledge, advanced degrees, and enlightenment.[10]

As the surface cleaning progressed, the images became more visible and their intent more obvious (fig. 12). For example, the slipper-shaped form on the splat shoe represented the Rite of Discalceation, where the apprentice removes one shoe before entering the lodge as a sign of humility before God and trust in his fellow lodge members. The date "1870" executed in gold-colored metallic powders on the top of the right side of the splat shoe indicated the year the chair was made. The curled form next to the slipper represented the cabletow, a symbol of brotherly love. A candidate for membership was traditionally initiated by being wrapped with the cabletow (or rope) and led blindfolded, wearing only one slipper, around the lodge room, ending up in the northeast corner where the cornerstone of a building is laid. There his blindfold was removed, and he saw "the light." This rite is symbolic of the light, or knowledge, of Masonry being revealed to the new member.[11]

Other important symbols on the chair include: silver stars that represent God and the five points of Masonic Fellowship; swords symbolizing the confidentiality that guards the purity of Masonic ritual and the jewels of office; acacia leaves symbolizing faith; a Masonic apron symbolizing the Rite of Investiture or Purification—one of the three great rites of Masonry—during which the new mason is presented with a lambskin or white leather apron. The level is a symbol of equality; the plumb rule, a symbol of uprightness; and the trowel, the symbol of brotherly love (see fig. 12).[12]

Of particular interest are a number of relatively recent Masonic symbols. The hourglass, the scythe, and the G centered between the square and compasses are all American forms (fig. 13). Masonic author Allan E. Roberts claims that around 1873 "some unknown inventor added a letter 'G' in the center of the square and compasses." If this information is correct, the Master's chair, dated 1870, may mark one of the first times the G in the center of the square and compasses was used. Representing God and geometry, the G is often depicted in Masonic drawings as shining, with radiating lines extending from the design.[13] The method of painting the G on the chair, using silver metallic powder, blue glazes, and large smalt particles, produced a shining, sparkling surface.

The pillars and candle stands figured less prominently in the conservation treatment because they were in stable condition and lacked painted Masonic symbols (see fig. 1). One pillar was painted blue, very similar to the color of the armchair, and the other was red-brown and had a thick, resinous varnish coating. The only major repair to the blue pillar was the replacement of the base with a felt-covered piece of wood, probably done years ago by a member of the lodge. Both candle stands had a dark brown stain and a wax coating. It is unclear whether the stained surface is original or the result of a later refinishing; however, candle wax attached to the sides and tops of both stands indicates that the stain dates to the period of their use. I used a mild nonionic surfactant cleaning system to remove accumulated grime on

Figure 13 Post-treatment detail of the crest rail, G, compass, and square. Although cleaning helped reveal the red paint and blue glaze, the metallic powder layers remained darkened and corroded. (Photo, David Bohl.)

all four objects. Then I waxed and buffed the dark red pillar and brown candle stands and sprayed the blue pillar with two coats of Soluvar Matte Varnish to match the surface coating on the chair.[14]

Most likely the two pillars represent Jachin and Boaz—the two columns at the entrance of Solomon's Temple, which are the symbolic foundations of many of the great truths of Freemasonry. The right pillar, Boaz, symbolizes strength, or power. The left pillar, Jachin, symbolizes the establishment, or choice and control. In general, the column form also symbolizes the five steps—Tuscan, Doric, Ionic, Corinthian and Composite—necessary to reach the second level, or Fellowcraft Degree.[15]

Although only two candle stands from the suite are known, lodges traditionally have three burning tapers symbolizing the sun, the moon, and the Worshipful Master. Light plays an important literal role in Masonic ceremonies, and the "three lights" are usually positioned in the middle of the center room of the lodge.[16] Swan Lodge No. 358 was dilapidated and abandoned when the suite was discovered in situ in 1966, so it is conceivable that a third taper had been removed or destroyed.

With its curule-style legs, fanciful painting, and massive crest ornament, the Masonic Master's chair undoubtedly was an unusual form for rural Ohio in the 1870s (see fig. 11). Luker chose bright, intensely colored raw pigments that would have been readily available and comparatively inexpensive. His choice of brass and pewter metallic powders meant that, although the metallic powder designs started out as highly reflective, bright gold and silver-colored areas, they started to corrode and change color as soon as the protective varnish coating broke down. This process may have begun while the Master's chair was still in use, so, by the time the lodge was abandoned, the surface was dark, unsightly, and not considered important enough to save.

Given the adverse conditions affecting the suite, it is miraculous that the pieces survived with most of the original material intact.[17] Recent technological developments now allow conservators to understand better the original intent of the maker, to reconstruct more effectively what an object might have looked like in use, and to conserve more appropriately the surfaces and structures that survive.

ACKNOWLEDGMENTS   Research funding for this project was provided in part by the Samuel H. Kress Foundation. The author thanks John Hamilton and Maureen Harper for their contributions to the treatment process and to this article.

1. Richard C. Wolbers and Gregory Landrey, "Use of Direct Reactive Fluorescent Dyes for the Characterization of Binding Media in Cross Sectional Examinations," 15th Annual AIC Meeting, Vancouver, British Columbia, 1987, pp. 168–202.

2. Jonathan Fairbanks and Elizabeth Bates, *American Furniture 1620 to the Present* (New York: Richard Marek Publishers, 1981), p. 361.

3. John Hamilton, curator of the Museum of Our National Heritage, suggests that the wear on the crest rail may be the result of abrasion from the rim of the top hat frequently worn by the Master during ceremonies.

4. To achieve a glassy surface, I polished the cross-sections with Micro-Mesh abrasive cloths with grits from 1,500 to 12,000. I examined the samples with an Olympus BHT Series 2 Fluorescence microscope with UV (300 to 400 nm with 420 nm barrier filter) and V (390 to 420 nm with 455 nm barrier filter) cubes. Richard C. Wolbers, Nanette T. Sterman, and Chris Stavroudis, *Notes for Workshop in New Methods in the Cleaning of Paintings* (Santa Monica: Getty Conservation Institute, 1988), pp. 11, 58–74.

5. I mounted the samples under cover slips on glass slides with Cargille Meltmount (refractive index of 1.66). For more on these pigments and their characteristics, see Rutherford J. Gettens and George L. Stout, *Paintings Materials* (New York: Dover Publications, 1966), pp. 150, 153, 158–59, 171.

6. Dr. Leon Stodulski of the Detroit Institute of Arts performed the SEM analysis.

7. Saliva worked too slowly and required too much volume to be practical. Saliva also contains a high percentage of water, so there was still a problem of cleaning the metallic powder areas with any form of an aqueous cleaning system that would encourage further corrosion.

8. Modified recipe from Richard C. Wolbers for artificial saliva: 0.50 g albumen; 0.25 g mucin; 0.15 g glucose; 1.80 g NaCl; 0.04 g diammonium citrate; 0.01 g uric acid; 0.44 g sodium phosphate; 0.44 g sodium phosphate dibasic; trace amounts of lipase, amylase, lysozyme, protease; pH adjusted to 8.5 with NaOH; water to produce a total volume of 200 ml; 3 g hydroxypropyl methyl cellulose; 2 ml Ancor LB-503 Corrosion Inhibitor.

9. John D. Hamilton, Maureen Harper (Registrar, Museum of Our National Heritage), and I decided to spray the painted surfaces lightly with Liquitex Soluvar Matte Varnish to provide a protective coating and to resaturate the areas that were badly abraded and damaged. There was also evidence of a plant resin varnish coating on the chair, so we decided that this reversible varnish coating appropriately replicated the earlier glossy surfaces.

10. Allen E. Roberts, *The Craft and Its Symbols: Opening the Door to Masonic Symbols* (Richmond, Va.: Macoy Publishing and Masonic Supply Company, 1974), pp. 6–8. The author thanks John Hamilton for information on the significance of the color red in Masonry.

11. Roberts, *Craft and Its Symbols*, p. 12.

12. Ibid., pp. 30, 56.

13. Ibid., pp. 12, 56. Roberts did not cite any references to support his claim, but he noted that "in other languages God does not start with the letter 'G,' nor does Geometry," implying that the use of G in non-English-speaking countries would not convey the same message and thus would not be used in this form.

14. I cleaned the pillars and candle stand using 0.2 percent Triton X-100 in deionized water, rinsed them with deionized water, and cleared them with odorless mineral spirits.

15. Waldwin Percival, *Masonry and Its Symbols in the Light of Thinking and Destiny* (New York: The WORD Publishing Co., 1952), p. 54. Roberts, *Craft and Its Symbols*, p. 56.

16. "More Light" is referred to as the true Masonic Prayer. For more on the symbolism of light, see Roberts, *Craft and Its Symbols*, p. 32; and Percival, *Masonry and Its Symbols*, p. 54.

17. Mr. J. Denny Kitchen discovered the suite in a ruined Masonic temple in rural Ohio over twenty-five years ago. The objects were wet from roof leaks and covered with bird droppings. To slow the drying process and save the painted surfaces, he coated them with a thick layer of beeswax-based furniture polish. Because the chair was too tall to fit into his house, he removed the casters and stored them away in a box (the author thanks Mr. Kitchen for this information).

Figure 1 James Smither, Benjamin Randolph trade card, Philadelphia, 1769. Line engraving on paper. 9" × 7". (Courtesy, Library Company of Philadelphia.)

Morrison H. Heckscher

English Furniture Pattern Books in Eighteenth-Century America

▼ THE EIGHTEENTH century in England was the golden age of books illustrating architecture and furniture designs. The approximately 250 different architectural titles and 40 furniture titles published were a principal means for the transmission of London designs throughout the English-speaking world, and they deserve much of the credit for the pleasing proportions and quality construction that characterize Georgian architecture and furniture, be it from London, Dublin, or Philadelphia.[1]

Early historians of American furniture, such as Irving W. Lyon and Luke Vincent Lockwood, acknowledged the influence of British pattern books, but the first serious student of published design sources for American furniture was Fiske Kimball. During the 1920s he incorporated the results of his research in articles on American architecture, Philadelphia furniture, and Thomas Chippendale. Over the ensuing years scholars assembled a sizeable body of information documenting the existence of these books in America. Helen Park's well-known *List of Architectural Books Available in America before the Revolution* itemizes more than 100 different architectural titles. This article provides a similar compilation of furniture design books.[2]

All told, we now have nearly seventy individual references to nineteen different furniture books, and a twentieth title is included in the checklist because Philadelphia artisans clearly utilized engravings from it. Most of the references were culled from the catalogues of colonial booksellers and libraries, newspaper advertisements, and estate inventories of architects and cabinetmakers.[3] In three instances the actual volumes owned by American craftsmen have been identified by signatures in the books. Although additional references undoubtedly will come to light as eighteenth-century manuscript and printed documentary sources are studied systematically, now that we have a journal devoted to American furniture it seems fitting and timely to bring together all the known material.

Modern distinctions between books of architecture and of design are not always accurate since some architectural books, such as Batty and Thomas Langley's *The City and Country Builder's and Workman's Treasury of Designs* (1740), contain patterns for furniture. In addition, some furniture design books, such as Thomas Chippendale's *Gentleman and Cabinet-Maker's Director* (1754), occasionally have engravings of chimneypieces and other interior details. The collections of ornamental designs by John Stalker and George Parker, P. Baretti, Henry Copland, Thomas Johnson, and Matthias Lock are included in this study because they were primarily for the decoration of furniture. However, catalogues illustrating brass furniture hardware made by Birmingham and Sheffield manufactories—a wide variety of drawer pulls, keyhole escutcheons, and casters—are excluded from the checklist because they were tangential to furniture design.[4]

Most of the furniture design books published in Britain during the eighteenth century were available in America. Notable among them were the major works in the rococo style by Chippendale, Johnson, William Ince and John Mayhew, Robert Manwaring, and the Society of Upholsterers. Absent are a number of books by late baroque (including Palladian) designers, such as Gaetano Brunetti's *Sixty Different Sorts of Ornaments* (1736), William Jones's *Gentlemen or Builder's Companion* (1739), or De La Cour's various *Books of Ornament* (1741–1747). Likewise, there is no record of the Chinese designs of Matthew Darly, William Halfpenny, and Sir William Chambers, nor is there evidence of any of Lock's suites of carver's ornaments and furniture designs in America before the 1780s.[5]

All the books recorded in America are British; so too are the individual designs, excepting the French and German plates pirated by the Langleys for the *Treasury* (1740). The books ran the gamut from princely folio size to pocket handbook, but most were modest volumes intended to guide tradesmen in constructing fashionable furniture. Aside from Thomas Jefferson's copy of Chippendale's *Gentleman and Cabinet-Maker's Director* (1755 edition), no other design book has a history of ownership by an American merchant, professional, or other member of the colonial elite.[6]

Several London booksellers settled in American cities in the decades before the Revolution. More than half of the references uncovered are from their advertisements and catalogues. Chief among these men were James Rivington and Garret Noel, who arrived in New York in 1760 and 1762, respectively; the firm of Cox and Berry, which opened a shop in Boston in 1766; Robert Wells, who immigrated to Charleston about 1766; and Robert Bell, a Scot who dominated the book trade in Philadelphia from 1768 until his death in 1784. Their presence helps explain the overwhelmingly London orientation of titles found in America.[7]

These booksellers brought with them, or later imported, a variety of titles, particularly modest pattern books such as P. Baretti's *New Book of Ornaments for the Year 1766*, John Crunden's *Joyner and Cabinet-Maker's Darling* (1765), Manwaring's *Cabinet and Chair-Maker's Real Friend and Companion* (1765), and the Society of Upholsterers' *Houshold Furniture in Genteel Taste* (1760). Chippendale's *Director* and Ince and Mayhew's *Universal System of Houshold Furniture* (1762) were not offered in America until 1766, presumably because these elegant folios were too costly to import on speculation.

The books of baroque designs had little influence on colonial furniture styles. Langley's *Treasury,* for example, was an important design source for American builders, but only two pieces of colonial furniture—altarpieces designed by Newport architect, Peter Harrison—derive from this book. Likewise, Stalker and Parker's *Treatise of Japanning and Varnishing* (1688) and John Vardy's *Some Designs of Inigo Jones and William Kent* (1744) appeared in America late in the eighteenth century and evidently had no influence whatsoever. The collections of rococo designs had a much greater impact. Manwaring's *Cabinet and Chair-Maker's Real Friend and Companion* determined the basic look, and occasionally the details, of much Boston seating furniture, whereas Chippendale's *Director* had a broad influence on furniture styles in the Middle Atlantic region, particularly Philadelphia, and in the South. Somewhat later, volumes of neoclassical designs such as George Hepplewhite's *Cabinet-Maker and Upholsterer's Guide* (1788) and Thomas Sheraton's *Cabinetmaker & Upholsterer's Drawing Book* (1793) had a broad and immediate influence in introducing the "antique" taste.

American pieces directly influenced by pattern books are, however, very much the exception, for most colonial furniture conforms more to regional styles than to pattern book designs. It is primarily with costly commissioned furniture—be it rococo or neoclassical—that we find precise borrowings. The reason for this is that the fashion for the rococo—an ornamental style promulgated through design books—coincided with a period of growing tension between England and her colonies during the 1760s. Although the American merchant elite hungered for fashionable London goods, there was broad-based sentiment for boycotting British goods and encouraging home manufactures. There was thus a market for American-made goods in the latest London style. To fill that need, highly skilled cabinetmakers and carvers immigrated to the colonies, there to make furniture that proclaimed its owner's familiarity with current London fashion. For example, Philadelphia cabinetmaker Benjamin Randolph paid for the passage of London-trained carvers Hercules Courtenay and John Pollard in 1765.[8]

Randolph's trade card (fig. 1) graphically illustrates the importance of pattern books in the transmission of London rococo designs to the colonies. In 1769 Randolph commissioned James Smither to engrave the card as an advertisement for his new shop, the Golden Eagle. The furniture designs that surround the cartouche were copied from popular pattern books. The message they imparted to Randolph's chosen market, those cosmopolitan Philadelphians who could afford to import furnishings from London but for political reasons deemed it expedient not to do so, was clear: "I can provide you with American-made furniture based upon designs that your peers will recognize as being in the latest London style."

The high chest illustrated in figure 2 shows how cabinetmakers and carvers in the colonies mined design books for motifs. In London the high chest—a flat-top chest of drawers with six turned legs—was a purely baroque form that went out of fashion by 1710, but in the colonies it evolved into a prestigious and uniquely American creation. During the 1730s New England craftsmen gave the high chest a scroll top with a central drawer, a large central bottom drawer (often with a carved shell), and cabriole legs. The evolution of this form continued in Philadelphia during the 1750s, when the pediment drawer was superceded by broad carved appliqués, and during the mid- to late 1760s, when an extended cornice separated the pediment from the drawers in an architecturally correct manner. Figure 2 is a perfect example of the last, and judging from the tentative and laborious

Figure 2 High chest, Philadelphia, 1762–1775. Mahogany with tulip poplar, white cedar, and yellow pine. H. 91 3/4", W. 44", D. 24 5/8". (Metropolitan Museum of Art, John Stewart Kennedy Fund, 1918, acc. 18.110.4.)

construction methods employed in fashioning the pediment, this object must be one of the first attempts at this design.

The cabinetmaker and carver responsible for this high chest (long-known as the "Pompadour") copied details from two pattern books published in London in 1762. The pediment, with scroll volutes metamorphosing into acanthus leaves, the cornice, and draped urn finials, and the bash lit corridor bust ornament come from two desk-and-bookcases illustrated in the third edition of the *Director* (figs. 3–5). The drawer appliqué, however, is copied

Figure 3 Design for a desk-and-bookcase illustrated on pl. 108 in the third edition of Thomas Chippendale's *Gentleman and Cabinet-Maker's Director* (London, 1762). (Metropolitan Museum of Art, The Elisha Whittelsey Fund, 1982, acc. 1982.1133.)

Figure 4 Design for a desk-and-bookcase illustrated on pl. 107 in the third edition of Chippendale's *Director*. (Metropolitan Museum of Art, The Elisha Whittelsey Fund, 1982, acc. 1982.1133.)

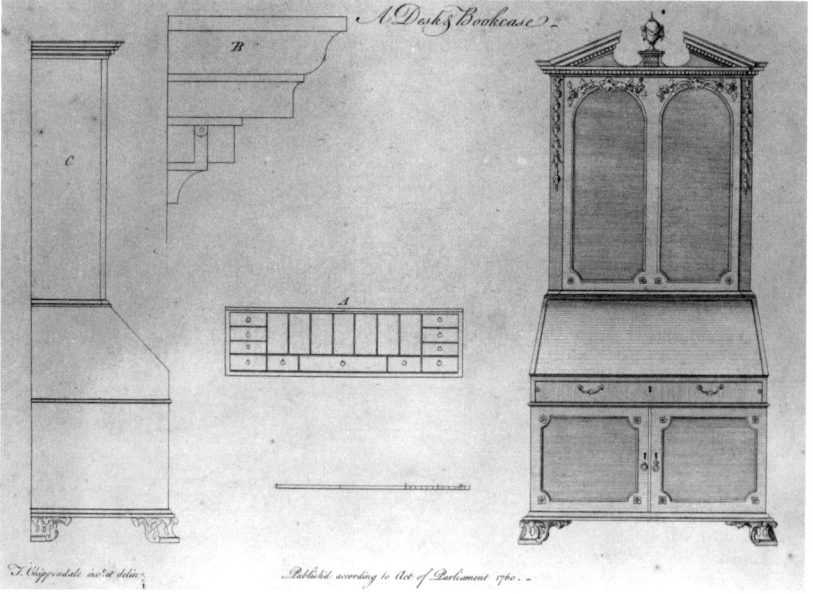

Figure 5 Detail of the cornice of the high chest illustrated in fig. 2. In both size and profile, the cornice exactly matches the full-scale cornice detail illustrated in fig. 4. (Photo, Metropolitan Museum of Art.)

Figure 6   Detail of the bottom drawer appliqué of the high chest illustrated in fig. 2. (Photo, Metropolitan Museum of Art.)

Figure 7   Design for a chimneypiece tablet on pl. 5 in Thomas Johnson's *New Book of Ornaments* (London, 1762). (Metropolitan Museum of Art, Gift of Harvey Smith, 1985, acc. 1985.1099.)

from a design for a chimneypiece tablet in Thomas Johnson's *New Book of Ornaments* (figs. 6, 7). These pattern book details clearly attest to a familiarity with modish London style, yet, as a whole, the high chest is an original American statement.

In the following checklist and catalogue, all of the furniture pattern books documented in America before 1800 are arranged, first by the style of their designs, then alphabetically by author. (The checklist gives only the dates of editions found in America; the catalogue gives the dates of all eighteenth-century editions.) The catalogue entries are numbered sequentially, and each begins with a bibliographical synopsis of the book and commentary about its availability and influence. Within each entry, individual references are listed chronologically. Where possible, all catalogue references have been checked against the original sources and page numbers given. The citations at the end of each reference are abbreviations for the publications listed under "References Consulted" at the end of the catalogue section.

Checklist of English Furniture Pattern Books in Eighteenth-Century America

▼ BAROQUE

1. Langley, Batty and Thomas. *The City and Country Builder's and Workman's Treasury of Designs*, 1745, 1750, 1756.
2. Stalker, John, and George Parker. *A Treatise of Japanning and Varnishing*, 1688.
3. Vardy, John. *Some Designs of Inigo Jones and William Kent*, 1744.

▼ ROCOCO

4. Baretti, P. *A New Book of Ornaments*, 1762 and/or 1766.
5. Chippendale, Thomas. *The Gentleman and Cabinet-Maker's Director*, 1754, 1755, 1762.
6. Copland, Henry. *A New Book of Ornaments*, 1746.
7. Crunden, John. *The Joyner and Cabinet-Maker's Darling*, 1765.
8. Ince, William, and John Mayhew. *The Universal System of Houshold Furniture*, 1762.
9. Johnson, Thomas. *One Hundred and Fifty New Designs*, 1758, 1761.
10. Johnson, Thomas. *A New Book of Ornaments*, 1762.
11. Lock, Matthias. *A New Book of Ornaments for Looking Glass Frames . . . &c.*, ca. 1752 or ca. 1768.
12. Lock, Matthias. *A Book of Tables . . . &c.*, 1768.
13. Lock, Matthias, and Henry Copland. *A New Book of Ornaments*, 1752 or 1768.
14. Manwaring, Robert. *The Cabinet and Chair-Maker's Real Friend and Companion*, 1765.
15. Manwaring, Robert. *The Chair-Maker's Guide*, 1766.
16. Society of Upholsterers. *Houshold Furniture in Genteel Taste*, 1760

▼ NEOCLASSICAL

17. Adam, Robert and James. *The Works in Architecture*, 1773–1778, 1779.
18. Hepplewhite, George. *The Cabinet-Maker and Upholsterer's Guide*, 1788, 1789, or 1794.
19. London Society of Cabinet Makers. *The Cabinet-Makers' London Book of Prices*, 1788 or 1793.
20. Sheraton, Thomas. *The Cabinet-Maker & Upholsterer's Drawing Book*, 1793.

Catalogue of English Furniture Pattern Books in Eighteenth-Century America

▼ BAROQUE

1. Batty and Thomas Langley, *The City and Country Builder's and Workman's Treasury of Designs*, London, 1740, 1745, 1750, 1756, 1770.

The *Treasury of Designs* was one of the most popular of the various architectural pattern books cobbled together by Batty Langley, an architect and drawing master, and his brother Thomas, an engraver. Its furniture designs are mostly copied from engravings of continental designers. There are two bracket clocks (after J. F. Lauch), six marble tables (after Nicolas Pineau), three table frames, one medal case, one chest on stand, one dressing table (after J. J. Schubler), eight bookcases, and six altarpieces. All plates but one are signed "Thomas Langley invent and sculp," and most are dated 1739. The exception, a design for a chest of drawers, is signed "Batty Langley Invent and Delin."[9]

Booksellers advertised the *Treasury* in Philadelphia, New York, and Boston. Artisans who owned a copy included Philadelphia carpenters Robert Smith and John King, Virginia and Maryland architect William Buckland, and Boston builder Thomas Dawes. Newport architect Peter Harrison based his designs for the altar in King's Chapel in Boston (1749) and the Ark in Touro Synagogue in Newport (1759) on plate 108, but there is no reference to the book in the catalogue of his library.[10] Most of the heavy baroque pier tables and bookcases illustrated in this volume were inappropriate for the scale and style of colonial life, and, with the exception of Harrison's alterpieces, the *Treasury* had no influence on American furniture designs.

1.1. 1751. "Robert Smith, his book, Philada 1751," inscribed in copy of the 1750 ed., Carpenters Company Library, Philadelphia (Hummel, 1955, p. 30).

1.2. 1755. "Langley's builder's designs," in advertisement, "Imported in the last vessels from London, and to be sold by David Hall, At the New-Printing-Office, in Market-street, Philadelphia, the following Books, viz," in *Pennsylvania Gazette*, January 21, 1755, p. 2 (Hummel, 1955, pp. 30–31).

1.3. After 1756. "John King" inscribed in copy of the 1756 ed., Carpenter's Company Library, Philadelphia (Hummel, 1955, p. 30).

1.4. 1760. "Langley's builder's and workman's treasury of designs," in broadside, "Books Imported in the last Vessel from London, and to be sold by David Hall, at the New-Printing-Office, in Market-street, Philadelphia," 1760 (Evans, 8362; Hummel, 1955, p. 31).

1.5. 1760. "Langley's Builder's Treasury, Designs for Builders and other Artists," in *A Catalogue of Books, lately Imported, and Sold by James Rivington Bookseller and Stationer from London, at his store over against the Golden Key, in Hanover-Square, New-York. And also at His Store next Door to Messrs. Taylor and Cox, in Front Street, Philadelphia*, New York, 1760 (Winans, 41; Hummel, 1955, pp. 30–31).

1.6. 1760. "Langley's City and Country Builders and Workman's Treasury of Designs, 4to," in advertisement, "The following new Books, &c To Be Sold, Enquire of the Printer," in *Boston News-Letter*, March 13, 1760 (Dow, p. 221; Park, 42).

1.7. ca. 1760. "Langley's City and Country Builders and Workmans Treasury of Designs," in *A Catalogue of Books, Just Imported from London, And to be Sold by W. Bradford, At the London-Coffee-House, Philadelphia*, ca. 1760, p. 9 (Evans, 8555; Winans, 34; Hummel, 1955, p. 31).

1.8. 1761. "Langley's Treasury of Designs, 4to," in advertisement, "Lately Imported, and to be Sold the following Books, &c. Among which are a Variety upon Architecture, Enquire of the Printers," in *Boston Gazette and Country Journal*, November 30, 1761, p. 2 (Dow, p. 222).

1.9. 1762. "Langley's Builder's and Workman's Treasury of Designs, 4to," in advertisement of books offered for sale "At Mr. Holbrook's House in the Common, Boston," in *Boston News-Letter*, February 18, 1762 (Dow, p. 222).

1.10. 1762. "Langley's Builder's Treasury, designs for Builders and other Artists," in *A Catalogue of Books, sold by Rivington and Brown, Booksellers and Stationers from London, At their Stores, over against the Golden Key, in Hanover-Square, New-York: and Over against the London Coffee-House, in Philadelphia. At both which Places will be found, a constant Supply of Books, with all the new Articles as they are published in Europe; and from whence all Orders directed to them from the Country, whether in a wholesale or retail Way, will be punctually complied with*, Philadelphia (?), 1762, p. 66, no. 750 (Evans, 9259; Winans, 45; Hummel, 1955, pp. 31, 132).

1.11. 1764. "Langley's Designs, 4to," in advertisement, "The following Books to be Sold cheap for Cash at Timothy White's Shop, a little above the Market," in *Boston Gazette*, December 10, 1764, p. 2 (Dow, p. 222).

1.12. 1773. "Langley's City and Country Builder's and Workman's Treasury of Designs: Or, the Art of drawing or working the ornamental Parts of Architecture, illustrated by upwards of 400 grand Designs, neatly engraved on 186 Copperplates," in *Robert Bell's Sale Catalogue of a Collection of New and Old Books, In all the Arts and Sciences, and in various Languages . . . with the Lowest Price Printed to each Book; Now Selling, at the Book-Store of William Woodhouse, Bookseller, Stationer, and Bookbinder, in Front-Street, near Chestnut-Street, Philadelphia*, July 15, 1773, p. 3, no. 31 (Evans, 12670; Hummel, 1955, p. 129).

1.13. Before 1774. "Langley's Designs -10-," in "An Inventory of the Goods and Chattels of William Buckland, late of Anne Arundel County deceased," Annapolis, December 19, 1774 (Beirne and Scarff, p. 150).

1.14. Before 1795. "The city and country builder's and workman's treasury of designs; or, the art of drawing and working the ornamental parts of architecture; with plates. London, 1745," in *A Catalogue of the Books belonging to The Loganian Library*, Philadelphia, 1795, p. 33, no. 650 (Johnston, p. 9, n. 44).

1.15. Before 1809. "Langley's Builder's Treasury, 4to.1," in Boston Athenaeum *Book of Donations, 1807–51*, p. 15. This copy of the 1756 edition was donated by Thomas Dawes, Jr., on January 16, 1809, and is signed "Thomas Dawes" (possibly by his father) on the title page (Park, p. 33).

2. John Stalker and George Parker, *A Treatise of Japanning and Varnishing*, Oxford, 1688.

This handsome quarto volume has a lengthy "how to" text on the subject of japanning in imitation of Oriental lacquer and twenty-four large copper-plate engravings, each illustrating numerous individual motifs. Alec Tiranti reprinted the *Treatise* in 1960 and 1971.

Stalker and Parker's book frequently is cited in publications on Boston japanned furniture of the 1730s and 1740s (the golden age of japanning in America), but, as a design source, the book apparently had absolutely no direct influence. Recent research suggests that the *Treatise* had a greater influence on the relief decoration for English stoneware and earthenware than on furniture.[11] Its availability in Philadelphia late in the century suggests an interest rekindled by the beginnings of the China trade.

2.1. 1783. "Art of Japanning and Varnishing, &c, with above 20 Chinese Designs on Copper-plates, three dollars," in *A Catalogue of a Large Collection of New and Old Books, in Arts, Sciences, and Entertainment, for Persons of all Denominations, With the selling Price Printed to each Book; Now on Sale, at said Bell's Book-Store, near St. Paul's Church, in Third-Street*, Philadelphia, 1783, p. 15, no. 190 (Evans, 17830; Winans, 99; Johnston, p. 25).

2.2. 1789. "A treatise of japanning and varnishing; with the method of gilding, burnishing and lackering; the art of separating and refining metals, and of painting mezzotinto prints; also of imitating tortoise-shell and marble, and of staining wood, ivory and horn. By John Stalker and George Parker. Oxford, 1688," in *A Catalogue of the Books, Belonging to The Library Company of Philadelphia*, 1789, p. 286, no. 314 (Evans, 22066; Winans, 131; Johnston, p. 25).

3. John Vardy, *Some Designs of Mr. Inigo Jones and Mr. Wm. Kent*, London, 1744.

A 1796 reference to "Varley's designs, folio," is undoubtedly a reference to John Vardy's *Designs of Inigo Jones and William Kent*. (The only other possible choice of author, Matthew Darly, is unlikely; none of his known books is of folio size, and his name is correctly given later in the same document.)

Vardy was an architect and designer whose only book is this handsome folio of fifty-three plates. Most of the engravings are architectural, but there are a few furniture (pls. 40–43) and silver designs. Gregg Press reprinted the volume in 1967.

William Kent's furniture designs are for massive, richly carved and gilded pier tables, pier glasses, and chairs—all suited to the grandest of English Palladian houses but not to smaller, simpler colonial houses. It is difficult to explain the presence of this volume in late-eighteenth-century Philadelphia.

3.1. 1796. "Varley's designs, folio," in [Thomas] *Bradford's Catalogue of Books and Stationary, Wholesale & Retail, for 1796*, Philadelphia, 1796, p. 56 (Evans, 30121; Winans, 212; Johnston, p. 22).

▼ ROCOCO

4. P. Baretti, *A New Book of Ornaments on 16 Leaves for the Year 1762*, London, 1762, 1766.

The 1762 edition, subtitled "Very useful for Cabinet Makers, Carvers, Printers, Engravers &c," is a slight assemblage of carvers' designs, some of which are reverse copies of plates in Henry Copland's *New Book of Ornaments* (1746) (see cat. 6). A second edition, no copy of which is known, was published in 1766 and offered for sale by London publisher Henry Webley. Both editions consisted of sixteen leaves and cost two shillings, but the second edition had the word "chasers" added to the subtitle. These publications are discussed and the 1762 edition (British Museum) is reprinted in *Furniture History* 11.[12]

Boston booksellers Cox and Berry advertised the second edition in 1767. If the first edition's designs are any guide, the book had no direct influence on Boston furniture carving. However, in Charleston, where London-trained architect and carver Ezra Waite owned a copy, architectural carving bears a general similarity to Baretti's designs. There is no record of the *Book of Ornaments* in Philadelphia, but some of Baretti's designs with symmetrically arranged patterns of C and S scrolls may have inspired the carved ornament on the skirts and pediments of high chests.[13]

4.1. 1767. "Baretti's new Book of Ornaments, very useful for Cabinet-makers, Carvers, Painters, Engravers, Chasers, &c," in advertisement, "Cox and Berry Arrived from London, In the John Galley, Captain Blake, Beg leave to acquaint the Publick, That they have just opened at the Store of the late Messirs. Green & Walker, opposite the Rev. Mr. Cooper's Meeting-House. . . . Also modern Books of all kinds . . . and of whom may be had the following very useful Books," in *Boston News-Letter*, January 1, 1767 (Park, 3; for January 8, 1767, advertisement, see Dow, pp. 222–23).

4.2. Before 1769. "Morris Architect & Chimneypieces with Barrettis Ornaments," in inventory of estate of Ezra Waite, November 29, 1769, Charleston Inventories, Book Y (1769–1771), pp. 180–82, South Carolina Department of Archives and History, Columbia (Dixon, p. 65, no. 4).

5 Thomas Chippendale, *The Gentleman and Cabinet-Maker's Director*, London, 1754, 1755, 1762.

Thomas Chippendale's *The Gentleman and Cabinet-Maker's Director* was the most widely owned furniture design book in eighteenth-century America. Chippendale published the first edition of this folio (with 160 engraved plates) in 1754; the second edition (with no substantive changes) in 1755; and the third edition (enlarged to 200 plates, of which 100 were new) in 1762. Dover Publications began reprinting the third edition in 1966.

Four references document the folio's presence in New England: a copy signed "Boston 1768," an advertisement by Boston booksellers Cox and Berry, the inventory of Salem cabinetmaker Nathaniel Gould, and a copy inscribed by Newport cabinetmaker Thomas Goddard (who presumably got the copy from his father, John). The rococo style had little following in New England, and the furniture associated with Gould and Goddard displays no hint of Chippendale's influence. No New York reference to the *Director* is known, but the splat design of a chair illustrated on plate 12 of the third edition (plate numbers refer to the third edition unless otherwise noted) was a recurrent favorite among that region's chairmakers, and a 1774 newspaper advertisement by Thomas Burling is illustrated with a woodcut of a ribbon-back chair inspired by plate 15 (center). Four copies of the *Director* are documented from the Chesapeake Bay region—three in Virginia and one used both in Virginia and Maryland by architect William Buckland. Much of the furniture attributed to Buckland's shop was influenced by *Director* designs (see Luke Beckerdite's article in this volume). Williamsburg cabinetmaker Edmund Dickinson (fl. 1770–1778) owned a copy, perhaps the same one that his predecessor (as master of the Anthony Hay shop), Benjamin Bucktrout, used as inspiration for the dolphin legs of a Masonic Master's chair. Thomas Jefferson also owned a copy, but it hardly informed his progressive tastes.[14]

The *Director* was available in Charleston, where bookseller Robert Wells advertised it in 1766 and 1772. His clients may have been immigrant craftsmen; carver and builder Ezra Waite (d. 1769) and upholsterer Walter Russell (d. 1776) owned copies at their deaths. Locally made furniture generally followed London styles, but a library bookcase based on plate 93 is the sole instance of direct borrowing. A pair of chairs attributed to New Bern, North Carolina, also have details copied from the *Director*.[15]

Several copies of the *Director* were owned by Philadelphians. Thomas Affleck, one of the city's preeminent makers, probably brought his copy with him when he left London in 1763. The Library Company of Philadelphia, the first subscription library in America, acquired a copy of the third edition sometime between 1764 and 1769. By 1769, subscribers to the Library Company included nine prominent furniture makers, the best-known being William Savery, James Gillingham, and Benjamin Randolph. Several related Philadelphia side chairs, including one labeled by Gillingham, have splat designs based on the left side chair in plate 10.[16]

Philadelphia booksellers carried the *Director* well into the 1780s. In 1776,

Figure 8 Desk-and-bookcase, Philadelphia, ca. 1765. Mahogany with yellow pine, white cedar, tulip poplar, and white oak. (Collection of Mr. and Mrs. George M. Kaufman; photo, Dirk Bakker.)

Robert Bell offered the first or second edition, in 1784, William Pritchard and printer Eleazer Oswald offered to order copies from a London dealer; and two years later one Thomas Dobson paid bookbinder James Muir for binding a copy.

The direct copying of designs, or portions thereof, was limited to a few plates in Philadelphia. Several sets of Philadelphia side chairs have design elements based on plates 9, 13, and 14; a Philadelphia "French" chair is derived from plate 19; a writing table combines details taken from plates 72 and 74; and the lower section of a Philadelphia desk-and-bookcase (fig. 8) and the pediment of a high chest are based on plate 108 (see fig. 3). Five of these plates were limited to the 1762 edition. In the 1770s, cabinetmaker John Folwell planned to print, by subscription, a furniture design book based on the *Director*; however, the Revolutionary War halted his scheme. A letterpress proposal for Folwell's *The Gentleman and Cabinet-Maker's Assistant* survives bound with some copies of the Philadelphia edition of Abraham Swan's *British Architect* (1775).[17]

5.1. 1766. "Chippendale's and Ince and Mayhew's designs of houshold furniture," in advertisement, "Robert Wells, At the Great Stationary and Book Shop on the Bay, has imported for sale . . . from London," in *South-Carolina & American General Gazette* (Charleston), July 18, 1766 (Dixon, p. 68, no. 19).

5.2. 1768. "[Name erased] Boston 1768," inscribed in copy of the 1762 ed., Boston Athenaeum (Jobe and Kaye, p. 19, n. 60).

5.3. Before 1769. "Chippendale's Book of Furniture designs £12," in inventory of estate of Ezra Waite, November 29, 1769 (for full reference see cat. 4.2) (Dixon, p. 68, n. 19).

5.4. 1770. "DIRECTOR: (The Gentleman and Cabinet-Maker's) being a large collection of the most elegant and useful designs of houshold furniture, in the most fashionable taste. . . . The whole comprehended in 200 copper plates, neatly engraved. By Thomas Chippendale, Cabinet-maker. The 3d edition. London, 1762," in *The Charter, Laws, and Catalogue of Books, of the Library Company of Philadelphia*, 1770, entry D, folio 8 (Evans, 11820; Winans, 74).

5.5. 1772. "The Gentlemen and Cabinet Maker's Directory; being a large Collection of the most useful Designs of Houshold Furniture in the most fashionable taste, &c. The whole comprehended in Two Hundred Copperplates neatly engraved. By Thomas Chippendale, Cabinet-maker, and Upholsterer. Third Edition," in advertisement, "Robert Wells, At the Great Stationary and Book Store, Has just received from London A great Variety of Maps, Prints, Books of Architecture and Drawing &c," in *South-Carolina & American General Gazette* (Charleston), March 30, 1772 (Dixon, p. 68, no. 19).

5.6. ca. 1772. "Chippendale's Designs of Houshold Furniture, 2 V. Fol.," in *A Catalogue of A very large Assortment of the most esteemed Books In every*

Branch of Polite Literature, Arts and Sciences . . . Which are to be Sold by Cox and Berry At their Store in King-Street, Boston, ca. 1772, p. 7 (Evans, 42336; Winans, 791).

5.7. Before 1774. "Chippendales Designs -6-," in "An Inventory of the Goods and Chattels of William Buckland, late of Anne Arundel County deceased," Annapolis, December 19, 1774 (Beirne and Scarff, p. 150).

5.8. Before 1776. "Chippend also Designs & Hattons Arithmetic £5," in inventory of estate of Walter Russell, July 10, 1776. Charleston Inventories, Book CC (1766–1778), p. 9, South Carolina Department of Archives and History (Dixon, p. 69, n. 19).

5.9. 1776. "Chippendale's 160 elegant and useful designs of household furniture," among "a variety of New and Old Books . . . now selling at Robert Bell's Book Store," in advertisement on inside back board of the Bell imprint *American Independence the Interest and Glory of Great Britain*, Philadelphia, 1776 (Shepherd and Forman, p. 196; see also Hummel, 1976, p. 11).

5.10. Before 1778. "Chippendales Designs £6," in "Appraisement of the Personal Estate of Major Edmund Dickenson decd. taken this 28th. July 1778," York County Wills and Inventories, vol. 22 (1771–1783), p. 40 (Gusler, pp. 182–83).

5.11. Before 1782. "Chipendales Designs 28/," in "An Inventory of the Estate of Mr. Nath Gould Gent of Salem, dec. . . . Salem March 10th 1782" (Forman, p. 52).

5.12. 1784. "Chippendale's Designs, fine plates," in advertisement, "Just imported from London, A Catalogue of Books Consisting of many valuable and scarce Articles in every Branch of Useful and polite Literature . . . Which are selling very reasonable, by Shepperson and Reynolds, Booksellers, Binders, and Stationers, No. 137, Oxford Street, London. . . . All orders will be received by Mr. William Prichard, Bookseller, in Market-street, between Front and Second streets, and by Eleazer Oswald, at the Coffee-house, Philadelphia," in *Independent Gazetteer* (Philadelphia), April 22, 1784, p. 2 (Johnston, p. 24, n. 14).

5.13. Before 1785. "Thomas Goddard" inscribed on inside back board of a copy of the 1762 ed., Museum of Fine Arts, Boston (Hipkiss, p. 32).

5.14. 1786. "November 24, 1786. To Binding Chippendales directory folio . . . 12/6," in Account Book of Philadelphia bookbinder James Muir, Historical Society of Pennsylvania (Forman, p. 52).

5.15. After 1789. "Chippendale's Cabinetmaker's Designs. fol," in Jefferson's manuscript *Catalogue of Books*, Massachusetts Historical Society (Kimball, p. 93).

5.16. Before 1794. "Shippendales [sic] Designs," in inventory of Thomas Affleck, Philadelphia, 1794 (Hornor, p. 73; Hummel, 1955, p. 53).

5.17. Before 1805. "Cabinet makers Guide," in inventory of Alexander Taylor (d. June 26, 1805). Also, "A parcel of books, among which is the *Gentleman and Cabinet-Maker's Director*, comprehending one hundred and sixty copper-plate engravings of the most elegant designs of household furniture, &c.," in inventory of Alexander Taylor, Jr. (d. 1820), Petersburg, Virginia (Prown, p. 148).

6. Henry Copland, *A New Book of Ornaments*, London, 1746.

All ten sheets of the *New Book of Ornaments* are signed by Copland and dated April 16, 1746, but their varied formats suggest that they were prepared at different times. This volume was Copland's first publication, and it contained a variety of designs for asymmetrical cartouches, scrolls, and leafage. Offered for sale at 3s 6d, the *New Book of Ornaments* was the earliest of the English pattern books in the rococo style known to have been available in colonial America. A second edition, which cannot be accurately dated, is reprinted in *Furniture History* 15.[18]

New York booksellers Noel and Hazard offered the title in 1771, but there is no evidence that this publication influenced local cabinetmakers. Peter Harrison, the distinguished Newport architect, probably purchased his copy—the only furniture or ornament title in his library—along with many of his architectural books while in London in 1747–1748. The avante garde rococo designs in this book found little favor in New England towns.

6.1. 1771. "Copeland's new Book of Ornaments," in *A Catalogue of Books, sold by Noel and Hazard, at their Book and Stationary Store, Next Door to the Merchants Coffee-House, Where the Public may be Furnished with all Sorts of Books and Papers*, New York, 1771, p. 18 (Evans, 12168; Winans, 76).

6.2. Before 1775. "Copland's Ornaments do. 1 vol. 0.5.-," in "An Inventory of the estate of Peter Harrison, Esqr. late of New Haven deceased," June 28, 1775, Connecticut State Library, Hartford (Bridenbaugh, p. 169; Park, 8).

7. John Crunden, *The Joyner and Cabinet-maker's Darling; or, Pocket Director*, London, 1765, 1770, 1786.

Of the six architectural books published by architect and surveyor John Crunden between 1765 and 1770, *The Joyner and Cabinet-maker's Darling* is the only one with a bearing on furniture design. It contains twenty-six plates with "Sixty different Designs, . . . Forty of which are Gothic, Chinese, Mosaic, and Ornamental Frets, Proper For Friezes, Imposts, Architraves, Tabernacle Frames, Book-Cases, Tea Tables, Tea Stands, Trays, Stoves, and Fenders." The other twenty designs are for fan lights and overdoors. The *Darling* was issued without revision in 1770 and 1786. Copies are in the Huntington Library and the Winterthur Library.

Boston booksellers Cox and Berry advertised the first edition in 1767, but none of the fret designs in it appear on Boston or Salem furniture. The book also may have been available in Charleston, where furniture and architectural frets with interlaced diamonds and figure-eights resemble that shown in plate 7 of the book.

Figure 9 China table attributed to Robert Harrold, Portsmouth, 1765–1775. Mahogany and mahogany veneer with maple and white pine. H. 28 5/8", W. 36 1/4", D. 22 7/8". (Courtesy, Carnegie Museum of Art, museum purchase: Richard King Mellon Foundation grant, acc. 72.55.2.)

Figure 10 Design for bureau dressing table illustrated on pl. 40 of William Ince and John Mayhew's *Universal System of Houshold Furniture* (1762). (Metropolitan Museum of Art, Harris Brisbane Dick Fund, acc. 34.100.)

7.1. 1767. "Crunden's Joiner and Cabinet maker's Darling, containing 60 new and beautiful Designs for all sorts of Frets for Friezes, Impost, Architraves, Tabernacle Frames, Tea-stands, Stoves, Fenders, and Fan lights over Doors"; in advertisement of Cox and Berry (transcribed at cat. 4.1), *Boston News-Letter*, January 1, 1767 (Park, 11; Dow, pp. 222–23).

8. William Ince and John Mayhew, *The Universal System of Houshold Furniture*, London, 1762.

Cabinetmaker William Ince and upholsterer John Mayhew went into business together in 1759 and operated one of the most important furniture manufactories in London. In 1762 they issued *The Universal System of Houshold Furniture*, a handsome folio volume with eighty-nine numbered plates of furniture designs, plus some smaller engravings of metalwork. The designs clearly derive from the *Director*; the original plan for the *Universal System* called for 160 plates, precisely the number in Chippendale's first edition. The publication of the enlarged 1762 edition of the *Director* forced Ince and Mayhew to bring out their volume only half finished. Alec Tiranti reprinted the *Universal System* in 1960.

The only reference to Ince and Mayhew's book in America is in Charleston, where bookseller Robert Wells advertised it, along with the *Director*, in 1766 and 1772. Those two books may have been instrumental in fostering a local preference for pierced and blind frets in Charleston. The book also must have been present in the northern colonies, for the interlaced diamond fret illustrated on plate 40 (fig. 10) is repeated on two pieces of Portsmouth, New Hampshire, furniture—a china table (fig. 9) and a library bookcase attributed to Robert Harrold, a British-trained cabinetmaker who immigrated to Portsmouth in 1767. The same fret pattern also occurs on a heavily restored Philadelphia desk-and-bookcase at the Metropolitan Museum of Art. If this fretwork is original, the *Universal System* probably was present in Philadelphia as well.[19]

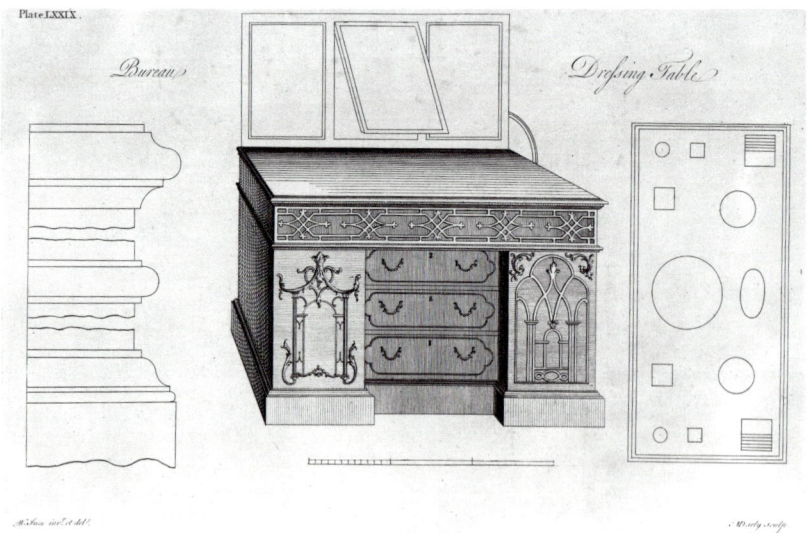

Figure 11 Wall bracket, Philadelphia, 1765–1775. White pine. H. 16 1/4", W. 12 7/8", D. 5 1/2". (Courtesy, Winterthur Museum, acc. 58.2242.)

Figure 12 Design for a wall bracket illustrated on pl. 42 of Thomas Johnson's *One Hundred and Fifty New Designs* (1761). (Metropolitan Museum of Art, Harris Brisbane Dick Fund, acc. 32.61.)

8.1. 1766. "Chippendale's and Ince and Mayhew's designs of houshold furniture," in advertisement of Robert Wells (transcribed at cat. 5.1), in *South-Carolina & American General Gazette* (Charleston), July 18, 1766. (Dixon, p. 74, no. 51).

8.2. 1772. "The Universal System of Houshold Furniture. Consisting of above Three hundred Designs in the most elegant Taste, both useful and ornamental; finely engraved, in which the Nature of Ornament and Perspective is accurately exemplified. By Ince & Mayhew, Cabinetmakers and Upholders," in advertisement of Robert Wells (transcribed at cat. 5.5), in *South-Carolina & American General Gazette* (Charleston), March 30, 1772 (Dixon, p. 74, no. 51).

9. Thomas Johnson, *One Hundred and Fifty New Designs*, London, 1758, 1761.

One Hundred and Fifty New Designs is by far the most comprehensive of English carvers' pattern books. The volume is a substantial quarto consisting of fifty-three plates with 135 individual designs. The first edition (1758) is untitled; the second edition (1761) is titled and the plates, including one new design, are reordered. The furniture forms illustrated were ones that could be made by carvers without the assistance of cabinetmakers: looking glass and picture frames, pier tables, stands, and chimneypieces. The 1758 edition is reprinted in Helena Hayward, *Thomas Johnson and English Rococo* (London: Alec Tiranti, 1964).

The only colonial references to Johnson's *Designs* are from Maryland. William Buckland (1735–1774), a house joiner who came to America in 1755, owned a copy, but there is no direct copying from the book in any of the houses he constructed in Virginia and Maryland. That the copy advertised by Baltimore bookseller John McLure in 1783 was titled suggests that it was the 1761 edition.

The book's influence is clearly visible in Philadelphia furniture and architectural carving. The clock in Benjamin Randolph's trade card (see fig. 1) is based on the flamboyantly carved tall case clock on plate 45 (1758 edition); a carved wall bracket at Winterthur is derived from a bracket illustrated on plate 42 (figs. 11, 12); and an elaborate Philadelphia high chest has a drawer appliqué (Aesop's fable of the Fox and Grapes) derived from plate 6 and urn-and-flower finials copied from plate 31.[20]

9.1. Before 1774. "Johnsons Carver's Designs . . . -2-," in "An Inventory of the Goods and Chattels of William Buckland, late of Anne Arundel County deceased," Annapolis, December 19, 1774 (Beirne and Scarff, p. 150; Park, 33).

9.2. 1783. "Ditto [A Book of Ornaments] containing 150 new Designs for Carvers, &c," in advertisement, "Collection of Books, At Mr. John M'Lure's Store. . . . Of this Collection (as large and elegant a one as ever imported here) there remains yet undisposed of, several hundred Volumes," in *Maryland Journal and Baltimore Advertiser*, November 18, 1783, p. 1.

10. Thomas Johnson, *A New Book of Ornaments*, London, 1762.
The only known complete copy of this suite of six patterns, "Designed for Tablets & Friezes for Chimney-Pieces," is at the Victoria and Albert Museum and is reprinted in *Furniture History* 11.[21]

There is no written documentation for this book in America, but the exact copying of its patterns in Philadelphia demonstrates its existence there. For example, the tablet of a chimneypiece from the Blackwell House (depicting a bull attacked by a dog) is copied from plate 3, and the drawer appliqués of a high chest and matching dressing table are copied from plate 5 (see figs. 6 and 7). In both instances the carving has been attributed to the "school" of Hercules Courtenay, one of Thomas Johnson's London apprentices who might reasonably be expected to have brought along his master's engraved designs when he immigrated in 1765.[22]

11. Matthias Lock, *A New Book of Ornaments for Looking Glass Frames, Chimney Pieces &c. &c. in the Chinese Taste*, London, ca. 1752, ca. 1768.
In addition to the decorative frame on the title page (drawn by Peter Glazier), Lock's suite consists of five plates of chimneypiece and pier glass designs in the rococo style. No copy of the first edition is known. London publisher and bookseller Robert Sayer printed the second edition. The book was published twice in the early nineteenth century, and most recently in *Furniture History* 15. It was one of several rococo titles available in Baltimore during the early 1780s (see also nos. 9, 12, 15, 16).[23] No American furniture based on designs in this book is known.

11.1. 1783. "A Book of Ornaments for Looking Glass Frames," in advertisement, "Collection of Books, At Mr. John M'Lure's Store" (transcribed at cat. 9.2), in *Maryland Journal and Baltimore Advertiser*, November 18, 1783, p. 1.

12. Matthias Lock, *A Book of Tables. Candle Stands, Pedestals, Tablets, Table Knees, &c.*, London, 1746, 1768.
This booklet, one of the earliest English suites of engravings in the rococo style, originally appeared in 1746 under the title *Six Tables*. As with Lock's *New Book of Ornaments*, London bookseller Robert Sayer published a second edition in 1768. Lock's *Book of Tables* was also reissued twice in the early nineteenth century and reprinted in *Furniture History* 15.[24] There are no pre-Revolutionary references to this book; it did not have any recognizable influence in America.

12.1. 1783. "Ditto [A Book of Ornaments] for Pedestals, Tables, &c," in advertisement, "Collection of Books, At Mr. John M'Lure's Store" (transcribed at cat. 9.2), in *Maryland Journal and Baltimore Advertiser*, November 18, 1783, p. 1.

13. Matthias Lock and Henry Copland, *A New Book of Ornaments*, London, 1752, 1768.
Lock and Copland's *New Book of Ornaments*, first published in 1752 and reissued by Robert Sayer in 1768, has twelve large etched plates with twenty-

Figure 13 Side plate from a six-plate stove attributed to Marlboro Furnace, Frederick County, Virginia, 1768–1780. H. 21 7/8", W. 27 1/2". (Colonial Williamsburg Foundation, partial gift of Liza and Wallace Gusler, acc. 1992–123.)

Figure 14 Design for a chimneypiece illustrated on pl. 7 of Matthias Lock and Henry Copland's *New Book of Ornaments* (1752, 1768). (Metropolitan Museum of Art, Harris Brisbane Dick Fund, 1928, acc. 28.88.7.)

nine rococo designs. The first edition was the most ambitious pattern book to predate the *Director* (1754). *The New Book of Ornaments* is reprinted in *Furniture History* 15.[25]

Although the only documented American reference to this volume is from late-eighteenth-century Philadelphia, there is compelling evidence that the book was available in New York and Philadelphia during the 1765–1775 period. The carved spandrel appliqués from the stairhall arch of the Van Rensselaer Manor house (now in the Metropolitan Museum) are copied from plate 10. Stephen Van Rensselaer probably acquired a copy from his father-in-law, Philip Livingston (who was sending him household goods from London), before completing the interior fittings of his house near Albany in 1768. Presumably, this copy was the second edition, published on January 1, 1768. An anonymous Philadelphia carver also adapted the flute player and Budda-like figure illustrated on plates 4 and 7 to designs for casting patterns for the side and back plates of two six-plate stoves attributed to Marlboro Furnace, Frederick County, Virginia (figs. 13, 14).[26]

13.1. 1796. "Lock and Copeland's ornaments," in [Thomas] *Bradford's Catalogue of Books and Stationary, Wholesale & Retail, for 1796*, Philadelphia, 1796, p. 56 (Evans, 30121; Winans, 212).

14. Robert Manwaring, *The Cabinet and Chair-Maker's Real Friend and Companion*, London, 1765.
The Cabinet and Chair-Maker's Real Friend and Companion, one of three modest publications by chairmaker and cabinetmaker Robert Manwaring, was readily available in America, and it had a considerable impact. It is a small book with thirty-eight engravings depicting a variety of chairs, stools, and settees, all modestly rococo in style. Boston booksellers Cox and Berry advertised the *Friend* early in 1767 and again in their ca. 1772 printed cata-

Figure 15 Side chair, Boston, 1765–1785. Mahogany with maple. H 38 3/4", W. 23 5/8", D. 21". (Metropolitan Museum of Art, Gift of Mrs. Paul Moore, 1939, acc. 39.88.1.)

Figure 16 Design for a "Parlour" chair illustrated on pl. 9 of Robert Manwaring's *Cabinet and Chair-Maker's Real Friend and Companion* (1765). (Metropolitan Museum of Art, Harris Brisbane Dick Fund, acc. 32.9.6.)

logue of books as "Pranker's Chairmaker's Friend," a reference to the engraver whose name figures as large as Manwaring's on the title page. The Essex Institute has a copy implausibly dated 1762 (possibly a misprint for 1772?), and the Boston Athenaeum has a copy originally owned by Boston builder Thomas Dawes (1731–1809). Tiranti reprinted the book in 1970.

Though the drawing is weak and the perspective poor, some of Manwaring's simpler designs are practical and attractive; or so, at least, many Bostonians must have believed, for this publication was the most influential rococo pattern book in New England. The splats and crest rails of chairs from a set owned by Clark Gayton Pickman and his wife Sarah Orne (m. 1770) are copied from plate 9 (figs. 15, 16), and there are many examples of New England chairs with strapwork splats indebted to Manwaring's designs. A common Portsmouth variety is based on plate 4. More idiosyncratic is a "Gothick Chair" attributed to Portsmouth cabinet-maker Robert Harrold. The splat of this chair—suggestive of a screen of interlaced strapwork crockets—is taken directly from the right chair on plate 15. Manwaring's book also was present in Philadelphia during the last decades of the eighteenth century, much too late for the *Friend* to have had a formative influence on local style.[27]

14.1. 1767. "The Cabinet and Chair-maker's real Friend and Companion, containing upwards of 100 new and beautiful Designs for all sorts of Chairs," in advertisement of Cox and Berry (transcribed at cat. 4.1), *Boston News-Letter*, January 1, 1767 (Dow, pp. 222–23).

14.2. 1772?. "Plate No 1 Bosto[n]," inscribed on plate 1 recto, and "From London/1762," inscribed on plate 9 verso of a copy, Essex Institute, Salem, Massachusetts (Fales, p. 50).

14.3. ca. 1772. "Pranker's Chairmaker's Friend, 4to sew'd," in *A Catalogue of . . . esteemed Books . . . Which are to be Sold by Cox & Berry* (full transcription at cat. 5.6), Boston, ca. 1772, p. 22 (Evans, 42336; Winans, 79).

14.4. 1783. "Cabinet makers companion," in advertisement of "Books lately imported and to be sold by Joseph Crukshank, in Market-Street, between Second and Third streets," in *Pennsylvania Journal and the Weekly Advertiser* (Philadelphia), December 3, 6, 13, and 20, 1783 (Johnston, p. 25).

14.5. 1796. "Cabinet and chair maker's companion, 12mo," in [Thomas] *Bradford's Catalogue of Books and Stationary, Wholesale & Retail, for 1796*, Philadelphia, 1796, p. 56 (Evans, 30121; Winans, 212; Johnston, p. 25).

14.6. Before 1809. Manwaring's *Chairmaker's Friend*, bound together with Isaac Ware's *Designs of Inigo Jones and Others* (1743) and catalogued as "Jones' Designs. 8vo.1" in Boston Athenaeum *Book of Donations, 1807–1851*, p. 15. The volumes were donated by Thomas Dawes, Jr., on January 16, 1809 (Park, p. 33; Jobe and Kaye, p. 19).

15. Robert Manwaring, *The Chair-Maker's Guide*, London, 1766. The *Guide*, subtitled "upwards of Two Hundred New and Genteel Designs

". . . for Gothic, Chinese, Ribbon and other Chairs, Couches, Settees, Burjairs, French, Dressing and Corner Stools . . . By Robert Manwaring, cabinetmaker and others," has seventy-five plates. The first twenty-eight constitute a reprint of plates in the Society of Upholsterer's *Houshold Furniture in Genteel Taste* (see no. 16). As with Manwaring's *Cabinet and Chair-Maker's Real Friend* (see no. 14), the plates are quite crude; yet unlike the *Friend*, the *Guide* had no influence on American furniture design and probably was not available in the colonies before the Revolution.

15.1. 1783. "The Chair-Makers Guide," in advertisement, "Collection of Books, At Mr. John M'Lure's Store" (transcribed at cat. 9. 2), in *Maryland Journal and Baltimore Advertiser,* November 18, 1783, p. 1 (Weidman, p. 77).

16. A Society of Upholsterers, *Houshold Furniture in Genteel Taste for the Year 1760,* London, 1760, 1762, 1763, 1764, or 1765.

Between 1760 and 1765, bookseller and printer Robert Sayer published four editions of *Houshold Furniture in Genteel Taste,* an octavo volume of relatively modest rococo designs for a wide variety of furniture forms. Sayer assembled and reissued a medley of designs including works by Manwaring, Ince and Mayhew, Chippendale, and Johnson. The first edition had sixty plates with approximately 180 designs; the second and third editions were identical and had 100 plates with about 300 designs; the fourth edition had 120 plates with about 350 designs. EP Publishing of East Ardsley, England, reprinted the latter edition in 1978.

Most of the designs were for modestly scaled furniture with restrained ornamentation, and the book found favor in cities like New York and Philadelphia. The first edition arrived in New York, hot off the press, when London bookseller James Rivington opened a store in Hanover Square in New York on September 25, 1760. The following month, his advertisement in the *New York Mercury* singled out this title for special attention. Two years later the same firm (operating in New York and Philadelphia under the name Rivington and Brown) offered the same first edition in its printed catalogue. Rival New York dealer, Garret Noel, also advertised a copy—probably the first edition—in his 1762 catalogue. The 1771 catalogue of books stocked by Noel and his partner Ebenezer Hazard also listed *Houshold Furniture,* and the description suggests that it, too, was a first edition. The reference by Baltimore bookseller John McLure is too abbreviated to identify by edition.[28]

The locally engraved trade card of New York cabinetmaker Samuel Prince is decorated with three furniture designs, two from the 1760 edition of *Houshold Furniture* (pls. 20 and 38 in the reprint); and Benjamin Randolph's trade card (see fig. 1) is festooned with fifteen pieces of furniture, eight of which are approximate copies (printed in reverse) of patterns from the same edition. For all this exposure, the book had little recognizable influence. The exception is a design for a candlestand on plate 72 (pl. 1 of the 1760 edition) that inspired the maker of a pair of stands at Mount Vernon—pieces thought to be of Williamsburg manufacture (figs. 17, 18).[29]

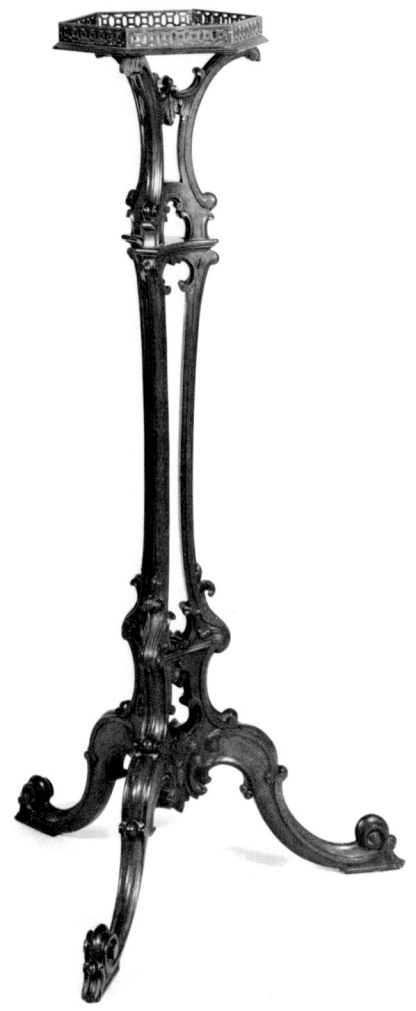

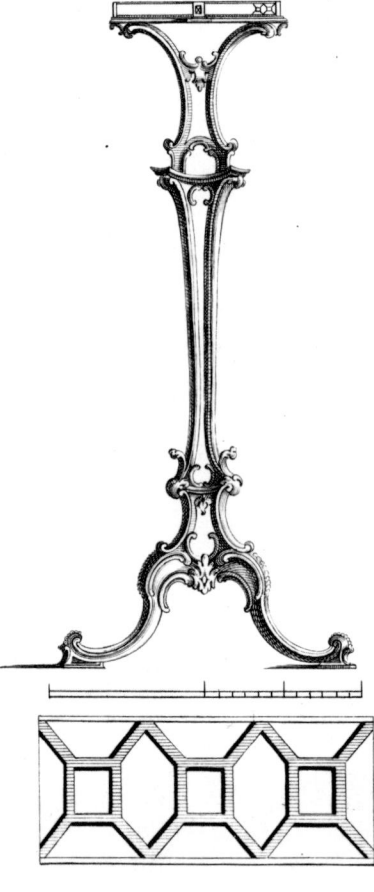

Figure 18 Design for a candlestand illustrated on pl. 1 of the Society of Upholsterers' *Houshold Furniture in Genteel Taste* (1760). (Metropolitan Museum of Art, Harris Brisbane Dick Fund, 1929, acc. 29.43.)

Figure 17 Candlestand attributed to the Anthony Hay shop, Williamsburg, Virginia, 1774–1776. Mahogany. H. 48", W. (top) 10". (Courtesy, Mount Vernon Ladies Association.)

16.1. 1760. "Houshold Furniture for the Year 1760, by a Society of Upholsterers, Cabinet makers, &c, containing upwards of 180 designs, consisting of Tea Tables, Dressing, Card, Writing, Library and Slab Tables, Chairs, Stools, Couches, Trays, Chests, Tea Kettles, Bureaus, Beds, Ornamental Bed Posts, Cornishes, Brackets, Fire Screens, Desk and Book Cases, Sconces, Chimney Pieces, Girandoles, Lanthorns &c, with Scales," in advertisement, "James Rivington, Bookseller, From London, [who] Has this Day opened a Store at the House of the late Doctor Ascough, in Hanover Square where he proposes to sell at the most reasonable Rates, all Sorts of Books . . . for Architects, Builders, Joiners, &c, particularly an entire new Work, entitled, Houshold Furniture," in *New York Mercury*, October 6, 1760, p. 3 (Lockwood, p. 19). The same title is listed in Rivington's *Catalogue of Books*, New York, 1760, p. 46 (full transcription at no. 1.5) (Hummel, 1955, pp. 53–54; Winans, 41).

16.2. 1762. "Houshold Furniture for the Year 1760, by a Society of Cabinet makers and other Artists, with 183 Designs for all Sorts of Workmen," in *A Catalogue of Books, sold by Rivington and Brown . . . in . . . New-York and . . .*

196   MORRISON H. HECKSCHER

Philadelphia, Philadelphia, 1762, p. 67, no. 763 (full reference at cat. 1.10) (Evans, 9259; Winans, 45; Hummel, 1955, p. 54).

16.3. 1762. "Houshold Furniture in the present genteel Taste, by a Society of Upholsterer's, Cabinet-makers, &c. Containing upwards of 140 Designs," in *A Catalogue of Books, &c. sold by Garrat Noel, Bookseller and Stationer, from London, At his Store next Door to the Merchant's-Coffee-House,* New York, 1762, p. 27 (Evans, 9222; Winans, 44).

16.4. 1771. "Designs in genteel Taste for Houshold Furniture," in *A Catalogue of Books Sold by Noel & Hazard,* New York, 1771, p. 18 (full reference at no. 6.1) (Evans, 12168; Winans, 76).

16.5. 1783. "A Book of Household Furniture," in advertisement, "Collection of Books, At Mr. John M'Lure's Store" (transcribed at cat. 9.2), in *Maryland Journal and Baltimore Advertiser,* November 18, 1783, p. 1 (Weidman, p. 77).

▼ NEOCLASSICAL

17. Robert and James Adam, *The Works in Architecture of Robert and James Adam,* vol. 1, 1773–1778; vol. 2, 1779.

The folio-sized engraved plates comprising volume 1 of the Adam brothers' monumental *Works in Architecture* were issued sporadically over a period of five years, and it was not until 1778 that complete copies of the first volume appeared. The second volume appeared the following year. In addition to architectural plans and elevations, *Works in Architecture* contains plates illustrating pier glasses, console tables, sideboards, and other furniture that the brothers designed.

The Library Company of Philadelphia ordered the book in 1773. After receiving the first part of volume 1 (eight plates of Sion House), the library apparently cancelled the order. The Library Company of Baltimore acquired both volumes sometime between the publication of their first institutional catalogue in 1797 and their second in 1802.

17.1. ca. 1771. "2 Adam's Designs . . . 2 vols . . . [@] 40/ . . . [£]4—," in bill, "Ebenr Battell Esqr/ Bot of Henry Knox," Boston, ca. 1771, *Henry Knox Papers* (microfilm ed., reel 48-6, Massachusetts Historical Society, Boston, 1960) (Park, 1).

17.2. 1774. "2 Adam's Architecture No 1, 2 . . . [£]4—," part of bill headed, "London, July 29, 1774. Shipped . . . for Boston in New England, by Thos Longman Bookseller in London, Five Packages of Merchandize in the Account and Risque of Mr. Henry Knox Merchant in Boston," in *Henry Knox Papers* (microfilm ed., reel 48-77, p. 3, Massachusetts Historical Society, Boston, 1960) (Park, 1).

17.3. 1775. "Architecture (The Works in) by Robert and James Adams [sic], with Explanations. London, 1773," in *The Second Part of the Catalogue of Books, of the Library Company of Philadelphia,* 1775, p. 6, no. 304 (Evans, 14392; Winans, 93; Park, 1; Hummel, 1955, p. 17). The Library Company's

Figure 19 Side chair, Salem, Massachusetts, 1790–1800. Mahogany and mahogany veneer with ash and birch. H. 38", W. 22 1/2", D. 18 3/8". (Metropolitan Museum of Art, Friends of the American Wing Fund, 1962, acc. 62.16.)

Figure 20 Design for a side chair illustrated on pl. 2 of George Hepplewhite's *Cabinet-Maker and Upholsterer's Guide* (1788). (Metropolitan Museum of Art, Rogers Fund, 1952, acc. 52.519.187.)

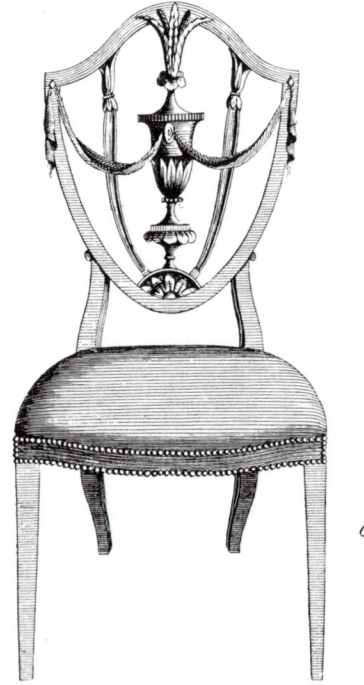

copy (Part 1 only) is now bound with Jan van Zyl, *Theatrum Machinarum Universale* (Amsterdam, 1734).

17.4. Before 1802. "Adam's Architecture. . . . 2 Vol.," in *A Catalogue of the Books, &c. Belonging to the Library Company of Baltimore*, 1802, p. 16 (Evans, 31769; Weidman, p. 77).

18. George Hepplewhite, *The Cabinet-Maker and Upholsterer's Guide*, London, 1788, 1789, 1794.

Hepplewhite published the *Guide* in 1788, then reissued it with slight revisions in 1789. The "improved" third edition (1794) consists of 128 plates; most of the cabriole-legged patterns found in the first two editions had been removed. Dover began reprinting the *Guide* in 1969.

Written evidence locates the *Guide* in Baltimore and Hartford at the very end of the eighteenth century, and surviving furniture demonstrates its presence in Salem as well. The splat design of a Hartford shield-back chair is based on that of the right chair illustrated in plate 6, and several Salem chairs owned by Elias Hasket Derby have urn-and-shield backs patterned after a chair shown in plate 2 (figs. 19, 20). On a more general level, Hepplewhite's easy chair design (pl. 15, left) may have helped establish what became the norm for American neoclassical examples of the 1790–1810 period.[30]

18.1. 1798. "Cabinet-Maker and Upholsterer's Guide," in *A Catalogue of the Books, &c. belonging to the Library Company of Baltimore*, 1798, p. 8 (Evans, 48345; Winans, 253; Weidman, p. 77).

18.2. 1799. "Cabinet Makers' Guide," in advertisement, "Hudson & Goodwin, Have for sale at their Store opposite the North-Meeting-House, Hartford, the following Books, which they have lately received from London, Dublin, and elsewhere," in *Connecticut Courant*, Hartford, December 9, 1799, p. 1 (Wadsworth Atheneum, p. 262).

19. The London Society of Cabinet Makers, *The Cabinet-Makers' London Book of Prices, and Designs of Cabinet-Work*, London, 1788, 1793, 1803.

The first edition of *The Cabinet-Makers' London Book of Prices* contains twenty engraved furniture designs, three of anonymous authorship and seventeen by Thomas Shearer, a little-known individual who may have been a journeyman. Alec Tiranti reprinted Shearer's designs under the title *Shearer Furniture Designs* in 1962. The revised 1793 edition of the *Book of Prices* had nine additional designs, six signed by Hepplewhite and three by William Casement. It was reissued, virtually unchanged, in 1803.

The revised London price book appeared shortly after publication in New York, Philadelphia, and Charleston. This volume was the model for several similar guides published in New York (1796 with eight subsequent versions by 1835) and in Philadelphia (1794 with four subsequent versions). The designs in the *London Book of Prices* were for furniture forms in common production, and the accompanying estimates were intended to aid woodworkers in determining how much to charge for certain standardized products. A Philadelphia winged bureau is based on plate 17, figure 1, whereas a Massachusetts library bookcase with wings and a secretary drawer in the

Winterthur collection is typical of American furniture more generally adapted from this book.[31]

19.1. 1793. "Robt Walker, Cupard[?] Scotland, 20th Aug. 1793," is inscribed on title page; "Robt Walker, Cabinet Maker, New York, North America, 20th October 1793" and "Octr 1st Novr. 1795, Charleston, South Carolina, North America," is inscribed on first page of index of a copy of the 1793 ed. Greenville County, South Carolina, Public Library (Dixon, pp. 77–78, no. 72).

19.2. 1796. "As there are many applications to the Philadelphia society of Cabinet and chair makers for hands, such as are willing to work for the prices in the London book (with 50 percent addition) lately published, will please call at William Cocks, No. 1. Grey's alley, Front Street between Chesnut and Walnut streets," in advertisement in *Federal Gazette* (Philadelphia), September 3, 1796 (Prime, 2:173).

19.3. 1797. "I hereby oblige myself to pay to any good workman, who is capable of doing the general run of Cabinet-work seventy-five percent advance on the New London book of Cabinet prices, published in 1793," in advertisement of Charles Watts, *The Diary* (New York), January 23, 1797 (Gottesman, 2:131).

20. Thomas Sheraton, *The Cabinet-Maker & Upholsterer's Drawing Book*, London, 1793, 1794, 1803.

Thomas Sheraton published *The Cabinet-Maker & Upholsterer's Drawing Book*, his most important work, in forty-two biweekly installments between 1791 and 1793. Parts 1 and 2 deal with geometry and perspective, and Part 3 illustrates thirty-six pieces of furniture. He published an "Appendix" containing thirty-three additional designs in 1793 and included it in the first complete edition (two volumes) of the *Drawing Book* (1793). The title page of volume 1 is dated 1791, whereas that of volume 2 is dated 1793. Sheraton added an "Accompaniment" with fourteen plates to the second edition (1794) and published a revised third edition in 1802. The 1972 Dover reprint omits most of Parts 1 and 2.

The only documentary reference to the *Drawing Book* in America is a copy of the first edition bearing the signature of Thomas Seymour. Thomas (1771–1848) was the son of John Seymour (d. 1818), an English cabinetmaker who immigrated to Portland, Maine, in 1785, and nine years later moved his family to Boston. Both father and son established commanding positions among the local artisans. Presumably Thomas acquired his copy of Sheraton shortly after arriving in Boston, but no furniture documented to either Seymour has features directly inspired by Sheraton's plates.

A number of designs in the *Drawing Book* are repeated on late-eighteenth- and early-nineteenth-century American furniture. Notable among them are plate 35, the inspiration for the archetypal Salem sofa with a carved tablet in the back; plate 33 (right), the source for a set of square-back chairs made about 1802 for the parlor of the Peirce-Nichols house, also in Salem (figs. 21, 22); and plate 36, whose six different "Chair Backs" provided popular

patterns for New York, Philadelphia, and Baltimore examples. Clearly, this book was widely available and influential. Perhaps the most graphic indication of the *Drawing Book*'s influence on early-nineteenth-century American furniture design is the trade card of Philadelphia cabinetmaker Joseph Barry (fig. 23) which is embellished with drawing room chairs and a sideboard copied exactly from the "Appendix" (pls. 6 and 21, respectively).[32]

20.1. After 1794. "Thomas Seymour" inscribed on verso of frontis; "Thos Seymour" inscribed on explanatory leaf to frontis of volume 1 of a copy of the 1793 ed., Museum of Fine Arts, Boston (Wood, pp. 1–2, pl. 1).

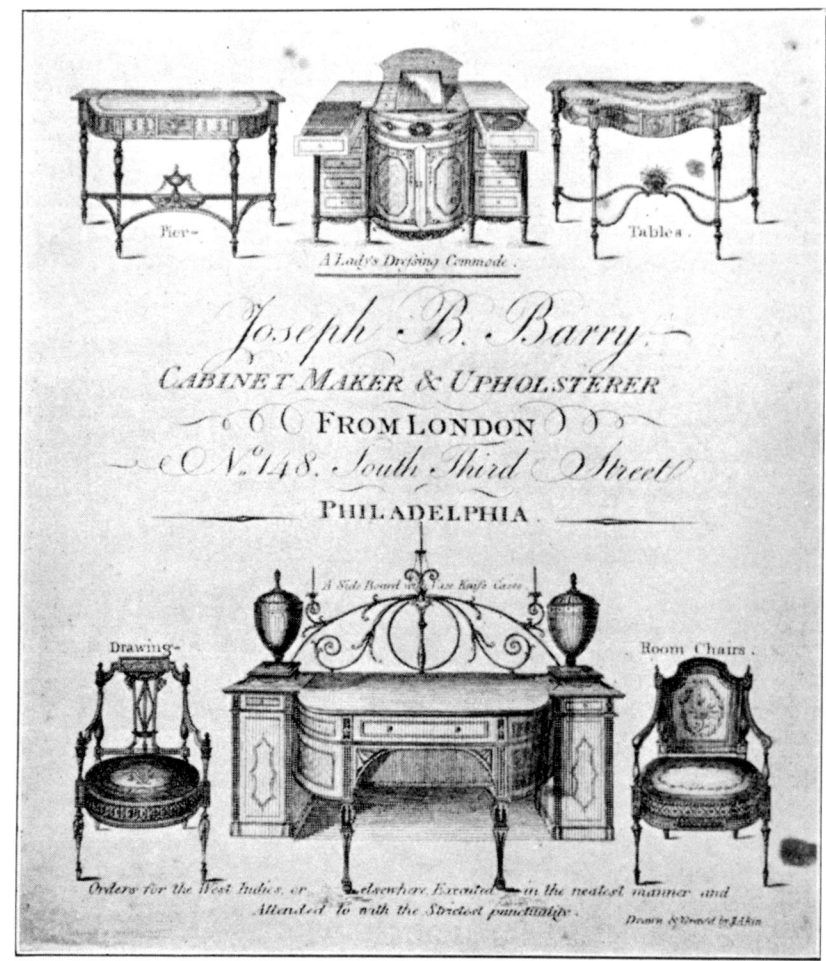

Figure 21 Side chair, Salem, Massachusetts, 1790–1800. Mahogany with birch and white pine. H. 37 7/8", W. 27 7/8", D. 18". (Metropolitan Museum of Art, Rogers Fund, acc.45.105.)

Figure 22 Design for a side chair illustrated in pl. 33 of Thomas Sheraton's *Cabinet-Maker & Upholsterer's Drawing Book* (1793). (Metropolitan Museum of Art, Rogers Fund, 1952, acc.52.519.25.)

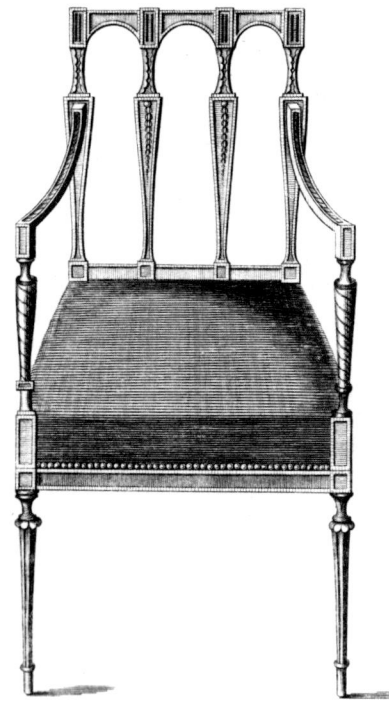

Figure 23 James Akin, Joseph B. Barry trade card, Philadelphia, ca. 1810. Line engraving on paper. From an advertisement by the Old Print Shop, in *Antiques* 34, no. 1 (July, 1938): 36.

▼ REFERENCES CONSULTED

Beirne, Rosamond Randall, and John Henry Scarff. *William Buckland, 1734–1774, Architect of Virginia and Maryland.* Baltimore: Maryland Historical Society, 1958.

Bridenbaugh, Carl. *Peter Harrison, First American Architect.* Chapel Hill, N.C.: University of North Carolina Press, 1949.

Dixon, Caroline Wyche. *A List of Architectural and Furniture Books Available in Charleston, South Carolina from 1750 through 1821.* Master's thesis, Columbia University, 1979.

Dow, George Francis. *The Arts and Crafts in New England, 1704–1775.* Topsfield, Mass.: Wayside Press, 1927. Reprint, New York: Da Capo Press, 1967.

Evans, Charles. *American Bibliography*, 14 vols. Chicago: privately printed, 1903–1934 (vols. 1–12); Worcester, Mass.: American Antiquarian Society, 1955–1959 (vols. 13–14). *Early American Imprints, 1639–1800* (microform) is a Readex microprint of the works listed in Evans.

Fales, Dean A. *The Furniture of Historic Deerfield.* New York: Dutton, 1976.

Forman, Benno M. "Thomas Chippendale in Salem, 1782." *Antiques* 97, no. 1 (January 1970): 52.

Garrett, Wendell. "Thomas Chippendale in Philadelphia, 1786." *Antiques* 97, no. 1 (January 1970): 52.

Gottesman, Rita Susswein, comp. *The Arts and Crafts in New York, 1726–1776: Advertisements and News Items from New York City Newspapers.* New York: New-York Historical Society, 1938.

Gottesman, Rita Susswein, comp. *The Arts and Crafts in New York, 1777–1799: Advertisements and News Items from New York City Newspapers.* New York: New-York Historical Society, 1954.

Gusler, Wallace B. *Furniture of Williamsburg and Eastern Virginia, 1710–1790.* Richmond: Virginia Museum, 1979.

Heckscher, Morrison H. "Philadelphia Chippendale: The Influence of the *Director* in America." *Furniture History* 21 (1985): 283–95.

Hipkiss, Edwin J. *Eighteenth-Century American Arts: The M. and M. Karolik Collection.* Boston: Museum of Fine Arts, Boston, 1941.

Hornor, William McPherson. *Blue Book: Philadelphia Furniture.* Philadelphia: by the author, 1935.

Hummel, Charles F. *The Influence of Design Books Upon the Philadelphia Cabinetmaker, 1760–1820.* Master's thesis, University of Delaware, 1955.

Hummel, Charles F. *A Winterthur Guide to American Chippendale Furniture: Middle Atlantic and Southern Colonies.* New York: Crown, 1976.

Jobe, Brock, and Myrna Kaye. *New England Furniture: The Colonial Era.* Boston: Society for the Preservation of New England Antiquities, 1984.

Kimball, Fiske. *Thomas Jefferson, Architect.* Cambridge, Mass.: Riverside Press, 1916.

Lockwood, Luke Vincent. *Colonial Furniture in America*, rev. ed. New York: Charles Scribner's Sons, 1913.

Johnston, Phillip M. *A Checklist of Books Relating to Architecture and the Decorative Arts Available in Philadelphia in the Three Decades Following 1780.* Master's thesis, University of Delaware, 1974.

Park, Helen. *A List of Architectural Books Available in America before the Revolution*, rev. ed. Los Angeles: Hennessey & Ingalls, Inc., 1973.

Prime, Alfred Coxe, comp. *The Arts and Crafts in Philadelphia, Maryland, and South Carolina, 1721–1785.* Series One. Topsfield, Mass.: Walpole Society, 1929. Reprint, New York: Da Capo, 1969.

——. *The Arts and Crafts in Philadelphia, Maryland, and South Carolina, 1786–1800.* Series Two. Topsfield, Mass.: Walpole Society, 1932. Reprint, New York: Da Capo, 1969.

Prown, Jonathan. "A Cultural Analysis of Furniture-Making in Petersburg, Virginia, 1760–1820." *Journal of Early Southern Decorative Arts* 18, no. 1 (May 1992): 1–173.

Shepherd, Raymond V., and Benno M. Forman. "Chippendale's Director for Sale, 1776." *Antiques* 98, no. 2 (August 1970): 196.

Wadsworth Atheneum. *The Great River: Art & Society of the Connecticut Valley, 1635–1820.* Hartford: by the museum, 1985.

Weidman, Gregory R. *Furniture in Maryland, 1740–1940.* Baltimore: Maryland Historical Society, 1984.

Winans, Robert B. *A Descriptive Checklist of Book Catalogues Separately Printed in America, 1693–1800.* Worcester: American Antiquarian Society, 1981.

Wood, Charles B., III. *Architecture, Landscape Gardening, and Furniture Design: Catalogue XII.* South Woodstock, Conn., 1970.

ACKNOWLEDGMENTS I am indebted to numerous people for help in assembling the material presented here, especially the late Edwin Wolf II, of the Library Company of Philadelphia, whose enthusiasm for books in colonial America was infectious, and Neville Thompson of the Winterthur Libraries for knowledgeable assistance over many years.

1. For more on English pattern books, see Eileen Harris, *British Architectural Books and Writers, 1556–1785* (New York: Cambridge University Press, 1990); and Peter Ward-Jackson, *English Furniture Designs of the Eighteenth Century* (London: Victoria and Albert Museum, 1958).

2. Irving W. Lyon cited the designs of Thomas Chippendale, George Hepplewhite, and Thomas Sheraton in *The Colonial Furniture of New England* (Boston and New York: Houghton Mifflin & Co., 1891), pp. 70, 71, 173–75; and Luke Vincent Lockwood devoted nearly a dozen pages to the publications of Chippendale, William Ince and John Mayhew, and the Society of Upholsterers in *Colonial Furniture in America* (New York: Charles Scribner's Sons, 1913), pp. 10–19. Fiske Kimball, "The Sources of the Philadelphia Chippendale," *Pennsylvania Museum Bulletin* 21, no. 104 (June 1926): 183–93; "The Sources of the Philadelphia Chippendale: II. Benjamin Randolph's Trade Card," *Pennsylvania Museum Bulletin* 23, no. 115 (October 1927): 5–8; "The Sources of the Philadelphia Chippendale. III. A Chair With the label of Benjamin Randolph," *Pennsylvania Museum Bulletin* 23, no. 117 (December 1927–January 1928): 15–19. Helen Park, *A List of Architectural Books Available in America Before the Revolution* (1961; rev. enlarged ed., Los Angeles: Hennessey and Ingalls, 1973). The principal recent studies of furniture design books in America are: Caroline Wyche Dixon, "A List of Architectural and Furniture Books Available in Charleston South Carolina From 1750 Through 1821," M.A. thesis, Columbia University, 1979; Morrison H. Heckscher, "Philadelphia Chippendale: The Influence of the *Director* in America," *Furniture History* 21 (1985), pp. 283–95; Charles F. Hummel, "The Influence of Design Books Upon the Philadelphia Cabinetmaker, 1760–1820," M.A. thesis, University of Delaware, 1955; Phillip M. Johnston, "A Checklist of Books Relating to Architecture and the Decorative Arts Available in Philadelphia in the Three Decades Following 1780," M.A. thesis, University of Delaware, 1974. In America the most complete collections of furniture pattern books are in the Department of Prints and Illustrated Books at the Metropolitan Museum of Art and in the library at Winterthur.

3. For American book catalogues, see Charles Evans, *American Bibliography*, vols. 1–12 (Chicago: privately published, 1903–1934), vols. 13–14 (Worcester, Mass.: American Antiquarian Society, 1955–1959) (*Early American Imprints, 1639–1800* [microform] is a Readex microprint of the works listed in Evans); Robert B. Winans, *A Descriptive Checklist of Book Catalogues Separately Printed in America, 1693–1800* (Worcester, Mass.: American Antiquarian Society, 1981). For transcriptions of newspaper advertisements, see George Francis Dow, comp., *The Arts and Crafts in New England, 1704–1775* (Topsfield, Mass.: Wayside Press, 1927); Rita Susswein Gottesman, comp., *The Arts and Crafts in New York, 1726–1776: Advertisements and News Items from New York City Newspapers* (New York: New-York Historical Society, 1938); Rita Susswein Gottesman, comp., *The Arts and Crafts in New York, 1777–1779: Advertisements and News Items from New York City Newspapers* (New York: New-York Historical Society, 1954); Alfred Coxe Prime, comp., *The Arts and Crafts in Philadelphia, Maryland, and South Carolina, 1721–1785* (Topsfield, Mass.: Walpole Society, 1929); Alfred Coxe Prime, comp., *The Arts and Crafts in Philadelphia, Maryland, and South Carolina, 1786–1800* (Topsfield, Mass.: Walpole Society, 1932).

4. Charles Hummel, "Samuel Rowland Fisher's Catalogues of English Hardware," in *Winterthur Portfolio One* (Winterthur, Del.: Winterthur Museum, 1964), pp. 188–97.

5. For more on Brunetti, Jones, De La Cour, Darley, Halfpenny, and Chambers, see Ward-Jackson, *English Furniture Designs*, pp. 34–35, 37–38, 47–48. For Lock, see Morrison Heckscher, "Lock and Copland. A Catalogue of the Engraved Ornament," *Furniture History* 15 (1979): 1–23.

6. The Langley furniture designs are discussed in Ward-Jackson, *English Furniture Designs*, pp. 35–36, pls. 30–34.

7. The chief source of information about these booksellers is their own imprints. See Clifford K. Shipton and James Mooney, eds., *National Index of American Imprints Through 1800: The Short-Title Evans*, 2 vols. (Worcester, Mass.: American Antiquarian Society, 1969).

8. Philadelphia Museum of Art, *Philadelphia: Three Centuries of American Art* (Philadelphia: by the Museum, 1976), pp. 111–14.

9. Ward-Jackson, *English Furniture Designs*, pp. 35–36, pls. 30–34.

10. Carl Bridenbaugh, *Peter Harrison: First American Architect* (Chapel Hill, N.C.: University of North Carolina Press, 1949), pp. 57–58, 98–101.

11. Leslie B. Grigsby, "John Stalker and George Parker's Treatise: An Inspiration for Relief Decoration on English Stoneware and Earthenware," *Antiques* 143, no. 6 (June 1993): 886–93.

12. Terry F. Friedman, "Two Eighteenth-Century Catalogues of Ornamental Pattern Books," *Furniture History* 11 (1975): 66–75, pls. 152–160.

13. See Caroline Wyche Dixon, "The Miles Brewton House: Ezra Waite's Architectural Books and other Possible Design Sources," *South Carolina Historical Magazine* 82, no. 2 (April

1981): 123; and John Bivins, Jr., "Charleston Rococo Interiors, 1765–1775: The 'Sommers' Carver," *Journal of Early Southern Decorative Arts* 12, no. 2 (November 1986): figs. 31e, 34d. Compare, for example, Baretti's plate 1 with the pediment head of the Philadelphia high chest illustrated in Morrison H. Heckscher, *American Furniture in the Metropolitan Museum of Art* (New York: Random House, 1985), no. 165.

14. The Goddard copy of the *Director* has a complicated provenance. Thomas (1765–1858) was the son of John Goddard (1724–1785) and a cabinetmaker in his own right. According to George C. Mason's *Reminiscences of Newport* (Newport: C. E. Hammett, Jr., 1884), p. 50, "Goddard's copy of Chippendale's quarto volume of designs is now owned by a cabinet-maker in Newport." Walter A. Dyer reported that the book belonged to Duncan A. Hazard ("John Goddard and his Block-Fronts," *Antiques* 1, no. 5 [May 1922]: 203–7). Hazard wrote collector Maxim Karolik: "The Chippendale book which you purchased of me I bought from an old lady in Newport, Miss Goffe. Her father was an old time cabinet-maker in Newport seventy-five years ago. This Chippendale book belonged to John Goddard the celebrated cabinet-maker of Newport. . . . Mr. Goffe purchased the book . . . at an auction of the effects of one of the descendants of John Goddard. . . . Later I had Albert W. Goddard the great-grandson of John Goddard identify his book. He . . . immediately recognized the book and said it was the one his great-grandfather owned and used." Edwin Hipkiss annotated the Hazard letter: "Thomas Goddard' was written inside the back cover—now just visible" (Duncan Hazard to Maxim Karolik, October 9, 1929, Museum of Fine Arts, Boston). The signature has since been reworked. Burling advertisement in *Rivington's New-York Gazetteer*, September 2, 1774. The woodcut is reproduced in *Antiques* 25, no. 1 (January 1934): 10. For more on the Masonic chair, see Wallace Gusler, *The Furniture of Williamsburg and Eastern Virginia, 1710–1790* (Richmond: Virginia Museum, 1979), pp. 75–79. On p. 113, n. 59, Gusler states that the pierced arm support of Bucktrout's Masonic chair probably derives from plate 17 of the first edition of the *Director*, an engraving omitted in the third edition. Thus, if Edmund Dickinson inherited Bucktrout's copy when he succeeded him as master of the Hay shop, the copy recorded in his inventory was the first or second edition. Jefferson acquired his copy of the *Director* sometime after 1789. Jefferson sold a portion of his library to the government in 1815, and subsequent Library of Congress catalogues identified the book as the 1755 edition. Jefferson's copy was destroyed in the Library of Congress fire of 1851 (E. Millicent Sowerby, *Catalogue of the Library of Thomas Jefferson*, 5 vols. [Washington: Library of Congress, 1952–1959], 4: 383, no. 4221). William B. O'Neal, *Jefferson's Fine Arts Library* (Charlottesville, Va.: University Press of Virginia, 1956), pp. 62–68, no. 26.

15. The library bookcase is illustrated in several publications on southern furniture and decorative arts. For recent illustrations, see John Bivins, Jr., and Forsyth Alexander, *The Regional Arts of the Early South* (Chapel Hill, N.C.: University of North Carolina Press for the Museum of Early Southern Decorative Arts, 1991), pp. 95–96; and Morrison H. Heckscher and Leslie Greene Bowman, *American Rococo, 1750–1775* (New York: Metropolitan Museum of Art and Los Angeles County Museum of Art, 1992), fig. 43. The New Bern chairs are illustrated in John Bivins, Jr., *The Furniture of Coastal North Carolina, 1700–1820* (Chapel Hill, N.C.: University of North Carolina Press for the Museum of Early Southern Decorative Arts, 1988), pp. 396–97.

16. For more on *Director*-influenced furniture from Philadelphia, see Morrison H. Heckscher, "Philadelphia Chippendale: The Influence of the *Director* in America," *Furniture History* 21 (1985): 283–95. The Library Company's copy of the *Director* is not in the 1764 catalogue of that institution's collection and thus must have been acquired between 1765 and 1769. Edwin Wolf II believed that (since there was no evidence of the book having been ordered) this copy probably entered the Library Company when it incorporated the Union Library Company in 1769. The *Director* appears in succeeding Library Company catalogues through 1835. A copy of the 1755 edition signed by Benjamin Randolph is said to exist, but the author has yet to examine it. A Philadelphia side chair based on plate 10 is illustrated in Heckscher, *American Furniture in the Metropolitan Museum of Art*, pp. 100–101, no. 54.

17. Folwell's proposal is illustrated in Heckscher and Bowman, *American Rococo*, p. 8, no. 5.

18. Heckscher, "Lock and Copland," no. 11, pp. 20–21, pls. 48–55.

19. See Brock Jobe, ed., *Portsmouth Furniture: Masterworks from the New Hampshire Seacoast* (Boston: Society for the Preservation of New England Antiquities, 1993), pp. 159–62, 223–26, nos. 27, 48. Heckscher, *American Furniture in the Metropolitan Museum*, p. 285, no. 185.

20. For an illustration of the high chest, see Philadelphia Museum of Art, *Three Centuries*, p. 133.

21. Helena Hayward, "Newly-discovered Designs by Thomas Johnson," *Furniture History* 11 (1975): 40–42 pls. 96–101. The Metropolitan Museum has an impression of plate 5 (see fig. 7).

22. Luke Beckerdite, "Philadelphia Carving Shops Part III: Hercules Courtenay and His School," *Antiques* 131, no. 5 (May 1987): 1044–63.

23. Heckscher, "Lock and Copland," no. 8, pp. 18–19, pls. 34–39. The author thanks Gregory R. Weidman for providing a copy of the McLure reference.

24. Heckscher, "Lock and Copland," no. 2, pp. 11–12, pls. 7A–10.

25. Heckscher, "Lock and Copland," no. 7, pp. 17–18, pls. 21–32.

26. John Bivins, Jr., "Isaac Zane and the Products of Marlboro Furnace," *Journal of Early Southern Decorative Arts* 11, no. 1 (May 1985): 47–49, figs. 16, 17.

27. Heckscher, *American Furniture in the Metropolitan Museum*, pp. 50–52, no. 13. Jobe, *Portsmouth Furniture*, pp. 316–21, nos. 85, 86.

28. The "*Book of Household Furniture*" in McLure's advertisement could refer to Ince and Mayhew's *Universal System of Houshold Furniture*, but given the other small, inexpensive volumes in McLure's list, *Houshold Furniture in Genteel Taste* is much more likely.

29. For more on the Prince card, see Heckscher and Bowman, *American Rococo*, pp. 52, 154–55. Kimball, "Randolph's Trade Card," pp. 5–8, identifies pls. 22, 25, 35, 36, 38, 41, 91. Gusler, *Furniture of Williamsburg*, pp. 125–26, makes the attribution for the stand.

30. For a Hartford example, see *The Great River: Art & Society of the Connecticut Valley, 1635–1820* (Hartford: Wadsworth Atheneum, 1985), pl. 262, cat. 150. William N. Hosley was the first to note that Hepplewhite's volume was available in 1799 from Hudson and Goodwin of Hartford.

31. See Charles F. Montgomery, *American Furniture: The Federal Period* (New York: Viking, 1966), p. 488, for the various American price books, and no. 183 for the library bookcase.

32. For American furniture based on Sheraton designs, see Montgomery, *American Furniture: The Federal Period*, nos. 269–70, 23, 98, 99. William Mcpherson Hornor published a later state of Barry's trade card in *Blue Book: Philadelphia Furniture* (Philadelphia, 1935), pl. 432.

Figure 1 William Goodacre, *Virginia Capitol in 1830*, Richmond, 1830. Watercolor on paper. (Courtesy, Valentine Museum, Richmond, Virginia.)

Sumpter T. Priddy III and Martha C. Vick

The Work of Clotworthy Stephenson, William Hodgson, and Henry Ingle in Richmond, Virginia, 1787–1806

▼ OF ALL *the Arts which are either improved or ornamented by Architecture, that of* CABINET-MAKING *is not only the most useful and ornamental, but capable of receiving as great Assistance from it as any whatever.*

Thomas Chippendale
The Gentleman and Cabinet-Maker's Director (1754)

The relationship between architecture and furniture in eighteenth-century America and the close associations between artisans who constructed buildings and those who constructed furniture are exemplified in the work of three talented tradesmen who moved to Richmond, Virginia, in the 1780s. The first, Clotworthy Stephenson, was an Irish joiner who arrived in Virginia by 1787 and executed the interior woodwork for the new Virginia Capitol. In 1793 he moved to Washington, D.C., and oversaw much of the construction of the United States Capitol. The second, British-trained carver William Hodgson, immigrated to Virginia by 1784 and resettled in Richmond by 1788. Over the following twenty years, he carved woodwork for the Virginia Capitol and for private dwellings, and he ornamented furniture for cabinetmakers in the Richmond area. The third, Philadelphia-trained cabinetmaker Henry Ingle, moved to Richmond in 1788 and established a shop at the base of Capitol Hill. Periodically working together, these three men produced some of the most significant woodwork and furniture in late eighteenth-century Virginia.[1]

Having moved from Williamsburg to Richmond for a safe haven from British troops in 1780, the Virginia legislature appropriated £30,000 for a capitol building in Richmond and appointed Governor Thomas Jefferson to oversee its design. Jefferson drew preliminary plans for the structure that year, but it was not until 1784 and his appointment to the position of minister to France that the project moved forward. With the assistance of French antiquarian Charles Louis Clérriseau, Jefferson completed the designs and provided specifications through correspondence with the nine Directors of Public Buildings for the Commonwealth of Virginia. Drawings for the design, based upon the Maison Carrée, arrived in Richmond in 1785, followed by a plaster model in 1786. This design called for the first freestanding temple-form building in the new nation, and it met with immediate acclaim (fig. 1). Slated for one of the highest prospects in Richmond, Shockoe Hill, the Capitol would overlook the James River and the agricultural lands of southern Virginia.[2]

The Capitol at Richmond was the largest public commission under con-

Figure 2 Interior of the rotunda of the Virginia State Capitol, Richmond, 1788–1789. The Carrara marble statue of Washington was sculpted by Jean Antoine Houdon in 1788. (Courtesy, Library of Virginia; photo, Katherine Wetzel.)

Figure 3 William Hodgson, Ionic capitals in the Senate chamber of the Virginia State Capitol, 1789. Painted wood. (Photo, Katherine Wetzel.)

struction in America during the 1780s, and the fledgling community of approximately 1,800 inhabitants, half of whom were slaves, was unable to provide enough skilled artisans to accomplish the task. From the beginning, the directors of the project understood that outside tradesmen would be needed to complete the building.[3]

Irish joiner Clotworthy Stephenson probably arrived in America in 1785. He moved to Richmond by August 28, 1787, when he took an Oath of Fidelity to the Commonwealth "in Order to entitle himself to the rights of a Citizen." The following January, Governor Edmund Randolph drew on the state's contingent fund to pay Stephenson £3.3.0 "for making a Table to a Copying press for the use of the Executive."

From 1789 to 1790, Stephenson worked with joiner John Hart, and together they constructed most of the interior woodwork for the new Capitol. Their £604.16.0 worth of "Joyners Work done in the Capitol in the year 1789" included over 1,000' of columns and pilasters, over 900' of entablature, dado, windows, moldings for chimneypieces and niches, balustrades, and the doorways' "Raking and level Cornices," the most elaborate of which appear in the Capitol rotunda (fig. 2).[4]

Assisting Stephenson and Hart was William Hodgson, a talented tradesman who had previously resided in Norfolk. In 1789, Hodgson submitted a voucher for carving two large and ten smaller trusses (also known as consoles or brackets) supporting the "Raking and level cornices," fourteen Ionic capitals for the Council chamber, and six Ionic capitals for the Senate. The carving came to £64.18.0, and with the labor for painting and putting up the capitals, his invoice totaled £75.[5]

The capitals of the Council chamber were destroyed when an overloaded courtroom above the chamber collapsed in 1870, but the capitals in the Senate chamber survive. Two are on the pilasters on the north wall, and the other four cap the paired pilasters in the corners of the room (fig. 3). Stylistically, these capitals differ from the ones that Jefferson designed for

the exterior and represent a departure generally attributed to the building's superintendent, Samuel Dobie. Each capital carved by Hodgson is deeply modeled, with the spiral of each volute separated from the preceding turn as it tightens inward. Egg-and-dart and bead-and-reel moldings span the volutes, and a central patch now occupies the space originally filled by a carved flower. Unlike Ionic capitals from antiquity, which have a single volute on each corner, Hodgson's have converging volutes that give a finished appearance from the front and side. Such capitals are based on designs by Italian Renaissance architect Vincenzo Scamozzi (1552–1616), a student of Andrea Palladio. Scamozzi capitals are rare in eighteenth-century America, where architects and builders preferred the single volute commonly found in antiquity.[6]

Careful inspection of the surviving trusses reveals four different designs. The first is found on the two principal doorways of the south entry (not illustrated); the second on the east, west, and south doorways of the rotunda (figs. 4, 5); the third on the north doorway of the rotunda (fig. 6); and the fourth on the doorways opening onto the balcony of the rotunda (fig. 7).[7] Despite the stylistic differences in their designs, the physical evidence suggests that William Hodgson carved all twenty-four of the trusses.

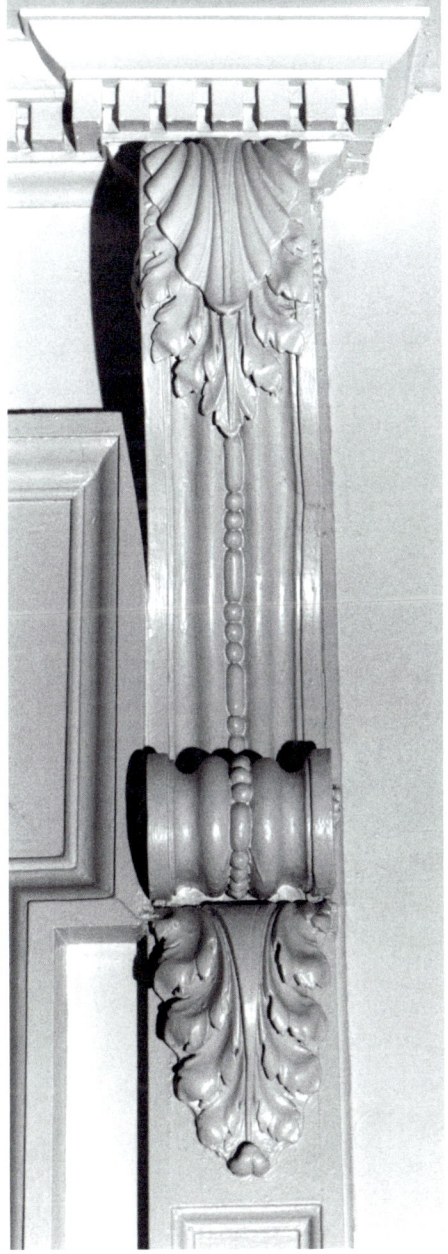

Figure 4 William Hodgson, truss over the east doorway of the rotunda of the Virginia State Capitol, 1789. Painted wood. (Photo, Katherine Wetzel.)

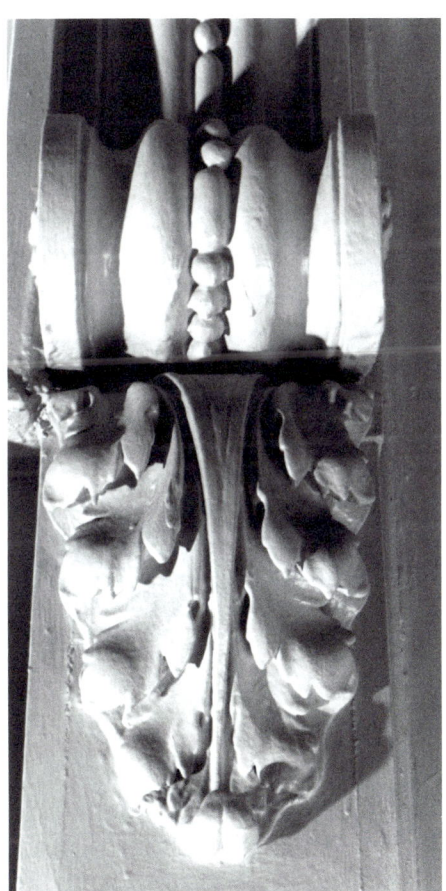

Figure 5 Detail of the acanthus carving on the truss illustrated in fig. 4. (Photo, Katherine Wetzel.)

Figure 7 William Hodgson, truss over the north central doorway on the balcony of the rotunda of the Virginia State Capitol, 1789. Painted wood. (Photo, Katherine Wetzel.)

Figure 6 William Hodgson, truss over the north doorway of the rotunda of the Virginia State Capitol, 1789. Painted wood. (Photo, Katherine Wetzel.)

Each leaf has a concave central channel (or flute) rather than a raised vein or rib, as is commonly found in the work of other carvers. As the channel approaches the tip of each leaf, it flows into a raised, rounded nodule. The tip of each leaf then falls away, as though clipped across the surface with a single gouge cut (see fig. 5). Such details are easily recognizable in the leafage at the base of the trusses on the south, east, and west doorways in the rotunda, on the doorways of the south entry, and below the smaller trusses on the balcony.

Certain details appear less refined than others and initially suggest that Hodgson's shop included a journeyman or apprentice of considerably less skill. This difference is most apparent on the north doorway of the rotunda and on the sides of the twelve smaller trusses on the balcony, where the acanthus leaves and husks (or bellflowers) are simpler in design and less finished than those on the sides of the trusses on the east and west doorways. However, other carving attributed to Hodgson indicates that, though he

Figure 8 Masonic canopy in Richmond Randolph Lodge 19, attributed to Clotworthy Stephenson and William Hodgson, Richmond, 1788–1791. (Courtesy, Richmond Randolph Lodge 19; photo, Katherine Wetzel.)

was capable of exceptional artisanry, he sometimes executed lesser work, particularly for areas of secondary importance.

William Hodgson also carved at least one piece of architectural furniture that Clotworthy Stephenson made for the Capitol. In November 1789, Hodgson billed the directors for "blocking & Carving Elbows for the Judge's Seat." Records of Stephenson's work strongly suggest that this seat was built-in like those in other eighteenth-century Virginia courtrooms. His invoice listed "Steps of Stairs to Judges Seat," along with 111'4" of "circular seats," 422'8" of "straight seats," and 120 "bracketts" that supported the straight seats in the court. All were destroyed in 1870.[8]

In addition to architectural joinery and built-in seating, Stephenson also made the finest of the conventional furniture for the building. He received £6.12.10 for a painted "Bookcase . . . with Double folding doors, Brackett feet Sliding Shelves Pedament Top &c." for the auditors office, and £6.0.0 for a similar "Book press" with "pidgeon holes" and £5.14.6 for a "Double Writing Desk Eight feet Long with Six Drawers and Slides at one End" for the High Court of Chancery.[9]

None of Stephenson's furniture survives, but one other example of his architectural joinery remains in Richmond—an elaborate Palladian canopy made to cover the Masonic Master's chair of Richmond Randolph Lodge 19, where he served as Senior Warden (fig. 8). The entablature moldings used on this remarkable structure are close enough in proportion and detail to those of the balcony doorways at the Capitol to suggest that Stephenson's shop executed all of them at approximately the same time (compare figs. 7 and 9).[10]

The carved details on the Masonic canopy are attributed to William Hodgson. The Ionic capitals vary only slightly from the documented examples in the Senate chamber (compare figs. 3 and 9), and the husks on the frieze are closely related to those on the sides of the balcony trusses in the Capitol (compare figs. 7 and 9). Only the backband of the arch, which has relief-carved acanthus leaves, is absent from the vocabulary of ornament recorded at the Capitol.

Although written documentation is lacking, evidence suggests that Stephenson and Hodgson collaborated on at least one private architectural project—Woodlands. Built in Amelia County by planter Stephen Cocke (1751–1794), Woodlands is remarkable for its pedimented facade and four-square plan. Temple-form houses with symmetrical wings were a popular Palladian convention, but such pedimented structures without wings were virtually unknown in America before the construction of the Virginia

Figure 9 Detail of the Masonic canopy illustrated in fig. 8. (Courtesy, Richmond Randolph Lodge 19; photo, Sumpter T. Priddy III.)

Capitol. Woodlands marks a point of departure from traditional domestic architecture in Virginia (fig. 10). Together with the John Marshall house, simultaneously under construction in Richmond just two blocks north of the new Capitol, Woodlands represents an important transition in acceptance of the neoclassical style in Virginia.[11] It is not known whether the Capitol inspired the design of these houses or whether Stephenson or another Capitol artisan introduced the temple form into the realm of domestic architecture.

The principal "undertaker" for Woodlands was Petersburg joiner James Crumpley, and the provincial character of most of the architectural details suggests that he directed the joiners who fabricated them.[12] The exception is the principal room on the first floor (fig. 11), which contains some of the

Figure 10 James Crumpley (builder), "Woodlands," Amelia County, Virginia, 1789–1794. (Courtesy, Helen Scott Townsend Reed; photo, Katherine Wetzel.)

Figure 11 Chimney wall in the principal parlor on the first floor of "Woodlands." The woodwork is attributed to Clotworthy Stephenson, and the carving is attributed to William Hodgson. (Illustrated in Mills Lane, *Architecture of the Old South: Virginia* [Savannah, Ga.: Beehive Press]; photo, V. J. Martin.)

Figure 12 Detail of the left Ionic capital of the chimney wall illustrated in fig. 11. (Photo, Sumpter T. Priddy III.)

finest interior woodwork made in Virginia during the last quarter of the eighteenth century. The pediment and raking cornice of the overmantle bear a striking resemblance to those of the Capitol rotunda (compare figs. 2 and 11) and probably represent the collaborative efforts of John Hart and Clotworthy Stephenson.

The carving in the principal room is attributed to Hodgson. The Ionic capitals have volutes carved in a manner similar to those in the Senate cham-

Figure 13 Detail of the right truss, rosette, and husk garland on the chimneypiece illustrated in fig. 11. (Photo, Katherine Wetzel.)

Figure 14 Detail of the urn ornament of the chimneypiece illustrated in fig. 11. (Photo, Sumpter T. Priddy III.)

Figure 15 Detail of the tablet appliqué of the chimneypiece illustrated in fig. 11. (Photo, Katherine Wetzel.)

ber (compare figs. 3 and 12), and the acanthus-draped trusses on the mantle (fig. 13) are simplified versions of those on the Capitol doorways (compare figs. 4–7 and 13). Two details in Woodlands provide benchmarks for identifying other carving by Hodgson. The urn finial of the chimneypiece (fig. 14) is related to the pediment ornaments of several late-eighteenth-century Richmond case pieces (see figs. 23 and 24 later in this article), and the acanthus reinceau, husks, and rosettes of the tablet appliqué (fig. 15) have direct parallels in local furniture carving and composition ornaments.[13]

Richmond-made furniture with carving attributed to Hodgson includes three desks-and-bookcases (figs. 16, 19, 21) with intricate latticework pediments and scroll volutes with "hollowed" acanthus leaves that are virtually identical to those on the Capitol trusses (compare figs. 5 and 17). One desk-and-bookcase also has an elaborate vase ornament with naturalistic flowers (figs. 16, 18) that are similar to those on the sides of the trusses over the doorways of the Capitol rotunda (figs. 6, 7). With its naturalistically modeled flowers and leaves, this ornament provides a significant gauge of Hodgson's most accomplished work.[14]

The desk-and-bookcase illustrated in figure 16 has two chalk inscriptions—"Jan 24th 1789" and "Dabney Minor." Dabney Minor (1749–1799) lived at Woodlawn, Orange County, Virginia, and was a prosperous carpenter appointed by the Directors of Public Buildings to work on the Capitol. Living in Richmond when construction began, he did not return to Orange County until 1796, just as finishing touches were being put on the building.[15]

Dabney Minor built several pieces of furniture for the Commonwealth of Virginia; however, documentary evidence discounts him as the maker of this desk-and-bookcase. In an indenture dated January 26, 1789, Minor described himself as a "carpenter" rather than as a cabinetmaker. Second, receipts pertaining to the construction of the Capitol reveal that he provided a wide range of modest services including carpentry and simple furniture joinery. In 1790 he billed the Directors of Public Buildings for a "Box to Send Books to Philadelphia," for a "pr Hinges for the Garden Gate," for "Repairing Roof of House," for "94 pannels [of] planking," and for three large tables for the General Court and "Committy" rooms. Two of the tables were painted, but the surface of the third—the cheapest one—was unspecified. His furnishings for the governor included "2 large pine tables" and "3 pine bedsteads for the Gov[ernor's]. Negroes." He also charged £1.16.0 for "1 large Oval Table for the Sennett," £3.15.0 for "3 large Tables painted w. 1. draw. for ye use of ye Assembly," and £32.8.0 for eight "large" bookcases for the offices "under . . . [the] portico" of the Capitol. Presumably these pieces were pine and unpainted, because no materials are specified.[16]

Another desk-and-bookcase is similar to the Minor example both in style and construction (fig. 19). Although lacking its ornament, this piece has its original acanthus-carved plinth block and arched prospect door (figs. 19, 20). Fitted with glazed doors sporting "Chinese" mullions, this item was undoubtedly the more expensive of the two. It has a chalk inscrip-

Figure 16 Desk-and-bookcase attributed to Henry Ingle and William Hodgson, Richmond, inscribed "Dabney Minor" and dated "Jan. 24th, 1789." Mahogany and mahogany veneer with yellow pine, tulip poplar, walnut, birch, and cherry. H. 92½", W. 44⅜", D. 21½". (Private collection; photo, Gavin Ashworth.)

Figure 17 Detail of the rosette of the desk-and-bookcase illustrated in fig. 16. (Photo, Gavin Ashworth.)

Figure 18 Detail of the urn-and-flower ornament of the desk-and-bookcase illustrated in fig. 16. (Photo, Gavin Ashworth.)

tion "B. Tanner" written by the same hand as that on the Minor example. Branch Tanner (d. 1794) was a wealthy planter who owned land near Woodlands in Amelia County and had another sizable tract just south of Richmond in Chesterfield County.[17]

These two desks-and-bookcases, together with a third whose history and current location are unknown (fig. 21), are among the most aspiring designs for case furniture produced in eighteenth-century Virginia. Stylistically, however, they are more closely indebted to Philadelphia prototypes than to currently recognized Virginia examples. Their ogee feet, graduated draw-

Figure 19 Desk-and-bookcase attributed to Henry Ingle and William Hodgson, Richmond, inscribed "B. Tanner," ca. 1790. Mahogany and mahogany veneer with yellow pine and tulip poplar. H. 93 1/2", W. 44 1/2", D. 21 3/4". (Private collection; photo, Museum of Early Southern Decorative Arts.)

Figure 20 Detail of the carved plinth block on the pediment of the desk-and-bookcase illustrated in fig. 19. (Photo, Sumpter T. Priddy III.)

Figure 21 Desk-and-bookcase attributed to Henry Ingle and William Hodgson, Richmond, ca. 1790. (Francis Clary Morse, *Furniture of the Olden Time* [1902; reprinted and enlarged 1917, New York: MacMillan, 1940], p. 143; photo, Museum of Early Southern Decorative Arts.)

ers, and desk interiors are relatively generic, but their latticework tympana, scroll pediments, and spiral, acanthus-carved volutes clearly derive from Philadelphia examples of the 1760–1780 period.

Similarly, several structural features seem strongly indebted to traditional Philadelphia cabinetmaking practices. The construction of the dustboards—which are thinner than the drawer blades and are wedged into dadoes ploughed in the case sides—is one of the most common construction methods on eighteenth-century Philadelphia case pieces. The attachment of the waist molding to the upper case and the practice of screwing the two sections together also is consistent with contemporary Philadelphia work. Despite these parallels, several structural features appear to be concessions to Virginia cabinetmaking traditions: the side-to-side orientation of the drawer bottoms (Philadelphia drawers often have bottom boards that run front to back), the use of birch as a secondary wood, and the employment of stack-laminated (or "composite") support blocks for the feet. This last detail is extremely rare in Philadelphia and is more commonly representative of furniture made in Williamsburg and eastern Virginia during the colonial period. Although these pieces could represent the work of a Virginia artisan inspired by an imported Philadelphia desk-and-bookcase, it is far more likely that they represent the work of a Philadelphia-trained cabinetmaker who employed regional workmen in his shop. This latter possibility is strongly suggested by the documentary evidence; of the cabinetmakers in Richmond during this period only Henry Ingle (1764–1822) had trained in Philadelphia.[18]

Henry Ingle was a talented, socially connected journeyman when he arrived in Richmond in 1788. Born in Germantown, just outside Philadelphia, Ingle was apprenticed at the age of nine to John Webb, variously referred to as a cabinetmaker and a house joiner. Ingle's apprenticeship papers committed him to serve for twelve years and eight months—an usually long term evidently owing to his age.[19]

Webb operated one of the largest and most successful cabinet shops in Philadelphia. No documented pieces are known, but the taxes assessed for his annual production in 1783 and 1786 were £60 and £75 respectively. Although less than the largest Philadelphia shops, his assessments were well ahead of those of such Philadelphia notables as William Savery and Thomas Tuft, whose annual production incurred £50 tax. Webb enjoyed a long career and is listed as a cabinetmaker and joiner in Philadelphia directories as late as 1800.[20]

Insights into the skills that Webb taught Ingle are suggested by the work of another Philadelphia cabinetmaker, Daniel Trotter (1747–1800), who was in partnership with Webb from 1771 to 1773. Documented pieces by Trotter are dated after that partnership; however, a desk-and-bookcase (fig. 22) that Trotter made for Philadelphia merchant Stephen Girard provides evidence of the level of artisanry in which Ingle was schooled.[21]

Henry Ingle was legally bound to remain in Webb's shop until 1785, but he packed up his tools and personal possessions in 1784 and headed south, most probably with his master's blessings. The young journeyman moved to Albemarle County, Virginia, the birthplace of Thomas Jefferson and, from the late 1760s onward, the site of his home, Monticello. Documentary evidence does not irrefutably link Ingle and Jefferson until 1791, when both men were living in Philadelphia. Yet, circumstances strongly suggest that they met earlier—perhaps during the Second Continental Congress (1783–1784)—for it is otherwise difficult to explain how a Pennsylvania

Figure 22 Desk-and-bookcase attributed to Daniel Trotter, Philadelphia, ca. 1780. Mahogany with tulip poplar and white cedar. Dimensions not recorded. (Courtesy, Girard College.)

Figure 23 Secretary-and-bookcase attributed to Henry Ingle and William Hodgson, Richmond, ca. 1790. Mahogany and mahogany veneer with white pine, cherry, and tulip poplar. H. 99" (less ornament), W. 49½", D. 23¼". (Private collection; photo, Museum of Early Southern Decorative Arts.)

tradesman who shared a lifelong allegiance to Jefferson would appear in rural Albemarle County and subsequently at the Capitol in Richmond at the precise moment that Jefferson left America to serve as minister to France.[22]

One hypothesis for Ingle's move to Virginia is suggested by a secretary-and-bookcase attributed to him and William Hodgson (fig. 23). According to oral tradition, this piece originally belonged to Colonel Nicholas Cabell (1750–1803) of "Liberty Hall" in Amherst County, which adjoins Albemarle. Colonel Cabell was a college classmate and friend of Jefferson, and the two frequently spoke and corresponded about architecture and the decorative arts. The Cabells were among the wealthiest and best-educated families in Virginia, and their success in agriculture and business enabled them to engage in extensive house building during the late eighteenth century. Jefferson may have recommended Ingle to his friend shortly before leaving for France; however, Cabell probably commissioned this particular piece five to ten years later.[23]

The design of the secretary-and-bookcase, having a writing compartment concealed in a drawer with a compass-hinged front, represents an important stylistic shift from the traditional slant-front desk. The raking cornice is the only such example from Ingle's Richmond period, and, though it bears an affinity to Clotworthy Stephenson's work at the Capitol, the cornice differs substantially in detail (compare figs. 2 and 23). In a further departure from the preceding desks-and-bookcases, Ingle employed cross-banding rather than a pierced guilloche for the bookcase frieze. Despite these differences, this piece shares a number of details with the preceding examples, including interior drawer construction and moldings profiles.

The carved vase ornament of the Cabell secretary-and-bookcase is very similar to the one at Woodlands (figs. 14, 24), and it sits on a rectangular plinth like the vase-and-flower ornament of the Tanner desk-and-bookcase (fig. 20). In the center of the plinth is a carved mahogany rosette that is similar to other rosettes attributed to Hodgson (figs. 7, 15, 34). As on the Minor and Tanner desks-and-bookcases, the plinth and vase of Colonel Cabell's piece are not carefully integrated into the design of the tympanum (figs. 16, 19, 23); rather, they appear to be placed on top of the cornice molding as an entity unto themselves, much like those that Hodgson carved for Clotworthy Stephenson's chimneypiece in Woodlands (fig. 11). This feature commonly appears in British design books and occasionally on furniture and architecture from eastern Virginia. Ingle's departure from conventional Philadelphia design, where the tympanum usually sweeps up and encompasses the base of the plinth, represents an important concession to regional preferences.

A mahogany clothespress and a painted yellow pine clothespress are the only examples of utilitarian furniture associated with Ingle (figs. 25, 26). Both have histories of descent in the Tabb family of Matthews County, Virginia. Although clearly related to the preceding desks-and-bookcases and secretary-and-bookcase, the presses differ in subtle detail. Their feet and

Figure 24 Detail of the plinth block and ornament of the secretary-and-bookcase illustrated in fig. 23. (Photo, Museum of Early Southern Decorative Arts.)

Figure 25 Clothespress attributed to the school of Henry Ingle, Richmond, ca. 1790. Mahogany and mahogany veneer with yellow pine. H. 80¾", W. 50", D. 22⅝". (Private collection; photo, Museum of Early Southern Decorative Art.)

Figure 26 Clothespress attributed to the school of Henry Ingle, Richmond, ca. 1790. Painted yellow pine. H. 83", W. 52¼", D. 26¼". (Colonial Williamsburg Foundation, acc. 1968–279.)

cornices are slightly larger in scale and have profiles slightly different from others in the group. There are no dustboards in the mahogany press, but the drawer construction is virtually identical to that of figures 16, 19, and 23. Construction differences notwithstanding, the presses have enough of an affinity with Ingle's other work that they can certainly be attributed to his sphere, if not to his shop.[24]

A secretary-and-bookcase made in Richmond and now known only from an early photograph is the most elaborate piece attributed to Ingle and Hodgson (fig. 27). Although aspects of the case design differ significantly from other work attributed to Ingle's shop, the cornice moldings and frieze are similar to those of the Cabell and Tabb pieces and the vase-and-flower ornament is virtually identical to that on the Minor desk-and-bookcase. The veneers and inlays of figure 27 also represent a departure from other work attributed to Ingle; however, these details are no less indebted to Philadelphia prototypes than his basketweave tympana or his scroll pediments. The unusual geometric medallions on the doors and the writing drawer are virtually identical in detail and placement to those on an elaborate library bookcase (fig. 28) made in Philadelphia about 1790 for Revolutionary War hero James Hunter (1729–1796). Initially, one might question the authenticity of the boldly carved ogee feet, the central pendant of the skirt, and the gadrooned waist molding, but under magnification they appear to be original and the feet bear a striking resemblance to those of contemporary Irish pieces. It is thus conceivable that Clotworthy Stephenson played some role in its design. An Ingle-Hodgson attribution for figure 27 is reinforced by another secretary-and-bookcase purchased in Richmond in 1904 (fig. 29). Although the latter example is later in date and technically less accomplished, it probably represents the work of an artisan on the periphery of the Ingle-Hodgson school.[25]

The quantity of furniture attributed to Henry Ingle's Richmond period is remarkable considering his brief career in the state. On October 27, 1789, he announced his intention of leaving the Commonwealth and requested those indebted to him to settle their obligations. In a separate advertisement published the same day, he reported that he would sell:

> at ... auction ... a large assortment of elegant new Mahogany furniture, consisting of CHAIRS, DESKS AND BOOKCASES, DINING AND CARD TABLES, SIDEBOARDS AND BREAKFAST DITTO. HIGH AND LOW POST BEDSTEADS, FIELD AND CANOPY DITTO, CRADLES AND CANDLESTANDS, &C.

Henry Ingle's precise date of departure and destination are unknown. He returned to Philadelphia by 1791 and subsequently moved to Washington.[26]

Hodgson continued to ply his trade in Richmond. A bookcase illustrated in Frances Clary Morse's *Furniture of the Olden Time* has one of Hodgson's most elaborate ornaments (fig. 30). Although the character of the carved feet bear a vague resemblance to the secretary-and-bookcase illustrated in figure 27, disparate stylistic and structural details—Ionic pilasters, paneled ends of the lower case, unconventional mullion design, and florid carved pediment—suggest that the bookcase was altered during the late nineteenth

Figure 27 Secretary-and-bookcase attributed to Henry Ingle and William Hodgson, Richmond, ca. 1790. Materials and dimensions not recorded. (Edward Wenham, *The Collector's Guide to Furniture Design* [New York: Collector's Press, 1928], p. 144; photo, Luke Beckerdite.)

century. Nonetheless, the exquisite ornament capping the piece differs only slightly from that of the Minor desk-and-bookcase, and it appears to be the most complete of Hodgson's surviving ornaments.[27]

Figure 28 Library bookcase, Philadelphia, 1785–1795. Materials and dimensions not recorded. (William Mcpherson Hornor, *Blue Book: Philadelphia Furniture* [1935; reprinted, Washington, D. C.: Highland House, 1977], p. 251; photo, Luke Beckerdite.)

Figure 29 Secretary-and-bookcase, Richmond, 1790–1800. Mahogany, mahogany veneer, and unidentified light and dark inlays with tulip poplar, oak, and yellow pine. H. 88 5/8", W. 46", D. 22 3/4". (Private collection; photo, Museum of Early Southern Decorative Arts.)

Figure 30 Desk-and-bookcase with an urn-and-flower ornament attributed to William Hodgson, Richmond, ca. 1790. Materials and dimensions not recorded. (Francis Clary Morse, *Furniture of the Olden Time* [1902; reprinted and enlarged 1917, New York: MacMillan Co., 1946], p. 143; photo, Luke Beckerdite.)

Hodgson's most important commission independent of Stephenson and Ingle was for furniture carving and architectural details for the principal first-floor parlor and dining room of John Marshall's house (built 1788–1790), just two blocks north of Capitol Square. Several artisans worked on Marshall's house, but Hodgson's name does not appear in any of the documents. Hodgson probably worked, in a modern sense, as a subcontractor. Because he received payment directly from the contractor or "undertaker," his name never appeared in the owner's accounts.[28]

Hodgson's furniture carving in the John Marshall house is represented by an ornament made for an English library bookcase owned by Marshall's wife, Mary Willis "Polly" Ambler, the daughter of Jaquelin and Rebecca Burwell Ambler (figs. 31, 32). Originally from Jamestown, the Amblers came to Richmond soon after the relocation of the capital, and they constructed a "mansion" between Marshall and Clay streets.[29] It is impossible to determine whether Hodgson carved the ornament when the piece was owned by the Amblers or, subsequently, by the Marshalls. Nonetheless, the ornament clearly is a composite of details from other examples carved by Hodgson (fig. 32).

The Marshall house also provides the only surviving evidence of William Hodgson's pattern carving for composition ornament (fig. 33). A variety of these cast ornaments are in the principal parlor on the first floor and in a small dining room adjoining it. The parlor has a classical entablature with composition paterae in the metopes (fig. 34). Alternately round and oval, these paterae are virtually identical to the carved mahogany paterae on the plinth block of the Cabell family secretary-and-bookcase (fig. 24). The finest composition ornaments are on the mantlepieces in the two rooms. Hodgson's most individualistic vase (or urn) carving is represented by the composition examples on the central tablets of the mantles in the parlor (fig. 35) and dining room. Unlike his furniture ornaments, the tablets' vases

Figure 31 Library bookcase with urn-and-flower ornament attributed to William Hodgson, England (library bookcase) and Richmond (ornament), 1770–1780 (library bookcase) and ca. 1790 (ornament). Mahogany with oak and deal. The library bookcase was altered to fit into a specific space in the principal first-floor room of the John Marshall house, built in Richmond between 1789 and 1791. (Courtesy, Association for the Preservation of Virginia Antiquities; photo, Katherine Wetzel.)

Figure 32 Detail of the ornament of the library bookcase illustrated in fig. 31. (Photo, Katherine Wetzel.)

Figure 33 Detail of the chimneypiece illustrated in fig. 31. The composition ornaments on the chimneypiece and in the metopes are attributed to William Hodgson. (Photo, Katherine Wetzel.)

Figure 34 Detail of one of the composition paterae in the metopes of the room illustrated in figs. 31 and 33. (Photo, Katherine Wetzel.)

Figure 35 Detail of the composition urn on the tablet of the chimneypiece illustrated in fig. 33. (Photo, Katherine Wetzel.)

are horizontally oriented and have spiral fluted necks and rectilinear handles with broad acanthus overlays.

The seasonal representations applied to the pilasters on the parlor mantle are the only figural ornaments attributed to Hodgson. Winter is represented by a winged cherub warming beside a tripod burner (fig. 36), whereas Spring is represented by a cherub draped in a floral garland (fig. 37). Each is contained within an oval wreath of acanthus leaves bound at the top by a triple bow with trailing ribbons. Hodgson's estate inventory provides

Figure 36 Detail of the composition ornament depicting "Winter" on the chimneypiece illustrated in fig. 33. (Photo, Katherine Wetzel.)

Figure 37 Detail of the composition ornament depicting "Spring" on the chimneypiece illustrated in fig. 33. (Photo, Katherine Wetzel.)

additional evidence for attributing these ornaments to his hand: "1 Nest of drawers with a quantity of composition" valued at $5 and "60 composition molds" valued at $2.[30]

The composition ornament in the John Marshall house clearly illustrates the work of an English-trained artisan adapting his skills to changing demands. As the rococo style gave way to neoclassicism, so tastes moved away from asymmetrical ornament and gravitated toward geometric repetition. To flourish, tradesmen such as Hodgson had to adopt a new stylistic vocabulary and expand their business to include the production of molds for composition ornament.

Aside from the architectural carving and the composition ornament that Hodgson executed between 1788 and 1794, his later work remains unrecognized. Of the sixty composition molds recorded in his inventory, only those that were used for the Marshall house can be identified. If Hodgson's style changed, it is not readily discernable among the small body of composition ornament and carving that survives in local buildings. He apparently never advertised. Moreover, none of the few building accounts that survive for Richmond structures from the last decade of the century provides evidence of his later work. Further identification is complicated by the massive destruction of Richmond's early buildings, which were lost through the vicissitudes of war, through neglect, and in more recent years, through demolition.

Although Hodgson's skills allowed him to flourish during the 1780s and early 1790s, he undoubtedly had difficulty competing with inexpensive, composition ornaments imported from abroad and from the north. His greatest domestic competition probably came from British immigrant George Andrews. Thomas Jefferson strongly encouraged Andrews to establish a composition manufactory in Washington, where the latter could provide decorations for the many public and private buildings under construction in the District of Columbia during the early nineteenth century. Andrews made ornaments for the White House in 1800 and for Monticello in 1804.[31]

Hodgson's local market was severely undercut by Andrews. James Oldham, a Philadelphia-trained joiner who moved to Richmond in 1804, informed Jefferson of the difficulty he was having finding suitable ornaments for a Richmond project: "The agreement with Mr. Hudson [Hodgson] and my self was that he should furnish his composition at the same price that it would cost at Washington." Yet, after comparing prices, Oldham reported that he had "declined having any that are made in this place," and that he would instead purchase the ornaments from George Andrews. Oldham continued, "I am persuaded his ornaments will meet with a ready sale in Richmond and hope he will send an assortment immediately." By 1805, Hodgson's local market was being displaced by products from over a hundred miles away.[32]

Hodgson died in the summer of 1806, and his body was interred in the burial ground at St. John's Church, Richmond, across Shockhoe Valley from the Capitol where he started his Richmond career. His son Joseph T. Hodgson was the administrator of his estate. There were no woodworking or carving tools enumerated, he owned no real estate, and the total value of his possessions was a modest $131. Submitting his estate accounts were Windsor-chairmaker Samuel Pointer, merchant Benjamin Wolfe, and William McKim, a builder and friend who also worked on the Capitol and the Marshall house.[33]

Henry Ingle's later career proved to be more successful than Hodgson's. After moving to Philadelphia by 1791, he joined his brother Joseph in the cabinetmaking business. Henry and Joseph Ingles' shop was located at 273 High Street, next door to the residence of Thomas Jefferson, who lived in Philadelphia while serving as secretary of state. In 1791, Henry married Mary Pechin, daughter of wealthy Philadelphia merchant Christopher Pechin and his wife Christina. During the next eight years, the Ingles resided in a small house owned by Pechin on Elfreth Alley. Joseph moved to Alexandria, Virginia, by 1793 and subsequently purchased a shop at 112 South Royal Street. Six years and several children later, Henry again joined his brother. From Royal Street, they conducted the funerals of George and Martha Washington.[34]

In 1800, Henry moved to New Jersey Avenue, near the construction site of the United States Capitol. From there, he concentrated on the building trades and reportedly constructed the first speculative housing in the District of Columbia, known during the period as "Ingle Row" (on the current site of the Offices of the House of Representatives). He established the District's first hardware store and shipped goods up the Potomac to western Maryland and Virginia and across the piedmont to Thomas Jefferson at Monticello. In 1806 Ingle served on the first Common Council for Washington, D.C., and, as a vestryman for Christ Church, Navy Yard, in 1807, he supervised the development of the burial ground designated as the Congressional Cemetery. Ingle eventually retired to his elaborate house,

"Ingleside," in the Mt. Pleasant section of Washington. He died in 1822, one the wealthiest and most revered men in the city.[35]

Clotworthy Stephenson's later career is no less illustrious. Leaving Richmond in 1792, he moved briefly to Annapolis where he served as Junior Warden of the newly established Grand Lodge. The Master of the Lodge was architect Joseph Clarke, who supervised the construction of several public buildings including the new Maryland State House. It is likely that Stephenson worked with Clarke on some of these projects. By 1793, Stephenson moved to Washington where, accompanied by Clarke and architect James Hoban, he served as Grand Marshall in the ceremony to lay the cornerstone of the United States Capitol.

It is not known whether Stephenson and Hoban knew each other in Britain, but the parallels in their careers are close enough to suggest that they did. Both probably arrived in America in 1785. In the summer of 1787, when Stephenson moved to Richmond to work on the new Capitol, Hoban moved to South Carolina and probably designed the new state house and supervised its construction. Both men had workshops that produced architectural joinery and furniture, and both moved to Washington within a year of each other. Hoban hired Stephenson to oversee the workmen building the United States Capitol, and together they laid the cornerstone in an elaborate Masonic ceremony.[36]

After leaving the employ of Hoban, Stephenson had a successful career on his own. In 1798 he helped the Fairfax County, Virginia, Commissioners select plans for public buildings and built the Alexandria Theater. In Washington, he collaborated with Benjamin Henry Latrobe on the design and construction of the Navy Yard and worked with Hoban on the Washington Market and Blodgett's Hotel. He died in Washington in 1819 and was buried in a Masonic ceremony.[37]

Clotworthy Stephenson, William Hodgson, and Henry Ingle dominated a brief but significant moment in the history of the arts in Virginia. Their legacy is one of the most cohesive yet diverse groups of material objects to survive from the late eighteenth century. Clotworthy Stephenson's accomplished architectural joinery; Henry Ingle's sophisticated casework; and William Hodgson's carving for architecture, furniture, and composition ornament attests to the versatility of eighteenth-century artisans and their adaptability in an agricultural society where the demand for specialized work clearly was limited.

ACKNOWLEDGMENTS For assistance with this article, the authors thank Luke Beckerdite, William Beiswanger, Chris Colby, Morgan Delaney, Viola Fleming, Peter Grover, Melissa Haines, Ronald Hurst, Jean Kling, Elizabeth Kostelny, Mills Lane IV, Calder Loth, Christine Meadows, Michael Miller, James and Marilyn Melchor, Stephen Patrick, Jonathan Prown, Helen Scott Townsend Reed, Charles Sale, Susan Shames, Edith Sprouse, Cinder Stanton, Susan Stein, Ibby Taylor and family, and Katherine Wetzel. We are especially grateful to Frank Horton, Martha Rowe, and the staff of the Museum of Early Southern Decorative Arts for assistance with our research and photography.

1. Clotworthy Stephenson Oath of Fidelity, August 8, 1787, Richmond Hustings Court Order Book 2, 1787–1792, p. 190. William Hodgson probably immigrated through Norfolk, Virginia, where he witnessed the will of Francis Hodgson in 1784 (Norfolk Will Book 2, no. 138, January 15, 1784, pp. 392–93). Francis Hodgson was a ship captain who sailed from the James River to Jamaica (*Virginia Gazette*, September 15, 1774). William Hodgson's son, Joseph, took an Oath of Allegiance in Norfolk in 1787 (Elizabeth and W. Bruce Wingo, *Naturalizations and Declarations of Intention, Norfolk* [Norfolk: Wingo Publishing, 1987], p. 17). The earliest reference to Hodgson in Richmond is in the City Personal Property Tax Lists, 1788, p. 7. The earliest reference to Ingle in Richmond is his advertisement in the August 20, 1788, *Virginia Independent Chronicle*.

2. For more on the design and construction of the Capitol, see Fiske Kimball, *The Capitol of Virginia: A Landmark of American Architecture*, ed. Jon Kukla, Martha C. Vick, and Sarah Shields Driggs (Richmond: Virginia State Library and Archives, 1989).

3. Population statistics for the city of Richmond are in *Heads of Families, First Census of the United States Taken in the Year 1790. Records of the State Enumerations of Virginia from 1782 to 1785* (1908; reprint, Bountiful, Utah: Accelarated Indexing Systems, 1978), pp. 111–19.

4. Stephenson Oath, Richmond Hustings Court Order Book 2, August 28, 1787, p. 190. Although Stephenson is not documented in Richmond until 1787, it is possible that he arrived in America about 1785. By 1790, federal law required a one-year residency in the state and a two-year residency in America prior to taking the Oath of Fidelity. If the law codified an earlier tradition, which is likely, Stephenson probably resided in Virginia before 1787 (Wingo, *Naturalizations,* p. 1). Edmund Randolph to Clotworthy Stephenson, January 1788, Contingent Fund, Auditor of Public Accounts, no. 2, 1787–1792, p. 190, Virginia State Library and Archives, Richmond (hereinafter cited as APA and VSLA). "The Directors of Public Buildings Dt. in Accot. with Hart and Stephenson for Joyners Work done in the Capitol in the Year 1789," "Measured and Accompted by S. Dobie," February 16, 1790, Vouchers, APA, 1788–1789, Capitol Square Data, Records, 1784–1931.

5. "Mr. Wm. Hodgsons proposals for the Caps of Columns &. Pilasters [illegible] Council Rooms &. of Work done already. Mar: 30. 1789," Vouchers, APA, 1788–1789.

1788 The Directors of the Public Buildings to Wm. Hodgson

To 2 Large Trusses @ £ 2.14	£ 5.8.0
10 Smaller Do. @ 1.6	18.0.0
14 Caps for Counl. Cham. @ 2	28.0.0
6 Do. for Sen. Room @ 2.5	13.10.0
	64.18.0
To getting out 6 Caps @ 12. . . .	3.12.0
To Do 14 Do @ 16	4.4.0
Painting and putting up 6 Caps a/3	0.0.18
Do 14 @ /2	1.1.8
Inspected S. Dobie	75.0.0

6. For an illustration of the Scamozzi design used on the exterior of the Capitol, see Kimball, *Capitol*, p. 94.

7. The number of trusses listed on Hodgson's voucher do not match the actual number of those in the rotunda and entry. The additional twelve trusses may have been listed on a now-lost voucher, or they may have been invoiced as unspecified work by another Capitol artisan if Hodgson was working as a subcontractor.

8. The Directors of Public Buildings to W. Hodgson, November 24, 1789, Vouchers, APA, 1788–1790. "Directors of Public Buildings Dr. in Accot. with Hart and Stephenson," February 16, 1790, Vouchers, APA, 1788–1789. For more on built-in furniture in Virginia courtrooms, see Carl Lounsbury, "The Structure of Justice, The Courthouses of Colonial Virginia," Thomas Carter and Bernard Herman, eds., in *Perspectives in Vernacular Architecture* (Columbia, Mo.: University of Missouri Press, 1989), pp. 214–26.

9. "Commonwealth of Virginia Dr. in Account with Hart & Stephenson," December 15, 1789, and "Commonwealth of Virginia Dr. in Account with C. Worthy Stephenson," January 4, 1790, Contingent Vouchers, 1789–1791, APA.

10. Stephenson served as Senior Warden of the Richmond Randolph Lodge 19 in 1787 (Charles P. Rady, *History of Richmond Randolph Lodge No. 19* [Richmond: Fergusson and Son,

1888], p. 2). The authors thank Mr. Charles Sale and the members of Richmond Randolph Lodge 19 for assisting with this research.

11. Temple-form houses with symmetrical wings are illustrated in several British design books, most notably in Robert Morris's *Select Architecture* (London, 1757). Among the best-known American examples are the Redwood Library in Newport, Rhode Island (1748–1750) and the Semple house in Williamsburg, Virginia (ca. 1782).

12. Records concerning the building of Woodlands are in the Cocke Family Papers at the Virginia Historical Society, Richmond. Accounts between merchants William and James Douglas of Petersburg, Virginia, and builder James Crumpley suggest that Crumpley was the undertaker at Woodlands. These accounts refer to Crumpley's purchase of materials for the hearth, front steps, shelving, closet fittings, and other building supplies (William Douglas to James Crumpley, n.d., Cocke Family Papers, Virginia Historical Society, Richmond).

13. Although elements of the chimneypiece in Woodlands are similar to details illustrated in Owen Biddle's *Young Carpenter's Assistant* (Philadelphia: Benjamin Johnson, 1805), the woodwork pre-dates this publication. For more on Woodlands, see Mary Jefferson, *Old Homes and Buildings of Amelia County, Virginia* (Amelia, Va.: privately published, 1964), p. 40; and Helen Scott Townsend Reed, "Chastain," *The Goochland County Historical Society Magazine* 9, no. 1 (Spring 1977): 6–14. Hodgson probably executed the carving for Woodlands in his shop in Richmond. During the eighteenth century, carvers often shipped architectural work great distances. For more on this practice, see Luke Beckerdite, "Philadelphia Carving Shops Part III: Hercules Courtenay and His School," *Antiques* 128, no. 3 (September 1985): 1044.

14. The Museum of Early Southern Decorative Arts (hereinafter MESDA) first recorded the desks-and-bookcases. Two of them and a related clothespress at Colonial Williamsburg are discussed in Wallace B. Gusler, *Furniture of Williamsburg and Eastern Virginia* (Richmond: Virginia Museum, 1978), pp 132–37. Two bookcases, long separated from their desk sections and pediments, have frieze designs identical to figures 16, 19, and 21. One was owned originally by Richmond merchant John Wickham.

15. State of Virginia to Dabney Minor, April 1791, Contingent Vouchers, APA. See also Aline H. Zeno, "The Furniture Craftsmen of Richmond, Virginia, 1780–1820," M.A. thesis, University of Delaware, 1987, p.177.

16. Indenture between Thomas Clark and Dabney Minor, January 26, 1789, Richmond Hustings Court Book 2, 1787–1792, p. 396. State of Virginia to Dabney Minor, 1790, Contingent Vouchers, APA, no. 139, 1789–1791. The furniture that Minor made for the governor is recorded in State of Virginia to Dabney Minor, December 6, 1792, Records of the Governor's Mansion, 1791–1826, folder 1791–1821, VSLA. The furniture for the Capitol is recorded in State of Virginia to Dabney Minor, April 24, 1791, Contingent Vouchers, APA, 1789–1791.

17. Will of Branch Tanner, January 9, 1794, Amelia County Will Book 5, p. 122. Amelia County Deed Book 16, 1781, p. 25. The complete provenance of the Tanner piece is published in Gusler, *Furniture of Williamsburg*, p. 137, n. 6.

18. The Dabney Minor desk-and-bookcase has structural features that are representative of this group. It has a removable cornice with a series of shaped glue blocks held to the top of the bookcase by screws. The waist molding is attached to the bookcase, and the bookcase is attached to the desk with two screws. The backboards are horizontal, and they are butted and glued together. The dustboards are tongue-and-grooved to the drawer blades and dadoed to the case sides. The large case drawers have yellow pine frames and bottoms. The bottom boards have beveled edges that are set into grooves in the fronts and sides. They are held in place along the sides with three rectangular glue blocks, the front one abutting the back of the drawer front, and the back one set in from the back of the drawer. The drawer bottom is nailed to the drawer back with a combination of small cut and wrought nails. Each drawer bottom is composed of several boards that are butt joined and glued. Deep, long kerfs on the inside of the drawer front remain from sawing out the dovetails. A secret compartment hidden beneath the prospect is made of birch. This wood occurs frequently on furniture made in the Richmond area and in the central and southern piedmont areas of Virginia. Laminated blocks support the front feet of the Minor desk-and-bookcase. The rear feet of the Minor example and all four feet of the Tanner piece have single-piece vertical support blocks. Composite feet are discussed in Gusler, *Furniture of Williamsburg*, pp. 42, 45, 55, 120, 121. Ellen W. Henson was the first to suggest Henry Ingle as a possible maker for these desks-and-bookcases. Her preliminary research on this group is in "Petersburg Cabinetmakers as Related to Three Desks-and-Bookcases

attributed to the Petersburg Area," Summer Institute Paper, Museum of Early Southern Decorative Arts, 1982.

19. William Mcpherson Hornor, *Blue Book of Philadelphia Furniture* (1935; reprint, Washington, D.C.: Highland House, 1977), pp. 321, 326.

20. Hornor, *Blue Book*, pp. 317–26.

21. Robert Schwartz, *The Stephen Girard Collection, A Selective Catalog* (Philadelphia: Girard College, 1980), figs. 14–17.

22. *Heads of Families, First Census of the United States Taken in the Year 1790, Records of the State Enumerations of Virginia from 1782–1785* (Baltimore: Genealogical Publishing Co., 1966), p. 80. Between May 20 and October 19, 1791, Jefferson hired Henry and his brother Joseph to make two tables and a writing desk, to put up Venetian blinds, and to carry out a host of miscellaneous repairs. The Ingle shop was adjacent to Jefferson's residence in Philadelphia (Julian Boyd et al., eds., *The Papers of Thomas Jefferson*, 22 vols. to date [Princeton, N. J.: Princeton University Press, 1965–present], 17: 359, 364, 366, 373).

23. For more on the Cabells and their plantations, see Marlene Heck, "Palladian Architecture and Social Change in Post-Revolutionary Virginia," Ph.D. dissertation, University of Pennsylvania, 1988.

24. Instead of a dustboard between the drawers, the mahogany press from the Tabb family has drawer runners that are dadoed to the case sides, mortise-and-tenoned to the drawer blades, and tapered and nailed at the back (Luke Beckerdite to Wallace B. Gusler, March 3, 1983, Colonial Williamsburg Archives). Two cabinetmakers associated with Henry Ingle possibly made these presses: Elijah Speakman or James McCormick. Speakman was in business with Ingle briefly in 1788 (*Virginia Independent Chronicle,* August 20, 1788). McCormick, who reportedly worked in "the first shops in Dublin," immigrated to Baltimore in February 1786 (*Maryland Journal & Baltimore Advertiser*, February 21, 1786). He moved to Alexandria the following May (*Maryland Journal & Baltimore Advertiser*, April 7, 1786; and *Virginia Journal and Alexandria Advertiser*, May 11, 1786) and subsequently relocated to Norfolk in 1787 (*Norfolk and Portsmouth Journal*, November 21, 1787). McCormick died in Petersburg, Virginia, in June 1791 (*Virginia Gazette, and Petersburg Intelligencer*, June 23, 1791). An orphan named James McCormack was apprenticed to Joseph Ingle in 1793 (Borough of Alexandria, Hustings Court Order Book, August 28, 1793, p. 146). The orphan may have been James McCormick's son. The aforementioned references are from MESDA research files and Ronald L. Hurst, "Cabinetmakers and Related Tradesmen in Norfolk, Virginia," M.A. thesis, College of William and Mary, 1989, pp. 123–25.

25. Dr. William H. Crim of Baltimore, Maryland, owned this piece in 1903 (*Catalogue of the Celebrated Collection of Dr. William H. Crim* [Baltimore: O. A. Kirkland Auctioneer, April 22, 1903], lot 748). It is illustrated in Edward Wenham, *Collector's Guide to Furniture Design* (New York: Collector's Press, 1928), fig. 363. The authors thank Luke Beckerdite and Michael Flanigan for these references. For more on the Hunter library bookcase, see Hornor, *Blue Book*, pl. 410. For more on the secretary-and-bookcase illustrated in figure 29, see MESDA Research File S-6534.

26. *Virginia Independent Chronicle and General Advertiser*, October 28, 1789. Clement Biddle, *The Philadelphia Directory* (Philadelphia: James & Johnson, 1791). No Henry Ingle appeared in the Philadelphia directories after 1794 except for an ironmonger by that name (information courtesy, Cinder Stanton). Henry Ingle first advertised in Washington in the October 21, 1801, *National Intelligencier*; however, he was living in Alexandria by 1799 when he assisted his brother with Washington's funeral ("The Estate of the late Genl. George Washington . . . to Henry and Joseph Ingle Alexandria July 16, 1800"). The authors thank Mount Vernon curator Christine Meadows for the information on Washington's funeral.

27. Frances Clary Morse, *Furniture of the Olden Time* (1903; reprinted and enlarged 1917, New York: MacMillan Co., 1946), p. 143. Morse identified the owner of the bookcase as J. J. Gilbert of Baltimore. The authors thank Luke Beckerdite for this reference.

28. The authors thank Melissa Haines, site coordinator for the John Marshall house, for documentary information on the Marshall house. The names of Hodgson, Ingle, and Stephenson do not appear in any published or nonpublished account kept by John Marshall. For more on Marshall and his house, see Charles T. Cullen and Herbert A. Johnson, eds., *The Papers of John Marshall* (Chapel Hill, N.C.: University of North Carolina Press, 1974); and J. Everete Fauber, Jr., "Report on Documentary Research John Marshall House, Richmond, Virginia" (typescript), 1970, and "Supplementary Report No. 2" (typescript), 1971, Association for the Preservation of Virginia Antiquities, Richmond.

29. For more on the Amblers and their mansion, see Samuel Mordecai, *Richmond in By-Gone Days* (Richmond: George M. West, 1856), pp. 64, 67. Jacquelin Ambler was treasurer of the Commonwealth in 1781. In 1784 he served as a Director of Public Building, and he undoubtedly participated in the planning for the Capitol. He probably knew the principal artisans who worked on the Capitol.

30. "Account of Sales made this day of the estate of William Hodgson, decd.," February 21, 1807, Richmond Hustings Deed Book 5, 1807–1810, pp. 10–11.

31. Thomas Jefferson to George Andrews, June 2, 1802; Thomas Jefferson to James Oldham, November 20, 1804, Thomas Jefferson Coolidge Collection of Manuscripts 1705–1827 (microfilm), Massachusetts Historical Society, Boston (information courtesy, William Beiswanger, Architectural Historian, Thomas Jefferson Memorial Foundation). See also Richard Cote, "The Architectural Workmen of Thomas Jefferson in Virginia," Ph. D. dissertation, Boston University, 1986.

32. James Oldham to Thomas Jefferson, March 5, 1805; James Oldman to Thomas Jefferson, June 30, 1805, Thomas Jefferson Papers (microfilm), Library of Congress.

33. Hodgson's tombstone reads, "Here lies the Body/ of Wm. Hodgson/ d. July 28, 1806/ Aged 58 Yrs." "Inventory of Estate of William Hodgson."

34. Edward Ingle, *Henry Ingle (1764–1822) His Ancestry and Descendants (1610–1914)* (Baltimore: privately published, 1914), pp. 1–4. Joseph Ingle first appears in Alexandria in 1793 (Borough of Alexandria, Hustings Court Order Book, 1791–1796, August 28, 1793, p. 146). "The Estate of the late Genl. George Washington . . . to Henry and Joseph Ingle Alexandria July 16, 1800."

35. Virginia Moore, "Reminiscences of Washington as Recalled by a Descendant of the Ingle Family," in *Records of the Columbia Historical Society* (Washington: Columbia Historical Society), vol. 3, pp. 96–114. Henry first advertised hardware in the December 10, 1802, *National Intelligencer and Washington Advertiser*. Jefferson's hardware purchases are discussed in Henry Ingle to Thomas Jefferson, June 28, 1802; John Ingle to Henry Ingle, March 24, 1806; and Henry Ingle to Thomas Jefferson, October 14, 1806 (letters transcribed by L. C. Stanton, research files, Monticello research department). Vestry Minutes of Christ Church, April 19, 1806. Henry Ingle and other vestrymen started a subscription to purchase land for a burial ground in 1807 (information courtesy, Jean Kling, Archivist, Christ Church, Washington, D.C.). The land for the burial ground was deeded to Christ Church on March 25, 1808 (*Evening Star* [Washington], May 11, 1808, clipping).

36. Edward T. Schultz, *History of Freemasonry in Maryland, of All the Rites Introduced into Maryland* (Baltimore: J. H. Mediary, 1884), pp. 182–191. Stephenson described himself as a resident of the "City of Washington" in an advertisement in the September 10, 1794, *Virginia Gazette*. Hoban advertised for employment soon after his arrival in America (*Pennsylvania Evening Herald*, May 25, 1785). For more on Hoban in Charleston, see Beatrice St. Julien Revenel, *Architects of Charleston* (Charleston: Carolina Art Association, n.d.), pp. 76–80. Stephenson served as Grand Marshall at the laying of the cornerstone (Kenton Harper, *History of the Grand Lodge and of Freemasonry in the District of Columbia* [Washington: R. Beresford, 1911], p. 17).

37. A description of the Alexandria Theater appeared in the May 17, 1798, *Times and Alexandria Advertiser*:

> It is a lofty edifice decorated with handsome pediments and deep cornices, the window-frames, trusses and rustic work are of stone. The pedestals on the South front are designed for the Statue of Shakespeare, with the tragic and Comic Muse at the West and East Corners.

The theater stood for many years and was later renamed Liberty Hall. In 1872, it burned in a devastating fire that destroyed much of Cameron Street (William Francis Smith and T. Michael Miller, *A Seaport Saga, Portrait of Old Alexandria, Virginia* [Norfolk: Duning Co., 1989], p. 54).

Book Reviews

Portsmouth Furniture: Masterworks from the New Hampshire Seacoast. Organized and edited by Brock Jobe, with contributions by Diane Carlberg Ehrenpreis, James L. Garvin, Anne Rogers Haley, Brock Jobe, Myrna Kaye, Johanna McBrien, Kevin Nicholson, Richard C. Nylander, Elizabeth Redmond, Kevin Shupe, Robert Trent, Gerald W. R. Ward, and Philip Zea. Photographs by David Bohl. Boston: Society for the Preservation of New England Antiquities, 1993. Distributed by University Press of New England, Hanover, New Hampshire. 454 pp., 14 color and numerous bw illustrations, appendixes, bibliography, index. $65.00 (cloth), $39.95 (paper).

In 1891 Irving W. Lyon published what is acknowledged as the first serious book-length study of American furniture, *The Colonial Furniture of New England*. One hundred two years later, *Portsmouth Furniture* offers impressive evidence of the inexhaustible richness of the field of early American furniture, as well as of the significant developments and refinements made to Lyon's pioneering scholarship during the past century.

Lyon made no references to Portsmouth in *Colonial Furniture*, and Portsmouth furniture has received little attention from scholars over the ensuing century. The foremost achievement of *Portsmouth Furniture*, therefore, is as the first book to be written on the subject. *The Architectural Heritage of the Piscataqua* (1937) by John Mead Howells, as well as James L. Garvin's more recent publications on the public and domestic buildings of Portsmouth, have brought the town's architecture to national attention; yet, other than research-in-progress published by Myrna Kaye and Brock Jobe and one or two short articles, the only existing survey of Portsmouth furniture has been Charles Buckley's five-page article, "Fine Federal Furniture Attributed to Portsmouth," in *Antiques* for February 1963. The exhibitions of New Hampshire decorative arts held by the Currier Gallery in 1964 and the New Hampshire Historical Society in 1973 included a few examples of Portsmouth furniture, but the New Hampshire Historical Society's landmark exhibition and catalogue, *Plain & Elegant, Rich & Common: Documented New Hampshire Furniture, 1750–1850* (1978), included nothing made in the Piscataqua region prior to 1802.

Much of both the artifactual and documentary evidence presented in *Portsmouth Furniture* is, therefore, newly rescued from obscurity. Brock Jobe and his colleagues have researched every possible source for information: public and private records, genealogies, and local histories. Their search for objects has been particularly exhaustive, involving public and private collections, auction catalogues, and periodical and secondary literature. Most importantly, their study has been grounded in the firsthand examination of 1,500 pieces of furniture. The detailed information provided for the 117 examples in this book offers any student of the subject an extraordinary resource. Two appendices provide the names of more than 250 craftsmen in the furniture trades and the identities of 48 individuals or families who branded their furniture, a practice more common in federal-period Portsmouth than anywhere else in the United States.

The subject has thus benefited from the delay: although it has taken the field a long time to focus on Portsmouth furniture, this particular treatment is an exemplary publication. The book's large format allows David Bohl's excellent photographs to be reproduced in large scale, and the high quality of the printing brings out every detail. The organization of *Portsmouth Furniture* was taken from Brock Jobe and Myrna Kaye's superb catalogue of the SPNEA collection, *New England Furniture: The Colonial Era* (1984), with interpretive essays followed by a catalogue section of entries on 117 objects. These objects have been scrutinized not only by curators but also by conservators, who have contributed important information concerning condition and original finishes; one desk (cat. 31) retains its original beeswax coating. Much of this evidence, as well as the documentation provided for upholstered objects in this study, would have been ignored as recently as fifteen years ago.

The three introductory essays are the heart of the book. James L. Garvin makes abundantly clear in his essay, "That Little World, Portsmouth," that the Piscataqua region was one of the primary centers of eighteenth-century Atlantic shipping. The great fortunes and the concomitant political power realized by such mercantile families as the Wentworths, Moffatts, Langdons, and Wendells allowed them to construct homes that emulated English patterns and models. Brock Jobe's essay, "Furniture Making in Eighteenth-Century Portsmouth," begins with a survey of the working environment and of the wide variety of tasks expected of a furniture maker in this period. He follows with a discussion of the stylistic development of Portsmouth furniture, contrasting the idiosyncratic, localized interpretations of later baroque styles by John Gaines III (1704–1743) and Joseph Davis (fl. 1726–1762) with the sophisticated work in the Georgian manner by English immigrant Robert Harrold (fl. 1765–1792). Harrold in particular represents this project's most significant discovery, a man who, as a London-trained craftsman producing exceptional forms for a wealthy clientele, was one of the most important furniture makers in America during the later eighteenth century. Just as these men dominated local production during their respective careers, so Langley Boardman (1774–1833) and Samuel M. Dockum (1792–1872) dominated the furniture trade in the federal period, as Johanna McBrien demonstrates in her essay, "Portsmouth Furniture Making, 1798–1837." Given an evident taste for Massachusetts-style objects and an increasing attempt to consolidate production into single large shops, the identity of Portsmouth furniture underwent a significant change during this period.

As in the *New England Furniture* catalogue, the entries on individual objects in *Portsmouth Furniture* are grouped by form: case furniture, tables, seating furniture, beds, and looking glasses and picture frames. Each entry also follows an identical sequence to the earlier book, with a one- or two-page discussion of the object's significance followed by notes on structure and condition, inscriptions, materials, dimensions, and provenance. This system is logical and easy to consult as a reference; however, I find the organization by form more suitable for a collection catalogue than for this regional study. Given the differences in makers, style, construction, and consumption between the colonial and federal periods, I would have preferred to see separate sections for the colonial and federal objects. Not only did this organization work well in the related exhibition, but it would have tied the entries more closely to the relevant essays by Jobe and McBrien.

The entries are by nine different authors, with almost half of the total being written by Diane Carlberg Ehrenpreis (thirty two) and Brock Jobe (twenty one), not counting the seventeen entries they wrote jointly with others. The remaining seven authors were tapped to contribute in areas of special expertise, such as Philip Zea on clocks and early turned chairs, Robert Trent on seventeenth-century furniture and upholstered objects, and Richard C. Nylander on beds. The editors of this volume (Jobe, Nancy Curtis, and Gerald W. R. Ward) are to be commended for not only the uniformly high standard of the writing but also for preserving the authors' individual voices. For example, Myrna Kaye's entries on English-style chairs by Robert Harrold and his contemporaries in the 1760s and 1770s communicate the excitement and suspense that accompanied the identification of this important group of objects.

The objects were chosen for the catalogue on the basis of three criteria: documentation to maker or owner, aesthetic quality, or "significance as a representative example of a common form" (p. 74). Not surprisingly, the last category represents the smallest number of objects, for only about a dozen—turned chairs and tables and board chests—represent relatively inexpensive furniture. In part this selection is a matter of survival, for the best documented objects tend to be the aesthetic successes and also tend to be the most costly furniture made for elites. Commonplace objects also receive less emphasis because, as Elizabeth Redmond notes with regard to a turned table (cat. 45), they are "ubiquitous and exhibit so little regional variation." *Portsmouth Furniture* has as one of its principal agendas the reversal of "the century-long process of misattribution" as objects made elsewhere, primarily the North Shore Massachusetts (p. 36). Diagnostic style features and construction details are less likely to be present on simple, inexpensive objects. One such reattribution is a type of scrolled support for armchairs (such as cat. 88) long considered typical of Newburyport; it is now conclusively identified as a Portsmouth trait, apparently later imitated by Newburyport craftsmen. A secretary-and-bookcase (cat. 28) resembles documented Salem work but features idiosyncratic construction features of Langley Boardman. Both the armchair and the desk are beautiful objects, but neither of them was representative of the furniture owned by the majority of Portsmouth residents.

The authors' collective effort to create an identity for Portsmouth furniture raises the larger issue of how, one hundred years after Irving Lyon, one approaches or defines a "region." In his essay "Regionalism in American Furniture Studies," published in *Perspectives on American Furniture* (1988), Philip Zimmerman identified three chronologically successive types of regional studies: descriptive, comparative or evaluative, and analytical. As the first book on the subject, *Portsmouth Furniture* is of necessity largely descriptive, providing detailed evidence concerning objects, makers, and owners. With the understandable zeal of archaeologists uncovering buried treasure, most of the authors take an all-or-nothing approach in identifying objects as Portsmouth products. Only eight objects in the catalogue are described as "probably Portsmouth" or "Portsmouth area," with one identified only as "coastal New Hampshire" (cat. 114). Of the objects described unequivocally as "Portsmouth," however, a few seem less secure than the majority. A blockfront chest of drawers (cat. 7) "closely adheres to Boston precedents" but is attributed to Portsmouth because of some construction features that deviate from the respected Boston norm. Jobe also notes that these features have little in common with chests made in Portsmouth, and it is only the chest's history of ownership in the Saltar and Wendell families that links it to the town. One could argue with equal validity that the idiosyncracies of its construction are the signature of a maverick Boston maker rather than the hallmark of a different center. A fancy dressing table (cat. 24) is presented as "the most outstanding piece of painted furniture from Portsmouth," although the only substantive connection to the town is the object's Wendell family ownership. The shape and turnings of this table appear in Boston and other areas of Massachusetts. None of the fancy chairs and settees (cats. 98–100) included in this study are definitely ascribed to Portsmouth, leaving little context in which to evaluate the table.

As these examples indicate, the authors of the entries bring in comparative examples from other areas only as influences on Portsmouth styles or as examples of what Portsmouth styles are not. For instance, federal-period card tables made in Salem are described as models for Portsmouth craftsmen but supposedly feature more monochromatic veneers than those made in Portsmouth (p. 260). Aside from the fact that documented Salem card tables exist with veneers of equal contrast, there is no systematic comparison of Portsmouth furniture with contemporary work in Massachusetts or elsewhere as a means of defining how Portsmouth fits into the larger picture of American furniture.

An analytical approach to the subject—answering the question of *why* specific styles were popular in Portsmouth—would require not only the foregoing comparative study but also a less chauvinistic view of Portsmouth furniture. In other words, as Philip Zimmerman frames the question, how is a "region" properly defined—by simple political boundaries, by geography, or by larger socioeconomic-cultural factors? In most instances the first choice seems to be the guiding definition for *Portsmouth Furniture*. A few examples of furniture made in outlying towns are included, but without any systematic observations concerning Portsmouth's relationship to the rest of New Hampshire. Moreover, after looking at much of the material from the federal period, one wonders if, despite certain distinctive forms, Portsmouth really did belong to the larger coastal Massachusetts-to-Maine region that has obscured it for so long. A few of the federal-period objects presented as Portsmouth products (in particular, cats. 23, 29, 62) are so similar to Boston and North Shore examples that the attempt to isolate them as Portsmouth products seems almost beside the point.

I raise these issues not to diminish in any way the splendid achievement realized in *Portsmouth Furniture*. In fact, it is only because Jobe and his colleagues have prepared such a detailed map of previously uncharted territory that anyone can begin to ask these questions. Synthetic conclusions have to build upon a rock-solid foundation of studies such as this one, grounded on a close examination of objects and documents. This book has filled a major gap in our understanding of New England's artifactual history. For anyone wishing to do further research and analysis into this important topic, *Portsmouth Furniture* will be both their starting point and guide.

David L. Barquist
Yale University Arts Gallery

David L. Barquist. *American Tables and Looking Glasses in the Mabel Brady Garvan and Other Collections at Yale University.* New Haven, Conn.: Yale University Art Gallery, 1992. 423 pp. ; 30 color and numerous bw illustrations, line drawings, appendixes, bibliography, index. $65.00.

David L. Barquist's *American Tables and Looking Glasses* is the fourth catalogue in a series covering the American furniture collections at Yale University. Beautifully presented and intelligently written, it follows in the scholarly tradition of its predecessors: Edwin A. Battison and Patricia E. Kane's *The American Clock, 1725–1865: The Mabel Brady Garvan and Other Collections at Yale University* (1972); Patricia E. Kane's *300 Years of American Seating Furniture: Chairs and Beds from the Mabel Brady Garvan and Other Collections at Yale University* (1976); and Gerald W. R. Ward's *American Case Furniture in the Mabel Brady Garvan and Other Collections at Yale University* (1988).

The comprehensive catalogue entries and excellent photography in *American Tables and Looking Glasses* constitute an invaluable reference, not only for the Yale collections, but for related objects in other institutions and private collections. The tables and looking glasses are arranged first by form, then by style and place of manufacture if, as in the case of neoclassical card tables, there are enough objects to warrant such divisions. Each entry specifies the period term of the object, maker (if known), place of origin, date of manufacture, materials, and dimensions, followed by detailed descriptions of the structure, condition, and provenance. Inscriptions, exhibition histories, and publication references are also given where appropriate.

The accompanying photographs consist of overalls and details carefully chosen to illustrate important points in the text. For example, a rare southern baroque oval table with falling leaves (cat. 43) — popularly referred to as a William and Mary gate-leg table — is illustrated open in color and black and white, closed, and upside-down to show the unusual draw-leg support. Photographs of related objects in other collections and additional close-ups and color illustrations of construction details, carving, turning, and inlay would have improved the catalogue, but space, budgets, and price constraints are a factor in any publication.

Engraved designs from British pattern books, prints, and paintings complement Barquist's excellent analysis of European influences on American furniture, both in design and use. The entry for a classical New York card table (cat. 120) is especially noteworthy in identifying the probable design source as Nicholas de Launay or Claude Ballin's illustration of two silver console tables made between 1670 and 1680 for the *Galerie des Glaces* at Versailles. Such information is very helpful in placing American furniture in a more global context.

The individual entries in *American Tables and Looking Glasses* are extremely well researched, with abundant references from primary sources—particularly from city directories, inventories, pattern and price books, letters, and newspaper advertisements—and published works. Not only do these entries record the physical properties of each object but they contain detailed discussions of related examples, structural and decorative options available to patrons (see cat. 108), and patterns of use. They also complement Barquist's interpretive essays examining the social and cultural factors that influenced the development and evolution of each major table and looking-glass form.

The chapter on looking glasses has a lengthy introduction with sections devoted to terminology and connoisseurship. Barquist's analyses of the importation of European looking glasses (primarily British), the technological and economic factors that made it difficult for American tradesmen to compete with imports, the problem of relying solely on woods to determine nationality (because woods were exported to Britain and some related American and European species are indistinguishable microscopically), and the absence of identifiable American looking-glass styles caution professionals and novices against making hasty conclusions about place of origin. At Christie's we have found that reliable attributions depend on wood analysis combined with a thorough understanding of structure, carving, and gilding techniques. Using this methodology, we were able to identify not only the city of origin (Philadelphia) but the carving shop (James Reynolds) that produced an important carved white rococo looking glass that sold at our gallery in January 1991. Catalogues like *American Tables and Looking Glasses* provide the source material that make such determinations possible.

Although every section in the book is noteworthy, the essay titled "Pillar Looking Glasses" (pp. 323–25) is a fascinating history of design and one of the few areas where objects outside the Yale collections are illustrated. Barquist discusses the British neoclassical origins of this form, the importation and sale of pillar looking glasses in the colonies, and American regional variants. With reverse-painted glass panels, carved ornaments, and relatively generic architectural elements, pillar looking glasses were intended to complement other furnishings and architectural details. *A Plan & Section of a Drawing Room* from Thomas Sheraton's *The Cabinet-Maker and Upholsterer's Drawing Book* (1793)—one of the earliest depictions of a pillar looking glass—makes the point abundantly clear.

In addition to Barquist's excellent research, *American Tables and Looking Glasses* contains brilliant essays by Gerald W. R. Ward and Elisabeth Donaghy Garrett. Ward's "The Intersections of Life: Tables and Their Social

Role" takes up where his essay for Yale's case furniture catalogue left off (see "Matter in Place: Some Thoughts on Case Furniture"). In "Intersections of Life," Ward uses the evolution of the table (in terms of size, shape, materials, etc.) to explore broader historical, social, and cultural topics such as human behavior, philosophy, social and familial hierarchies, and perceptions of equality and status. Drawing on modern studies of proxemics—the manner by which people "establish territories, create privacy, avoid intrusions, and . . . regulate their interaction with others" (p. 18)—and research into changing attitudes toward dining, card playing, and social interaction from the seventeenth century to the mid-nineteenth century, he demonstrates that furniture forms are intimately related to social relationships and attitudes about correctness. To use a simple example, rectangular table tops suggest formality and hierarchy, whereas round or oval ones have the opposite effect.

Garrett's introductory essay, "Looking Glasses in America, 1700–1850," eloquently reveals how "the looking glass . . . bespeaks ritual and symbolic meaning as much as utility and household use, metaphor as much as mirror" (p. 27). Using information from inventories, diaries, housekeeping guides, and other period documents, Garrett shows how looking glasses evolved from pocket size to full length and how they became reflections of status, both personal and societal. She also ties the proliferation of looking glasses and the evolution of accompanying forms, such as dressing tables, dressing glasses, and commodes, with increased concerns for personal hygiene. Even the problems of caring for looking glasses—subjected as they were to the vagaries of climate, clumsy owners and servants, and neglect—are covered in this excellent essay.

In recent years, museum catalogues have been criticized for being descriptive rather than interpretive and for being somewhat redundant; yet, they are essential references for academics, curators, auction professionals, dealers, and collectors. The objects illustrated and described in them are the building blocks for books and articles on individual tradesmen, shops, and regional groups; technology, industry, and connoisseurship; consumerism and patronage; and the social and cultural implications of material culture. With its thought-provoking essays, interpretive catalogue entries, and excellent photography, *American Tables and Looking Glasses* is a testimony to the importance of collection catalogues, both public and private.

John Hays
Christie's

Philip Zea and Robert C. Cheney. *Clock Making in New England, 1725–1825: An Interpretation of the Old Sturbridge Village Collection.* Edited by Caroline F. Sloat. Sturbridge, Mass.: Old Sturbridge Village, 1992. 173 pp., numerous color and bw illus., line drawings, appendixes. $34.95.

For cultural historians and others who study and interpret the decorative arts, clocks are exceptionally rich objects. Typically combining the skills of clockmakers, cabinetmakers, inlaymakers, brassfounders, silversmiths, engravers, and decorative painters, clocks are usually signed by their makers and often bear additional clues to their ownership, cost, distribution, and subsequent repairs. For curators and collectors faced with the same clues, clocks can be daunting objects, the genuine article being costly and rare and even the simple examples requiring a broad knowledge of different media (metal, wood, glass) and historical trades. As a result, the literature on American clocks over the past century has naturally divided along disciplinary lines of technology and art, lines that often fail to converge. Caught somewhere in between is a long tradition of pictorial survey begun by N. Hudson Moore (*The Old Clock Book* [New York: Frederick A. Stokes, 1911]), maintained by Wallace Nutting (*The Clock Book* [Framingham: Old American Company, 1924]), and revived by William Distin and Robert Bishop (*The American Clock: A Comprehensive Pictorial Survey, 1723–1900* [1976; reprint, New York: Bonanza Books, 1983]).

In the past two decades, only a few books on American clocks have successfully combined two or more of these approaches, often with contributions by two or more authors. In the case of *The American Clock, 1725–1865* (Greenwich, Conn.: New York Graphic Society, 1973), a catalogue of American clocks in the collection of the Yale University Art Gallery, Edwin A. Battison, Curator of Horology at the Smithsonian, supplied extensive technical notes for Patricia E. Kane's entries. Published two years later, *Two Hundred Years of American Clocks and Watches* (Englewood Cliffs, N. J.: Prentice Hall, 1975) by Chris H. Bailey is still the best overview of American clocks and clockmaking, a subject worthy of several volumes by now and one that may be better addressed by regional surveys such as the late Charles Parsons's lifetime pursuit of New Hampshire clocks.

The present volume by Philip Zea and Robert C. Cheney, *Clockmaking in New England, 1725–1825: An Interpretation of the Old Sturbridge Village Collection*, is a successful synthesis of both models. Ultimately, Zea and Cheney, like Bailey, have written much more than a collection catalogue or a regional checklist. Indeed, a checklist of clocks appears only at the end of the book as "Technical Data" (Appendix A), arranged by accession number and printed in minuscule type. (It is not clear whether the list includes all the clocks in the collection or just those under consideration for this book.) Technical notes on the movement, escapement, and strike train are a significant improvement over the first publication on the Sturbridge collection by Charles Avery issued in 1955. The usefulness of *Clockmaking in New England* as a reference book, however, is diminished by the regrettable omission of an index, alphabetical list of clockmakers, concordance, or any other means of locating these objects in the body of the text. Considering the early formation of the Wells collection, it also would have been instructive to know where these clocks had been published previously. It is even more regrettable that such a well-researched book lacks even a general bibliography.

As stated in the introduction, the goals of the book are to interpret clocks "in their historical context" and to show how clocks are "part of the fabric of New England life" (p. 5). For this project, Philip Zea and Robert Cheney are the ideal collaborators. Zea has written eloquently about rural New England furniture and craftsmen in Brock Jobe and Myrna Kaye, *New England Furniture: The Colonial Era* (Boston: Houghton Mifflin, 1984), and his earlier article on Jedidiah and Jabez Baldwin, published by the Dublin Seminar (1981), is an exemplary comparison of the lives and livelihoods of an urban and a rural New England clockmaker and their patrons. Cheney, a third-generation clockmaker who has served for years as a consultant to Old Sturbridge Village, knows the J. Cheney Wells collection intimately. Through training, experience, and his own research, he has a thorough knowledge of New England clocks and is eminently well qualified to discuss alterations, replacements, and forgeries in the final chapter titled "Spurious Timepieces: Alarming Signs and How to Recognize Them." It is a tribute to the editor Caroline F. Sloat that the individual voices of the authors do not emerge separately.

Organized into six chapters, the book begins with an overview titled "Clockmaking in Colonial New England." Citing tall clocks by Gawen Brown of Boston and the Claggetts of Newport, Zea and Cheney discuss the transmission of British clockmaking traditions to coastal New England cities during the second quarter of the eighteenth century. Later tall clocks with wooden movements by Jonas Fitch and John Bailey of Massachusetts and by the Cheneys of Connecticut speak for the adaptation of these traditions by inland craftsmen lacking access to imported raw materials. Despite the limitations of the Sturbridge collection, this essay makes thorough use of early-eighteenth-century newspapers, account books, manuscripts, and secondary sources as well as the clocks themselves to portray the environment in which the first American clocks were made and owned. Throughout the book, the authors maintain an effective balance between technological, aesthetic, and cultural concerns. Unlike more narrowly focused studies, this interpretation reflects the broad interests of Zea, a seasoned historian who draws insight from a number of sources ranging from Puritan sermons to urban workshop practices, rural blast furnaces, and merchants' best parlors, which serve to supplement Cheney's technical analysis of clocks.

For many readers, the main appeal of *Clock Making in New England* will be its three central chapters that address the Willard phenomenon, the work of their many apprentices, and their impact on clockmaking in New England during the early national period. Since the publication in 1911 of *A History of Simon Willard, Inventor and Clockmaker* by his great-grandson, John Ware Willard, the name of Simon Willard has loomed larger than life and arguably out of proportion to his historical contribution. In the absence of shop records or account books, the authors have combined close scrutiny of every kind of clock made by the Willards with every known scrap of documentation to present a full account of "their developing business and scientific interests" (p. 29). In the process, some new information emerges, such as Benjamin Willard's removal to York, Pennsylvania, during the Revolutionary War (pp. 31–32).

The authors' analysis of six tall clocks by Simon and Aaron in the collection leads to the reasonable conclusion that "opulent cases masked standardized production," the bread and butter that allowed Simon Willard and his sons to pursue more experimental designs and scientific instruments. Though it is helpful to know that the cost of the average tall clock represented approximately half the annual salary of hired agricultural labor (p. 37), it is less obvious how these clocks could be "in the mainstream of urban clockmaking on both sides of the Atlantic," with cases based on recognizably old-fashioned, "mid-century London styles" (p. 38). As with bombé case furniture, it may be that some wealthy buyers preferred a more conservative, English expression of opulence. By comparison, the design of the patented timepiece (the so-called "banjo clock") was completely original, and the authors' discussion of various cost options in light of accounts kept by John Doggett and nearby ornamental painters gives an excellent sense of the extensive collaboration and subcontracting among Boston artisans in the first quarter of the nineteenth century. The real value of chapter 2, "'Elegant Faces and Mahogany Cases': Clocks by the Willard Family," is its frank reevaluation of famous designs (the thirty-hour timepiece, weight-driven shelf clocks, tall clocks, patented timepieces and alarm clocks, gallery clocks, and regulators) and the factors behind their development.

The chapter that follows, "The Willard Legacy: Clocks by Their Apprentices," addresses the impact of the Willards on clocks made by nearly a dozen of their apprentices, several of whom were related by marriage to each other and to the Willards. As Zea and Cheney demonstrate, the similarities among their work are more striking than the differences, and they help shed light on the business of clockmaking and its evolution by mid-century. One wonders how many superior mechanics like Gardner Parker of Westborough were overshadowed by the self-perpetuating success of their masters. Those like Elnathan Taber and William Cummens who remained in Roxbury continued to produce clocks that are nearly indistinguishable from the work of Simon and Aaron. Those who left the Boston area still found it difficult to compete against the Willards' well-established reputation and far-flung apparatus for marketing and distribution.

The last of the three main chapters, titled "As Neat as at Roxbury: Clock Making in Federal New England," examines the careers of clockmakers who were not trained by the Willards and of the vast majority who worked in the Yankee hinterland. Although rural patrons sought elegant timepieces for the same reasons as their urban counterparts, rural artisans tended to work seasonally while marching "to agricultural rhythms" (p. 101). In a barter economy, clockmakers typically lacked the cash necessary to purchase cast metal and imported materials for fine clockmaking. This territory is familiar for Zea, and he does a superb job of discerning both innovation and compromise in a disparate group of clocks from Maine, New Hampshire, and central Massachusetts. Original research in primary documents produces occasional nuggets, such as Nichols Goddard of Shrewsbury, Massachusetts, who ordered steel and clock parts from Germany in 1789 (p. 107). For readers satiated by the "immutable" elegance of Roxbury-style clocks, several of the cases in this chapter display interesting abstractions of familiar ornament, such as the attenuated fretwork in the hoods of clocks by John Edwards and Alexander T. Willard of Ashby, Massachusetts.

The final interpretive chapter, "A Clock for Every Home: Connecticut's Clock Makers Show the Way," inevitably shifts gears with the industrialized manufacture of clocks in Connecticut between 1800 and 1830. Admittedly not a primary collecting interest of J. Cheney Wells (p. 119), the shifts from craft to industry and from patron to consumer are important themes in the interpretation of Old Sturbridge Village as a museum. This period has been well covered elsewhere, particularly by Chris Bailey, and is better represented in other museum collections. Nevertheless, Zea and Cheney make good use of the extensive secondary literature as well as of contemporary letters and account books at the libraries of the American Clock and Watch Museum and the Connecticut Historical Society. The result is a very readable account of Silas Hoadley, Seth Thomas, Eli Terry, and others who gradually transformed the manufacture and ownership of clocks.

Considering the decision to illustrate and discuss only clocks in the collection at Old Sturbridge Village (except for one lantern clock), the authors of this book are remarkably successful in their effort to provide an historical and cultural interpretation of clocks and clockmaking in New England. Where the collection is relatively weak (chapters 1 and 5), the narrative is bolstered by historical documents; where it is strong (chapters 2–4), the technical and historical portions are well balanced.

In this context, one might normally regard a final "how to" chapter on identifying fakes and forgeries as a thinly veiled ploy to appeal to a wider audience. Thanks to Robert Cheney's familiarity with the clocks at Sturbridge and the wisdom inherited from his father and grandfather, however, this chapter is a fascinating guide across the treacherous terrain of altered cases, dials, reverse-painted glass, patent timepieces (where the stakes are especially high), high-quality reproductions from the 1920s and 1930s, and "updated" antiques, "marriages," and "improvements." Although Cheney stops short of describing certain tricks of the trade ("It is not the author's intent to create a 'faker's handbook'" [p. 142]), his essay based on the study collection at Sturbridge provides many useful lessons not available elsewhere.

Throughout this book, Zea and Cheney manage to elucidate complicated objects without ever losing sight of the larger context of clockmaking in nineteenth-century New England. The clarity of the text and the logical juxtaposition of consistently clear photographs set this book apart from dozens of previous attempts to cover the same material. Thanks to the determination of J. Cheney Wells to amass a comprehensive collection of work by the Willards, their apprentices, and their competitors, the collection at Sturbridge is well qualified to serve as the basis for a study of New England clocks. Historians, curators, and collectors are all well served by this lucid interpretation.

Thomas S. Michie
Museum of Art, Rhode Island School of Design

Sheila Connor. *New England Natives: A Celebration of People and Trees.* Cambridge, Mass., and London: Harvard University Press, 1994. xi + 274 pp.; 24 color and 194 bw illus., bibliography, index. $39.95.

Three Windsor chairs, an Eli Terry tall-case clock, and a painted triangular white-pine hatbox are the only pieces of furniture illustrated in this beautiful book, yet *New England Natives* will be of great interest to readers of *American Furniture*.[1] It is no less than an engaging narrative of the evolving relationship between New England's people and New England's trees from the last ice age in the Pleistocene Era to the chestnut blight and reforestation of the twentieth century. Although the book can serve as a guide to the appearance and characteristics of trees found in the area, Sheila Connor also weaves into her story the importance of trees to the many crafts and industries that have been dependent on the products of trees: for instance, tailoring, shoemaking, cranberry and blueberry harvesting, in addition to the more obvious ones of papermaking, gunsmithing, lumbering, clockmaking, chairmaking, cooperage, boatbuilding, and other types of woodworking in its various guises. Serious students of furniture will be familiar with much of the material presented here about various common types of furniture wood, but the overall breadth of the discussion of the material culture of wood will surely illuminate new corners of "This Wooden World" (to borrow the title of chapter 2) for nearly every reader.[2]

Whereas the book's content will be valuable to furniture historians, its broad interpretive format may also serve as a model for curators and others charged with caring for furniture collections and interpreting them for the public. This book grew out of the desire to prepare a guidebook to the collections of living trees and shrubs on the grounds of the Arnold Arboretum, a 265-acre site in Boston, Massachusetts, operated by Harvard University since 1872. Rather than prepare a traditional guidebook that emphasizes description and taxonomic identification, the Arboretum staff decided "instead to capture the imaginations of our visitors by telling them something about the history of the plants and their interactions with people — stories of how people have sought out plants and used them for various economic, cultural, and esthetic purposes" (p. ix). In other words, they wanted to write a book that someone who isn't a plant or tree nut (so to speak) might like to read, both for knowledge and for enjoyment. Thus the text discusses all of New England and a multitude of subjects, while using specific trees, shrubs, and landscape formations in the Arboretum as illustrations, both pictorial and literary, to illuminate the general discussion.

The National Endowment for the Humanities gave its support to this project, and Sheila Connor, Horticultural Research Archivist at the Arboretum, has accomplished the goal admirably. Her text mixes the general with the specific, avoids oversimplification, and provides an overview that will instruct and entertain laymen without making scholars cringe.

One wonders how many, if any, American furniture collections can boast an interpretive guidebook of such quality that has appeal beyond the inbred world of curators, collectors, and dealers. *New England Natives* proves that it can be done, although it seems ironic that the hefty price tag may prevent the book from reaching the general audience for whom it is designed. Detailed catalogues of collections and exhibitions will always be needed, whether in printed or electronic form, as the basic building blocks of research and the cutting edge of scholarship, but *New England Natives* reminds us that contextual, interpretive handbooks are a viable supplement.

Gerald W. R. Ward
Museum of Fine Arts, Boston

1. The Windsor armchair and two side chairs, illustrated as fig. 95 on page 117, are not identified in the caption. They are Rhode Island braced bow-back chairs, part of a set of six side and two armchairs, ca. 1780–1800, in the collection of the Museum of Fine Arts, Boston (anonymous gift and Helen and Alice Colburn Fund; 1976.774-779, 1976.819-820). The chairs are of pine, ash, and maple, painted green, with unpainted mahogany arms on the two armchairs. They descended in the Richmond family until acquired by John Walton and, in turn, the Museum.

2. For a brief recent overview of the use of wood in American furniture, see Edward S. Cooke, Jr., "Beyond Aesthetics: Wood Choice in Historical Furniture," in *Conservation by Design*, ed. Scott Landis (Providence, R.I.: Museum of Art, Rhode Island School of Design, and Woodworkers Alliance for Rainforest Protection, 1993), pp. 19–28, in which he argues that the selection of wood at any given time was more than a simple aesthetic choice, but rather it was "embedded within the values of a society and can reveal issues about cultural cohesion, social dominance, and even labor exploitation" (p. 19). This innovative book, which features a number of essays by various people and a catalogue of modern furniture by seventy-six craftsmen, examines both the craftsmans' "responsibilities for their materials and the patrons' for their patterns of consumption" (p. 9), and is perhaps the first book to deal with what Cooke calls the "ecological history of furnituremaking."

*Compiled by
Gerald W. R. Ward*

Recent Writing on
American Furniture:
A Bibliography

▼ THE MORE than two hundred titles listed in this bibliography suggest that the study of American furniture is perhaps not as devoid of intellectual energy or serious scholarly purpose as some writers might suggest. In 1993, for example, a major survey of Portsmouth, New Hampshire, furniture, and Jeremy Adamson's study of American wicker have brought strong, new light to bear on subjects that have been largely in the shadows. The classical style has been revisited in major retrospectives by the Baltimore Museum of Art (on the national level) and the Maryland Historical Society (in a regional context); and the Victorian era in Quebec has been examined in an impressive exhibition and catalogue. Monographs have ranged from a thick tome on Shaker furniture to a slender, but equally valuable, study of Joseph P. McHugh of the arts and crafts period. The first volume of *American Furniture*, containing eleven articles and four book reviews, made its own strong contribution toward developing a more rounded and sophisticated knowledge of furniture and the people who made and used it. In all, the titles in the following lists attest to the interests and the skills of a diverse body of authors—some amateurs, some professionals—who are trying their best to understand and to enjoy American furniture of many types and all ages, and, in turn, to learn more about the nature of human experience. The results are perhaps uneven, but the intentions are sincere, and the best works enrich the study of History immeasurably.

These lists have been prepared along the same lines as the compilations published in the 1993 issue of *American Furniture*. This year's list, however, includes citations for substantive book reviews as well as one auction catalogue that is tightly focused on neoclassical furniture and contains an unusual number of exemplary entries. The compilation begins with a number of 1991 and 1992 titles not included last year, either because they escaped attention or because they were actually published after the last issue went to press. The 1993 and 1994 titles follow; the 1994 list only includes titles seen through the time this issue went into production in May 1994.

Although it is not included in the list, a new journal entitled *Studies in the Decorative Arts* began publication in 1993. Published semiannually by the Bard Graduate Center for Studies in the Decorative Arts, Bard College, New York City, and edited by Sarah B. Sherrill, this journal contains articles and book reviews that will be of interest to many readers of *American Furniture*. Although to date it has not contained any articles on American furniture, the journal's guidelines indicate that it is "devoted to the examination and interpretation of the decorative arts without restriction as to medium, culture, era, or region."

Once again, it is a pleasure to record my debt to the staffs of the various libraries that have helped me compile this material, principally the Museum of Fine Arts, Boston, the Portsmouth Public Library, and the Portsmouth Athenaeum. Neville Thompson of the Winterthur Museum Library, as always, has been of great assistance. Any errors or omissions are my responsibility.

I would be glad to receive information about books and articles, especially those in museum journals and bulletins, that should be included in these annual lists. Please send references and suggestions to:

Gerald W. R. Ward
Carolyn and Peter Lynch Associate Curator of American Decorative Arts
   and Sculpture
Museum of Fine Arts, Boston
465 Huntington Avenue
Boston, Massachusetts 02115

ADDITIONS TO 1991 AND 1992 LISTS

Andrews, John. *Victorian and Edwardian Furniture: Price Guide and Reasons for Values*. Woodbridge, England: Antique Collectors' Club, 1992. 298 pp.; 80 color and 1,020 bw illus., bibliography, index. (English furniture.)

Campbell, Nina, and Caroline Seebohm. *Elsie de Wolfe: A Decorative Life*. New York: Crown Publishers, 1992. 160 pp.; illus.

Coleman, Feay Shellman. *Nostrums for Fashionable Entertainments: Dining in Georgia, 1800–1850*. Savannah: Telfair Academy of Arts and Sciences, 1992. xii + 133 pp.; bw illus., appendixes, bibliography.

Connecticut Masters: The Fine Arts and Antiques Collections of The Hartford Steam Boiler Inspection and Insurance Company. Hartford, Conn.: Hartford Steam Boiler Inspection and Insurance Company, 1991. 271 pp.; numerous color illus., index.

Cooke, Edward S., Jr. Review of John Bivins, Jr., *The Furniture of Coastal North Carolina, 1700–1820*. In *Winterthur Portfolio* 26, nos. 2/3 (Summer/Autumn 1991): 195–97.

Flood, Elizabeth Clair. *Country High Style: Thomas Molesworth to the New West*. Salt Lake City, Utah: Gibbs Smith, 1992. Illus.

Foa, Linda. *Furniture for the Workplace*. New York: Library of Architecture and Interior Design, 1992. 240 pp.; illus., index.

Hinckley, F. Lewis. *Georgian Furniture and Looking Glasses*. Washington Square, N.Y.: A Washington Mews Book, 1992. 154 pp.; 269 bw illus., index.

Hinckley, F. Lewis. *The More Significant Regency Furnitures, 1800–1830+*. Washington Square, N.Y.: A Washington Mews Book, 1991. 82 pp.; 105 bw illus., index.

Ingram, K. E. "Furniture and the Plantation: Further Light on the West Indian Trade of an English Furniture Firm in the Eighteenth Century." *Furniture History* 28 (1992): 42–97. 5 tables, 27 bw illus.

Kraus, Bill, and Jon F. Sikes, eds. *American Furniture Makers*. Madison, Wis.: Kraus Sikes, 1991. 160 pp.; illus. Distributed by Rockport Publications.

Lahvis, Sylvia Leistyna. "Icons of American Trade: The Skillin Workshop and the Language of Spectacle." *Winterthur Portfolio* 27, no. 4 (Winter 1992): 219–34. 21 bw illus.

Mack, Daniel. *Making Rustic Furniture*. New York: Sterling Publishing Co., 1992. 160 pp.; numerous color and bw illus., source list, index.

Munger, Jeffrey H. "Royal French Furniture in Eighteenth-Century Boston." In *Versailles: French Court Style and Its Influence*, pp. 113–25. Edited Lectures of the Decorative Arts Institute. Toronto: University of Toronto School of Continuing Studies, 1992. 4 bw illus.

Naeve, Milo M. "John Glinn's Clock Case of 1750 for Henry Bromfield of Boston, Massachusetts." *Furniture History* 28 (1992): 22–34. 12 bw illus.

Parissien, Steven. *Regency Style*. Washington, D.C.: Preservation Press of the National Trust for Historic Preservation, 1992. 240 pp.; numerous color illus., directory of designers, glossary, contacts and sources, bibliography, index.

Pocius, Gerald L., ed. *Living in a Material World: Canadian and American Approaches to Material Culture*. Social and Economic Papers, No. 19. St. John's, Newfoundland, Canada: Institute of Social and Economic Research, Memorial University of Newfoundland, 1991. xix + 290 pp.; bw illus., references, index. (See especially Jules David Prown, "On the 'Art' in Artifacts"; Dell Upton, "Form and User: Style, Mode, Fashion, and the Artifact"; Michael J. Ettema, "The Fashion System in American Furniture"; and Stanley Johannesen, "Invisibility, Embodiment, and American Furniture.")

Regional Furniture 6 (1992): 1–100. Numerous bw illus. (Anthology of articles on Scottish, Irish, and Welsh furniture.)

Reinish, James L., and Ann Yaffe Phillips. *The Craftsman Table: Dining Rooms by Greene & Greene, Gustav Stickley, Frank Lloyd Wright*. New York: Hirschl & Adler Galleries, 1992. Not paged; 6 color illus., checklist of exhibition. (Brochure.)

Roberts, Derek. *A Collector's Guide to Clocks*. Secaucus, N.J.: Chartwell Books, 1992. 128 pp.; numerous color illus., index.

Rowan, Michael J. *Ukrainian Pioneer Furniture*. Toronto: Ukrainian Museum of Canada, 1992. 24 pp.; color illus., bibliography.

Semowich, Charles. "The Life and Chairs of William Buttre." *Furniture History* 28 (1992): 129–36. 7 bw illus.

Scherer, John L. Review of Peter M. Kenny, Frances Gruber Safford, and Gilbert T. Vincent, *American Kasten: The Dutch-Style Cupboards of New York and New Jersey, 1650–1800*. In *Newsletter of the Decorative Arts Society* 1, no. 1 (Winter 1992): 11–12.

Sypher, F. J. "Sypher & Co., A Pioneer Antique Dealer in New York." *Furniture History* 28 (1992): 168–79. 6 bw illus.

Ward, Gerald W. R. Review of Bernard D. Cotton, *The English Regional Chair*. In *Winterthur Portfolio* 26, no. 4 (Winter 1991): 277–78.

Zimmerman, Philip D. Review of David L. Barquist, *American Tables and Looking Glasses in the Mabel Brady Garvan and Other Collections at Yale University*. In *Winterthur Portfolio* 27, no. 4 (Winter 1992): 293–95.

Zonderman, David A. *Aspirations and Anxieties: New England Workers and the Mechanized Factory System, 1815–1850*. New York: Oxford University Press, 1992. viii + 357 pp.; bibliography, index. (Contains references to clock factories.)

1993 TITLES

Adamson, Jeremy. *American Wicker: Woven Furniture from 1850 to 1930*. Washington, D.C.: The Renwick Gallery of the National Museum of American Art, Smithsonian Institution, in association with Rizzoli, 1993. 175 pp.; numerous color and bw illus., bibliography, index.

Anderson, Mark J., and Robert F. Trent. "The Case of the Desk-and-Bookcase." *Winterthur Magazine* 39, no. 2 (Spring 1993): 8–9. 1 color and 1 bw illus. (Re conservation of Gardiner family desk and bookcase attributed to Nathaniel Dominy V, East Hampton, N.Y., ca. 1800, in Winterthur collection.)

Anderson, Mark J. "A Catalogue of American Easy Chairs." In *American Furniture 1993*, ed. Luke Beckerdite, 1993, pp. 212–234. Milwaukee, Wis.: The Chipstone Foundation, 1993. 35 bw illus.

Arkansas: Year of American Craft, 1993. Little Rock: Arkansas Arts Center Decorative Arts Museum, The Pike-Fletcher-Terry House, 1993. 65 pp.; color illus, biographies. (Includes some contemporary furniture.)

Arrowsmith, James. *An Analysis of Drapery*. 1819. Thomas King. *The Upholsterers' Accelerator*. 1833. Reprint. Introduction by Gail Caskey Winkler. New York: Acanthus Press, 1993. 144 pp.; 55 line drawings.

Baarsen, Reinier. *Nederlandse Meubelen, 1600–1800: Dutch Furniture, 1600–1800*. Amsterdam: Rijksmuseum, 1993. 143 pp.; numerous color illus., bibliography.

Barder, Richard C. R. *The Georgian Bracket Clock, 1714–1830*. Woodbridge, England: Antique Collectors Club, 1993. 233 pp.; 39 color and 267 bw illus., bibliography, index. (Mainly English examples.)

Baron, Donna, and Caroline Sloat. "Cabinet Furniture & Chairs, Cheap: Making and Selling Furniture in Central New England." *Antiques and the Arts Weekly* (November 12, 1993): 1, 72–74. bw illus.

Baron, Donna, and Caroline Sloat. "Cabinet Furniture & Chairs, Cheap: Making and Selling Furniture in Central New England, 1790–1850." *Old Sturbridge Visitor* (Spring 1993): unpaged. 2 color and 1 bw illus.

Baumgarten, Linda. "Protective Covers for Furniture and Its Contents." In *American Furniture 1993*, ed. Luke Beckerdite, pp. 1–14. Milwaukee, Wis.: The Chipstone Foundation, 1993. 1 color and 16 bw illus.

Beckerdite, Luke. "Origins of the Rococo Style in New York Furniture and Interior Architecture." In *American Furniture 1993*, ed. Luke Beckerdite, pp. 15–38. Milwaukee, Wis.: The Chipstone Foundation, 1993. 2 color and 44 bw illus.

Beckerdite, Luke. Review of Graham Hood, *The Governor's Palace in Williamsburg: A Cultural Study*. In *American Furniture 1993*, ed. Luke Beckerdite, pp. 271–74. Milwaukee, Wis.: The Chipstone Foundation, 1993.

Beckerdite, Luke, ed. *American Furniture 1993*. Milwaukee, Wis.: The Chipstone Foundation, 1993. xiii + 298 pp.; numerous color and bw illus., bibliography, index. Distributed by University Press of New England.

Bivins, John, and J. Thomas Savage. "The Miles Brewton House, Charleston, South Carolina." *Antiques* 143, no. 2 (February 1993): 294–307. 17 color and 2 bw illus.

Brooks Manufacturing Co. *Arts and Crafts Furniture: The Complete Brooks Catalogue of 1912*. New York: Dover Publications and the Athenaeum of Philadelphia, 1993. 80 pp.; 1 color and 150 bw illus., 20 line drawings. (Facsimile reprint of *Brooks Arts and Crafts Furniture Catalog No. 14*, January 1912.)

Clark, Ginna. "Winterthur Opens the Henry S. McNeil Gallery." *Antiques and the Arts Weekly* (July 16, 1993): 1, 72–75. bw illus.

Collins, Philip. *Pastime: Telling Time from 1879 to 1969*. San Francisco: Chronicle Books, 1993. 95 pp.; color illus.

Common Ground/Uncommon Vision: The Michael and Julie Hall Collection of American Folk Art in the Milwaukee Art Museum. Milwaukee, Wis.: Milwaukee Art Museum, 1993. 335 pp.; numerous color and bw illus., biographies, bibliography, index. (Includes a few examples of furniture.)

Conradson, David H. "The Stock-in-Trade of John Hancock and Company." In *American Furniture 1993*, ed. Luke Beckerdite, pp. 38–54. Milwaukee, Wis.: The Chipstone Foundation, 1993. 1 color and 6 bw illus., appendix.

"Conservation Reveals Neoclassical Splendor." *SPNEA Conservation Center Update* (Summer 1993): unpaged. In *SPNEA Newsletter*, series 59 (Summer 1993). 3 bw illus. (Re eight pieces of Maryland furniture.)

Cooke, Edward S., Jr. "New Netherlands' Influence on Furniture of the Housatonic Valley." In *The Impact of New Netherlands upon the Colonial Long Island Basin*, ed. Joshua W. Lane, pp. 36–43. New Haven, Conn., and Washington, D.C.: Yale-Smithsonian Seminar on Material Culture, 1993. 5 bw illus.

Cooke, Edward S., Jr. "Scandinavian Modern Furniture in the Arts and Crafts Period: The Collaboration of the Greenes and the Halls." In *American Furniture 1993*, ed. Luke Beckerdite, pp. 55–74. Milwaukee, Wis.: The Chipstone Foundation, 1993. 2 color and 27 bw illus., appendix.

Cooke, Edward S., Jr. Review of Bernard D. Cotton, *The English Regional Chair*. *Antiques* 143, no. 5 (May 1993): 716, 718. 1 bw illus.

Cooper, Wendy A. "Classical Taste in America, 1800–1840." *Antiques* 143, no. 5 (May 1993): 764–75. 18 color illus.

Cooper, Wendy A. *Classical Taste in America, 1800–1840*. New York: Baltimore Museum of Art and Abbeville Press, 1993. 308 pp.; numerous color and bw illus., bibliography, exhibition checklist, index.

Copeland, Peter A., and Janet H. Copeland, eds. *The 1912 Quaint Furniture Catalog: Stickley Brothers Company, Grand Rapids Michigan*. Grand Rapids, Mich.: Stickley Brothers Co., 1912. Reprint. Introduction by Don Marek and Richard Weiderman. Parchment, Mich.: Parchment Press, 1993. xii + unpaged facsimile reprint, numerous bw illus.

Cotton, Bernard D. *Manx Traditional*

Furniture: A Catalogue of the Furniture Collections of Manx National Heritage. Douglas, Isle of Man: Manx National Heritage, Manx Museum and National Trust, 1993. l + 286 pp.; 25 color and numerous bw illus., appendixes, glossary, bibliography.

Crump, Nancy Carter. "Foodways of the Albemarle Region: 'Indulgent Nature Makes Up for Every Want.'" *Journal of Early Southern Decorative Arts* 19, no. 1 (May 1993): 1–36. 16 bw illus.

D'Ambrosio, Anna Tobin, and Leslie Greene Bowman. *"The Distinction of Being Different": Joseph P. McHugh and the American Arts and Crafts Movement*. Utica, N.Y.: Munson-Williams-Proctor Institute, 1993. 64 pp.; color and bw illus., line drawings, bibliography, exhibition checklist.

De Gary, Marie-Noël, and Geneviève Musin. *Objects d'usage & de goût dans les premières années du 19e siècle*. Paris: Union Centrale des Arts Dècoratifs, Réunion des Musées Nationaux, 1993. 157 pp.; numerous color illus., bibliography.

De Noblet, Jocelyn, ed. *Industrial Design: Reflection of a Century*. Paris: Flammarion/APCI, 1993. 431 pp.; numerous color and bw illus., bibliography, index.

Donald Judd Furniture: Restrospective. Rotterdam: Museum Boymans-van Beuningen, 1993. 134 pp.; numerous color and bw illus., biography, bibliography.

Dormer, Peter. *Design Since 1945*. London: Thames and Hudson, 1993. 216 pp.; 25 color and 145 bw illus., chronology, bibliography, index. See esp. chapter 5, "Furniture Design."

Edwards, Clive. *Victorian Furniture: Technology and Design*. Manchester, England: Manchester University Press, 1993. xii + 209 pp.; illus. Distributed by St. Martin's Press, New York. (English furniture.)

Ehresmann, Donald L. *Applied and Decorative Arts: A Bibliographic Guide*. 2d ed. Englewood, Colo.: Libraries Unlimited, Inc., 1993. xxxvii + 629 pp.; author-title index, subject index. (See esp. chapter 9, Furniture.)

Einarsson, Magnus, and Helga Benndorf Taylor, eds. *Just for Nice: German-Canadian Folk Art*. Hull, Quebec: Canadian Museum of Civilization, 1993. 124 pp.; color and bw illus., bibliographies. Distributed by University of Chicago Press.

Evans, Nancy Goyne. "Design Transmission in Vernacular Seating Furniture: The Influence of Philadelphia and Baltimore Styles on Chairmaking from the Chesapeake Bay to the 'West.'" In *American Furniture 1993*, ed. Luke Beckerdite, pp. 75–116. Milwaukee, Wis.: The Chipstone Foundation, 1993. 34 bw illus.

Fennimore, Donald. "Survivals and Revivals: An American Fascination." *Winterthur Magazine* 39, no. 2 (Spring 1993): 6–7. 3 bw illus.

Fiell, Charlotte, and Peter Fiell. *Modern Chairs*. Cologn, Germany: Benedikt Taschen, 1993. 160 pp.; numerous color illus., appendix, biographies, bibliography, index.

Fifty Years on Chestnut Street. Philadelphia: Schwarz Gallery, 1993. Unpaged; color and bw illus., index.

Fowble, E. McSherry. "Classical Maryland, 1815–1845: Fine and Decorative Arts from the Golden Age: An Exhibition Review." *Winterthur Portfolio* 28, nos. 2/3 (Summer/Autumn 1993): 159–65. 3 bw illus.

Frankel, Candie. *Encyclopedia of Country Furniture*. New York: Michael Friedman Publishing Group, 1993. vii + 192 pp.; numerous color illus., glossary, sources, bibliography.

Frelinghuysen, Alice Cooney. "Louis Comfort Tiffany and the H. O. Havemeyers." *Antiques* 143, no. 4 (April 1993): 596–607. 12 color and 7 bw illus.

Frelinghuysen, Alice Cooney, et al. *Splendid Legacy: The Havemeyer Collection*. New York: Metropolitan Museum of Art, 1993. xvi + 415 pp.; 176 color and 624 bw illus., chronology, appendix, bibliography, list of exhibition, index. (See esp. Frelinghysen's chapter entitled "The Havemeyer House," pp. 173–98.)

Garrett, Wendell. "History in Houses: Dumbarton House in Georgetown, District of Columbia." *Antiques* 143, no. 1 (January 1993): 154–61. Color illus.

Garrett, Wendell. *Victorian America: Classical Romanticism to Gilded Opulence*, ed. David Larkin. New York: Rizzoli, 1993. 300 pp.; 180 color and 20 bw illus.

Garrett, Wendell, and Elisabeth Garrett. "Living with Antiques: The Clark-Haskell House, Lisbon, Connecticut." *Antiques* 144, no. 2 (August 1993): 212–21. Color illus.

Gaynor, James M., and Nancy L. Hagedorn. *Tools: Working Wood in Eighteenth-Century America*. Williamsburg, Va.: Colonial Williamsburg Foundation, 1993. xiv + 126 pp.; numerous color and bw illus., glossary, bibliography, index.

Giblin, James Cross. *Be Seated: A Book About Chairs*. New York: Harper-Collins, 1993. 136 pp.; bw illus., bibliography, index. (Juvenile literature.)

Gilbert, Christopher. "Comments from Leeds." *Newsletter of the Decorative Arts Society* 2, nos. 3–4 (Summer/Fall 1993): 2.

Gilbert, Christopher, and Tessa Murdoch. *John Channon and Brass-Inlaid Furniture, 1730–1760*. New Haven and London: Yale University Press in association with Leeds City Art Galleries and the Victoria and Albert Museum, 1993. viii + 164 pp.; 28 color and 186 bw illus., appendixes, bibliography, index. (English furniture.)

Gusler, Elizabeth Pitzer. Review of Clement E. Conger and Mary K. Itsell; Alexandra W. Rollins, ed.; Will Brown, photographer, *Treasures of State: Fine and Decorative Arts in the Diplomatic Reception Rooms of the U.S. Department of State*. In *American Furniture 1993*, ed. Luke Beckerdite, pp. 263–67. Milwaukee, Wis.: The Chipstone Foundation, 1993.

Gustafson, Eleanor H. "Museum Accessions." *Antiques* 143, no. 5 (May 1993): 692, 694. 2 color and 2 bw illus. (Re Stickley Brothers Co. desk acquired by the Metropolitan Museum of Art; a Charleston federal linen press acquired by MESDA; a Meeks gaming table, ca. 1836–1855, and other nineteenth-century objects acquired by the Munson-Williams-Proctor Institute Museum of Art; and a tall-case clock, ca. 1775, by Jonathan Mulliken acquired by the Museum of Our National Heritage.)

Halle, David. *Inside Culture: Art and Class in the American Home.* Chicago: Chicago University Press, 1993. xvi + 261 pp.; 91 bw illus., appendix, index.

Handbook for Winterthur Interpreters: A Multidisciplinary Analysis of the Winterthur Collection. Pauline K. Eversmann, Project Director; Rosemary Troy Krill, Project Coordinator; Gerald W. R. Ward, Editor. 2 vols. Winterthur, Del.: Winterthur Museum, 1993. Typescript. Numerous bw illus. and line drawings.

Hayes, John, and Debra Force. "The Elizabeth Blaney Cram Collection." *Christie's International Magazine* 10, no. 4 (June/July 1993): 36–37. 1 color and 1 bw illus.

Herman, Lloyd E., and Matthew Kangas. *Tales and Traditions: Storytelling in Twentieth-Century American Craft.* St. Louis: Craft Alliance, 1993. 94 pp.; color and bw illus., checklist. Distributed by University of Washington Press.

Heydenryk, Henry, Jr. *The Art and History of Frames: An Inquiry into the Enhancement of Paintings.* 1963. Reprint. New York: Lyons & Burford, 1993. 119 pp.; numerous bw illus., bibliography.

Hiesinger, Kathryn B., and George H. Marcus. *Landmarks of Twentieth-Century Design: An Illustrated Handbook.* New York: Abbeville Press, 1993. 430 pp.; 100 color and 300 bw illus., designer biographies and bibliographies, general bibliography, index.

Hood, Graham. "American or English Furniture? Some Choices in the 1760s." In *American Furniture 1993*, ed. Luke Beckerdite, pp. 117–46. Milwaukee, Wis.: The Chipstone Foundation, 1993. 3 color and 11 bw illus., appendix.

Hosley, William. Review of Brock W. Jobe, et al., *American Furniture with Related Decorative Arts, 1660–1830: The Milwaukee Art Museum and the Layton Art Collection.* In *Newsletter of the Decorative Arts Society* 2, nos. 1–2 (Winter/Spring 1993): 9–12.

Hough, Katherine Plake. *American Arts and Crafts from the Collection of Alexandra and Sidney Sheldon.* Palm Springs, Calif.: Palm Springs Desert Museum, 1993. 104 pp.; 93 color and 5 bw illus., biblio. Distributed by University of Washington Press.

Hughes, Debra K. *Artifacts of Invention: Patent Models at the Hagley Museum and Library.* Wilmington, Del.: York Publishing Services, 1993. 112 pp.; color illus. (Includes several models for furniture.)

Huitson, John. "The American Museum in Britain: Visions of Heaven on Earth." *Antiques* 143, no. 3 (March 1993): 436–41. 9 color illus.

Hurst, Ronald L. Review of Morrison H. Heckscher and Leslie Greene Bowman, *American Rococo, 1750–1775: Elegance in Ornament.* In *American Furniture 1993*, ed. Luke Beckerdite, pp. 268–71. Milwaukee, Wis.: The Chipstone Foundation, 1993.

"Is It Phyfe? Museum of the City of New York." *Antiques and the Arts Weekly* (April 2, 1993): 1, 72–75. bw illus.

Jacobson, Dawn. *Chinoiserie.* London: Phaidon Press, 1993. 240 pp.; numerous color and bw illus., glossary, bibliography, index.

Jobe, Brock, ed., with contributions by Diane Carlberg Ehrenpreis, James L. Garvin, Anne Rogers Haley, Brock Jobe, Myrna Kaye, Johanna McBrien, Kevin Nicholson, Richard C. Nylander, Elizabeth Redmond, Kevin Shupe, Robert Trent, Gerald W. R. Ward, and Philip Zea. *Portsmouth Furniture: Masterworks from the New Hampshire Seacoast.* Boston: Society for the Preservation of New England Antiquities, 1993. Distributed by University Press of New England. 454 pp.; 14 color and numerous bw illus., appendixes, bibliography, index.

Julier, Guy. *The Thames and Hudson Encyclopedia of 20th-Century Design and Designers.* London: Thames and Hudson, 1993. 216 pp.; numerous bw illus., subject index, chronological chart, bibliography.

Kamil, Neil Duff. "Of American Kasten and the Mythology of 'Pure Dutchness': A Review Article." In *American Furniture 1993*, ed. Luke Beckerdite, pp. 275–82. Milwaukee, Wis.: The Chipstone Foundation, 1993.

Kane, Patricia E. *Furniture of the New Haven Colony: The Seventeenth Century Style, with an Addendum.* New Haven: New Haven Colony Historical Society, 1993. 110 pp.; numerous bw illus. (First published 1973.)

Kane, Patricia E. "New Netherlands' Influence on Connecticut Decorative Arts." In *The Impact of New Netherlands upon the Colonial Long Island Basin*, ed. Joshua W. Lane, pp. 28–32. New Haven, and Washington, D.C.: Yale-Smithsonian Seminar on Material Culture, 1993. 6 bw illus.

Kardon, Janet, ed. *The Ideal Home, 1900–1920: The History of Twentieth-Century American Craft.* New York: Harry N. Abrams in association with the American Craft Museum, 1993. 304 pp.; 100 color and 169 bw illus., appendixes, bibliography, index. (See esp. Edward S. Cooke, Jr., "Arts and Crafts Furniture: Process or Product?" pp. 64–76, and related catalogue entries.)

Kaye, Myrna, and Brock Jobe. "Robert Harrold, Portsmouth Cabinetmaker." *Antiques* 143, no. 5 (May 1993): 776–83. 12 color and 6 bw illus.

Ketchum, William C., Jr. *Collecting the West: Cowboy, Indian, Spanish American, and Mining Memorabilia.* New York: Crown Publishers, 1993. 174 pp.; numerous color illus., glossary, bibliography, index. (Includes a few examples of furniture.)

Kinmonth, Claudia. *Irish Country Furniture, 1700–1950.* New Haven and London: Yale University Press, 1993. x + 249 pp.; 320 color and bw illus., line drawings, appendix, gazetteer, map, glossary, bibliographic note, index.

Kugelman, Thomas P., and Alice K. Kugelman. "The Hartford Case Furniture Survey." *Maine Antique Digest* 21, no. 3 (March 1993): 36A–38A. 10 bw illus.

Kylloe, Ralph. *Rustic Traditions*. Salt Lake City, Utah: Gibbs Smith, 1993. vii + 176 pp.; numerous color and bw illus., list of contemporary makers and sources, bibliography.

Landis, Scott, ed. *Conservation by Design*. Providence, R.I.: Museum of Art, Rhode Island School of Design, and Woodworkers Alliance for Rainforest Protection, 1993. 160 pp.; numerous color and bw illus. (See esp. Edward S. Cooke, Jr., "Beyond Aesthetics," pp. 19–28.)

Landrey, Greg. "The Conservator as Curator: Combining Scientific Analysis and Traditional Connoisseurship." In *American Furniture 1993*, ed. Luke Beckerdite, pp. 147–59. Milwaukee, Wis.: The Chipstone Foundation, 1993. 11 color and 5 bw illus.

Larason, Lew. *Buying Antique Furniture: An Advisory*. Chalfont, Pa.: Scorpio Publications, 1993. 172 pp.; 65 line drawings.

Levy, Frank M. "A Maker of New York Card Tables Identified." *Antiques* 143, no. 5 (May 1993): 756–63. 12 color and 1 bw illus.

Lindquist, David P., and Caroline C. Warren. *Colonial Revival Furniture with Prices*. Radnor, Pa.: Wallace-Homestead Book Co., 1993. 166 pp.; numerous bw illus., bibliography, index.

Linley, David. *Classical Furniture*. New York: Harry N. Abrams, 1993. 192 pp.; numerous color illus., index.

Lubar, Steven, and W. David Kingery, eds. *History from Things: Essays on Material Culture*. Washington, D.C.: Smithsonian Institution Press, 1993. xvii + 300 pp.; 54 bw illus., 12 line drawings.

Martin, Ann Smart. "Makers, Buyers, and Users: Consumerism as a Material Culture Framework." *Winterthur Portfolio* 28, nos. 2/3 (Summer/Autumn 1993): 141–57.

McLary, Kathleen. *Amish Style: Clothing, Home Furnishings, Toys, Dolls, and Quilts*. Bloomington and Indianapolis: Indiana University Press, 1993. 104 pp.; 80 color and 15 bw illus., bibliography.

Metropolitan Museum of Art. "Recent Acquisitions: A Selection, 1992–1993." *Metropolitan Museum of Art Bulletin* 51, no. 2 (Fall 1993): 56, 58–59, 80, 82. (Entries by Morrison H. Heckscher on a finial bust of John Locke, Philadelphia, ca. 1765–1775; Catherine Hoover Voorsanger on a Hunzinger settee, ca. 1876–1885, a Greene and Greene armchair, 1907–1909, and a Stickley Bros. desk, 1904; and Alice Cooney Frelinghuysen on a Tiffany and Colman armchair, ca. 1891.)

Miller, Alan. "Roman Gusto in New England: An Eighteenth-Century Boston Furniture Designer and His Shop." In *American Furniture 1993*, ed. Luke Beckerdite, pp. 160–200. Milwaukee, Wis.: The Chipstone Foundation, 1993. 5 color and 50 bw illus.

Miller, Judith, and Martin Miller. *Victorian Style*. London: Mitchell Beazley, 1993. 240 pp.; numerous color illus., directory, glossary, bibliography, index.

Morley, John. *Regency Design, 1790–1840: Gardens, Buildings, Interiors, Furniture*. New York: Harry N. Abrams, 1993. 473 pp.; 132 color and 339 bw illus., index. (Focus on English objects.)

Mowl, Timothy. *Elizabethan and Jacobean Style*. London: Phaidon Press, 1993. 240 pp.; numerous color and bw illus., glossary, bibliography, index.

Naeve, Milo M. Review of "Hadley Chests" exhibition and *Hadley Chests*, by Philip Zea and Suzanne L. Flynt. In *Newsletter of the Decorative Arts Society* 2, nos. 1–2 (Winter/Spring 1993): 6–8.

"New Accession: Museum Adds Portsmouth Couch to Collection." *Winterthur Magazine* 39, no. 2 (Spring 1993): 11. 1 bw illus. (Re couch attributed to Robert Harrold, with upholstery attributed to Joseph Bass, 1760s, ex coll. Wendell and Manney.)

Nichols, Sarah. "The American Museum in Britain: The Furniture." *Antiques* 143, no. 3 (March 1993): 442–55. 22 color illus.

Nylander, Jane C. *Our Own Snug Fireside: Images of the New England Home, 1760–1860*. New York: Alfred A. Knopf, 1993. xiv + 317 pp.; 162 bw illus., bibliography, index.

Paston-Williams, Sara. *The Art of Dining: A History of Cooking and Eating*. London: The National Trust, 1993. 318 pp.; 200 color and 56 bw illus., bibliography, index. Distributed by Harry N. Abrams, Inc., New York.

Pearce, Susan M. *Museums, Objects, and Collections: A Cultural Study*. Washington, D.C.: Smithsonian Institution Press, 1993. 296 pp.; bw illus., bibliography, index.

Phillips, Patricia C. "Sitting Up: Critical Chairs." *Sculpture* 12, no. 4 (July–August 1993): 24–31. 6 color illus.

Plante, Ellen M. *Country Furniture*. Radnor, Pa.: Wallace-Homestead Book Co., 1993. 150 pp.; bw illus., bibliography, index.

Porter, John R., ed. *Living in Style: Fine Furniture in Victorian Quebec*. Montreal and Quebec: Montreal Museum of Fine Arts and Musée de la Civilisation, 1993. 527 pp.; 64 color and 490 bw illus., bibliography, index.

Regional Furniture 7 (1993): 1–135. Numerous bw illus. ("An Anthology of Regional Furniture with Maker's Identification"; primarily English furniture.)

Rieman, Timothy D., and Jean M. Burks. *The Complete Book of Shaker Furniture*. New York: Harry N. Abrams, 1993. 400 pp.; 117 color and 283 bw illus., bibliography, glossary, index.

Rinker, Harry L., ed. *Warman's Furniture*. Radnor, Pa.: Wallace-Homestead Book Co., 1993. xxii + 312 pp.; bw illus., line drawings, index.

Roberts, Derek. *Carriage and Other Travelling Clocks*. Atglen, Pa.: Schiffer Publishing Co., 1993. 368 pp.; 400 color and 285 bw illus., glossary, index.

Rogers, Alan W. "The Horn Furniture of Herman F. Metz." *Maine Antique Digest* 21, no. 8 (August 1993): 8B–9B. 4 bw illus.

Rogers, Bryan, and Snowden Taylor. *Eight Day Wood Movement Shelf Clocks: Their Cases, Their Movements, Their Makers*. NAWCC Bulletin Supplement

19, Spring 1993. Columbia, Pa.: National Association of Watch and Clock Collectors, Inc., 1993. 60 pp.; 153 bw illus., tables.

Sack, Albert. *The New Fine Points of Furniture: Early American — Good, Better, Best, Superior, Masterpiece*. New York: Crown, 1993. 320 pp.; 650 color and bw illus., bibliography, index.

Sack Archives of Portsmouth Furniture. 3 vols. Boston: Society for the Preservation of New England Antiquities, 1993. Unpaged typescript, numerous xerographic illus., computer disks. (Available only at SPNEA, Portsmouth Atheneum, Winterthur Museum, Israel Sack, Inc., and a few other locations.)

Sack, Israel, Inc. *Celebrating Our 90th Anniversary*. New York: By the firm, 1993. 112 pp.; numerous color and bw illus.

Sands, John O. "An effect which far exceeds any conception . . ." *Colonial Williamsburg: The Journal of the Colonial Williamsburg Foundation* 15, no. 3 (Spring 1993): 72–73. 6 color illus. (Re Philadelphia painted and gilt neoclassical chairs in the Hennage collection.)

Saumarez Smith, Charles. *Eighteenth-Century Decoration: Design and the Domestic Interior in England*. New York: Harry N. Abrams, 1993. 407 pp.; 379 color and bw illus., bibliography, index.

Savage, Bert. "Rustic American Furniture." *Antiques and the Arts Weekly* (August 6, 1993): S18–S19. 7 bw illus.

Savage, J. Thomas. "Decorative Arts Discoveries at the Miles Brewton House." *Newsletter of the Decorative Arts Society* 2, nos. 3–4 (Summer–Fall 1993): 4. (Abstract.)

Schultz, Ronald. *The Republic of Labor: Philadelphia Artisans and the Politics of Class, 1720–1830*. New York: Oxford University Press, 1993. xv + 298 pp.; illus., bibliography, index.

"Scott Collection, Baltimore Museum of Art." *Antiques and the Arts Weekly* (March 5, 1993): 1, 76–78. bw illus.

Shaw, Robert. *America's Traditional Crafts*. New York: Hugh Lauter Levin Associates, 1993. 312 pp.; numerous color and bw illus., glossary, index.

Sisco, Mark. "A $40,000 Desk with a $125,000 History: Jim Julia, Rockport, Maine." *Maine Antique Digest* 21, no. 11 (November 1993): 1D–3D. bw illus.

Smith, A. Lee. "Elisha Manross: The Clockmaker's Clockmaker." *Bulletin of the National Association of Watch and Clock Collectors, Inc.* 35, no. 5 (October 1993): 541–56. 24 bw illus., 4 tables.

Solis-Cohen, Lita. "Connoisseurship." *Maine Antique Digest* 21, no. 11 (November 1993): 36A–37A. 8 bw illus.

Sparke, Penny, ed. *The Plastics Age: From Bakelite to Beanbags and Beyond*. Woodstock, N.Y.: Overlook Press, 1993. 160 pp.; 65 color and 85 bw illus., bibliography, index. (Includes a few examples of furniture.)

Stein, Susan R. "Furnishings at Monticello." *Antiques* 144, no. 1 (July 1993): 70–79. 15 color and 1 bw illus.

Stein, Susan R. *The Worlds of Thomas Jefferson at Monticello*. New York: Harry N. Abrams in association with the Thomas Jefferson Memorial Association, 1993. 472 pp.; 107 color and 220 bw illus., appendixes, index.

Stevens, John Taylor. "A Case, Willard & Co. Triple-Decker Clock." *Bulletin of the National Association of Watch and Clock Collectors, Inc.* 35, no. 5 (October 1993): 563–66. 7 bw illus., bibliography.

Swedberg, Robert W., and Harriett Swedberg. *Collector's Encyclopedia of American Furniture*. Vol. 3, *Country Furniture of the Eighteenth and Nineteenth Centuries*. Paducah, Ky.: Collector Books, 1994. 125 pp.; numerous color illus., price guides.

Taragin, Davira S., et al. *Contemporary Crafts and the Saxe Collection*. New York: Hudson Hills Press and Toledo Museum of Art, 1993. 216 pp.; 26 bw and 122 color illus., index. (See esp. Edward S. Cooke, Jr., "Wood in the 1980s: Expansion or Commodification?" pp. 149–62.)

Trent, Robert F. "Mid-Atlantic Easy Chairs, 1770–1820: Old Questions and New Evidence." In *American Furniture 1993*, ed. Luke Beckerdite, pp. 201–11. Milwaukee, Wis.: The Chipstone Foundation, 1993. 1 color illus.

Trapp, Kenneth R., et al. *The Arts and Crafts Movement in California: Living the Good Life*. Oakland, Calif. and New York: Oakland Museum; and Abbeville Press, 1993. 328 pp.; 213 color and bw illus., biographies and company histories, bibliography, checklist of exhibition, index.

Troyen, Carol. "The Incomparable Max: Maxim Karolik and the Taste for American Art." *American Art* (Summer 1993): 65–87. 19 color and bw illus.

Troyen, Carol. "The Karoliks and Their Collections." In *A Significant Story: Treasures of American Painting and Decorative Arts from the M. and M. Karolik Collections of the Museum of Fine Arts, Boston*, pp. 15–51. Newport, R.I.: Newport Art Museum, 1993. 34 bw illus.

Ward, Gerald W. R. "The Karolik Collections of American Decorative Arts." In *A Significant Story: Treasures of American Painting and Decorative Arts from the M. and M. Karolik Collections of the Museum of Fine Arts, Boston*, pp. 53–64. Newport, R.I.: Newport Art Museum, 1993. 16 bw illus.

Ward, Gerald W. R., and Karin E. Cullity. "The Wendell Family Furniture at Strawbery Banke Museum." In *American Furniture 1993*, ed. Luke Beckerdite, pp. 235–62. Milwaukee, Wis.: The Chipstone Foundation, 1993. 46 bw illus.

Ward, Gerald W. R., comp. "Bibliography of Works on American Furniture Published in 1991 and 1992." In *American Furniture 1993*, ed. Luke Beckerdite, 1993, pp. 283–89. Milwaukee, Wis.: The Chipstone Foundation, 1993.

Warren, David B. "The Reopening of Bayou Bend in Houston, Texas." *Antiques* 144, no. 3 (September 1993): 328–37. 15 color and 2 bw illus.

Warren, Winthrop D., and Christopher B. Nevins. "Clocks and Clockmakers of Colonial Fairfield, Circa 1736–1813." *Bulletin of the National Association of Watch and Clock Collectors, Inc.* Part I,

35, no. 5 (October 1993): 515–40. 36 bw illus., appendix, bibliography. Part II, 35, no. 6 (December 1993): 659–97. 72 bw illus., bibliography, appendixes.

Webb-Deane-Stevens Museum. *"Please Be Seated": A Catalogue of the Exhibit, July 13 to October 3, 1993.* Wethersfield, Conn.: By the museum, 1993. 51 pp.; 26 bw illus. (Essays by Beth Ann Spyrison, Kevin M. Sweeney, and Florence Mellowes Montgomery.)

Weidman, Gregory R. "The Painted Furniture of John and Hugh Finlay." *Antiques* 143, no. 5 (May 1993): 744–55. 20 color illus.

Weidman, Gregory R., and Jennifer F. Goldsborough, with Robert L. Alexander, Stiles Tuttle Colwill, Mary Ellen Hayward, and Catherine A. Rogers. *Classical Maryland, 1815–1845: Fine and Decorative Arts from the Golden Age.* Baltimore: Maryland Historical Society, The Museum and Library of Maryland History, 1993. xiii + 185 pp.; 231 color and bw illus. (See esp. Gregory R. Weidman, "The Furniture of Classical Maryland, 1815–1845," pp. 89–140.)

Weinhagen, Robert F., Jr. *Assume Nothing: A Manual for Buyers of American and English Antique Furniture.* Alexandria, Va.: Highland House Publishers, 1993. viii + 104 pp.; 55 line drawings, bibliography.

Wells, Camille. "Interior Designs: Room Furnishings and Historical Interpretations of Colonial Williamsburg." *The Southern Quarterly* 31, no. 3 (Spring 1993): 89–111. Illus., bibliography.

Whitehead, John. *The French Interior in the Eighteenth Century.* New York: Dutton Studio Books, 1993. 256 pp.; 247 color and 16 bw illus., appendix, bibliography, index.

Wilk, Christopher. "A Frank Lloyd Wright Room in the Victoria and Albert Museum, London." *Antiques* 143, no. 2 (February 1993): 280–83. 4 color and 1 bw illus.

Wilk, Christopher. *Frank Lloyd Wright: The Kaufman Office at the Victoria and Albert Museum.* London: Victoria and Albert Museum, 1993. 80 pp.; illus.

"Windsor Added to Historic Deerfield Collection." *Antiques and the Arts Weekly* (October 8, 1993): 40–K. 1 bw illus. Re Writing-arm Windsor by Ebenezer Tracy (1744–1803) of Lisbon, Conn.

Zelleke, Ghenete, Eva B. Ottillinger, and Nina Stritzler. *Against the Grain: Bentwood Furniture from the Collection of Fern and Manfred Steinfeld.* Chicago: Art Institute of Chicago, 1993. 124 pp.; 200 + bw illus., appendix, bibliography.

Zimmerman, Philip D. "History Repeats Itself: Another Desk Used by Washington to Sign Andre's Death Warrant." *Maine Antique Digest* 21, no. 11 (November 1993): 4D. 2 bw illus.

Zogry, Kenneth Joel. "On the Trail of Vermont Furniture." *Maine Antique Digest* 21, no. 10 (October 1993): 8E–9E. 12 bw illus.

Zogry, Kenneth Joel. "Vermont Furniture in the Bennington Museum, 1765–1840." *Antiques* 144, no. 2 (August 1993): 190–201. 19 color and 1 bw illus.

1994 TITLES

Burks, Jean M. "The Evolution of Design in Shaker Furniture." *Antiques* 145, no. 5 (May 1994): 732–41. 13 color and 3 bw illus.

[Christie's]. *The Collection of Ronald S. Kane: Important American Classical Furniture and Decorative Arts.* Sale 7822. New York: Christie's, January 22, 1994. 108 pp.; numerous color and bw illus.

Connor, Sheila. *New England Natives: A Celebration of People and Trees.* Cambridge, Mass., and London: Harvard University Press, 1994. xi + 274 pp.; 24 color and 194 bw illus., bibliography, index. (A narrative of the relationship between the people and the trees of New England, based on horticultural collections of Harvard's Arnold Arboretum.)

Contemporary Art in Rhode Island. Providence, R.I.: Museum of Art, Rhode Island School of Design, 1994. 111 pp.; numerous color and bw illus. (Includes a few examples of furniture.)

"Costly as Well as Ornamental: 25 Examples on Display." *Antiques and the Arts Weekly* (January 21, 1994): 92–93. 8 bw illus. (Re exhibition at Levy, Inc., of the blockfront form.)

Craven, Wayne. *American Art, History and Culture.* New York: Harry N. Abrams, 1994. 687 pp.; 700 + color and bw illus., glossary, bibliography, index. (A survey primarily of painting and architecture that includes some mention of the decorative arts.)

Cummings, Abbott Lowell, comp. *Bed Hangings: A Treatise on Fabrics and Styles in the Curtaining of Beds, 1650–1850.* 1961. Reprint. Introduction by Jane C. Nylander. Boston: Society for the Preservation of New England Antiquities, 1994. 136 pp.; 58 bw illus., 5 figs. Distributed by University Press of New England.

"The Distinction of Being Different: Joseph P. McHugh and the American Arts and Crafts Movement." *Antiques and the Arts Weekly* (January 14, 1994): 1, 72–74. bw illus.

Ducoff-Barone, Deborah. "Philadelphia Furniture Makers, 1816–1830." *Antiques* 145, no. 5 (May 1994): 742–55. 7 color and 3 bw illus., checklist.

Evans, Nancy Goyne. "A Pair of Distinctive Chairs from Newport, Rhode Island." *Antiques* 145, no. 1 (January 1994): 186–93. 8 color and 9 bw illus.

Foy, Jessica H., and Bradley C. Brooks. *Back in Style: Selections from the McFaddin-Ward House Reserve Collection.* Beaumont, Tex.: McFaddin-Ward House, 1994. 104 pp.; 92 color and bw illus. (Includes some furniture.)

Freund, Thatcher. *Objects of Desire: The Lives of Antiques and Those Who Pursue Them.* New York: Pantheon, 1994. 291 pp.

Freund, Thatcher. "The Tales a Table Could Tell." *The New York Times Magazine* (January 16, 1994): 22–27, 38–40, 48, 54, 60. Color and bw illus. (Excerpts from Freund, *Objects of Desire.*)

Gaynor, James M. "Woodworking Tools in Early America." *Antiques* 145, no. 5 (May 1994): 714–23. 17 color illus.

Gere, Charlotte, and Michael Whiteway. *Nineteenth-Century Design from Pugin to Mackintosh*. New York: Harry N. Abrams, 1994. 312 pp.; 200 color and 150 bw illus., appendix of architects, designers, and manufacturers, bibliography, index.

Gustafson, Eleanor H. "Museum Accessions." *Antiques* 145, no. 5 (May 1994): 656. 1 color and 1 bw illus. (Re slant-front desk by William Carwithen [1704–1770] of Charleston, S.C., acquired by MESDA; and Windsor writing armchair by Ebenezer Tracy [1744–1803], Lisbon, Connecticut, acquired by Historic Deerfield.)

Gustafson, Eleanor H, ed. "Collectors' Notes." *Antiques* 145, no. 1 (January 1994): 68–72, 78. 1 color illus. (Re Charles Bullard [1794–1871]), ornamental painter in Boston.)

Harrison, Stephen. "'C. Lee': Maker of Bedsteads for the Southern Market." *Maine Antique Digest* 22, no. 4 (April 1994): 28A-29A. 5 bw illus. (Re Charles Lee [1817–1889] of Manchester, Massachusetts, active in the mid nineteenth century.)

Heinz, Thomas A. *Frank Lloyd Wright: Interiors and Furniture*. London: Academy Editions; Berlin: Ernst & Sohn, 1994. 264 pp.; 396 color and bw illus., bibliography index. Distributed by St. Martin's Press, New York.

Hewett, David. "Home Reveals Fretwork Furniture Bonanza." *Maine Antique Digest* 22, no. 5 (May 1994): 8B–9B. 13 bw illus. (Re elaborate fretwork-sawn furniture of the 1880s and 1890s made by Charles E. Bacheller [1848–1915] of Lynn, Massachusetts, and sold at auction.)

"Highchest and Dressing Table Acquired." *Decorative Arts Guild of North Texas* (Newsletter) 4, no. 2 (Winter 1994): 4–5. 2 bw illus. (Re Boston case furniture in the William and Mary style, with a history in the Sever family, acquired by Dallas Museum of Art.)

"Historic Deerfield Adds Eliakim Smith High Chest." *Antiques and the Arts Weekly* (April 15, 1994); 22. 1 bw illus. (Re cherry high chest, ca. 1760-1775, from Hadley, Massachusetts.)

Koster, John, with contributions by Sheridan Germann and John T. Kirk. *Keyboard Musical Instruments in the Museum of Fine Arts, Boston*. Boston: Museum of Fine Arts, 1994. xl + 368 pp.; 16 color and 242 bw illus., 79 line drawings, appendixes, bibliography, index. Distributed by Northeastern University Press, Boston. (International in scope, but includes important American examples.)

Kugelman, Alice, Thomas Kugelman, and Robert Lionetti. "The Hartford Case Furniture Survey, Part II: The Chapin School of East Windsor, Connecticut." *Maine Antique Digest* 22, no. 1 (January 1994): 12D–14D. 14 bw illus.

Levison, Deanne. "The Symbolism of Floral Inlay." *Antiques* 145, no. 5 (May 1994): 704–13. 14 color illus.

McNerney, Kathryn. *American Oak Furniture, Book II*. Paducah, Ky.: Collector Books, 1994. 222 pp.; numerous bw illus., glossary, index.

McNerney, Kathryn. *Victorian Furniture, Book II*. Paducah, Ky.: Collector Books, 1994. 271 pp.; numerous bw illus., glossary, index.

Murdoch, Tessa. "John Channon and English Brass-Inlaid Furniture, 1730–1760." *Antiques* 145, no. 2 (February 1994): 286–95. 14 color and 3 bw illus.

Pile, John. *The Dictionary of 20th-Century Design*. 1990. Reprint. New York: Da Capo Press, 1994. viii + 312 pp.; numerous bw illus., index.

Podmaniczky, Michael, and Philip D. Zimmerman. "Two Massachusetts Bombé Desk-and-Bookcases." *Antiques* 145, no. 5 (May 1994): 724–31. 14 color and 3 bw illus.

Rauschenberg, Brad. "Does MESDA Now Own the Earliest Known Signed Example of Southern Furniture? We Think We Do!" *The Luminary* (Newsletter of the Museum of Early Southern Decorative Arts) 15, no. 1 (Spring 1994): 1, 5. 4 bw illus. (Re walnut and cypress desk, ca. 1732-1740, stamped by William Carwithen [d. 1770] of Charleston; also refers to a corner chair, Charleston, ca. 1740–1750, and a Charleston press, ca. 1790–1800, both recently acquired by MESDA; p. 4 of same issue illustrates a tea or gaming table, ca. 1746–1775, from the Virginia Tidewater area, also added to the collection recently.)

Stillinger, Elizabeth. "The Folk Art Collection of Nina Fletcher and Bertram Kimball Little: The Documented Context." *Maine Antique Digest* 22, no. 1 (January 1994): 1E–3E. 7 bw illus.

Swedberg, Robert W., and Harriett Swedberg. *Collector's Encyclopedia of American Furniture*. Vol. 3, *Country Furniture of the Eighteenth and Nineteenth Centuries*. Paducah, Ky.: Collector Books, 1994. 125 pp.; numerous color illus., price guide.

"Virginia MFA Adds to its Collection." *Antiques and the Arts Weekly* (January 14, 1994): 66. 2 bw illus. (Re Pottier & Stymus slipper chair, ca. 1875, acquired by Virginia Museum of Fine Arts, and silverplated tilt-top tea table, Tiffany & Co., 1893, acquired by the Munson-Williams-Proctor Institute, Utica, New York.)

Volk, Joyce Geary. "The Knotty Problem of the Pine Desks: Twins?" *Maine Antique Digest* 22, no. 2 (February 1994): 12B–14B. 8 bw illus.

Wahlberg, Holly. *Everyday Elegance: 1950s Plastic Design*. Atglen, Pa.: Schiffer Publishing Co., 1994. 112 pp.; numerous color illus., bibliography, index. (Includes a few examples of furniture.)

Wood, Lucy. *The Lady Lever Art Gallery Catalogue of Commodes*. London: HMSO, 1994. xii + 367 pp.; numerous color and bw illus., appendix, glossary, index of botanical names of timbers, concordances, bibliography, index. (English furniture.)

Index

Adam, James, 197–98
Adam, Robert, 29, 197–98
Adams, Abigail, 85, 98
Adams, John, 74, 78, 95
Adams, Samuel, 74, 81
Adamson, Jeremy, 247
Aesthetic style, and Marcotte firm, 53, 66–68
Affleck, Thomas, 185, 188
Aging, surface, 13
Alexandria Theater, 229, 233(n37)
Allard et Fils, Jules, 69
Alling, David, 20
Alterations: and clocks, 244; definition of, 3; and eighteenth-century chairs, 34–35; to Windsor furniture, 15–18, (& figs.)
Ambler, Jaquelin, 225, 233(n29)
American Tables and Looking Glasses (Barquist), 238–40
Amory, John, 74, 101(nn 24, 27)
Amory, Jonathan, 74, 79, 101(n27)
Amory, Martha Babcock (née Greene), 96
Amory, Thomas, Jr., 73, 81(& fig.), 83, 101(n27), 102(n30)
Amory, Thomas, Sr., 101(n27)
Amory, Thomas Coffin, 83
Amory, William, 83
Andrews, George, 227–28
Anglo-Dutch hybrids, 112–13, 131, 132(n9)
Appliques. *See* Carving
Architects, 29, 45, 49–50, 55; relationship with furniture makers, 207
Architectural furniture, 29–30, 38, 40, 41, 44, 50, 65, 66, 211–12
Architectural Heritage of the Piscataqua, The (Howells), 234
Architecture: design books, 173, 181–83, 197 (see also Design books); Portsmouth, 234; temple-form houses, 211–12, 231(n11)
Arms, restoring, 5, 6(fig.), 14, 14(fig.)
Arnsmear, 55, 57, 61
Arnold Arboretum, 245
Atkins, Gibbs, 79
Atlas Chinensis (Nieuhof), 139
Attributions, maker: and construction/style details, 126, 128 (& figs.), 130(& fig.), 236–37; factors in making, 239; and oval tables, 113, 118–19, 128–30; and regional characteristics, 116–17, 128–30, 135(n32), 175. *See also* Inscriptions

Badlam, Stephen, 83–85
Bagatelle, The, 91
Bailey, Chris H., 241
Bailey, John, 242
Bailey, Samuel, 47(n22)
Bair, John M., 18
Baldwin, Jedidiah and Jabez, 242
Ballin, Claude, 139
Baltimore, 198, 200
Baltimore Museum of Art, 247
Baretti, P., 174, 184
Barger, Philip, 137
Barnes, Elizur, 15
Baroque style: design books on, 174–75, 180, 181–84; in eighteenth century, 30, 75, 77; Huguenot painter-stainers and, 137, 140; and oval tables with falling leaves, 108, 110, 115–31, 133(nn 17, 18), 134(n24)
Barquist, David L., 108, 238–40
Barrell, Joseph, 73, 74, 75, 79, 87–91, 102(n40)
Barry, Joseph, 200, 200(fig. 23)
Battison, Edwin A., 241
Bedloe, Catherine, 127, 128
Beekman, Thomas, 130. *See also* Elting-Beekman shop
Bell, Robert, 174, 185, 188
Berain, Jean, 139–40
Berger, Jean, 137–41, 160(n9); pattern book by, 142–59, 160(n1)
Berger, M. le Sr., 137
Berry, Richard, 129
Birch wood, 231(n18)
Bishop, Robert, 241
Boardman, Langley, 235, 236
Bombé furniture: Cogswell's, 81–96, 104–105; eighteenth-century Bostonian, 73, 75, 77, 81, 87(fig.), 99(n2), 101(n21)
Bookcases, library: eighteenth-century Philadelphia, 222, 224(fig. 28); Marshall house, 225(fig.), 226(fig. 32). *See also* Desk-and-bookcases
Book of Architecture, A (Gibbs), 37(fig 17), 46(n7), 77
Book of Tables. Candle Stands, Pedestals, Tablets, Table Knees, &c. (Lock), 180, 192
Booksellers, 174. *See also* Design books
Books of Ornament (De La Cour), 174
Boston: design books and style in, 175; eighteenth-century, 73, 74(fig. 1), 78–79, 98, 136(fig.); Huguenot com-

257 INDEX

munity, 160(n3); leather chair, 118(fig. 21), 124(fig.), 125; oval tables with falling leaves, 108
Boston Museum of Fine Arts, 126
Bow repairs, 2 (fig. 1), 4
Bowdoin, James, 74
Boylston, Thomas, 74
Boyse, Antipas, 108
Braces, 4
Bradford, Seth, 55
Brands. *See* Inscriptions
Brass Founders Catalog of Accessories for Cabinetmakers and Upholsterers, 95(fig. 35)
Brattle Square Church, Boston, 73–77, 74(fig. 2), 75(fig.), 76(figs.), 77(fig. 7)
Brent, James, 33
Brested, Andrew, 129
Bright, George, 79
Brinley, Col. Francis, 94
Brinley, Edward, 87, 94, 103(n42)
British Architect (Swan), 46(n7), 187
Broeck, Abraham Ten, 110(fig. 3)
Brown, Gawen, 242
Brown, Joseph, Jr., 127
Buckland, James, 29
Buckland, William, 28(fig.), 29, 30–45, 47(nn 15, 22), 48(n23); library of, 46(n7), 181, 183, 185, 188, 191
Buckley, Charles, 234
Bucktrout, Benjamin, 185, 204(n14)
Builder's Companion and Workman's General Assistant, The (Paine), 31
Bulfinch, Charles, 74, 91
Bulfinch, Thomas, 74
Burbeck (Burbank), William, 76–77, 78, 92, 100(nn 10, 12)
Burling, Edward, 129, 134(n29)
Burling, Thomas, 185

Cabell, Col. Nicholas, 221
Cabinet and Chair-Maker's Real Friend and Companion (Manwaring), 174, 175, 180, 193–94, 194(fig. 16)
Cabinetmaker & Upholsterer's Drawing Book (Sheraton), 175, 180, 199–200, 200(fig. 22), 239
Cabinet-Maker and Upholsterer's Guide (Hepplewhite), 175, 180, 198(& fig. 20)
Cabinet-Makers' London Book of Prices, 185, 204(n14): *and Designs of Cabinet-Work* (London Society of Cabinet Makers), 180, 198–99

Cabinets: attributed to Marcotte firm, 57–58, 60(fig. 13), 63, 65(fig. 25)
Callis, John Ariss, 47(n22)
Candlestands, 162(fig.), 169–70, 195, 196(figs.)
Canopies, 35–36, 36(fig. 15), 211(& figs.)
Carter, Robert Wormley, 45
Carving: attributed to Hodgson, 208–11, 208(fig. 3), 209(figs.), 210(figs.), 211(figs.), 212–14, 212(figs. 11, 12), 213(figs.), 216(figs.), 217(figs.), 221(& fig.), 222–27, 226(figs.), 227(figs.); on Buckland and Sears furniture, 34, 35(fig. 13), 38, 39(fig. 22), 40–41, 40(figs.), 42(fig. 27), 43–44, 43(figs.), 44(fig. 32); on Cogswell furniture, 83–85, 85(figs. 15, 16), 86, 89–91, 90(figs.), 92–94, 92(figs.), 96, 98(fig. 42); and design books, 177, 179(figs.), 184, 189, 191–93; Gunston Hall (Buckland and Sears), 31(fig. 6), 32–34, 32(fig. 7), 33(fig.), 34(fig. 10); Mt. Airy (Buckland and Sears), 37(fig. 18), 37–38; on pulpit of Brattle Square Church, 75, 76–77, 76(figs.). *See also* Ornamentation
Casement, William, 198
Casting patterns, 193(& fig. 130)
Catalogue of Manuscripts and Relics in Washington's Head-Quarters, 128
Caucus system, 78, 98
Caulton, William, 4
Centennial Exposition at Philadelphia, 63
Chair-maker's Guide, The (Manwaring), 180, 194–95
Chair(s), attributed to Marcotte firm, 53(fig.), 54, 55–57, 56(fig.), 57(fig. 7), 58(fig.), 59(figs.), 60(fig. 11), 61, 62(figs. 18, 20, 21), 66–67, 66(fig. 30), 67(fig.), 68(fig. 32), 71(n21), 72(n27); Boston leather, 118(fig. 21), 124(fig.), 125; by Buckland and Sears, 34–35, 35(figs.), 47(n12); in design books, 36(fig. 14), 44(fig. 34), 194(figs.), 198(figs.), 200(figs. 21, 22); English cane armchair, 120(& fig.); Masonic Master's, 162(fig.), 163–69, 164(figs. 3, 4), 167(fig. 11), 168(fig.), 169(fig.), 170(& n3), 171(n17), 185, 204(n14); New York leather, 120–21, 133(n18); Rhode Island braced bow-back, 246(n1); with twisted legs, 122–23; Windsor alterations, 15–18, 15(fig.),

16(figs.); Windsor enhancements, 26(& fig.); Windsor reconstructions, 18–20, 19(fig.); Windsor repairs, 2(figs.), 4–5(& figs.), 15; Windsor reproductions, 20–25, 21(figs.), 22(fig.), 23(figs.), 24(fig.), 25(fig.); Windsor restorations, 5–11, 6(fig.), 7(fig.), 9(fig.), 10(fig.), 11(fig.), 12(fig. 12), 13–14(& figs.), 15
Chambers, Sir William, 174
Chardon, Peter, 74
Charleston, S.C., design book influence in, 184, 185, 189, 190
Chase-Lloyd house, 45, 47(n17)
Chastellux, Marquis de, 81
Chateau-Sur-Mer, 54(fig.), 55, 59, 63 (fig. 22)
Cheney, Robert C., 240–44
Cheney, Silas, 15
Cherry: in New York oval tables, 116
Chesapeake Bay region, design book influence in, 185
Chest-on-chests, attributed to Cogswell, 83–85, 84(fig.), 85(figs.), 102(nn 31, 32)
Chests: attributed to Cogswell, 87, 89(figs. 21, 22), 94–96, 94(fig. 33), 95(fig. 36), 96(figs.), 97(figs.), 103(n48); and design books, 175–79, 176(fig.), 178(fig. 5), 179(fig. 6)
Chimneypieces, 179(fig. 7), 193(fig. 14); carved by Hodgson, 212(& figs. 11, 12), 213(figs.), 214, 225–27, 226(fig. 33), 227(figs.)
China case, Chippendale, 36(fig. 16)
Chinese elements. *See* Oriental elements
Chinnery, Victor, 107, 119
Chippendale, Thomas, 185–89, 195; and rococo style, 174. *See also Gentleman and Cabinet-Maker's Director, The*
Chipstone Foundation, ix
Christiana, Pa., 5
City and Country Builder's and Workman's Treasury of Designs (Langley and Langley), 33, 75, 77(& fig. 6), 173, 174, 180, 181–83
Clarke, Elizabeth Copley, 96
Clarke, Joseph, 229
Clark-Frankland house, 140
Classical style: Marcotte firm and French, 58. *See also* Palladian classicism
Cleaning systems, 165, 166–68, 169–70, 171(nn 7, 14)
Clérriseau, Charles-Louis, 207

Clock Making in New England, 1725–1825: An Interpretation of the Old Sturbridge Village Collection (Zea and Cheney), 240–44
Clothespresses, 221–22, 222(figs.), 232(n24)
Cocaille forms, 30
Cocke, Stephen, 20
Codman, Ogden, Sr., 59, 66–67
Cogswell, Abiel (Abiall) (née Page), 79, 100(n12)
Cogswell, Abigail (née Gooding), 77, 100(nn 11, 12)
Cogswell, Francis, 77–78
Cogswell, John, 73, 77–81, 100(n11), 101(n19); furniture by, 81–96, 104–105
Cogswell, Mary (née Caznau *or* Cazneau), 100(n12)
Cogswell, Sarah (née Tuckerman), 100(n12)
Cogswell, William, 79
Colbert, Jean Baptiste, 137
Cole, Solomon, 8
Colles, James, 50–51, 54
Colonial Furniture in America (Lockwood), 126
Colonial Furniture of New England, The (Lyon), 234
Colt, Samuel, 55, 57, 61
Congressional Cemetery, 229, 233(n35)
Connor, Sheila, 245–46
Conservation: of Masonic suite, 163–70, 171(n9)
Construction: of Buckland and Sears furniture, 35, 38–40, 39(figs. 20, 21), 41–42, 42(figs. 28, 29), 44, 47(n12); of Cogswell furniture, 81–83, 83(fig. 11), 86, 87, 89(figs.); dating and identifying makers through, 126, 128(& figs.), 130(& fig.), 236–37; and identifying furniture repairs, 5, 14, 15–18, 20–21, 21(fig. 25), 23–25, 23(fig. 28), 25(fig.), 26; and Ingle furniture, 219, 221, 222, 231(n18), 232(n24); and New York oval tables, 114, 119
Cooper, John, 138, 139(& fig.)
Cooper, William, 74
Copland, Henry, 184, 189, 192–93
Copley, John Singleton, 74, 103(n46)
Cotelle, Jean, 139, 141(fig. 6)
Courtenay, Hercules, 175, 192
Cox and Berry (booksellers), 174, 184, 185, 187–88, 189, 190, 193–94
Crafts, Thomas, 78

Crafts, William, 75–76, 77, 78, 79, 100(n10)
Creese, Thomas, Jr., 139
Crests, 13(figs.); repairs/restorations to Windsor, 5(& fig.), 13; Windsor peaked, 23
Cross-section analysis, 164–66, 165(figs.), 166(figs.), 167(fig. 10), 171(n4)
Crumpley, James, 212, 231(n12)
Crunden, John, 174, 189–90
Crystal Palace Exhibitions, 61
Cummens, William, 243
Currier, True, 8
Currier Gallery, 234
Curtis, George William, 49
Curtis, Nancy, 236

Dachet House, 103(n42)
Damage: and eighteenth-century chairs, 34–35; and restored Windsor furniture, 16–17. *See also* Repairs; Restorations
Darly, Matthew, 33, 174, 183
Dating, of New York oval tables, 126–30, 135(n30)
Davis, Joseph, 235
Davis, Robert, 139
Dawes, Thomas, 77, 78, 79, 95, 99(n6), 100(n10), 102(n32); and Brattle Square Church, 73, 74; library of, 75, 181, 183, 194
de Forest, Emily (née Johnston), 58
de Launay, Nicholas, 239
Deacon, Mr., 50
Dehon, Bishop Theodore, 160(n1)
Dehon, Frances Dickson, 160(n3)
Dehon, Theodore, 160(n3)
Delaplaine, Joshua, 127, 129, 134(n29)
Delhonde, Laurence, 138
Derby, Elias Hasket, 79, 83–85, 96, 198
Design books: Berger's, 139–40, 141, 142–59, 160(n1); Buckland's, 46(n7); Buckland reliance on, 33, 44; catalogue of, 181–200; checklist of, 180; for chinoiserie designs, 139, 140(figs.), 141(figs.); influence of English, 173–79; temple-form houses, 231(n11); use by eighteenth-century Bostonian artisans, 75, 77, 92, 100(n10). *See also* Style/design; *specific design books*
Desks-and-bookcases: attributed to Cogswell, 85–86, 87–94, 88(fig.), 89(fig. 23), 90(figs.), 91(fig.), 92(figs.), 102(n35); attributed to

Daniel Trotter, 219(& fig.); attributed to Ingle and Hodgson school, 214–19, 215(fig.), 216(figs.), 217(figs.), 218(fig.), 220(fig.), 221(& fig.), 222–25, 223(fig.), 224(figs. 29, 30), 231(n18); and design books, 177(& fig.), 178(fig. 4), 186(fig.)
Desks: attributed to Cogswell, 81–83, 82(figs.), 83(fig. 11), 86–87, 86(fig. 17); attributed to Marcotte firm, 61, 62(fig. 19). *See also* Desks-and-bookcases
Dexter, Samuel, 99(n2)
Dickinson, Edmund, 185, 188, 204(n14)
Dickson, David, 160(n3)
Dickson, Margaret (née Berger), 160(n3)
Distin, William, 241
Diviat, Joseph, 129
Dobie, Samuel, 209
Dobson, Thomas, 187
Dockum, Samuel M., 235
Doggett, John, 243
Dominy, Nathaniel, V, 20
Douglas, Samuel, 8
Draw-bar tables, 109–16, 129–30, 132(n10), 133(nn 20, 25); illustrations of, 110(fig. 4), 111(figs.), 112(figs.), 113(figs.), 114(fig. 14)
Ducerceau, Paul Androuet, 139
Dun, R. G., appraisals (Dun and Bradstreet), 52
du Pont, Henry Francis, 12
Dupuis (Dupee), Jean, 160(n3)
Dutch: draw tables, 106(fig.), 108–109; and oval tables with falling leaves, 112–13, 123–24, 131

Eastlake style, 61, 67
Edwards, George, 33
Edwards, John, 244
Ehrenpreis, Diane Carlberg, 236
Elmendorf family table, 130, 132(n10)
Elting, Jan, 130. *See also* Elting-Beekman shop
Elting-Beekman shop, 110(fig. 4), 111(figs. 5, 6), 112(fig. 10), 114(fig. 14), 122(fig.), 130
England: cane armchair from, 120(& fig.), 125; design books from, 173–79 (*see also* Design books); as design source for New York oval tables, 119–20, 123, 131; evolution of dining tables in, 107–108
Enhancements: definition of, 3; to Windsor furniture, 26(& fig.)

Erving, John, 74
Exposition Universelle (Paris), 63

Family ownership histories: and dating furniture, 127–28; and regional attributions, 237
Fayerweather, John, 74
Ferguson, John, 37
Fitch, Jonas, 242
Fitzgerald, Gen. Louis, 128
Folwell, John, 99(n2), 187
Fontaine, Pierre, 61
Forman, Benno, 120, 123, 126, 133(n18), 135(n30)
Fourdinois, Alexandre Georges, 61
Fredin, Augustus, 52
Freemasons: furniture suite, 163–70; Richmond lodge, 211(& figs.), 230(n10); and Stephenson, 229; symbols of, 168–69, 170, 171(n13)
French elements: in Marcotte designs, 54, 55–63; and New York oval tables, 123–24; nineteenth-century popularity of, 49; and post-Revolutionary America, 81, 91
French Huguenots, 123–24, 137, 139–40, 141, 160(n3)
Frost, James, 4
Furniture of the Olden Time (Morse), 222
Furniture Treasury (Nutting), 44, 45(fig.), 121

Gaines, John, III, 235
Galerie des Glaces, 239
Gardner, William Amory, 83
Garrett, Elisabeth Donaghy, 239, 240
Garvin, James L., 234, 235
Gate-leg tables, 108, 109, 116–20, 133(nn 13, 20), 134(n25); illustrations of, 109(fig.), 110(fig. 3), 114(fig. 15), 115(figs.), 116(fig.), 117(fig.), 118(figs.), 119(figs.), 127(fig.)
Gautier, James and Daniel, 129
Gentleman and Cabinet-Maker's Assistant, The (Folwell), 187
Gentleman and Cabinet-Maker's Director, The (Chippendale): American distribution and influence of, 174, 175, 180, 185–89, 190, 204(nn 14, 16); architectural designs in, 173; desk-and-bookcase in, 177(fig.), 178(fig. 4); French chair design, 44(& fig. 34); Oriental elements, 33, 34, 35, 36(& figs. 14, 16); rococo style in, 30; table designs, 41, 42(& fig. 26)
Gentleman or Builder's Companion, The (Jones), 30(fig. 2), 174
Gibbs, James, 33(fig. 17), 46(n7), 77
Gillingham, James, 185
Gleaves, Thomas and Jonathan, 129
Goddard, John, 204(n14)
Goddard, Nichols, 243
Goddard, Thomas, 185, 188, 204(n14)
Goodacre, William, 206(fig.)
Gooding, Timothy, Jr., 100(n11)
Gooding family, 77
Gothic elements, 30, 31, 34, 35, 43–44
Gould, Nathaniel, 185, 188
Grange, The, 59, 61
Greene, Gardiner, 73, 95–96, 103(n46)
Greenleaf, William, 99(n2)
Grigg, Thomas, 129
Gunston Hall, 30–33, 30(fig. 3), 31(figs.), 32(figs.), 33(fig.), 34(figs.), 35–36, 36(fig. 15), 41

Hagen, Ernest, 49
Halfpenny, William, 33, 77, 174
Hall, Thomas, 47(n22)
Hancock, John, 74, 76–77, 95, 100(n10)
Hardware: catalogue patterns for, 95(fig. 35); dating furniture through, 128; in design books, 173–74; drawer pulls, 83(& fig. 12), 94(& fig. 34), 95(fig. 37), 96, 101(n27), 102(n30), 103(n47); hinges, 128(& fig. 32)
Harrison, Peter, 174, 181, 189
Harristy, John, 138
Harrold, Robert, 190(& fig. 9), 194, 235
Hart, John, 208, 212
Harvard Hall, 100(n10)
Hayward, Helena, 191
Hazard, Duncan A., 204(n14)
Hazard, Ebenezer, 195
Henderson, Mrs., 50
Hepplewhite, George, 175, 198
Herter Brothers, 49, 52, 63, 65, 69, 71(n23)
Herzog, Adrian, 52, 53, 69
Hinges, 128(& fig. 32)
Hoadley, Silas, 244
Hoban, James, 229, 233(n36)
Hodgson, Francis, 230(n1)
Hodgson, Joseph T., 228, 230(n1)
Hodgson, William, 207, 208–11, 214, 221, 222–28, 229, 230(nn 1, 5, 7), 231(n13)
Houdon, Jean Antoine, 208(fig. 2)
Houshold Furniture in Genteel Taste (Society of Upholsterers), 93(figs.), 174, 180, 195–97, 196(fig. 18)
Houston, J. H. M., 163
Howarding, Thomas, 127
Howells, John Mead, 234
Hunt, Edward, 129
Hunt, Richard Morris, 69
Hunter, James, 222

Ince, William, 174, 190–91, 195
Ingle, Henry, 207, 219–22, 228–29, 230(n1), 232(nn 22, 26), 233(n35)
Ingle, Joseph, 228, 232(n22), 233(n34)
Ingle, Mary (née Pechin), 228
Inscriptions, 26(& fig.); and clocks, 241; on Cogswell furniture, 83, 85(fig. 14), 86(fig. 18), 89(fig. 23), 94; on Ingle and Hodgson desks-and-bookcases, 214, 216; on Masonic suite, 163; and Portsmouth furniture, 234
Interior decorators, 49, 51
Ives, George F., 11–12
Ives Tavern and Colonial Museum, 12

Japanning, 139–41, 183
Jarrard, John, 138
Jaudon, Mrs. Samuel, 50, 51
Jefferson, Thomas, 174, 185, 204(n14), 207, 219–21, 227–28, 232(n22)
Jobe, Brock, 234–38
Johnson, Sir William, 127; table of, 114(fig.), 116, 117, 125, 126–27, 128, 129
Johnson, Thomas, 46(n7), 174, 179, 191–92, 195
Johnston, John Taylor, 54, 55, 57–58
Johnston, Thomas, 139
Johnston, Thomas, Jr., 139
Joinery: Brattle Square Church pulpit, 75; dating and identifying makers through, 119, 126, 127, 128, 130; eighteenth-century, 39–40, 42; illustrated details of, 16(fig. 19), 23(fig. 28); and repairs to Windsors, 5(& fig.). *See also* Construction
Jones, William, 29, 30(fig. 2)
Joy, Benjamin, 91, 102(n40)
Joyner and Cabinet-maker's Darling; or, Pocket Director, The (Crunden), 174, 180, 189–90

260 INDEX

Kammen, Michael, 108
Kane, Delancy, 50
Kasten, 114, 130, 131
Kaye, Myrna, 234, 236
Kent, William, 29
Keteltas, Eugene, 58–59
Keys, 4, 21
Kimball, Fiske, 173
Kinder, John, 159
King, John, 181
Kingston, Joseph, 129
Kingston area. *See* Ulster County
Kitchen, J. Denny, 171(n17)
Knowlton, Abraham, 99(n2)

Labrouste, Henri, 49
Landon, George, 15
Langley, Batty and Thomas, 173, 181–83; *City &. Country Builder's and Workman's Treasury of Designs*, 33, 75, 77(& fig. 6), 173, 174, 180, 181–83
Lansmeer, 58–59
Le Chevalier, John, 129
Le Magasin de Meubles, 67
Le Mercier, Rev. Andrew, 160(n3)
Latrobe, Benjamin Henry, 229
Lead, red, 166
Legs: baroque turnings on table, 121–26, 121(figs.), 122(fig.), 123(fig.), 133(nn 17, 18, 20), 134(n24), 135(n32); restoring Windsor, 8–13, 9(fig.), 10(fig.), 11(fig.), 14; twisted, 111, 113(figs.), 122–24, 132(n10)
Lenox, Charlotte, 109
Le Pautre, Jean, 139
Leprince Ringuet, Edmond, 53, 69, 71(n12)
Library Company of Baltimore, 197, 198
Library Company of Philadelphia, 185, 187, 197–98, 204(n16)
Lienau, Detlef, 50, 51, 52, 63, 70(n7)
List of Architectural Books Available in America before the Revolution (Park), 173
Livingston, Margaret (née Howarding), 127, 128
Livingston, Philip, 193
Livingston, Robert, Jr., 128
Livres des Ornemens pour Plafonds (Cotelle), 141(fig. 6)
Lloyd, Edward, IV, 45, 47(n22)
Lock, Matthias, 174, 192–93
Lockwood, Luke Vincent, 116, 126, 173

Lockwood (LeGrand) mansion, 63, 63(fig. 23), 64(fig.), 71(n23)
London Art of Building (Salmon), 46(n7), 77
London Society of Cabinet Makers, 198–99
Looking glasses, Yale University collection, 107–19
Low, Abraham, 8
Luker, John, 163
Lyman, Theodore, 74
Lyon, Irving W., 173, 234

McBrien, Johanna, 235
McCormick, James, 232(n24)
McCormick (Cyrus Hall) house, 63–65, 65(fig. 26), 66(fig. 28), 67, 68(figs. 33, 34), 72(n25)
McHugh, Joseph P., 247
McKim, Mead, & White, 69
McKim, William, 228
McLure, John, 191, 192, 195, 197
Mahogany: and New York oval tables, 116, 128; use in Windsor furniture, 20
Maine, 125
Makers. *See* Attributions, maker
Manwaring, Robert, 174, 175, 193–95
Maple: in New York oval tables, 116; use in Windsor furniture, 20
Marcotte, Charles, 52
Marcotte, L. & Co., 51(fig.), 52–53, 60(fig. 12), 69–70, 71(n10); and Rococo revival style, 54. *See also* Ringuet-Leprince, Marcotte and Co.
Marcotte, Leon Alexandre, 49–70, 70(nn 5, 7), 71(n9)
Marcotte, Louise-Marie (née de Rudder), 52
Marlboro Furnace, 193(& fig. 13)
Marot, Daniel, 137, 139, 140, 141(fig. 5)
Marquand, Henry, 55
Marshall, Mary Willis "Polly" (née Ambler), 225
Marshall (John) house, 212, 225–27, 225(fig.), 226(figs.), 227(figs.)
Maryland Historical Society, 247
Mason, George, 30, 36–37
Mason, Thomas, 30
Massachusetts, 125. *See also* Boston
Mathews (Lockwood) Mansion, 51, 57
Mathias Hammond house, 45
Mattocks, Samuel, Jr., 138
Mayhew, John, 174, 190–91, 195

Medallions, 222
Medieval Europe, 107
Mercantile Agency. *See* Dun, R. G., appraisals
Metallic powders, 166, 170
Metropolitan Museum of Art, 57
Mexican elements, 66–67, 67(fig.)
Miller, Fanny, 214
"Modern" style, 30
Montgomery, Charles, *ix*
Monticello, 228
Moore, N. Hudson, 241
Moorish style, 69
Morgan, Mathew, 50
Morris, Robert, 46(n7), 231(n11)
Morton, Perez and Sarah, 81
Moyers, Thomas J., 4
Mt. Airy, 37–44, 37(figs.)
Muir, James, 188
Museum of Our National Heritage, 163

Nelson, Temple, 138
Neoclassicism, 98; design books on, 175, 180, 197–200; and temple-form houses, 212
New Bern, N.C., 185
New Book of Chinese Designs, A (Edwards and Darly), 33
New Book of Ornaments, A (Copland), 180, 184, 189
New Book of Ornaments, A (Johnson), 179(& fig. 7), 180, 192
New Book of Ornaments, A (Lock and Copland), 180, 192–93, 193(fig. 14)
New Book of Ornaments for Looking Glass Frames, Chimney Pieces &c. &c. in the Chinese Taste (Lock), 180, 192
New Book of Ornaments on 16 Leaves for the Year 1762/1766 (Baretti), 174, 180, 184
New Design's for Chinese Temple's, Triumphal Arches, Garden Seats, Palings &c. (Halfpenny), 33
New England: design book influence in, 185, 194, 198, 199; oval tables, 116–17, 119; and twisted legs, 123. *See also* Boston; Portsmouth, N.H.
New England Furniture: The Colonial Era (Jobe and Kaye), 235, 242
New England Natives: A Celebration of People and Trees (Connor), 245–46
New Hampshire Historical Society, 234
New Netherland, 108–109. *See also* Dutch
New North Church, 100(n12)

New York: design book influence in, 185, 193, 195, 198, 200; mid-nineteenth-century styles and fashions, 49; oval tables with falling leaves from, 108–31; population figures for, 131(n5)
Newell, Timothy, 78
Nieuhof, Johan, 139
Noel, Garret, 174, 195, 197
Noel and Hazard (booksellers), 189, 195, 197
Nutting, Wallace, 11–12, 18, 22(fig.), 23(& figs.), 116, 241; *Furniture Treasury*, 44, 45(fig.), 121
Nylander, Richard C., 236

Old Sturbridge Village collection, 241–44
Oldham, James, 228
Oliver, Daniel, 74
One Hundred and Fifty New Designs (Johnson), 46(n7), 180, 191(& fig. 12)
Oriental elements: and design books, 174; in Marcotte firm designs, 67, 68(& fig. 32); popularity in eighteenth century, 30, 33, 34, 35
Ornamentation: canopies, 35–36, 36(fig. 15); decoupage decoration on Windsors, 5; in design books, 173, 183; influence of classicism, 29–30; and New York tables with falling leaves, 120–26, 121(figs.), 122(fig.), 123(fig.); painted decoration, 137, 139–41, 140(figs.), 141(figs.), 142–59. See also Carving
Oswald, Eleazer, 187, 188
Otis, Samuel, 74

Page, Capt. Thomas, 79
Page, Edward, 79
Page, Sarah (née Cogswell), 79
Paine, William, 31
Paint chronology, 8, 9, 12, 14, 18, 20
Painter-stainers, 137, 160(n9)
Palladian classicism: and Cogswell furniture, 92; eighteenth-century popularity of, 29–30, 77; example of, 30(fig. 2); and Gunston Hall, 31–33
Pallado, Andreas, 30
Parish, Truro, 37
Park, Helen, 173
Parker, Gardner, 243
Parker, George, 139, 140(figs.), 174–75, 183

Parsons, Charles, 241
Partridge, Nehemiah, 139
Patterson (Robert W.) house, 69
Pechin, Christopher and Christina, 228
Pediments: Cogswell chest-on-chest, 83, 85(fig. 15); in design books, 175–77, 177(fig.), 178(fig. 5). See also Carving
Peirce-Nichols house, 199
Pelham, Peter, 160(n9)
Pennsylvania, 123. See also Philadelphia
Percier, Charles, 61
Philadelphia: cabinetmaking practices in eighteenth-century, 219; design books and style in, 175, 185–87, 190, 191, 192, 193, 194, 198, 200; Windsors, 21
Phillipse family table, 106(fig.), 112, 131(n6), 135(n30)
Pickman, Clark Gayton, 194
Pickman, Sarah (née Orne), 194
Pigments, 166(& figs.), 170
Pillars, Freemason, 162(fig.), 169–70
Platt, George, 71(n23)
Pleasant Hill, 91, 102(n40)
Pointer, Samuel, 228
Polarized light microscopy (PLM), 166(& fig. 9)
Pollard, John, 175
Portsmouth, N.H., 190, 234–38
Portsmouth Furniture: Masterworks from the New Hampshire Seacoast (Jobe), 234–38
Pottier and Stymus, 49, 52, 63
Powell, Felix, 138
Price, William, 139
Prince, Samuel, 195
Pritchard, William, 185–87, 188
Proxemics, 240
Prussian blue, 166
Pulpit, 77(figs.), 99(nn 2, 8); Brattle Square Church, 73, 74, 75–76(& figs.), 77, 92

Quakers, 129
Quincy, Edmund, 78
Quincy, Josiah, 74, 99(n2)

Randall, John, 45, 47(n22)
Randle, William, 139
Randolph, Benjamin, 172(fig.), 175, 185, 191, 195, 204(n16)
Randolph, Edmund, 208
Rea, Daniel, 139

Reconstructions: definition of, 3; of Windsor furniture, 18–20, 19(fig.), 20(fig.)
Red gum, 117, 129
Redmond, Elizabeth, 236
Reeve, Tapping, 15
Regions: defining, 237; and oval table attributions, 116–17, 128–30, 135(n32); and studies of Portsmouth furniture, 236–38; and styles, 175
Renaissance: dining tables of, 107
Repairs: definition of, 3; and eighteenth-century chairs, 34–35; to Masonic suite, 169; to Windsor furniture, 2(figs.), 4–5,(& figs.), 15
Reproductions: and clocks, 244; definition of, 3; of Windsor furniture, 20–25, 21(figs.), 22(fig.), 23(figs.), 24(fig.), 25(fig.)
Restorations: definition of, 3; of Windsor furniture, 5–14, 6(fig.), 7(fig.), 9(fig.), 10(fig.), 11(fig.), 12(figs.), 13(figs.), 14(fig.), 15
Revivalist styles, 49, 53, 54, 59–63, 65, 69
Revolutionary War, 78, 79, 96–98
Rhode Island Windsors, 21
Rich, Fleming K., 4
Richmond, Va., 207–29
Richmond Randolph Lodge 19, 211(& figs.), 230(n10)
Ringuet, Julien-Daniel-René, 70(n5)
Ringuet-Leprince, Auguste-Emile, 49, 50–52, 70(n5), 71(n8)
Ringuet-Leprince, Marcotte and Co., 50(fig.), 51–52. See also L. Marcotte & Co.
Ringuet-Leprince, Marie-Felicité, 50
Rivington, James, 174, 195, 196
Robbins, Philemon, 6
Roberts, Allan E., 169, 171(n13)
Roberts, Joshua, 139
Rocaille forms, 30
Rockers, 15
Rococo style: design books on, 174, 175, 180, 184–97; in eighteenth century, 30, 31, 92, 94
Roudillon, Eugène, 51, 71(n8)
Roux, Alexander, 49
Russell, Walter, 185, 188

Saliva, 166, 167, 171(nn 7, 8)
Salmon, William, 46(n7), 77
Sans Souci Club, 81

Savery, William, 185, 219
Sayer, Robert, 192, 195
Scamozzi, Vincenzo, 209
Scanning electron microscope (SEM), 166
Schuyler, Margareta, 109
Sears, Clark, Jr., 11
Sears, William Bernard, 33–34, 37, 38, 41, 43, 44
Seats: repairs to Windsor, 2(fig. 2), 4(& fig.); restorations to Windsor, 6–7
Seaver, William, 4
Select Architecture (Morris), 231(n11)
Serpentine shaping. *See* Bombé furniture
Settees, 27(n10); alterations to Windsor, 17(fig.), 18(& fig.)
Seventh Regiment Armory, 65–66, 66(fig. 29)
Seymour, John, 199
Seymour, Thomas, 199, 200
Shearer, Thomas, 198
Shepherd, Margaret Vanderbilt, 69, 72(n30)
Sheraton, Thomas, 175, 199–200
Sherburne, Thomas, 79
Shiff, Hart M., 70(n7)
Shrinkage, 13
Sibley, John, 129
Sideboards by Marcotte firm, 61(fig. 17), 63–65, 65(fig. 27)
Singleton, Esther, 116
Sixty Different Sorts of Ornaments (Brunetti), 174
Skillin (Skillings), John and Simeon, 83–85, 86, 89–91, 94, 100(n12)
Skimmer, Capt. John, 79
Sloane, Emily Vanderbilt, 69, 72(n30)
Sloat, Caroline F., 242
Smalt, 166
Smith, Robert, 181
Smith, Thomas, 138
Smither, James, 175
Social factors: and business relations, 76–77, 78, 79, 98; and evolution of furniture, 240; and wood choice, 246(n2)
Society for the Preservation of New England Antiquities Conservation Center, 163
Society of Upholsterers, 174, 195–97
Soluvar Matte Varish, 170, 171(n9)
Some Designs of Inigo Jones and William Kent (Vardy), 174–75, 180, 183–84
South Carolina, 124, 184, 185, 189, 190
Speakman, Elijah, 232(n24)

Spindles, restoring, 14
Spofford, Harriet, 55
Sprague, Col. Joseph, 96, 103(n48)
Staats, Dr. Samuel, 127–28
Stalker, John, 139, 140(figs.), 174–75, 183
Stearns, Dr. William, 96
Stearns, Richard Sprague, 96, 103(n48)
Steenwyck, Cornelis, 108
Stephenson, Clotworthy, 208, 211–12, 222, 229, 230(nn 4, 10), 233(n36)
Stoddard Solvent, 166, 167
Stone, Polly Mariner, *ix*
Stone, Stanley, *ix*
Stools: reconstruction of Windsor, 20(& fig.); restoration of Windsor, 11–13, 12(figs. 10, 11)
Storer, Ebenezer, II, 73, 74, 78, 95, 103(n45)
Stretchers: on oval tables with falling leaves, 111–13, 116; replacing Windsor, 7(fig.), 8
Studies in the Decorative Arts, 247–48
Style/design: architectural elements in furniture, 29–30, 38, 40, 41, 44, 50, 65, 66, 211–12; bombé, 75, 77, 81–96, 87(fig.); and composition ornament, 227; Gunston Hall (Buckland), 31–33; Huguenots and diffusion of baroque, 137–41; and identifying furniture repairs, 8–10, 13–14, 18–20, 23–25, 27; influence of English design books on, 174–79 (*see also* Design books); and Ingle's case furniture, 221; and Marcotte firm, 53, 54, 55–69; and New England clocks, 242–44; nineteenth-century popularity of French, 49; and Portsmouth furniture, 235, 236–38; Scamozzi capitals, 208–209; sources for New York oval tables, 112–13, 119–20, 120–21, 123–24, 125
Swan, Abraham, 46(n7), 187
Swan Lodge No. 358, 164(fig. 2), 170
Symbols, Masonic, 168–69, 170, 171(n13)

Taber, Elnathan, 243
Tables: attributed to Buckland and Sears, 38–44, 38(fig.), 39(figs.), 40(figs.), 41(fig.), 42(figs. 27, 28, 29), 43(figs.), 44(figs. 32, 33), 45(fig.), 47(n18); attributed to Marcotte firm, 55, 57(fig. 6), 58–59, 60(fig. 14), 61(figs. 15, 16), 67–68; in design books, 42(& fig. 26), 190(figs.); history of, 107–108; New York oval, with falling leaves, 107, 108, 109–31, 131(n4), 134(nn 24, 25, 26), 135(n32) (*see also* Draw-bar tables; Gate-leg tables); rectangular draw, 106(fig.), 107, 108–109, 131(n5), 132(n8); square, with falling leaves, 132(n11); Yale University collection, 238–40

Tanner, Branch, 216
Tayloe, John, II, 37, 42, 45, 47(n15)
Taylor, Alexander, 188–89
Terry, Eli, 244
Thomas, Seth, 244
Thomas Johnson and English Rococo (Hayward), 191
Tiranti, Alec, 198
Townsend, Christopher, 129
Townsend, John, 129
Trade cards, 172(fig.), 175, 191, 195, 200(& fig. 23)
Treatise of Japanning and Varnishing (Stalker and Parker), 139, 140(figs.), 174–75, 180, 183
Trent, Robert, 236
Trotter, Daniel, 219
Tuft, Thomas, 219
Twain, Mark, 70
Two Hundred Years of American Clocks and Watches (Bailey), 241

Ulster County, N.Y., 129–30, 131, 135(n32)
Ultraviolet light analysis, 163, 164, 165(fig. 6), 166(fig. 8), 167(fig. 10)
United States Capitol, 207, 229, 233(n36)
Universal System of Houshold Furniture (Ince and Mayhew), 174, 180, 190–91, 190(fig. 10)
Useful Architecture (Halfpenny), 77

Van Cortlandt, Gertruy, 117–18, 133(n14)
Van Cortlandt table, 109(fig.), 116, 117–18, 121(fig. 26), 128, 133(n20)
Vanderbilt, William Henry, 68–69
Vanderbilt (William K.) house, 69(& figs.)
Vanderlyn family table, 114(fig. 14)
Van Rensselaer, Stephen, 193
Van Rensselaer Manor house, 193
Vardy, John, 174–75, 183–84
Veenendaal, Jan, 123
Vermilion, 166

263 INDEX

Vernon house, 141
Verplanck family table, 128, 135(n30)
Virginia State Capitol, 206(fig.), 207–11, 208(figs.), 209(figs.), 210(figs.), 230(nn 5, 7)

Waite, Ezra, 184, 185, 187
Wall brackets, 191(figs.)
Walnut: in New York oval tables, 116, 128; use in Windsor furniture, 20, 22
Walpole, Horace, 29
Ward, Gerald W. R., 236, 239–40
Warne, Francis, 129
Warren, Dr. Joseph, 74, 81
Washington, D.C., 228–29
Washington's Headquarters, 118(fig. 21), 128, 135(n30)
Webb, John, 219
Welch, John, 79
Wells, J. Cheney, 244
Wells, Robert, 174, 185, 187, 190, 191
Wetmore, Edith and George, 59, 61
Wetmore, William Shepard, 55, 61–63
White, Robert and Peter, 129
White House, 69, 228
Willard, Alexander T., 244
Willard, Benjamin, 242
Willard, Simon, 242–43
Windsor furniture: detecting problems in, 3–27. *See also* Chair(s); Settees; Stools
Winterthur, 126, 191
Wolfe, Benjamin, 228
Wood: and furniture origin attributions, 239; historical uses of, 245–46, 246(n2); in oval tables, 116; in Windsor furniture, 20
Wood, Eliphalet, 57
Woodlands, 211–14, 212(figs.), 213(figs.), 231(nn 12, 13)
Works in Architecture of Robert and James Adam, The, 180, 197–98
Writing chairs: converting Windsors into, 15; reproductions of Windsor, 20–23, 21(figs.)

Yale University American furniture collections, 238–40, 241

Zea, Philip, 236, 240–44
Zimmerman, Philip, 236, 237